Managing Social Change and Social Policy in Greater China

East Asia is at the heart of the global economic transformation, and the countries of the region are witnessing rapidly changing labour markets, alongside the pressure to cut production costs and lower taxes in order to become successful 'competition states'. These changes have resulted in increased welfare demands which governments, organisations and agencies across the region have had to address.

This book examines welfare regimes in the Greater China region, encompassing mainland China, Hong Kong, Macao and Taiwan. In so doing, it explores the ways in which the rapid growth and internationalisation of the economy across Greater China is presenting new social policy challenges that governments, social welfare organisations and agencies in the region are having to respond to. Rather than simply describing and categorising welfare systems, the contributors to this volume add to our understanding of how one of the major economic transformations of the contemporary era in East Asia is shaping welfare provision in the region. In turn, in this context of economic change, they examine the new strategies and measures that have been adopted in order to reduce the heavy burden on the state in terms of welfare provision, whilst also attempting to diversify funding and provision sources to meet the pressing welfare needs.

Based on extensive fieldwork by leading scholars of social policy, this book will appeal to students and scholars of Asian social policy, comparative development and social policy, social welfare and Chinese studies.

Ka Ho Mok is chair professor in comparative policy; Department of Asian and Policy Studies of The Hong Kong Institute of Education.

Maggie Lau is assistant professor in the Department of Public Policy at the City University of Hong Kong.

Routledge Research on Public and Social Policy in Asia
Edited by M Ramesh
National University of Singapore

Managing Social Change and Social Policy in Greater China

Welfare regimes in transition

Edited by
Ka Ho Mok and Maggie K. W. Lau

Routledge
Taylor & Francis Group

LONDON AND NEW YORK

First published 2014 by Routledge

2 Park Square, Milton Park, Abingdon, Oxfordshire OX14 4RN
711 Third Avenue, New York, NY 10017

Routledge is an imprint of the Taylor & Francis Group, an informa business

First issued in paperback 2017

British Library Cataloguing in Publication Data
A catalogue record for this book is available from the British Library

Library of Congress Cataloging in Publication Data
Managing social change and social policy in greater China : welfare regimes in transition / edited by Ka Ho Mok and Maggie Lau.
     pages cm. – (Routledge research on public and social policy in Asia; 6)
     Includes bibliographical references and index.
     1. China — Social policy.   2. Public welfare — China.   3. Social change — China.   I. Mok, Ka Ho,   II. Lau, Maggie.
     HN733.5.M353 2014
     303.3'720951—dc23

                                                                2013017665

ISBN: 978–0-415–70634-6 (hbk)
ISBN: 978-1-138–57918-7 (pbk)

Typeset in Times New Roman
by RefineCatch Limited, Bungay, Suffolk

Contents

Tables

Figures

x   *Figures*

About the contributors

Yu-Fang Chang was awarded M.Phil at Manchester Metropolitan University, United Kingdom and is currently Senior Lecturer in the Department of International Business Studies at the National Chi Nan University in Taiwan. Her research interests focus on social indicators and their implications to marketing, social enterprises and policy issues. She has been involved in a research project on poverty reduction in Taiwan, has published journal papers (e.g. in the *Asia Pacific Journal of Social Work and Development*) and many book chapters written in Chinese.

Lijun Chen is senior researcher with Chapin Hall at the University of Chicago. His research interests include the development and general well-being of vulnerable children from disadvantaged backgrounds and the welfare of the elderly in both developed and developing countries, along with the analysis and evaluation of government policies and programmes to promote the well-being of children and the elderly. He has worked with different survey and administrative data sets from China and the US to examine the effects of personal attributes and contextual factors on the well-being of children and the elderly. He holds a Ph.D. in sociology from the University of Chicago, and has published in *Social Service Review* and *Children and Youth Service Review*.

Genghua Huang is a research member of Centre for Greater China Studies at the Hong Kong Institute of Education. His research interests focus on social policy in China. His research has been published in The Journal of Current Chinese Affairs, China Social Work Research and Journal of Zhengjiang University (Humanities and Social Science).

John Hudson is deputy head of the Department of Social Policy and Social Work at the University of York, United Kingdom. His research and teaching interests centre around comparative social policy analysis, the political economy of welfare and the policy-making process. He is co-author of *Understanding the Policy Process* (The Policy Press, 2009) and *The Short Guide to Social Policy* (The Policy Press, 2008). His research has appeared in a wide range of journals including *Critical Social Policy*, the *Journal of European Social Policy*, the *Journal of Social Policy, Policy & Politics, Social Policy & Administration* and *Social Policy & Society*.

Yeun-Wen Ku is currently professor in the Department of Social Work at the National Taiwan University. He was awarded his Ph.D. at the University of Manchester, United Kingdom in 1995, and taught social policy in the Department of Social Policy and Social Work at the National Chi Nan University, Taiwan until 2007. He helped to set up Ph.D. programmes in both these universities. Together with some important social policy scholars, Professor Ku founded the Taiwanese Association of Social Policy (TASP) and is now the President. He has written widely on welfare development and policy debates in Taiwan, extending to comparative study on East Asian welfare.

Stefan Kühner is lecturer in Social Policy at the Department of Social Policy and Social Work at the University of York, United Kingdom. His academic interest centres on comparative and international social policy with a particular focus on historical institutionalist theory and the politics of welfare state reform. His research has been published in the *Journal of European Social Policy*, the *Journal of Social Policy* and the *Journal of Comparative Policy Analysis: Research and Practice*, among others. Stefan is co-author of *The Short Guide to Social Policy* (Policy Press, 2008) and worked as an external consultant for the International Labour Organisation (ILO) and the Organisation of Economic Co-operation and Development (OECD). He is a frequent visitor to Greater China and has spoken at academic events in Beijing, Hong Kong, Guangzhou and Wuhan among others in recent years.

Dicky W. L. Lai obtained his Ph.D. from the University of Hong Kong and is currently Associate Professor at the Social Work Programme, Macao Polytechnic Institute, where he teaches social policy and social welfare. He is the author of several journal articles, book chapters and research reports on social policy issues in Macao. His articles have appeared in journals such as the *Journal of Macau Studies*, the *Hong Kong Journal of Social Work*, the *Journal of Contemporary Asia*, the *China Journal of Social Work*, the *Journal of Macao Polytechnic Institute* and *International Social Work*.

Maggie K. W. Lau is assistant professor in the Department of Public Policy at the City University of Hong Kong. She obtained her Ph.D. from the University of York, United Kingdom. She has extensive research and teaching experience in development and policy studies, and contemporary China studies, poverty and social exclusion, children and youth well-being, as well as adolescent health. Her publications appeared in *Policy Studies* (2002), the *Journal of Societal and Social Policy* (2005), *Nicotine and Tobacco Research* (2008), *Asia-Pacific Journal of Public Health* (2010), *Child Indicators Research* (2010 & 2012), *Health Policy* (2010), the *Journal of Asian Public Policy* (2010), *Children and Youth Service Review* (2011), the *Journal of Community Health* (2012) and *Drug and Alcohol Review* (2013).

Kam-Yee Law is currently associate professor in the Department of Social Sciences at the Hong Kong Institute of Education, and also the executive editor of the *Hong Kong Journal of Social Sciences*. Co-authored with Lee Kim-ming, he has recently published a number of papers on the issues of social marginalisation in Hong Kong, including "Citizenship, Economy and Social Exclusion: Mainland Chinese Immigrants in Hong Kong" in the *Journal of Contemporary Asia*, and "Socio-political Embeddings of South Asian Ethnic Minorities' Economic Situations in Hong Kong" in the *Journal of Contemporary China*. He is also the co-editor of *Nations, National Narratives and Communities in the Asia-Pacific*, published by Routledge.

Kim-Ming Lee received his M.Phil in sociology at the Chinese University of Hong Kong, and is currently lecturer in the Division of Social Studies at Community College, City University of Hong Kong. In recent years he has published extensively on the issues of social marginalisation in Hong Kong, including *A Qualitative Research on Hong Kong Marginal Workers: Trap, Exclusion & the Way Out*, published by Oxfam Hong Kong and *The Economy of Hong Kong in Non-economic Perspectives*, published by Oxford University Press (co-edited with Kam-Yee Law).

Susie Yieng-Ping Ling is an administrative officer and project researcher at in the Institute of China Studies at the University of Malaya, Malaysia. She holds a Master of Economics degree from the University of Malaya.

Ka Ho Mok is chair professor of comparative policy and concurrently associate vice president (research and international exchange) of the Hong Kong Institute of Education (HKIEd). He served as a consultant for UNICEF and UNDP, and to the Information Service Department/Central Policy Unit of the HKSAR government. He was conferred as Changjiang chair professor by the Ministry of Education, People's Republic of China in 2010. Professor Mok is no narrow disciplinary specialist but has worked creatively across the academic worlds of sociology, political science and public and social policy while building up his wide knowledge of China and the region. He has published extensively in the fields of comparative education policy, comparative development and policy studies, and social development in contemporary China and East Asia. He has contributed to the field of social change and education in a variety of additional ways, not least of which has been his leadership and entrepreneurial approach to the organisation of the field.

King-Lun Ngok is professor and director of the Institute for Social Policy, Centre for Chinese Public Administration Research, School of Government at Sun Yat-sen University, China. His research interests include education policy, labour policy, social security and social development in China. His articles have been published in academic journals such as *Social Policy and Administration, Public Administration Review, Chinese Law and Government*, the *International Review of Administrative Sciences* and *Problems of Post-communism*. Kinglun serves as an editor of *Chinese Public Policy Review*. His most recent books include *Social Policy in China: Development and Well-being* (with Chak-kwan Chan and David Phillips, Policy Press, 2008), and *Welfare Reform in East Asia: Towards Workfare* (with Chak-kwan Chan, Routledge, 2011).

M. Ramesh is chair professor of governance and public policy in the Department of Asian and Policy Studies at the Hong Kong Institute of Education. Specialising in public policy and governance in Asia, Professor Ramesh has authored and edited many books, including *Public Policy Primer* (2010), *Studying Public Policy* (3rd ed. 2009), *Transforming Asian Governance* (2009), *Deregulation and Its Discontents* (2006), *Social Policy in East and Southeast Asia* (2004), *Welfare Capitalism in Southeast Asia* (2000) and *The Political Economy of Canada* (1999). He has also published extensively in reputed international journals. He is the co-editor of *Policy and Society* as well as *World Political Science Review*.

Shih-Jiunn Shi is associate professor at the Graduate Institute of National Development at the National Taiwan University. He received his Ph.D. in 2007 from the Department of Sociology at the University of Bielefeld, Germany. He has published papers in several journals including the *Journal of Social Policy, Social Policy & Administration* and *Policy & Politics*. Currently he is conducting research projects on the development of social policy in Greater China, and also collaborates with other scholars in research on East Asian social policy.

Dali L. Yang received his Ph.D. at Princeton University in 1993. He is now professor in the Department of Political Science at the University of Chicago and the founding faculty director of the University of Chicago Center in Beijing. He is the author of many books and articles on the politics of China's development.

Chung-Yang Yeh is a Ph.D. student in the Division of Sociology and Social Policy at the University of Southampton, United Kingdom. His thesis compares pension development in Japan, Korea and Taiwan through an integrated political economic approach. His main research interests including comparative welfare, pension policy and life course research.

Emile Kok-Kheng Yeoh is director and associate professor of the Institute of China Studies, University of Malaya, Malaysia. He graduated with a Ph.D. from the University of Bradford, West Yorkshire, England, and his research interests include institutional economics, China studies, decentralisation, fiscal federalism, socioracial diversity and the role of the state in economic development. His works have been published in journals and occasional paper series such as *The Copenhagen Journal of Asian Studies, GeoJournal: An International Journal on Human Geography and Environmental Sciences*, the *Journal of Asian Public Policy*, the *International Journal of China Studies*, the *International Journal of Business Anthropology, China-ASEAN Perspective Forum*, the *Malaysian Journal of Economic Studies*, the *International Journal of East Asian Studies* and the *Copenhagen Discussion Paper* series.

1 Introduction

The search for a new social policy paradigm: managing changing social expectations and welfare regimes in transition in Greater China

Ka Ho Mok and Maggie K. W. Lau

Introduction: welfare regime debates in Asia

Discussion of welfare regimes and ideal types of welfare state continues to dominate comparative social policy analysis, but the focus of the debate has expanded considerably since the publication of Esping-Andersen's groundbreaking *The Three Worlds of Welfare Capitalism* in 1990. Shifts in this debate have been prompted by a mixture of theoretical and empirical concerns raised by comparative social policy scholars, but they have also resulted from a more general internationalisation of social policy research agendas within the academy (see, for example, Abrahamson, 1999, 2011; Hwang, 2011) and debates have continued over the most appropriate indicators (Clasen and Sigel, 2007; Kühner, 2007) and methods (Hudson and Kühner, 2010). In particular, there has been a strong desire to expand the scope of the debate to encompass nations and regions not included in Esping-Andersen's initial study of just 18 high-income OECD states (Hudson and Kühner, 2011, 2012).

Arguably the largest body of work in this regard has been that focusing on East Asia, not least because the flowering of a very active East Asian social policy research network has provided a space for sustained discussion, debate and comparison of welfare regimes in this region. That said, debate about an "East Asian" model has featured prominently since the early 1990s, with some of the earliest critiques of Esping-Andersen's typology pointing to a potential mismatch between his ideal types and the foundations of welfare systems in the region (Jones, 1993; Goodman *et al.*, 1998) in which, broadly stated, governments emphasised economic development over social policy. Since then, a substantial body of literature has developed, such the work of Holliday (2000, 2005) and Kwon and Holliday (2007) which challenges Esping-Andersen's typology. According to Holliday (2000: 711), it is "impossible to place [East Asian cases] in Esping-Andersen's framework" because a "productivist" world of welfare exists in the region.

Nonetheless, the concern with productive welfarism has not been limited to East Asia, as vividly reviewed by Hwang's edited volume, with a special focus on new welfare states in East Asia (2011). Indeed, researchers in other parts of the globe, writing from a rather different perspective, have argued that – in response to globalisation – all high-income states have shifted the emphasis of their social policies towards that of a supporting and subjugated role *vis-à-vis* economic policy (see, for example, Cerny and Evans, 1999; Evans and Cerny, 2003; Horsfall, 2010). Confronted with declining economic growth, together with the dismantling of traditional income protections, a number of countries in Europe have begun to face the harsh reality of bankruptcy. In countries struggling for survival against the context of unmanageable welfare burdens and with stagnating economic growth, the call for replacing the welfare state with a competition state has become increasingly popular, favouring policies that can boost economic competitiveness (see Hudson and Kühner chapter in this volume).

The search for new social policy paradigm in Greater China and East Asia

In his recent work, Mok (2010) conducted a comparative review of how selected East Asian countries/economies have responded to the global financial crisis which started in the USA and extended to other parts of the globe, especially Europe. His research findings suggest that most East Asian governments have put economic recovery first by introducing various kinds of economic stimuli instead of adopting sufficient/comprehensive social protection measures to help those people (particularly the urban working poor) facing intensified poverty, inequalities and unemployment. As Sherraden (2009) has rightly suggested, there are broadly four major types of strategy being adopted by governments across the globe in handling the current economic crisis, namely, investment in infrastructure and public works, economic stimuli packages helping the business, banking and industrial sectors, cash transfer (consumption coupons) and social protection measures. Taking the global financial crisis of 2008 as a case, the governments of mainland China, Hong Kong, Singapore, South Korea and Taiwan have adopted massive countercyclical economic measures to help rescue the financial market, steer the economy and boost employment by increasing public spending on improving people's lives, in areas such as education, health care and environmental protection. While the stimulus packages and relief plans adopted by these countries/cities are too complex and comprehensive to be fully documented and discussed in this chapter, it is clear that the measures they have taken focus similarly on short-term relief as well as long-term prospects, indicated by the huge amount of money spent on infrastructures (Mok, 2011).

Comparing and contrasting the measures being adopted by Asian governments in handling the global financial crisis, we have not found major policy paradigm shifts in terms of post-economic crisis strategies. How far are these governments willing to set aside the market and redistribute wealth? Whether these Asian states have oriented towards a "pro-poor" development approach still remains an open question, although more attention seems to have been given to social protection issues. For China, in the face of huge investments in public development projects and massive tax cutting programmes, Liu Tienan, vice minister of the National Development and Reform Commission, has said that an increased fiscal deficit is "necessary" in times like this, as long as the increase is in a "controllable range" and the risk bearable (Gov.cn, "Official: China Confident of Achieving 8% GDP Growth in 2009", 27 February 2009). Mainland China is committed to boosting stable economic growth, as it has done in recent years, which can be broadly shared across different sectors in society, even though failing to retain fiscal discipline for the time being.

In terms of the East Asian "Four Tigers", in the years after the Asian financial crisis, scholars started to pay attention to the transformation of social policies. Kwon (2009) notes that Korea and Taiwan have seized the moment to extend social policies, while Hong Kong and Singapore remain restrained on in this area. Therefore, the different developmental trajectories of these late industrialising states suggest a formation of two clusters of developmental welfare states in East Asia, rather than an overarching "East Asian Welfare Model". In this financial crisis, we can still see the legacy of this transformation, although the governments in Taiwan and South Korea are becoming increasingly open to welfare and social protection (Ku, 2009). For South Korea, not only has the government addressed the concerns of investors and businessmen, it has also put efforts into helping people in the lower social and economic strata, best indicated by the provision of unemployment benefits. For Taiwan, its stimulus package focuses on stimulating consumption/demand (notably by giving aid to low-income households to maintain their houses and buy daily goods), job creation and large investments in infrastructure. Comparing the approaches for national development adopted by the Kuomintang (KMT) and Democratic Progressive Party (DPP) in Taiwan, we can see that a major difference between the two parties is that a pro-growth policy is adopted by the existing ruling party KMT, whereas the DPP adheres to "pro-poor" development principles (Huang, 2009).

Similarly, the Hong Kong government still commits itself in this financial crisis to its conventional governing philosophy of "big market, small government", best indicated by its reluctance to dig into the money reserve to distribute money directly to all residents and its unwillingness to pay extra benefits to the unemployed. For Singapore, the government has claimed that it is trying to solve the economic problems using a supply-side approach (helping business to retain workers) rather than a demand-side approach (stimulating consumption/demand), which closely resembles the idea of "trickle-down" theory. "Pro-poor growth" policies can hardly be found in the stimulus packages of Hong Kong and Singapore. Despite the fact that these East Asian countries seem to be able to maintain their existing welfare arrangements in the changing political and economic context, the questions being raised are closely related to whether and how these governments can continue to sustain their existing welfare practices.

Central to the critical challenges confronting Asian societies is how far they can excuse themselves from addressing the heightened welfare demands and politicised contexts resulting from fast-changing labour market conditions, while they have to cope with the pressure to become "competition states" by cutting production costs and lowering taxes, since they are increasingly dependent upon the globalising economy. Most important of all, trickle-down economic development has been hailed as the most desirable wealth distribution process in the past few decades. But the belief in this process is often challenged in times of economic crisis. Whether wholeheartedly solving the economic problems or just gaining political appeal, in this financial crisis many governments, democratic or authoritarian, have actually taken breathtaking measures that have not been seen for decades to intervene in the market and secure people's livings. In this regard, puzzling questions arise: "Will the big moves by the governments at this moment lead to a paradigm shift of social policy delivery? Or are they just special moves in a special time?" To answer these questions, the contributors of the present volume have tried to critically examine whether and how governments in Greater China and the East Asian region have moved beyond their current welfare approaches or just attempted to maintain an essentially productivist welfare regime to balance the tensions between competing demands: the need to address people's heightened welfare needs on the one hand and to enhance national competitiveness in the globalising world economy on the other.

Mok and Lau (2013, forthcoming) examine Guangzhou residents' subjective perceptions of social welfare needs (including minimum standard of living, health care security, housing security and education), discussing what major strategies the government has adopted in coping with the changing welfare expectations of local residents in Guangzhou. For instance, in December 2010, the local government promulgated the adjustment of the minimum living standard guarantee, addressing increasing living costs and the inflation rate in Guangzhou. However, the adjustment still lagged behind changes in prices and consumption. One single mother with a son in junior high school receiving the minimum living standard guarantee in *Jingtai* Street, Guangzhou, said that "the changes cannot match the rises in price levels. When the allowance level began to rise, I felt very happy. However, the price levels rose even faster. My son is now growing up, who needs to eat more meat, so I have to let him have my share as well". Such field observations clearly show that the minimum living standard guarantee cannot meet basic needs in the face of price inflation. The current welfare system in Guangzhou is following the logic of "supporting the poor and relieving the needy". Policy priorities are always given to people in such circumstances. Yet in the face of rapid economic, social and demographic changes, policy-makers also have to be alert to the living difficulties facing the general public, especially in the areas of medical, educational and housing services. Although the Guangzhou Municipal Government has already taken certain measures to address the changing needs of its residents in the past few years, without big changes in the underlying policy philosophy, the outcomes of the policies have been piecemeal and limited.

Citizens' welfare expectations have increased in recent years, not only in Guangzhou, China, but also in Hong Kong, Macau and Taiwan, as Mok, Ngok and Huang's recent book points out. Social development challenges, changing social welfare expectations and policy responses in these Chinese societies have clearly suggested that citizens living in the Greater China region have higher expectations for their governments to act more proactively in managing tensions between rapid economic growth and social harmony (Mok *et al.*, 2013). Most recently, a number of scholars in Hong Kong have reviewed social development issues and argued for new pathways in addressing poverty problems, especially when citizens' expectations for welfare and social protection have heightened (see, for example, Cheung, 2012; Lau, 2012; Wong, 2012). Similarly, the chapter by Chang and Ku in this volume points out how the heightened welfare expectations in the context of democratisation have placed immense pressure on the government in Taiwan for social welfare provision. Without sufficient economic drives for growth, Taiwan society is now experiencing difficult times in meeting people's pressing welfare demands (see Chapter 5).

In addition, Mok's recent research related to university students' perceptions of social mobility and career development opportunities in Guangzhou, Taipei and Hong Kong has clearly suggested that the younger generations are losing faith and confidence in their future, particularly when they believe the opportunities for upward social mobility are becoming less promising because economic growth is not sufficiently sustained. During field interviews with university students in these three Chinese cities, Mok found that the students expect their governments to provide them with more social protection, and especially more job opportunities and welfare services (Mok, 2013; Mok and Huang, 2013).

Major arguments of this book

This book uses the theoretical and policy backgrounds outlined above to examine issues related to major social development challenges and social policy responses in the Greater China region. The book includes chapters from leading scholars in the field of social policy, with a focus on comparative perspectives in Greater China and the East Asian region. Their contributions are based upon very rich research findings generated from projects and fieldwork conducted in the last decade. With particular reference to critical reflections on how Asian governments in particular and social welfare organisations/agencies in general have responded to the growing challenges of globalisation, the chapters in this volume critically examine what new strategies and measures governments in the area are adopting to reduce the heavy burden on the state in terms of welfare provision, while making other attempts to diversify funding and provision sources to meet pressing welfare needs.

The debates and discourses on welfare transformation in Greater China and East Asia are highly relevant to scholars, researchers, policy analysts, practitioners and students in policy studies/social policy in Europe and other parts of the world when searching for ways of resolving the intensified welfare crisis currently sweeping through Europe and the USA. More specifically, this book focuses on an examination of welfare regimes in the Greater China region, examining welfare development in mainland China alongside discussion of Hong Kong, Macao and Taiwan. In so doing, a key goal is to examine how the rapid growth and internationalisation of the economy in the Greater China region is presenting new social policy challenges that welfare regimes are having to respond to. Rather than simply aiming to describe and categorise welfare systems, the present volume aims to add to our understanding of how one of the major economic transformations of the contemporary era in East Asia is shaping welfare provision in the region.

Chapter 2 by Ka Ho Mok and M. Ramesh has chosen a focus to critically examine major social development challenges and social policy responses of two special administrative regions of the People's Republic of China, namely Hong Kong and Macau. In this chapter, the authors engage in the debate about East Asian welfare systems, using European social policy regimes as a reference point to examine social development challenges and social welfare responses. Mok and Ramesh elucidate how the Hong Kong and Macau governments have reformed their social welfare models to cope with rapid social, economic, demographic and political changes, especially analysing any major paradigm shifts in social welfare arrangements and social policy formulation in the post-2008 global financial crisis. They ask whether productivist welfare capitalism can be sustained in the context of complex social development problems resulting from an imbalance between economic growth and social and human development in these two Chinese societies.

Maggie Lau, in **Chapter 3**, uses the notions of social equity and equality of opportunity to frame her analysis on the extent to which welfare restructuring attains productive employment and sustainable livelihoods, and ensures equal opportunities for people's future development in Hong Kong. The analysis highlights the informalisation of labour markets, with lack of job security, unstable income and limited coverage of social security benefits, which has limited family resources and restricted working groups and their families in terms of taking part in normal activities in the community. Lau further argues that expanding precarious employment in the labour market not only contributes to a significant impact on sustainable retirement protection for the older population, but also brings about negative effects in terms of intergenerational mobility and equality of opportunity. In particular, it may intensify the educational inequality among students from different socio-economic backgrounds under the New Senior Secondary Curriculum in Hong Kong. The increasing nuclearisation of families and changing family structures puts too much pressure on care and support outside the family. The chapter discusses "productivist welfare capitalism", emphasising the subordination of social policy to economic policy, and the heavy reliance on family mutual support in addressing new social risks arising from a breakdown of traditional and informal risk-sharing mechanisms.

In **Chapter 4**, Kim-Ming Lee and Kam-Yee Law focus on the effects of globalisation generating economic insecurity, particularly unemployment, in Hong Kong, and scrutinise what roles social policies can play in protecting people against this insecurity. By examining the social policy packages adopted by the Hong Kong government in fighting against the financial tsunami, Lee and Law demonstrate the lack of "proactive" strategies and long-term commitment of the Hong Kong government in protecting people against adversity. By drawing on the experiences of other countries, Lee and Law suggest that active labour market policies should be adopted as policy tools to reform the social protection system.

Yu-Fang Chang and Yeun-Wen Ku, in **Chapter 5**, discuss whether the Taiwanese developmental welfare regime is sustainable to achieve both economic growth and social equity in the twenty-first century. Chang and Ku argue that:

> Taiwan has long been regarded as a model for economic growth with equity. Up to the 1990s, nearly all indicators showed significant improvement in every aspect. However, this did not last long and, especially after the 1990s, economic growth slowed down, and this was combined with higher unemployment and stagnation of incomes ... With democratic elections, how to acquire both economic growth and social equality has become the greatest challenge for the state and the measure of its legitimacy ... the vulnerability of Taiwan's current social policy ... fails to satisfy the expectations of the middle classes. Full employment and a massive number of small and medium-sized businesses contributed to wealth and income equality in Taiwan, but were no longer sustainable after the 1990s.

Kinglun Ngok adopts a theme of "bringing the state back in" to discuss how the Chinese government has tried to revitalise the importance of social welfare and social policy provision in order to address the growing intensity of social problems resulting from rapid economic growth without sufficiently corresponding social development and social welfare strategies. In **Chapter 6**, Ngok critically examines the development of social policy and social spending in China since 2003. Ngok elucidates the trajectory of the changes in China's social policy in the post-Mao era, and argues that a process of "bringing the state back in" is taking place in China's social policy expansion. Social policies in post-Mao China have changed dramatically in order to enhance market competition, increase economic efficiency and accelerate economic growth. The "marketisation of social welfare" has brought about negative effects on the livelihood of low-income citizens, including unemployed urban people, migrant workers and peasants, and consequently contributed to social instability and social unrest. After the Severe Acute Respiratory Syndrome (SARS) epidemic, the leadership, led by Hu Jintao and Wen Jiabao, made a fundamental policy change to reposition the role of the state in public welfare and social justice.

In **Chapter 7**, Mok and Huang adopt a case study approach to examine changing social welfare needs and expectations in Guangzhou, a relatively developed city in southern China. They examine what major strategies the Guangzhou government has adopted in managing people's welfare needs, and focus on how far the new measures have met the changing welfare expectations of citizens in China's mainland. The case of Guangzhou clearly indicates how the Chinese government has begun to take people's needs and interests into consideration when it designs social policy and seeks measures appropriate for addressing growing social welfare needs against the context of a widening gap between the rich and the poor and a deepening intensity of poverty, inequality and other unintended social consequences. China has tried to seek "GDPism" without striking for balanced economic and social development, as Ngok argued in Chapter 6. The authors conclude their chapter by highlighting the fact that even though the government in Guangzhou has taken people's needs and interests into serious consideration, welfare regionalism and social policy variations do exist in the Chinese mainland and the implementation of social policy/social protection measures greatly depends upon the political will and capacity of local governments in the policy context of fiscal decentralisation (Mok and Wu, 2013).

Chapter 8 shifts the focus to Macau, another special administrative region of China. Dicky Lai identifies the specific features of Macao's social policy that typify its welfare regime, and pays particular attention to its social security and housing policies. Lai examines the extent to which prominent welfare models (like Holliday and Wilding's productivist welfare regime and Kwon's welfare developmentalism) can explain Macao's current welfare model. Lai gives a historical account of Macao's social security and housing policies, and argues that these have been expected to perform different regulatory functions for maintaining the development of the capitalist system (i.e. restoring the government's political legitimacy, maintaining social stability, reproducing labour power and maintaining labour discipline). Macao is a regulatory welfare regime, characterised by the low modification impact and the strong regulatory role of social policy.

In **Chapter 9**, Lijun Chen and Dali L. Yang examine old age care concerns and state–society relations in China by discussing the changing public attitudes towards old age care (such as the cost of old age care, the availability of caregivers and care arrangements in old age) among urban and rural residents, and public attitudes towards the role of the state. It is argued that China's policies to expand the coverage of social security and boost investment in care for the elderly are well intentioned, but appear to have fallen short of public expectation to date. The increasing demand for old age care poses a significant challenge to China's state–society relationship.

Chung-Yang Yeh and Shih-Jiunn Shi's contribution in **Chapter 10** moves beyond the Greater China region to compare the cases of Japan and Taiwan, as they are typically categorised as "developmental welfare states" in which the pension systems consist of social insurance institutions. The authors demonstrate the public–private pension mix and governance modes that are embedded in specific welfare production regimes. Japan has well-developed occupational and private pension schemes embedded in its corporate conglomerate welfare production regime, while there is a limited role for private companies as providers of occupational pensions in Taiwan. Yeh and Shi argue that "The rationales and directions of recent pension reforms in East Asia can be further understood only by considering the historical contexts of political and economic structures."

"Poverty reduction, welfare provision and social security challenges in China in the context of fiscal reform and the 12th Five-year Plan" is the topic of **Chapter 11**. Emile Kok-Kheng Yeoh and Susie Yieng-Ping Ling describe issues related to fiscal reform and fiscal decentralisation in China in the context of the country's 12th Five-year Plan, and explore the Plan's implications for poverty alleviation and enhancing stability. They argue that fiscal reform during the 12th Five-year Plan:

will mainly involve the rationalisation of intergovernmental fiscal relations (fiscal IGR) as well as a sounder tax sharing system. Such rationalisation of fiscal IGR will inevitably involve dealing with the transfer payment system – the increase of the size and ratio of the regular general grants and the adjustment and reduction of earmarked grants (sub-provincial fiscal institutional reform), as well as moving towards direct provincial administration of counties so as to ensure and strengthen the county's fiscal capacity for the provision of public services, and exploring the institution of local government bonds.

John Hudson and Stefan Kühner, in **Chapter 12**, attempt to update their earlier work (e.g. Hudson and Kühner, 2011) with reference to the detailed case studies covered in this book, and offer a more nuanced analysis. They conclude that "the chapters within the book underline the diversity of policy frameworks in Greater China. They also, we might add, highlight what appears to be the gradual but significant expansion of income protection in all cases. Both these factors together lead us to believe that the simple labelling of the region as being home to a common 'productive welfare' model remains too simple to be convincing."

Putting together a very fine collection of chapters in this volume, as editors of the present book, we hope to present a more updated but critical review of social development and social policy responses with a focus on the Greater China and East Asia region. The transformations of social welfare and social policy that have taken place in the region also offer a unique perspective to comparative social policy analysts. With the publication of this volume, we hope researchers and scholars in the field of social policy will continue dialogue and comparative work to search for better approaches and strategies in managing growing challenges resulting from rapid social, economic, demographic and political changes.

Note

The editors of the present volume would like to thank the editors of the *Journal of Asian Public Policy* (JAPP) for allowing some of the authors in this book to reproduce their articles originally published in JAPP with a revised version being incorporated in this volume. Part of the materials adopted here is based upon the authors' previous publications. Thanks also goes to John Hudson and Stefan Kühner for engaging with the authors in welfare regime debates in East Asia.

References

Abrahamson, P. (2011). "The Welfare Modelling Business Revisited", in G. Hwang (ed). *New Welfare States in East Asia: Global Challenges and Restructuring*. London: Edward Elgar, 15–34.

Abrahamson, P. (1999). "The Welfare Modelling Business", *Social Policy and Administration*, 33: 394–415.

Cerny, P. and Evans, M. (1999). *New Labour, Globalization, and the Competition State*. Working Paper No. 70, Centre for European Studies, Harvard University.

Cheung, Y. L. (2012). "The Social Responsibility of the Government and the Business Sector in Addressing Poverty Problems in Hong Kong", *Bauhinia Tibune*, No. 3, May: 6–10 (in Chinese).

Clasen, J. and Sigel, N. (eds) (2007). *Investigating Welfare State Change: the 'Dependent Variable Problem' in Comparative Analysis*. London: Edward Elgar.

Esping-Andersen, G. (1990). *The Three Worlds of Welfare Capitalism*. Oxford: Polity Press.

Evans M. and Cerny P. (2003). "Globalisation and Social Policy", in N. Ellison and C. Pierson (eds) *Developments in British Social Policy 2*. Basingstoke: Palgrave.

Goodman, R., White, G. and Kwon, H. (eds) (1998). *The East Asian Welfare Model*. London: Routledge.

Holliday, I. (2000). "Productivist Welfare Capitalism: Social Policy in East Asia", *Political Studies*, 48(4): 706–723.

Holliday, I. (2005). "East Asian Social Policy in the Wake of the Financial Crisis: Farewell to Productivism?", *Policy and Politics*, 33(1): 145–162.

Horsfall, D. (2010). "From Competition State to Competition States?", *Policy Studies*, 31: 57–76.

Huang, C. T. (2009). "Introduction of Party Politics in Taiwan: Perspectives of the Democratic Progressive Party, Taiwan". Paper presented at the Global Citizenship Summer Institute, Democratic Progressive Party Headquarter, 26 June 2009, Taipei.

Hudson, J. and Kühner, S. (2010). "Beyond the Dependent Variable Problem: the Methodological Challenges of Capturing Productive and Protective Dimensions of Social Policy", *Social Policy and Society*, 9(2): 167–179.

Hudson, J. and Kühner, S. (2011). 'Analysing the Productive Dimensions of Welfare: Looking Beyond East Asia', in G.J. Hwang (ed) *New Welfare States in East Asia: Global Challenges and Restructuring*. 'Globalisation and Welfare' Series, London: Edward Elgar.

Hudson, J. and Kühner, S. (2012). "Analyzing the Productive and Protective Dimensions of Welfare: Looking Beyond the OECD", *Social Policy & Administration*, 46: 35–60.

Hwang, G. J. (ed.) (2011). *New Welfare States in East Asia: Global Challenges and Restructuring*. London: Edward Elgar.

Jones, C. (1993). "The Pacific Challenge: Confucian Welfare States", in C. Jones (ed.) *New Perspectives on the Welfare State in Europe*. London: Routledge.

Kühner, S. (2007). "Country-level Comparisons of Welfare State Change Measures: Another Facet of the Dependent Variable Problem within the Comparative Analysis of the Welfare State?", *Journal of European Social Policy*, 17(1): 5–18.

Ku, Y. W. (2009). "Comparative Welfare Policy Instruments in East Asia: Embedding Trust in Policy", in K.H. Mok and R. Forrest (eds) *Changing Governance and Public Policy in East Asia*. London: Routledge.

Kwon, H. J. (2009). "The Reform of the Developmental Welfare State in East Asia", *International Journal of Social Welfare*, 18: S12–S21.

Kwon, S. and Holliday, I. (2007). "The Korean Welfare State: a Paradox of Expansion in an Era of Globalisation and Economic Crisis", *International Journal of Social Welfare*, 16(3): 242–248.

Lau, M. (2012). "Analyzing Poverty and Social Exclusion in Hong Kong: Multi-dimensional Perspectives", *Bauhinia Tibune*, No. 3, May: 11–17 (in Chinese).

Mok, K. H. (2010). "The Impact of Global Economic Crisis: Social Policy Responses and Social Protection Strategies in East Asia", in T. Yang and J.G. Gao (eds) *Contemporary Social Policy Studies*. Beijing: Labour and Social Security Press (in Chinese).

Mok, K. H. (2013). "A Comparative Study of University Student Perception of Social Mobility in Guangzhou, Taipei and Hong Kong", *Bauhinia Tibune*, No. 7, January: 2–7 (in Chinese).

Mok, K. H. and Huang, G. H. (2013). "Asserting the 'Public' in Welfare Provision: A Study of Resident Evaluation and Expectation of Social Services in Guangzhou, China". Paper accepted for publication at *Current Issues in Contemporary China*, forthcoming.

Mok K. H. and Lau, M. (2013). "The Quest for Sustainable Livelihoods: Social Development Challenges and Social Policy Responses in Guangzhou, China", *Social Policy and Society*, forthcoming.

Mok, K. H. and Wu, X. F. (2013) "Dual Decentralization in China's Transitional Economy: Welfare Regionalism and Policy Implications for Central-Local Relationship", *Policy & Society*, 32(1): 61–75.

Mok, K. H., Ngok, K. L. and Huang, G. H. (2013). *Managing Social Change and Social Policy Responses in China: Theory, Practice and Comparative Perspectives*. Completed co-authored book manuscript in press by Social Sciences Documentation Publisher House, Beijing (in Chinese), forthcoming.

Sherraden, M. (2009). "The Global Economic Crisis and Social Policy". Paper presented at the Fifth International Symposium and Lecture on Social Policy, Shandong University, Jinan China, 27–29 July.

2 After the regional and global financial crises

Social development challenges and social policy responses in Hong Kong and Macau

Ka Ho Mok and M. Ramesh

Introduction

Hong Kong and Macau, like many other East Asian countries, have been experiencing enormous economic hardships due to rapid economic restructuring, especially after the Asian financial crisis in 1997 and the global financial crisis in 2008. Without satisfactorily dealing with the consequences resulting from the economic restructuring, "deep-seated conflicts" have driven the governments of Hong Kong and Macau very hard to try and devise new and appropriate measures to tackle these economic and social problems. Before the 1997 Asian financial crisis, both governments strongly believed that rapid economic growth would eventually resolve social and economic difficulties. However, such a growth-driven economic strategy, together with the "productivist welfare regime" typically characterised by attaching heavy weight to economic growth but ignoring the importance of social protection, has been exposed to challenges of rising unemployment and growing poverty (Lin, 2010). Wilding (2008) has rightly raised the question whether the "productivist welfare regime" is still productive in addressing heightened welfare expectations from people and handling social and economic problems resulting from rapid demographic and socio-economic changes in Asia. Moreover, political changes after the handover have also affected the development of welfare policies, and the mantras of "Hong Kong people are to run Hong Kong" and "Macau people are to run Macau" have raised the public expectation for better governance and higher living standards.

Experiencing the negative socio-economic consequences resulting from the regional and global economic crises, the governments of Hong Kong and Macau have been under tremendous pressure to change the way they manage social development and social welfare issues. Openly recognising the huge political price when they fail to meet people's social needs, especially having confronted social unrest in the context of unstable economic growth, rising unemployment, intensified income inequality and emerging social forces in questioning the legitimacy of their political regimes, the governments of Hong Kong and Macau have made attempts to change their social welfare strategies to cope with these challenges. It is against this context that this chapter attempts to critically examine the major social development challenges that the governments of the two special administrative regions of China have confronted, with particular reference to how far they have developed policies/strategies addressing the rapid socio-economic and socio-demographic changes taking place.

Pro-growth approach in managing changing socio-economic crises

Hong Kong and Macau have been adopting so-called "laissez-faire" policies in governance since the colonial era. The neoliberal idea of "small government, big market" has been hailed in both places as the gospel to ensure prosperity and maintain competitiveness. Both Hong Kong and Macau are conventionally characterised as "productivist welfare capitalism" economies, in which social policies are subordinated to economic policies and social development is giving way to economic productivity and growth (Holliday, 2000, 2005; Lai, 2003, 2006). In short, the productivist welfare model is oriented by a GDP-first strategy of development. The characteristic of low social spending of this welfare model lies on the premise that continuing economic growth can offset the under-development of social policies. Social policy and social welfare aim to serve the interests of economic growth and primarily to maintain a productive labour force (Holliday, 2005). Gough (2004) categorises the East Asian systems as "productivist welfare regimes" because social policy-making does not act as an autonomous sphere of governance. The adoption of a very "instrumental" role of social policy certainly undervalues the importance of social protection. However, after the burst of the "East Asian economic miracle" bubble in the economic crisis, the public demand for various social policy remedies has begun to rise (Lau and Mok, 2010). Having experienced both the regional financial crisis in 1997 and the global financial crisis in 2008, both Hong Kong and Macau have found existing welfare arrangements less than satisfactory in meeting people's growing welfare demands. It is against this context that this chapter sets out to critically examine how well the productivist welfare arrangements can survive and sustain in dealing with increasingly complex social, economic and political environments.

Hong Kong's welfare system has long been criticised for its lack of long-term vision and welfare policies are remedial and incremental in nature (Chui *et al.*, 2010). Adopting the principle of "positive non-intervention", the Hong Kong government is prudent in its welfare spending. While recognising the growing demand for social welfare following the Asian financial crisis, as social assistance spending as a share of total government recurrent expenditure has jumped drastic-ally from 2.6 per cent in 1993/1994 to 8.6 per cent in 1999/2000, the Hong Kong government decided to raise the bar for application with the introduction of welfare-to-work programmes since 1999 and also to reduce the amount of benefits (Lai, 2005). For example, able-bodied recipients were required to conduct a certain account of volunteer work in order to receive benefits. Since July 1999, benefits have been cut for larger households by 10 per cent for three-person households and 20 per cent for those households with more than three persons (Tang, 2000: 59–60). All these changes clearly suggest that the government has been very reserved in its intervention in the market. Despite this, in 2000 the Hong Kong government did finally put into place a social security programme, the Mandatory Provident Fund (MPF), which has been designed and debated since the mid-1960s. It is argued that the adoption of a social insurance plan "was constantly blocked by the business representatives who had overwhelmingly predominated the decision-making bodies of the colonial government" (Lai, 2005: 18). Since the Asian financial crisis in 1997, the situation in Hong Kong has been gradually changing as there is pressure for competitive direct elections in the Legislative Council and District Council (Lee, 2009). Besides, in order to reduce the financial burden of the raising demand for welfare, many workfare programmes have been introduced since the crisis to promote an ideology of self-reliance (Tang, 2006).

In response to the crisis, the Macau government expanded the Social Security Fund[1] by injecting a special funding of 50 million patacas in 1998, which was used for a training allowance, an employment subsidy, employment support for the disabled, a training allowance for career counsellors, the First Employment Allowance for Youth, along with unemployment relief. Starting from the twenty-first century, Macau has shifted the emphasis to vocational training and lifelong learning as solutions to poverty (Lai, 2008, 2010: 68–75). Similar to Hong Kong, workfare programmes were introduced in Macau in 2004 to enhance the working incentives for and employability of welfare recipients (Tian and Jiang, 2006). Taken together, in tackling the economic restructuring, the Asian financial crisis and its aftermath, the virtue of self-reliance was embraced by the Hong Kong and Macau governments and incorporated into the formulation of welfare policies.

Although employment has gradually improved in the past few years, people in the two places soon recognised that having a job alone is not enough for good living: desirable wages matter too. After the crisis, businesses started to under-stand that economic growth would not be as previously promised, and therefore opted for a more flexible business model. New business tools, such as short-term contracts, part-time employment, outsourcing and forcing employees to switch to self-employed status, etc. are common nowadays in order to reduce production costs and maintain flexibility in business scale. Similar to other global cities, the "working poor" has emerged and class polarisation has intensified. Such people may have to work for long hours yet earn insufficient money to meet basic living standards (Chiu and Lui, 2009). Concerned academics and NGOs have argued further that such a phenomenon will not only do harm to the livelihoods of the workers but will also affect their family lives, especially in creating or exacer-bating the problem of intergenerational poverty (Chan, 2006, 2009; HKCSS, 2008; Oxfam Hong Kong, 2007; Tang and Lin, 2005). In response to these emerging problems, the Hong Kong and Macau governments have devised various policies in the past few years.

Hong Kong's responses to major socio-economic challenges

Working poverty[2]

Working poverty has become a serious issue in recent years. According to the Subcommittee to Study the Subject of Combating Poverty, Legislative Council of the HKSAR (2006: 11), the number of working poor households has remained steady at 173,100 in 1998 and 170,400 in the second quarter of 2005. The level of "50 per cent of median monthly household income" dropped from HK$9,000 in 1998 to HK$7,800 in 2005 for all households, indicating a decrease in overall monthly income levels in Hong Kong after the handover. The number of working poor households increased to 186,900 in 2006 and reached 192,500 in the second quarter of 2010 (Oxfam Hong Kong, 2010).

The growing prominence of working poverty was indirectly confirmed and lawmakers began to take it seriously. In 2006, the Subcommittee to Study the Subject of Combating Poverty of the Legislative Council released the *Report on Working Poverty*. It has identified several causes of working poverty in Hong Kong: (a) economic re-structuring and a shift of industries to the mainland; (b) lack of manpower planning; (c) over-emphasis on cost reduction in both the public and private sectors which led to part-time employment; (d) contracting-out of government services and insufficient monitoring of the contractors on employees' benefits; (e) unequal opportunities for disadvantaged groups, such as new immigrants and ethnic minorities; (f) the need to take care of young children; (g) lack of employment opportunities in remote areas (2006: 18). Responding to the problems, the subcommittee, whose members include legislators of different political parties with varying economic philosophies, has come up with several recommendations: (a) enabling community participation and empowerment of the working poor in formulating strategies to reduce working poverty; (b) developing the economy and creating employment opportunities; (c) providing community support and developing local economies; (d) reviewing the contracting-out arrangements for government services; (e) safeguarding employees' benefits; (f) enhancing the competitiveness of the working poor through education and training; (g) providing financial assistance to the working-poor households; and (h) providing support services for working-poor households (2006: 24–5).

While a minimum wage was discussed in the Subcommittee, due to opposition from some pro-market political groups it was not included in the final recommendations. *The Report* simply notes that, "as regards the suggestion of setting a minimum wage, the Subcommittee considers that the Government should take note of the various views expressed on this subject in this report" (2006: 31). Lee argues that in Hong Kong, "the absence [of] electoral democracy coupled with interest pluralism makes it possible for the authoritarian state to pursue neoliberal reform in its social policy" (Lee, 2009: 173). In fact, after the SARS crisis that almost destroyed Hong Kong's economy, despite more frequent calls for setting up a minimum wage for income maintenance of low-waged labour, the government has refused to do so immediately and has instead launched the two-year

Wage Protection Movement in October 2006 to enourage businesses to offer higher wages for cleaning and security workers. Due to its voluntary nature, the Movement did not yield significant results, and because of that the government finally agreed to proceed to the legislation. Because of the negative impacts of globalisation and economic vulnerability, and threat to political and social stability, the government set up the Provisional Minimum Wage Commission, bringing representatives from the labour and business sectors, government departments and academia together to decide on the initial statutory minimum wage rate in February 2009. Some employers' organisations advocated the level of HK$23–5 per hour, while labour unions requested HK$33 per hour. After a few days of intermittent debate in the legislature, the minimum wage legislation bill was finally passed in late July 2010 but the debates related to the initial rate has not ended even though a minimum wage policy began in May 2011.

Apart from the minimum wage, labour unions, welfare NGOs and some left-wing politicians in Hong Kong have been advocating for years for maximum working hours, the rights to collective bargaining, unemployment benefits and policies against unreasonable dismissal. While the minimum wage bill is set to be signed into law, other policy suggestions have not been put in place by the government as yet. Nevertheless, certain small-scale support measures have been implemented quite successfully, such as the Transport Support Scheme (TSS), which aims to encourage and support low-wage workers from certain remote areas to find jobs and work across districts.

Long-term economic growth and employment opportunities are still the top priority for the Hong Kong government, with the belief that making the pie bigger can finally feed everyone. After the 2008 financial crisis, the government immediately set up the Task Force on Economic Challenges to recruit leading academics and business leaders to generate new ideas for future economic development. The previous chief executive, Donald Tsang, said in 2008 that the Hong Kong government would adhere to the strategy of "stabilising the financial system, supporting enterprises and preserving employment" (Task Force on Economic Challenges, 2009a) in striving for economic recovery. The Task Force also reasserted the preponderant role of the financial sector in Hong Kong's economy and proposed to establish six new economic industries, including testing and certification, medical services, innovation and technology, cultural and creative industries, environmental industry and educational services (Task Force on Economic Challenges, 2009b).

Other social protection policies maintaining the livelihoods of Hong Kong people during and after the financial crisis were short term and remedial in nature. In the first budget after the crisis, Financial Secretary John Tsang pledged in February 2009 that the government would spend HK$1.6 billion to create 62,000 jobs and internship opportunities in the next three years. One of the most controversial programmes in the budget was to launch an "Internship Programme for University Graduates" of about 4,000 places with a recommended minimum monthly salary of HK$4,000. This proposal has sparked criticisms of various kinds in the community: (1) the money should be devoted to helping low-skilled labour and the underprivileged instead to university students, who should have more choices and bargaining power in the employment market; (2) the recommended minimum salary level for university students was too low and would trigger a decrease of salary level for workers with lower educational levels; (3) although the HK$4,000 level was the required minimum, critics feared that it may become a standard scale for companies to hire fresh graduates. This incident clearly indicated how worried Hong Kong people were about the problem of working poverty and "wage exploitation" by employers.

The reluctance of the government to offer direct financial help has also stirred up controversy. While the people were expected to receive a direct cash refund from the government, the government decided instead to inject HK$9 billion into the Mandatory Provident Fund account for workers earning $10,000 or less per month. This measure was criticised as "saving market, but not saving people" by providing the fund managers with a new pool of money for further investment and speculation in the stock market. Taken together with the internship incident, both measures have unexpectedly reinforced the notorious image of the government's collusion with the business sector.

Intergenerational poverty

The establishment of the Commission on Poverty in 2005, consisting of government officials, legislators, NGO leaders and academics aims to address the issues of income disparity, unemployment, child and elderly poverty (Commission on Poverty, 2007). In the *Report of the Commission on Poverty*, the government stated that promoting employment is core to reduce poverty and achieving self-reliance. Based upon this premise, the government vowed to solve the poverty problem through the following means (Commission on Poverty, 2007: ii):

- For those with working abilities, the core strategy is to promote the policy of "From Welfare to Self-reliance" through enhancing employability, promoting employment opportunities, providing effective employment support and suitable work incentives.
- To prevent intergenerational poverty, besides providing children and families at-risk with additional support, we should adopt the right approaches to encourage them to move out of poverty by building up their capacities so that they can plan for their own future.
- For the needy elders and other disadvantaged groups who cannot support themselves, we should continue to provide them with welfare support and a safety net to ensure a dignified standard of living for the needy in our community.

The above policy rhetoric suggests that the underlying philosophy of Hong Kong has not changed in the face of enormous social and economic problems. In essence, it is stated in the report that the idea of " 'Market leads, Government facilitates' has been a core principle in driving the economic development and increasing employment opportunities in Hong Kong" (Commission on Poverty, 2007: 24).

Following the recommendations of the *Report* to tackle intergenerational poverty, the Hong Kong government set up the HK$300 million Child Development Fund (CDF) in 2008 which aspires to "draw on and consolidate the resources from the family, the private sector, the community and the Government effectively in support of the longer-term development of children from a disadvantaged background" (Child Development Fund, 2008). Children aged between 10 and 16 from disadvantaged backgrounds are eligible for application, and the project is expected to serve at least 13,600 such children. The CDF is comprised of three components: (a) "Personal Development Plans" which require participant children to draw up plans with short-term and long-term goals – operating NGOs will provide necessary training programmes for the children with a budget of HK$15,000 per head; (b) a "Mentorship Programme" which identifies each child with a personal mentor to advise on his/her personal development plan; and (c) "Targeted Savings" which encourages participating families to save up to HK$200 per month for two years. It also includes a one-to-one matching contribution with donations from the community. On the completion of the two-year period, the government will offer each child a special financial incentive of HK$3,000. The "target savings" coincides with the "asset building" approach coined and developed by Michael Sherraden, which encourages poor families to accumulate their capital rather than simply relying on short-term income maintenance measures offered by the government (Sherraden, 2000, 2001; Sherraden *et al.*, 1995). The element of self-reliance is again reflected in this policy design.

In fact, before the establishment of the CDF, the government had also set up the HK$200 million Partnership Fund for the Disadvantaged (PFD) in 2005, with the aim to "incentivise the welfare sector to expand their network in seeking and securing corporate participation, and to encourage the business sector to take up more social responsibility in helping to create a cohesive, harmonious and caring society" (Social Welfare Department, Hong Kong, 2005). In May 2010, the legislature approved an injection of another HK$200 million into the fund. Thereafter, NGOs can apply for the fund for programmes and activities relating to the underprivileged such as the disabled and elderly people, children from poor families and victims of family abuse. In regard to child poverty, for example, in 2005, the Society for Community Organisation launched the "Project for Equal Opportunity Development of Children Living in Poverty" with KPMG, providing support to the physical, mental, learning needs and social skills of children up to 18 from poor families. The Boys' & Girls' Clubs Association of Hong Kong partnered with Amway Hong Kong Limited to launch a relief and support programme for mentally distressed children from poor families in 2008.

The government has made attempts to address the intensified problems related to working poverty by establishing a social care matching grant in order to attract donations from big business corporations in Hong Kong to support socially and economically disadvantaged groups, while the government also announced that it would offer a cash allowance of HK$6,000 to all citizens who are eligible for sharing the economic success in the previous financial year. However, these measures have been criticised as short-sighted and many educated people, especially those serving in the social welfare sector, have openly urged the government to devise more long-term and strategic policies in support of the poor rather than deploying resources in coming up with short-term but ineffective measures to tackle the intensification of urban poverty issues.

Having discussed major strategies that the Hong Kong government has devised to address the major socio-economic challenges resulting from the significant economic changes after the regional and global economic crises in recent years, we have not found that the Hong Kong government has attempted to change its long-standing welfare approach. With a heavy emphasis on workfare and productivist approaches in handling social development/welfare needs, the measures outlined above to cope with the post-regional and global financial crises clearly show the Hong Kong government's reluctance in terms of long-term welfare and commitment to social protection.

Macau's responses to major socio-economic challenges

Working poverty

Macau has been experiencing a burgeoning economy in recent years, brought on by the rapid development of the gambling industry and tourism. Compared with Hong Kong, it seems that the Macau government is more generous to the people, especially in terms of the welfare packages being adopted in meeting people's welfare demands. In response to the latest global financial crisis, while the Hong Kong government was reluctant to provide direct cash refunds to citizens before 2011, the Macau government reacted swiftly to reduce 25 per cent of salary tax and distribute M$5,000 to each resident in late 2008. In April 2009, it delivered M$6,000 to each resident again. However, social conflicts in Macau are still frequently seen. For example, the protests on Labour Day (1 May) in recent years have become more confrontational because workers have become more frustrated with the loss of working opportunities to foreign labour. A survey conducted by a labour union in 2005 and 2009 indicated over 70 per cent of local workers thought that foreign labour had infringed upon their job opportunities and other work benefits (*Macau Daily*, 17 March 2010). Wages in different industries have shifted between 1998 and 2007. While the salaries of people working in "construction" and "cultural, recreational, gambling and other services" have increased significantly, the monthly income of people who work in "manufacturing" and "public administration and social security" has only slightly increased (Liu, 2009). More recently, a commissioned research project by the government of the Special Administrative Region of Macau to examine the most important social development concerns perceived by Macau citizens has discovered that the majority of citizens disapprove the growing number of migrant workers from the Chinese mainland and Hong Kong, criticising them for taking over their job opportunities (Consultant Team, 2010).

To target these problems, the Macau government launched the Temporary Income Supplement (TIS) scheme in 2008. Workers aged 40 or above who earn less than M$12,000 per quarter and work for at least 152 hours per month can apply for the TIS, implying that even a worker who can earn M$10,000 per quarter can apply for a TIS of an additional M$2,000 in order to reach the standard. In 2008 and 2009, there were 18,180 successful cases, and 3,800 low-wage workers have benefited, which costs about M$65 million. Similar to Hong Kong, there are frequent calls for setting up a minimum wage in Macau. In responding to such demands, in 2007 the Macau government stipulated that workers for the government's outsourcing jobs relating to cleaning and security are guaranteed a minimum wage of M$21 per hour. Yet comprehensive legislation that covers all jobs remains absent. But while the legislature of Macau is very pro-establishment in nature, whether the minimum wage legislation can finally be achieved depends on the political will of the strong executive-led government.

Intergenerational poverty

The discussion of child poverty or intergenerational poverty is relatively scarce in Macau as compared to Hong Kong. In recapping the 10-year development of Macau after the handover, former chief executive Edmund Ho said that the rapid expansion of the gambling industry had drawn many young people into this relatively high-paid profession, which in turn had alleviated intergenerational poverty. But some academics fear that although these young people do not suffer from economic poverty, they do suffer from "cultural poverty" (i.e. lack of educational qualifications and social exposure), which will affect their social mobility in the long run. In fact, school dropout rates of Macau students increased from 4.2 per cent in 2002/3 to 4.8 percent in 2004/5, which has been partly due to the rapid labour adsorption by the gambling industry. According to the official explanation, this is because those students wished to find jobs (*Oriental Daily*, 12 September 2006). Highly-paid work in the gambling industry is of course an attraction. A government-funded survey conducted in 2007 found that there were lots of youngsters willing to work in casinos (27.9 per cent of interviewees aged 13–18; 48.3 per cent of those aged 19–24; and 52.9 per cent of those aged 25–29). Respondents were further asked whether they were willing to do gambling-related work, and the ratios were even higher (68.5 per cent, 76.0 per cent and 67.6 per cent respectively) (Macau Youth Research Association and General Association of Chinese Students – Macau, 2007: 14). The lopsided economic development centred on the gambling industry is a worrying picture for the government. A recent study regarding educational development in Macau also clearly indicates that people feel that their educational qualifications are inadequate in the labour market, yet they do not have any specific plan for further education and training (Mok and Leung, 2011). This social phenomenon reinforces the argument that Macau's economic poverty is heavily linked with "cultural poverty".

In order to offer better prospects for young people and respond to calls for further developing human capital, the Macau government has turned to education for a solution. Not only in terms of satisfying domestic needs, Macau's educational development has become a national strategic issue, and as President Hu Jintao and Premier Wen Jiabo have said on various occasions, education is vital to the future development of Macau (*Macau Daily*, 21 December 2004, 29 December 2005, 21 December 2009). After the handover, the Macau SAR government started to develop education very aggressively. During the colonial era, the education sector of Macau was largely market-oriented. Until 2009, among all kindergartens, primary and secondary schools, 66 were privately owned, and 10 were public schools. In the 2010 Policy Address of the new administration, chief executive Fernando Chui declared that "social development has a close relationship with educational development. The nurturing of talents and the exploration of technologies also heavily depends on education. The future of society and the development of economy ultimately hinges upon the accumulation of 'human capital' " (Chui *et al.*, 2010: 14). In this connection, he proposed "boosting Macau through education" as the guiding principle to reform the educational administration, push for cross-border educational cooperation and increase educational inputs (Chui *et al.*, 2010: 63). In fact, the educational development of Macau in the past few years has been astonishing. Government expenditure on education has increased from about M$180 million in 2003 to M$370 million in 2008. In 2005, the government decided to expand the 10-year compulsory and free education to 15 years. Students are also exempted from various kinds of miscellaneous fees. These policies have been well received by Macau people because they have greatly alleviated their financial burden, especially in economic hard times (Mok and Leung, 2011). It is also not surprising to see the majority of Macau citizens' support for the further development of higher education by grasping the opportunity to develop the new campus of the University of Macau by dipping into the land offered by the Zhuhai government, just across the border between Macau and Zhuhai (Consultant Team, 2010). Like Hong Kong, the Macau government has not altered its strong workfare orientation when approaching social development/welfare matters but has chosen flexible welfare arrangements through short-term cash allowances in addressing the rapid social and economic changes.

A brief comparison of social welfare spending in Hong Kong and Macau

By and large, the Hong Kong and Macau governments' responses to social challenges are feeble. However, it is envisaged that there will be a surge in social welfare spending in Macau. The Hong Kong SAR Government spent HK$6,453 million in the fiscal year 2000/1. The spending was stagnant before the fiscal year 2008/9. The share of social welfare spending in terms of total government operating expenditure declined from 3.46 per cent to 3.13 per cent during the period of the fiscal years 2000/1 and 2008/9. The figure increased slightly, staying at 3.56 per cent in the fiscal year 2009/10.

In the meantime, the share of social services in terms of total operating expenditure stood very low at 2.82 per cent in 2000 in Macau. Nevertheless, the share jumped later on. In absolute terms, social services cost M$161.15 million in 2000, M$404.42 million in 2005 and M$971.268 million in 2010; thus the ratio of social services spending to government operating expenditure rose from 4.98 per cent in 2005 to 10.65 per cent in 2010.

Selective developmental welfare states and no change of tune in social welfare

Like other Asian economies, maintaining and raising living standards in Hong Kong and Macau is vital to maintaining the political legitimacy of the two governments (Lai, 2005, 2008, 2010; Lee, 2009). In the past, many governments in East Asia proved to be very successful in raising their political popularity by engaging the whole society in developing the economy by adopting the role of "developmental state" (Mok and Forrest, 2009). With the significant social, economic and political changes resulting from domestic economic restructuring and regional and global economic crises, a growing number of Asian states have found it difficult to maintain political popularity if their coping strategies are rendered inappropriate in managing crisis situations (Mok, 2011).

In recent years, the people of Hong Kong have been very concerned about their living standards, upon which the approval ratings of the government are often rated. According to a series of population-wide surveys in various years, issues related to economic problems and sustainable livelihoods have always been the top concerns for the people. In a survey conducted by the University of Hong Kong in late June 2010, Hong Kong people said that their greatest concerns are related to livelihood problems (53.8 per cent), followed by economic problems (31.1 per cent) and then political problems (11.9 per cent) (Public Opinion Programme of the University of Hong Kong, 2010). The situation is similar in Macau. In 2009, the Research Centre for Sustainable Development Strategies of the Macau government conducted a survey to examine how the Macau people assessed the development of Macau. The results indicated that their top five concerns were "employment" (19.0 per cent), "housing" (18.8 per cent), "economic development" (17.1 per cent), "livelihood" (12.4 per cent) and "social welfare" (8.9 per cent) (Consultant Team, 2010).

Yet public demands for better standards of living after the handover are different in Hong Kong and Macau as people in the two places have different assessments of the colonial regimes and thus have different expectations for the SAR governments. In a survey conducted before the handover of the two cities, 68.6 per cent of Hong Kong people said they were somewhat or very satisfied with British colonial rule, and only 7.2 per cent said they were somewhat or very unsatisfied with it. The respective answers of Macau people were 22.3 per cent and 36.4 per cent. In assessing the contributions and mistakes of the colonial regimes to the development of the society, 64.5 per cent of Hong Kong people said that the colonial government had offered "more contributions", and only 2.9 per cent said "more mistakes". The respective answers of Macau people were 19.8 per cent and 18.4 per cent respectively (Chung *et al.*, 2000). The high level of affirmation and appreciation for the colonial regime in Hong Kong has undoubtedly created pressure for the SAR government to keep up its achievements. While the democratic movement has been gaining momentum in recent years, the Hong Kong government has to be more accountable to the public in order to assert its political legitimacy. In contrast, the Macau SAR government has been in a better position to win over the people's hearts after the handover given the mediocre governance of its predecessor in the eyes of the Macau people. This may partly explain why the Hong Kong government has made more effort to eradicate working poverty and intergenerational poverty, as discussed above.

Despite the two governments having attempted to initiate new policies in addressing the major social development challenges, we have not witnessed a fundamental change in the philosophy and approach in social welfare and social development, especially given that these newly adopted policies/measures are in fact piecemeal in nature. In Hong Kong, one of the strong reasons against welfare expansion is the concern of "value for money". For example, some social policy scholarshave raised concerns about the financial sustainability of the welfare system, where the tax base is narrow and the tax rate is low. It is feared that increasing the rights of Hong Kong people to welfare without acknowledging their responsibility to pay for it will unreasonably heighten the public expectation for unlimited welfare. The inability of satisfying such expectations will ultimately undermine governance and political legitimacy (Wong, 2008). In recent years, the failure of the Hong Kong government to levy the Goods and Services Tax (GST) and introduce a means-tested mechanism for the old age allowance for the elderly clearly indicates its limitations in "squaring the welfare circle".

Recognising that reform is needed to respond to growing demands for welfare, in April 2010 the Social Welfare Advisory Committee of the Hong Kong government issued the second *Long-term Social Welfare Planning in Hong Kong* consultation paper, inviting suggestions and comments from the community on the future development of Hong Kong's welfare system. The consultation paper firstly points out the major economic (e.g. economic restructuring), social (e.g. crisis of traditional family) and technological (e.g. hidden youth) challenges facing Hong Kong in recent years. Questions concerning financial sustainability and the provision of welfare services are also raised in the paper. In a nutshell, the paper still places the importance on the concept of "self-reliance" to Hong Kong's welfare system. This is reflected in the proposed strategic direction of social investment which aims to build up the capacity of individuals, families and communities in order to cope with coming challenges. The "user pays" principle advocates shared responsibility for the sustainability of the welfare system. In addition, the paper also attaches much weight to the idea of multi-partite partnership between the government, NGOs and the business sector, which suggests that the government will not be the sole player in Hong Kong's welfare system in the future. Not only are businesses invited to enact their corporate social responsibilities to engage in welfare provision, the idea of business is also incorporated in the paper, such as the promotion of social enterprise, which aims to run a welfare agency using a business approach (Social Welfare Advisory Committee, HKSAR, 2010).

Yet the consultation paper was poorly received in the community, as concerned academics and NGOs immediately pointed to the lack of policy direction, policy substance and political will as reflected in the cliché of the consultation paper (*Oriental Daily*, 23 May 2010). For example, the Society for Community Organisation (2010) challenges the absence of discussion on tax structure, philosophy of public finance and human rights in the consultation paper. More specifically, it opposes the "user pays" principle, which will commodify the provision of welfare and make the underprivileged more vulnerable. It also casts doubt on the prospect of social enterprise in a market as competitive as Hong Kong. Similarly, the Hong Kong Council of Social Service (HKCSS 2010) also points to the lack of discussion on tax structure, public financing and social security insurance. Taken together, the major criticism of the consultation paper lies in the reluctance of government to alter its social welfare philosophy of "big market, small government". It is also clear that the Hong Kong government has no intention to propose major changes to the institutional welfare arrangements but still very much treats welfare as tool to boost the economy and to legitimise the regime (Hwang, 2011).

In Macau, though social conflicts related to working and intergenerational poverty have already surfaced, it seems that the government does not plan to pursue a comprehensive overview of welfare policies for the long run, at least for the time being (Tang, 2009). Though the government successfully reformed the social security system into a two-tiered one in 2008 to extend coverage to all citizens, it seldom mentions other social protection measures relating to working and intergenerational poverty. For example, as stated in the 2010 Policy Address, one of the major five policy objectives of the government is to "implement short-term livelihood enhancing measures to cope with the post-financial crisis impacts" (Chui, 2010: 24). In talking about social protection measures, chief executive Fernando Chui said that "the government needs to analyze clearly on how the public policies for social protection can balance the citizens' rights and responsibilities, long-term accumulation and short-term sharing, and the relationship with the market . . ." (2010: 13). Although Chui has announced more plans to support the socially and economically poor in Macau, such as the recent plan to construct social housing in the city-state, social policy experts do not foresee any fundamental change in Macau welfare ideology (Lai, 2011). From this rhetoric, it is expected that there will not be any vast changes for Macau's welfare system in the short term.

Recent studies related to social development challenges in Macau also suggest that despite the growing demands for social welfare protection, the Macau government has not committed itself to change its social welfare model. Notwithstanding that the Macau government has tried to make its citizens happier by offering them occasional vouchers or cash in the midst of economic crises, these short-term measures seem not to be very successful in containing growing social dissatisfaction. The riot turning from a protest staged on 1 May in Macau demonstrated the social unrest deeply rooted in the society, especially bearing in mind that Macau has experienced intensified income inequality, unstable economic growth and social development resulting from the domestic economic restructuring and global economic turmoil (Consultant Team, 2010; Wong *et al.*, 2011). After critical reflections on the socio-economic transformations in the globalised world, Standing argues that we have growing "dangerous classes" coming from unprotected social classes in the highly unequal capitalist world, and such a development may pose a potential threat to social and political stability (Standing, 2010). As Kwon *et al.* (2009) have rightly suggested, Hong Kong maintained the basic structure of a selective developmental welfare state after the financial crisis. Similarly, Mok (2013) argues that Macau remains a reluctant welfare regime even when the city-state has been confronted with increasing demands for social welfare protection for socially disadvantaged groups. Analysing the welfare developments of Hong Kong and Macau against the wider context that Standing has outlined, we would be interested to see how far the welfare state adaptations of Hong Kong and Macau would succeed in addressing rapid socio-economic, political and welfare changes. Judging from what we have discussed above, the ideal of productivism is not dead in these Chinese societies.

The most recent government policies being adopted by these two SAR governments do not reveal any clear signal of departure from a "productivist" welfare model, especially when these governments still maintain a relatively "conservative" approach in social welfare. In the most recently published *Policy Address of 2013* and *Budget of 2013*, both the chief executive and financial secretary of the HKSAR have not committed to long-term welfare provision despite the fact that the government is well aware of the heightened welfare expectations and the growth of the ageing population in Hong Kong (see Leung, 2013; Tsang, 2013). As the chief executive of the HKSAR openly declared, without fundamental taxation reform, the government would not significantly change its welfare provision approach, while the financial secretary does not commit to offer long-term welfare and more social protection for Hong Kong citizens as he still considers it is too risky to commit the government to unmanageable financial resources for welfare against the unstable global economic context (Tsang, 2013). Similarly, the chief executive of Macau SAR continued to hand out one-off cash allowances to the people rather than committing the government to any medium- or long-term welfare reforms (Macau SAR Government, 2013).

Analysing the welfare approaches in Hong Kong and Macau in the light of the social policy debate in Europe that focused on "state-market-class" relations seems less applicable, since these Asian societies are more concentrated on the triple relation of "family-collective-state" in welfare resource provision, especially bearing in mind that they have no rapidly institutionalised public or state insurance like their counterparts in Japan, South Korea and Taiwan. The steady growth of the economy and positive outcomes such as improved living standards has induced people to support a productivist strategy of development. But how far this development approach will sustain remains an open question which requires further evidence-based research. When comparing Hong Kong and Macau in terms of challenges for future welfare development, we should note that Hong

Kong is becoming more democratised, with a direct election scheduled in the near future. How far might Hong Kong follow the pathways of Taiwan and South Korea in social welfare expansion, with democratisation creeping in (Mok and Lau, 2013)?

One may argue that democracy would certainly affect welfare approaches as Haggard and Kaufman (2008) have argued; nonetheless we must be aware of how local politics operates and how the legacy of welfare templates will affect the choice of welfare approach. More importantly, the values and ideologies shared by the people, the fiscal capacity of the government and the commitment of people to transformation of the tax regime would certainly affect future directions in terms of welfare regimes. Despite the fact that more people in Hong Kong have been promoting long-term welfare development in the handling of rapid socio-economic and demographic changes, we also witness growing countering forces formed by business coalitions and the middle class, guarding against Hong Kong becoming a welfare state. The same set of questions also confront the Macau government when society opens up and democracy comes onto the scene. As in Hong Kong, the social and political foundations would certainly affect the way the Macau government handles future welfare expansion. Hence, we have to search for more empirical evidence to test the thesis of democracy and welfare expansion, critically examining the impact of the legacy of welfare templates on future welfare approaches in these two SARs (Mok, 2010, 2011).

Conclusion

Putting the cases of Hong Kong's and Macau's recent responses to major socio-economic challenges into the wider context of theoretical debates related to the sustainability of the "productivist welfare regime" in managing changing welfare expectations and handling the major social and economic challenges discussed above, we would argue with caution that both the Hong Kong and Macau governments have to conduct comprehensive reviews of their existing social development and social welfare strategies in order to properly address the unmatched social welfare needs resulting from the rapid social, economic and political changes in the increasingly complex, globalised world. These SAR governments will encounter major challenges in asserting their political legitimacy, especially when they are not directly elected. The popularity of political regimes is built upon the citizens' approval of the policies proposed to handle the complicated social and economic problems affecting people's livelihoods. With the rise of unemployment, intensi-fied income inequality, deeply rooted social and economic problems because of fundamental economic restructuring, together with the rise of civil society fighting for protecting a diversity of social and economic rights of the citizens, these SAR governments will eventually have to review their strategies and policies in order to legitimate their regimes by transforming their social development and welfare poli-cies/strategies. Whether the two SARs can maintain the status of "selective devel-opmental welfare state" (or for Macau seemingly more like a "reluctant welfare regime") would require further research for an answer.

Notes

1 The authors want to thank the Research Grant Committee of the HKSAR Government for supporting a GRF project entitled "Social Safety Nets during Economic Crisis: Hong Kong, Malaysia Singapore and Thailand" (Project Number: GRF/751510).
2 Macau's social security system consists of the Social Security Fund (SSF), Financial Assistance (FA) and the Old-age Allowance. The SSF is funded from the government's allocation with minimal employers' and employees' contributions.
3 The present chapter is a revised version based upon Muk's previous publication for incorporating in this volume.

References

Chan, R. K. H. (2006). "Risk and its Management in Post-financial Crisis Hong Kong", *Social Policy and Administration*, 40(2): 215–229.

Chan, R. K. H. (2009). "Risk Discourse and Politics: Restructuring Welfare in Hong Kong", *Critical Social Policy*, 29(1): 24–52.

Child Development Fund (2008). *Introduction of Child Development Fund*. Available at: http://www.cdf.gov.hk/english/introcdf/introcdf.html.

Chui, E., Tsang, S. and Mok, K. H. (2010). "After the Handover in 1997: Development and Challenges for Social Welfare and Social Work Profession in Hong Kong", *Asia Pacific Journal of Social Work and Development*, 20(1): 52–64.

Chui, S. (2010). *Policy Address for Fiscal Year 2010*. Macau: The Government of the Macau SAR.

Chiu, S. and Lui, T. (2009). *Hong Kong: Becoming a Chinese Global City*. London: Routledge.

Chung, T., Ma, K. and Lee, P. (2000). "Comparison of Public Opinions of Hong Kong and Macau before the Handover", The Public Opinion Program of the University of Hong Kong. Available at: http://hkupop.hku.hk/chinese/macau/pdf/Macau_HO_1999.pdf

Commission on Poverty (2007). *Report of the Commission on Poverty*. Hong Kong: Commission on Poverty.

Consultant Team (2010). *Research of Social Development and Social Indicators in Macau*. Macau: The Government of the Macau SAR.

Gough, I. (2004). "East Asia: The Limits of Productivist Regimes", in I. Gough and G. Wood G. (eds) *Insecurity and Welfare Regimes in Asia, Africa and Latin America*. Cambridge: Cambridge University Press, pp. 169–201.

Haggard, S. and Kaufman, R. R. (2008). *Development, Democracy and Welfare States: Latin America, East Asia and Eastern Europe*. Princeton, NJ: Princeton University Press.

HKCSS (Hong Kong Council of Social Services) (2008). "Social Development Index 2008" press release, 27 July. Available at: http://www.socialindicators.org.hk/chi/sd_highlight (in Chinese).

HKCSS (Hong Kong Council of Social Service) (2010). *Position Paper on the Long-term Social Welfare Planning in Hong Kong Consultation Paper*, 5 June.

Holliday, I. (2000). "Productivist Welfare Capitalism: Social Policy in East Asia", *Political Studies*, 48: 706–723.

Holliday, I. (2005). "East Asian Social Policy in the Wake of the Financial Crisis: Farewell to Productivism?" *Policy and Politics*, 33(1): 145–162.

Hwang, G. J. (2011). *New Welfare States in East Asia: Global Challenges and Restructuring*. Cheltenham: Edward Elgar.

Kwon, H. J., Mkandawire, T. and Palme, J. (2009). "Introduction: Social Policy and Economic Development in Late Industrializers", *International Journal of Social Welfare*, 18(s1): S1–S11.

Lai, D. W. L. (2003). *Macao Social Policy Model*. Macao: Macao Polytechnic Institute.

Lai, D. W. L. (2005). "Diffusion and Politics: Social Security Developments of Hong Kong and Macao in the Colonial Era", *Asian Journal of Social Policy*, 1(1): 9–24.

Lai, W. L. (2006). "Macao's Social Welfare Model: A Productivist Welfare Regime", *The Hong Kong Journal of Social Work*, 40(1/2): 47–59.

Lai, W. L. (2008). "The Regulatory Role of Social Policy: Macao's Social Security Development", *Journal of Contemporary Asia*, 38(3): 373–394.

Lai, W. L. (2010). "The Political Economy of Social Security Development in Macao", *China Journal of Social Work*, 3(1): 65–81.

Lai, W. L. (2011). "The Regulatory State of Macao in Social Policy Development", Paper presented at the Workshop on Social Welfare Regimes in Greater China, May. Hong Kong: Hong Kong Institute of Education.

Lau, M. and Mok, K. H. (2010). "Is Welfare Restructuring and Economic Development in Post-1997 Hong Kong in Search of a Cohesive Society?", in K. H. Mok and Y. Ku (eds) *Social Cohesion in Greater China: Challenges for Social Policy and Governance*. Singapore: World Scientific, pp. 287–318.

Lee, E. W. Y. (2009). "Social Mobilization, Blame Avoidance and Welfare Restructuring in Hong Kong", in M. Sing (ed.) *Politics and Government in Hong Kong*. London: Routledge, pp. 162–175.

Leung, C. Y. (2013). *Address by the Chief Executive The Honourable CY Leung*. Hong Kong: Government Printer.

Lin, K. (2010). "A Critical Analysis of the Productive Welfare Approach in Social Development", in T. Yang and J. G. Gao (eds) *Contemporary Social Policy Studies*. Beijing: Chinese Labour and Social Security Press.

Liu, C. W. (2009). "Labor, Employment and Human Resources in Macao", in Y. Hao and Z. Wu (eds) *Annual Report on Economy and Society in Macau 2008–2009*. Beijing: Social Sciences Academic Press, pp. 153–170 (in Chinese).

Macau Daily (21 December 2004). "Hu Jintao States Four Aspirations to Encourage the Macau People", p. A01 (in Chinese).

Macau Daily (29 December 2005). "Premier Wen: 15-year Compulsory Education is Extraordinary", p. A02 (in Chinese).

Macau Daily (21 December 2009). "Hu Jintao Wishes Macau to Build First Class Universities", p. A04. Available at: http://www.macaodaily.com/html/2009–12/21/content_406595.htm (in Chinese).

Macau Daily (17 March 2010). "Push for Minimum Wage, Alleviate Working Poverty", p. D09 (in Chinese).

Macau SAR Government (2013). *Policy Address of 2013–14*. Macau: Macau Government.

Macau Youth Research Association and General Association of Chinese Students – Macau (2007). *The Impacts of the Opening Up of the Casino Industry on Macau: Opinion Survey of the Youth*. Macau: Macao Youth Studies (in Chinese).

Mok, K. H. (2010). "The Impact of Global Economic Crisis: Social Policy Responses and Social Protection Strategies in East Asia", in T. Yang and J. G. Gao (eds) *Contemporary Social Policy Studies*. Beijing: Labour and Social Security Press (in Chinese).

Mok, K. H. (2011). "Right Diagnosis and Appropriate Treatment for the Global Financial Crisis?: Social Protection Measures and Social Policy Responses in East Asia", in G. J. Hwang (ed.) *New Welfare States in East Asia*. London: Edward Elgar.

Mok, K. H. (2013, forthcoming). "Can the Reluctant Welfare Regime Sustain? Managing Social Change and Welfare Expectations in Macau", in W. Y. Yu and M. K. Chan (eds) *China's Macao Transformed: Challenge and Development in the 21st Century*. Hong Kong: City University of Hong Kong Press.

Mok, K. H. and Forrest, R. (2009). "Introduction: The Search for Good Governance in Asia", in K. H. Mok and R. Forrest (eds) *Changing Governance and Public Policy in East Asia*. London: Routledge, pp. 1–22.

Mok, K. H. and Lau, M. (eds.) (2013, forthcoming). *Welfare Regimes in Transition: Managing Social Change and Social Policy in Greater China*, London: Routledge.

Mok, K. H. and Leung, K. K. (2011). "Establishing Macau further through Education: Citizens' Evaluations of Educational Development in Macau", in S. L. Wong *et al.* (eds) *Social Development and Social Indicators in Macau*. Hong Kong: Chinese University Press.

Oriental Daily (12 September 2006). "Students' Competition to be Casino Dealers has Driven the Wave of School Dropouts", p. A06.

Oriental Daily (23 May 2010). "Lack of Government Responsibility in Welfare Planning". Available at: http://www.orientaldaily.on.cc/cnt/news/20100523/00176_014.html.

Oxfam Hong Kong (2007). *Employed, but Poor: Poverty among Employed People in Hong Kong*, briefing paper]. Hong Kong: Oxfam Hong Kong.

Oxfam Hong Kong (2010). *Employment and Poverty in Hong Kong Families*, briefing paper. Hong Kong: Oxfam Hong Kong.

Public Opinion Programme of the University of Hong Kong (2010). "People's Level of Concern about Political, Economic and Livelihood Problems", June.

Sherraden, M. (2000). "From Research to Policy: Lessons from Individual Development Accounts", *The Journal of Consumer Affairs*, 34(2): 159–181.

Sherraden, M. (2001). "Assets and the Poor: Implications for Individual Accounts and Social Security", invited testimony to the President's Commission on Social Security. Washington DC, 18 October.

Sherraden, M., Nair, S., Vasoo, S., Liang, N. T. and Sherraden, M. S. (1995). "Social Policy Based on Assets: The Impacts of Singapore's Central Provident Fund", *Asian Journal of Political Science*, 3(2): 112–133.

Social Welfare Advisory Committee, HKSAR (2010). *Long-term Social Welfare Planning in Hong Kong – Consultation Paper*, April.

Social Welfare Department, Hong Kong (2005). *Partnership Fund for the Disadvantaged*. Available at http://www.swd.gov.hk/en/index/site_pubsvc/page_supportser/sub_partnership/.

Society for Community Organization (2010). *Position Paper on the Long-term Social Welfare Planning in Hong Kong Consultation Paper*, May.

Standing, G. (2010). "Work After Globalization: Building Occupational Citizenship", Paper presented at the Seventh East Asia Social Policy Network Annual Conference *Searching for New Policy Paradigms in East Asia*, 20–21 August, Sogang University, South Korea.

Subcommittee to Study the Subject of Combating Poverty, Legislative Council of the HKSAR (2006). *Report on Working Poverty* (LC Paper No. CB(2)1002/05–06). Hong Kong: Hong Kong SAR Government.

Tang, K. L. (2000). "Asian Crisis, Social Welfare, and Policy Responses: Hong Kong and Korea Compared", *International Journal of Sociology and Social Policy*, 20 (5/6): 49–71.

Tang, K. L. (2006). "Welfare-to-work Programs in Hong Kong: A New Direction in East Asian Social Welfare?", in Y. Yang (ed). *Development of Macau Social Welfare System:*

Characteristics and Tendency. Macau: Centre for Macau Studies of the University of Macau, pp. 166–179 (in Chinese).

Tang, K. L. and Lin, J. (2005). "How to Design Social Policies for Reducing Intergenerational Poverty" (Occasional Paper No. 161). Hong Kong: Hong Kong Institute of Asia-Pacific Studies.

Tang, Y.W. (2009). "Development and Reforming of Social Security in Macao", in Y. F. Hao and Z. L. Wu (eds) *Annual Report on Economy and Society in Macau 2008–2009*. Beijing: Social Sciences Academic Press, pp. 171–188 (in Chinese).

Task Force on Economic Challenges (2009a). "CE Announces New Measures to Tackle Financial Tsunami", press release, 22 January. Available at: http://www.info.gov.hk/gia/general/200901/22/P200901220263.htm.

Task Force on Economic Challenges (2009b). "Transcript of Remarks by CE at Media Session after Meeting of Task Force on Economic Challenges", press release, 3 April. Available at http://www.info.gov.hk/gia/general/200906/22/P200906220250.htm.

Tian, B. H. and Jiang, C. (2006). " 'From Welfare to Work' – The Development of Macau's Social Welfare", in Y. Z. Yang (ed.) *Development of Macau Social Welfare System: Characteristics and Tendency*. Macau: Centre for Macau Studies of the University of Macau, pp. 166–179 (in Chinese).

Wilding, P. (2008). "Is the East Asian Welfare Model Still Productive?", *Journal of Asian Public Policy*, 1(1): 18–31.

Wong, C. K. (2008). "Squaring the Welfare Circle in Hong Kong: Lessons for Governance in Social Policy", *Asian Survey*, 48(2): 323–342.

Wong, S. L. *et al.* (eds) (2011). *Social Development and Social Indicators in Macau*. Hong Kong: Chinese University Press.

3 Welfare restructuring and social (in)equity across generations in Hong Kong

Maggie K. W. Lau

Introduction

Economic restructuring and social transformation have significantly challenged the established structure of the welfare regime in Hong Kong (Chan and Lee, 2010; Mok, 2011). Like other East Asian economies, new social risks arising from increasingly global and complex societies and a breakdown of traditional and informal risk-sharing mechanisms bring enormous difficulties for certain social groups in Hong Kong (Chan, 2009; Chiu and Wong, 2011). It is also realised that global processes of economic change give governments impetus to adopt a welfare mix approach to ensure economic competitiveness (Powell, 2007). The extent to which welfare restructuring attains productive employment and sustainable livelihoods, and also ensures equal opportunities for people's future development in Hong Kong, is the focal point of the current debate.

This chapter adopts the notions of social equity and equality of opportunities to frame an analysis of the effects of financial crises, demographic change and social transformation on welfare restructuring that have shaped people's lifestyles in Hong Kong over the past two decades. It begins with conceptual discussion on sustainable livelihoods and equal opportunities and examines how they matter in rapidly changing economies. The next section focuses on the effects of economic restructuring, population ageing, and changing family structure on the caring-giving functions of traditional extended families in the Hong Kong context. The discussion further explores how an increase in atypical forms of employment with lack of adequate stable income and limited coverage of social security benefits shapes the lifestyles of working groups and their families. It also examines the extent to which welfare restructuring ensures social equity across generations. Finally, it argues whether "productivist welfare capitalism", emphasising the subordination of social policy to economic policy, and heavy reliance on family mutual support (Holliday, 2005) is still effective in addressing the increasing demand for care and support from a rapidly changing society.

Welfare restructuring, sustainable livelihoods and equality of opportunities

As Bonoli (2006: 5–6) argues, "de-industrialisation and tertiarisation of employment, as well as the massive entry of women into the labour force, have increased the instability of family structures and the de-standardisation of employment". In a knowledge-intensive economy, new social risks can be understood by an inability to reconcile work and family life, an increase in rates of single parenthood as a result of change in family structures and behaviour, low-skilled workers seriously exposed to the risk of being poorly paid and an increase in atypical working patterns with insufficient social security benefits (Bonoli, 2006).

The global financial crisis in the second half of 2008 further led to a sharp fall in employment and significant increase in unemployment, with serious repercussions for those in a disadvantaged position in the labour market, especially for those low-skilled and youth, and those in temporary or atypical jobs (International Labour Organisation, 2010; OECD, 2009a, 2009b). The plights of low-paid and unemployed workers and their families echo Standing's analysis of "precarious" labour insecurity, such as absence of protection against loss of employment (i.e. "labour market" insecurity), lack of adequate stable income and comprehensive social security protection (i.e. income insecurity) (Standing, 2011). Their labour insecurity raises concerns about how to enable all people to attain secure and sustainable livelihoods – which ensures "people's capacities to exercise choice, access opportunities and resources, and use them in ways that do not foreclose options for others to make their living, either now, or in the future" (Singh and Gilman, 1999: 540). Meanwhile, population ageing and changing family structures have weakened traditional risk-sharing mechanisms in many nations of the world, and engendered growing demand for care and support. For instance, the financial viability of the ongoing commitment to pay for the old-age entitlements has become a global policy debate on how to address the fairness and sustainability of resources transfer between the elderly and the working-age population (Morgan and Kunkel, 2011; Williamson *et al.*, 2003).

In the past decade, there have been several debates about the viability of "productivist welfare capitalism" in East Asian societies (Chan and Lee, 2010; Mok, 2011; Wilding, 2008). The post-1997 Asian financial crisis has intensified flexibilisation and informalisation of production processes (Standing, 2011). The family acts as a major player in welfare provision and is now further weakened in the globalising economy and changing family structures. Meanwhile, the global processes of economic change have significantly shaped governments' economic and social policies. There has been an increasing emphasis on marketisation of social services, promoting the work ethic and workfare, and individual and family responsibility, around the globe. To ensure economic competitiveness, a welfare mix approach is adopted to shift responsibilities of welfare provision to individuals, family, market and the community (Powell, 2007). It is argued that "the new risks are compounded by new risk management policies, which reflect the growing dominance of neoliberal values and are often based on a critique of the inability of old welfare strategies that emphasised collectivity and public schemes ... The new strategies are concerned primarily with mobilising individuals to be more responsible for themselves and to be competitive in the market, revealing a weakened belief in social solidarity and the efficacy of the public sector" (Chan, 2009: 27). A recent analysis of intergenerational patterns of reciprocity and exchange in the broader socio-economic context highlights that social and economic changes arising from globalisation limit the scope of government provisions (such as pension schemes), instead of promoting private and voluntary welfare (Phillipson, 2010). Izuhara and Forrest's recent study shows the co-existence of de-familisation and familisation in the housing sphere. As they argue, "While socio-economic and policy change supported increasing independence of the older generations from their adult children, the recent economic crisis and house price inflation reinforced family dependence of the younger generation" (Izuhara and Forrest, 2012: 17).

The Hong Kong government shares similar experiences to other developed countries in terms of how to achieve a fair and equitable distribution of public services to all walks of life in the midst of its economic and social transformation (Chan and Lee, 2010; Lee, 2008). Social equity refers to "the goal that the members of all social groups will have the same prospects for success and the same opportunity to be protected from the adversities of life ... Class, or more generally socioeconomic status, is associated with differing levels of resources, but should not be linked to differences in the availability of basic public services nor to the quality of those services" (Johnson and Svara, 2011: 3). It emphasises equal access to the "opportunities that allow people to pursue a life of their own choosing and to avoid extreme deprivations in outcomes" – that is, equality in rights, resources and voice (Buss and Ahmed, 2011: 56). This chapter sets out against this wider context to examine significant impacts of changing family structure on family support in the midst of global financial crises, and further explores the extent to which welfare restructuring addresses social equity across the generations in Hong Kong.

Expanding precarious employment in the labour market

The Hong Kong economy had begun to run into difficulties since the late 1990s, partly as a result of the financial crises and partly as a result of economic change and increased competition from other cities on the mainland or from other neighbouring countries in the region. Hong Kong has turned itself into an economy heavily relying upon the service sector since the late 1970s. The manufacturing sector of Hong Kong lost its competitiveness. The number of people engaging in manufacturing industry has dropped significantly from 207,816 in 2000 to 117,590 in 2010, while the numbers of people serving in the import/export trade and wholesale, retail, financing and insurance, and real estate have grown steadily from 1,028,615 in 2000 to 1,122,185 in 2010 (Census and Statistics Department, 2011a). The secondary industry's share of GDP declined significantly from 14.2 per cent in 2000 to 6.9 per cent in 2010. Meanwhile, the contribution of tertiary industry to GDP grew significantly from 85.7 per cent to 93 per cent in the same period of time (see Table 3.1). The growth of advanced finance and producer services, such as legal services, accounting and auditing services, is accompanied by the growth in professional and managerial jobs, while the decline in traditional manufacturing industry has resulted in the growth of low-skilled, low-paid, part-time jobs. As a result, income disparities have further intensified in Hong Kong over the last decade. The widening gap between the rich and the poor has been clearly indicated by the increase in the Gini coefficient in Hong Kong. The Gini coefficient rose from 0.518 in 1996, to 0.525 in 2001. The situation became worse in 2011 when the Gini coefficient rose to 0.537 (see Table 3.1). Hong Kong has the worst income disparities, compared to other East Asian societies such as South Korea and Singapore (Hong Kong Council of Social Service, 2012b).

In addition to the drastic economic restructuring, Hong Kong has also confronted global economic uncertainties and vulnerabilities since the late 1990s. Severely hit by the Asian financial turmoil, GDP growth significantly decreased from 10.4 per cent in 1996 to –4.7 per cent in 1998, while per capita GDP growth decreased from 5.6 per cent to –5.5 per cent at the same time. There has been slow economic growth in 2003 and in 2009 followed by the recession after the prevalence of Severe Acute Respiratory Syndrome (SARS) and the global financial crisis in 2008 respectively. Not surprisingly, the economic downturn contributed to a high unemployment rate, particularly among middle-aged people with low skills and educational attainment. The unemployment rate increased significantly from 2.8 per cent in 1996 to 4.7 per cent in 1998, and sharply increased to 7.9 per cent in 2003 and 5.4 per cent in 2009. The proportion of workless households was recorded as 9.8 per cent in 2003 and 9.2 per cent in 2009, compared to 7.1 per cent in 2001 (see Table 3.1). Meanwhile, the proportion of unemployed people receiving Comprehensive Social Security Assistance[1] (CSSA) to the whole pool of CSSA recipients has increased significantly since 1994. The tax-funded CSSA scheme places a large financial burden on the government and creates pressures for welfare reforms from a passive system of benefit payment to the unemployed to an active system encouraging personal responsibility and facilitating return to employment. The workfare programmes were first introduced in 1999 and further extended to both employable CSSA recipients and other near-CSSA recipients. Nonetheless, the effectiveness of these workfare programmes is related to several key issues, including: (i) how to create more employment opportunities; (ii) how to enhance the employability of the unemployed with low skills and low educational attainment; (iii) how to 'make work pay' and reduce the number of working poor; and (iv) how to ensure accessibility of support services (like care support services) (Gilbert, 2005; Rafferty and Wiggan, 2011).

According to Standing's analysis of "precarious" labour insecurity, people engaged in the informal economy (i.e. part-time, temporary and flexible employment) will not benefit from social security systems. Labour market informalisation has contributed to a massive number of precarious jobs, and consequently exclusion from social protection (Standing, 2011). In 2011, the Hong Kong Council of Social Service estimated that there were 17.1 per cent of people living in low-income households with a monthly household income less than or equal to half of the median monthly domestic household income of the corresponding household size, compared to 15 per cent in 1996 and 17.7 per cent 2001 (see Table 3.1). People who kept their jobs have suffered from taking a drop in salary and/or having longer working hours, especially for those workers who are low-skilled and/or low-educated. They were more likely to find part-time, temporary or low-paid jobs. In 2009, the median ages of all causal and part-time employees were 46 and 45 respectively, compared to 41 and 40 in 1999. Employees with low educational attainment had higher rates of taking up causal employment. It is also recorded that a high proportion of the causal employees engaged in the construction sector have a high vulnerability to economic uncertainties. In 2009, almost 45 per cent of causal employees did not work in permanent job because of the custom of trade or norm/business arrangements of their companies. Over one-third of casual employees could not find permanent jobs (12.6 per cent) and a tenth were tied to the home, engaging in housework or caring for dependants. The proportion of female part-time employees (64.4 per cent) was higher than their male counterparts (35.6 per cent) in 2009. Owing to caring responsibilities, over one-third (37.4 per cent) of employees worked part-time (Census and Statistics Department, 2010a). This indicates that attachment to the labour market does not guarantee a life free from poverty owing to the informalisation of employment.

Weakening traditional extended families' caring-giving functions

Apart from the repercussions of the global financial crises, Hong Kong has also faced demographic shifts in family structure and changing patterns of family caring. Divorce decrees as a percentage of marriages rose from 25.6 per cent in 1996 to 40.4 per cent in 2002. There have been at least one-third of cases since 2003. Female or male-headed single parents with dependent children may not find it easy to get full-time jobs because of caring responsibilities and thus they are more likely to encounter financial difficulties. There were at least one-tenth of CSSA single parent families with dependent children after the Asian financial crisis. As shown in Table 3.1, there have been at least one-fifth of children aged 0–14 living in low-income households in Hong Kong since the mid-1990s. Children in low-income households not only encounter financial deprivation but also suffer from service exclusion and non-participation in common social activities (Levitas *et al.*, 2007). Children living in low-income households are deprived of equal chances of growth and development, such as the use of information technology and access to the information-abundant internet, and taking part in activities and tuition classes after school. The next section will further explore how an increase in atypical employment patterns shapes the lifestyles of working groups and their families. In particular, there has been growing public concern about intergenerational poverty in Hong Kong.

Furthermore, Hong Kong has already confronted an ageing population resulting from a low fertility rate and an increase in life expectancy. The official statistics

Table 3.1 Selected socioeconomic indicators

	1996	1997	1998	1999	2000	2001	2002	2003	2004	2005	2006	2007	2008	2009	2010	2011
Average household size (person)[1]	3.4	3.3	3.3	3.3	3.3	3.2	3.2	3.1	3.1	3.0	3.0	3.0	3.0	2.9	2.9	2.9
Divorce decrees as a % of marriages[2]	25.6	27.9	41.5	42.9	42.9	40.9	40.4	39.0	37.7	34.8	34.6	38.8	37.5	33.2	34.7	—
GDP (year-on-year % changes)[3]	10.4	11.2	−4.7	−1.7	4.0	−1.2	−1.8	−3.1	4.8	7.2	6.5	9.8	3.4	−2.8	7.1	8.9
GDP per capita (year-on-year % changes)[4]	5.6	10.2	−5.5	−2.6	3.1	−1.9	−2.2	−2.9	4.0	6.8	5.8	8.9	2.8	−3.0	6.4	8.1
GDP by industry (%)[5]																
Primary industry	0.1	0.1	0.1	0.1	0.1	0.1	0.1	0.1	0.1	0.1	0.1	0.1	0.1	0.1	0.1	—
Secondary industry	15.5	14.7	14.9	14.6	14.2	13.4	12.3	10.7	10.0	9.3	8.7	7.6	7.3	7.2	6.9	—
Tertiary industry	84.4	85.2	84.9	85.3	85.7	86.5	87.5	89.2	89.9	90.6	91.2	92.3	92.6	92.7	93.0	—
Unemployment rate (%)[6]	2.8	2.2	4.7	6.2	4.9	5.1	7.3	7.9	6.8	5.6	4.8	4.0	3.6	5.4	4.4	3.4
Proportion of workless households (%)[7]	—	—	—	—	—	7.1	8.7	9.8	9.2	9	8.9	8.5	8.3	9.2	9.1	—
Gini coefficient[8]	0.518	—	—	—	—	0.525	—	—	—	—	0.533	—	—	—	—	0.537
% of people living in low-income domestic households[9]	15.0	15.6	18.1	17.2	18.3	17.7	18.3	17.6	18.1	17.4	17.6	17.7	17.6	17.7	17.9	17.1
% of children aged 0–14	22.8	23.7	26.2	22.9	25.9	22.3	23.7	21.6	23.1	22.0	22.4	22.4	22.8	22.4	22.9	22.3
% of youth aged 15–24	11.5	12.3	15.0	15.5	17.2	15.2	16.5	16.2	16.9	16.1	16.0	16.8	17.2	18.2	19.3	17.5
% of adults aged 25–44	—	—	—	—	—	11.0	11.9	11.2	11.2	10.4	10.7	10.7	10.5	10.8	11.1	10.4
% of adults aged 45–64	—	—	—	—	—	17.0	17.6	17.1	17.3	16.4	16.1	16.0	15.8	16.2	16.0	14.8
% of persons aged 65 and above	26.9	28.0	34.2	33.9	34.5	36.4	33.7	33.4	33.6	34.0	35.6	35.8	34.4	33.0	32.5	32.7

Source: [1] Census and Statistics Department (2001a, 2006: Table 1.9, 2011a: Table 1.11, 2012a: Chart 4); [2] Census and Statistics Department (2006, 2011a: Table 1.1); [3,4] Census and Statistics Department (2012c: Table 1); [5] Census and Statistics Department (2001b, 2004, 2007, 2009a: Table, 12.4, 2012b: Table, 4.4); [6] Census and Statistics Department (2001a, 2006, 2011a: Table 2.2); [7] Financial Secretary's Office (2011:Indicator 19); [8] Census and Statistics Department (2012d: Table 5.5); [9] Hong Kong Council of Social Service (2005, 2012a, 2012b).

show that the proportion of elderly people in the population (aged 65 and above) is expected to increase from 13 per cent in mid-2011 to 30 per cent in mid-2041. Meanwhile, the proportion of the population aged 0–14 is expected to decrease from 12 per cent to 9 per cent respectively. The ratio of persons aged 65 or over to those of working age (i.e. the old-age dependency ratio) is projected to grow from 21.6 per cent in mid-2016 to 49.7 per cent in mid-2041. It is projected that the old-old population (i.e. elderly people aged 80 and older) will gradually grow from 5 per cent to 11 per cent at the same time (see Table 3.2). It is an undeniable fact that physical and mental health conditions among the old-old population are more vulnerable than their younger-old counterparts. The growth of the old-old population in Hong Kong may imply that they need more care and support from family members and medical services, and emotional support from the community. Nonetheless, the rising number of divorce and separation cases, together with smaller families and increasing nuclearisation of families, have undoubtedly weakened the abilities of families to fulfil the obligations of filial piety and have led to an increasing demand for institutionalisation for long-term care in Hong Kong (Census and Statistics Department, 2009b). As Fernandez and Forder (2010: 4) observe, "relying on informal care networks in the future will be increasingly difficult, because of significant decreases in the number of informal carers per dependent older people, and other factors leading to a reduction of informal care

Table 3.2 Hong Kong population projections (2011–2041)

	Mid −2011	Mid −2016	Mid −2021	Mid −2026	Mid −2031	Mid −2036	Mid −2041
Total population (thousands)	7 071.6	7 370.5	7 662.0	7 937.1	8 160.9	8 337.2	8 469.0
Percentage of population							
Aged 0–14	12%	11%	11%	11%	10%	10%	9%
Aged 15–64	75%	73%	70%	66%	63%	62%	61%
Aged 65–79	**9%**	**11%**	**14%**	**18%**	**19%**	**20%**	**19%**
Aged 80+	**4%**	**5%**	**5%**	**5%**	**7%**	**9%**	**11%**
Elderly dependency ratio*	177	216	272	346	418	467	497
Life expectancy (years) (2011–2041)							
Males (Hong Kong)	**80.5**	**81.4**	**82.2**	**82.9**	**83.5**	**84.0**	**84.4**
Males (Japan)	79.4	80.4	81.0	81.5	82.0	82.4	82.8
Males (Sweden)	79.8	80.6	81.4	82.0	82.5	83.1	83.5
Females (Hong Kong)	**86.7**	**87.6**	**88.5**	**89.2**	**89.8**	**90.3**	**90.8**
Females (Japan)	85.9	87.2	87.8	88.3	88.7	89.1	89.5
Females (Sweden)	83.7	84.1	84.6	85.0	85.4	85.8	86.0

Note: *refers to the number of persons aged 65 and over per 1,000 persons aged between 15 and 64.

Source: Census and Statistics Department (2012e: Tables 1, 3, 15).

supply in the future (e.g. changes in the role of women in society, increases in female labour force participation, increases in divorce rates and in the number of one-person households, migration patterns and reductions in the rates of cohabitation across generations)".

In addition, Hong Kong has never had any comprehensive retirement protection schemes for the elderly. Despite the implementation of the Mandatory Provident Fund Scheme since 2000, the scheme will not offer any benefits to those people who have already retired or will retire in the near future. A recent study of *Socio-demographic Profile, Health Status and Self-care Capability of Older Persons* shows less than one-fifth of older persons who had retirement protection. A majority of older persons (70.1 per cent) expect to use their savings and interest to maintain daily living after retirement, compared to one-third from their children's financial support (Census and Statistics Department, 2009b). This explains why about one-third of elderly persons aged 65 and above have been living in low-income households in Hong Kong following the Asian financial crisis (see Table 3.1). A massive number of CSSA old age cases clearly demonstrates the financial difficulties confronted by a rising number of senior citizens looking for government support. All the evidence also points to the fact that women are more vulnerable to living in poverty (Hong Kong Council of Social Service, 2012a) since they are living longer (see Table 3.2), but they will not benefit from any contribution-based and employment-related retirement protection schemes. Some of them who have spent time caring for their own family members when they were young can neither receive sufficient family support nor benefit from employment-related retirement protection schemes. An ageing population results in growing demand for medical services and also exerts a heavy financial burden on those elderly people who are non-CSSA claimants. It raises concerns about the extent to which the younger generation can bear caring responsibilities for older people amid changing family structures and economic uncertainties in Hong Kong.

The extent to which welfare restructuring is ensuring social equity across generations in Hong Kong

Promoting decent work and sustainable livelihoods?

The preceding analysis indicates that people not in the working population are more likely to be poor. The greater the number of workers in a household, the less likely people are to be deprived of basic necessities. Owing to growing informalisation of employment, attachment to the labour market may not guarantee a life free from poverty. People in low-income households are more likely to have multi-dimensional experience of exclusion shaping their lifestyles. As Levitas *et al.* (2007: 25) explain, "social exclusion is a complex and multi-dimensional process. It involves the lack or denial of resources, rights, goods and services, and the inability to participate in the normal relationships and activities available to the majority of people in a society, whether in economic, social, cultural, or political arenas. It affects both the quality of life of individuals and the equity and cohesion of society as a whole". They further elaborate that people are socially excluded with limited economic and social "resources", "participation" (e.g. poor quality of working life; low social participation in common social activities on the grounds of affordability) and/or low "quality of life" (e.g. poor physical and health well-being) (Levitas *et al.*, 2007).

Oxfam Hong Kong recently published a report entitled *Before and After the Statutory Minimum Wage Ordinance in Hong Kong* (2012), which showed that 69.9 per cent of low-income workers' families benefited from the newly implemented ordinance. However, those low-income workers who remained in the same jobs before and after the statutory minimum wage ordinance suffered from a reduction of 5.6 per cent, were also deprived of paid rest days and lost paid meal breaks. Low-income families with dependent children still experienced material deprivation. The study also highlighted several key issues in terms of how to ensure sustainable livelihoods in Hong Kong, including work incentives derived from the disregarded earnings under the existing CSSA scheme; childcare support for low-income families; and assurance of better remuneration and benefits (i.e. how to "make work pay") with the implementation of the minimum wage (Oxfam Hong Kong, 2012). These findings are consistent with those of a qualitative study titled "Poverty and Social Exclusion in Hong Kong" (PSEHK).[2] Focus group participants expressed their concerns about employment opportunities in the midst of economic restructuring, and quality of working life among informal workers in Hong Kong, noting that people excluded from the labour market may find that their ability to generate material/economic resources is reduced:

> we cannot afford but it is necessary for ordinary families to have big meals at special occasions. Our financial situation does not allow us to spend a lot on food; therefore we cannot enjoy nice meals in many festivals.
>
> (Lone mother with dependent children from low-income family)

Female participants also explained that childcare responsibilities might hinder their employment opportunities or restrict their ability to participate in the labour market, even in a part-time capacity:

> As you have to look after your children, a part-time job is much better because it is much more flexible . . . You cannot go to work during weekends. You cannot leave them at home . . . [Until] your children have grown up, you cannot work in full-time job.
>
> (A married female with dependent children from low-income family)

Ensuring intergenerational mobility and equality of opportunity

There is public debate about the effectiveness of current education systems in terms of equalisation of opportunities. The educational inequality among students from various different socio-economic backgrounds may be further intensified under the New Senior Secondary Curriculum Other Learning Experiences in

Hong Kong. These "other learning experiences" (like aesthetic development and physical development) are directly related to various kinds of family effect (i.e. the "money" effect, the "time investment" effect and the "learning culture" effect) (Esping-Andersen, 2009b: 122). There are several financial assistance schemes for primary and secondary students, namely the School Textbook Assistance Scheme, the Student Travel Subsidy Scheme and the Subsidy Scheme of Internet Access Charges. To a large extent, these financial assistance schemes can reduce the financial burden on low-income families. However, children may need to have supplementary references, attend after-school tutorial classes and/or extra-curriculum activities to ensure their competitiveness under the 334 curriculum. Focus group participants of the PSEHK study also expressed clear support for items related to children's learning opportunities and/or environment to enhance their development (such as supplementary examination exercises, a suitable place at home to study or do homework and a home computer with an internet connection). However, recent official statistics show that there is a close relationship between monthly household income and the number of households having a home computer with an internet connection. Nearly two-fifths of households with a monthly household income less than HK$10,000 (38.3 per cent) had a home computer with an internet connection, compared to 76.4 per cent of all households in Hong Kong (Census and Statistics Department, 2011b). All the evidence points to children living in low-income households being deprived of equal chances of growth and development.

As Esping-Andersen (2009b: 113) argues, "A great paradox of our times is the lack of any serious equal opportunities progress despite so much effort invested in the pursuit thereof . . . What is now firmly understood is that education systems, no matter how progressive and egalitarian in design, are institutionally ill equipped to create equality". He further explains that "Both cognitive and non-cognitive skills are partially transmitted genetically and partially the result of nurturing . . . Since cognitive (and non-cognitive) abilities influence school success and, subsequently, adults' life chances, the policy challenge is to ensure a strong start for all children. Investing well in our children will yield very large returns both for individuals' life chances and for society at large (Esping-Andersen, 2009b: 115). This argument is substantiated by Wu's Hong Kong study of *Family Resources and Educational Stratification* (2007). He argues that "educational expansion does not lead to better chances for disadvantaged groups to make the transition and will not change the association between family backgrounds and the given level of school transitions . . . intergenerational transmission [of disadvantage] is enhanced; the role of education as an important channel for socioeconomic mobility is weakened. The society may become increasingly polarised as a result" (Wu, 2007: 21).

Offering dignified care and support for the older people

There are serious concerns about the far-reaching repercussions of Hong Kong's ageing population for sustainable economic development and in terms of the caring responsibilities of the younger population. First, there is concern about income security for older people in the midst of social and economic transformation in Hong Kong (Chui and Ko, 2011). The official statistics show that children often/very often give support to their parents, including "financial support" (38.5 per cent), "advice on important matters" (23.4 per cent), "listening to their concerns and views" (21.9 per cent) and "helping with household chores and with taking care of children or family members" (9.4 per cent) (Census and Statistics Department, 2010b). A recent study called "Poverty, Deprivation and Social Exclusion in Hong Kong" (2012)[3] indicated that a high proportion of older people who did not receive any financial support from their families encountered material deprivation.

Second, the informalisation of employment poses a challenge by placing a substantial number of the workforce outside the employment-based social security schemes in Hong Kong. In the long run, it creates a financial burden on the existing tax-funded CSSA schemes. In particular, women's career interruptions (such as caring responsibilities and other family work) and their part-time working status aggravate the risk of poverty in old age (Esping-Andersen, 2009b). The newly proposed Old Age Living Allowance is the first step towards alleviating the plight of poor older people in Hong Kong. In the long term, the government should explore a sustainable retirement protection scheme to ensure older people are able to live in dignity. The argument is substantiated by the PSEHK study which shows that older people are excluded from basic income security, and from taking part in social activities. They also have restricted access to medical services on the grounds of affordability. Their ill-health may directly affect their daily lives and level of social participation.

Third, a growing older population, changes in family structure, increasing female labour force participation and the number of nuclear families have resulted in a decline in traditional family support for older people, and engendered the need for care outside the family. For instance, the Nursing Home Places Purchase Scheme for older people aims to shorten waiting times and ensure good quality of residential care services in Hong Kong. The effectiveness of these subsidised residential care places depends predominantly on statutory service quality control checks. Some senior participants in the PSEHK study also pointed out that "Ageing in Place"[4] has not been fully implemented to address increasing demand for home care services for elderly people.

> I applied for cleaning service two years ago and it was approved last year. It was offered once a month and one hour each time. Eventually, a social worker informed me that I wouldn't receive the service . . . She said there wasn't enough manpower. I asked, the government advocated for "Ageing in Place", why not? The social worker replied that resources were insufficient.
>
> (A woman receiving old age CSSA)

Conclusion

In conclusion, the government of Hong Kong Special Administrative Region has remained committed to its philosophy of "small government, big society" in the midst of rapid demographic, socio-economic and political changes. As Lee (2005: 303, emphasis added) argues, "re-commodification and cost containment have become the major approaches in restructuring social programs, and are regarded as measures for bringing Hong Kong back to the 'correct' path of 'small government, big market'. *The restructuring of welfare programs is thus entirely budget driven and the policy implication – that is the effect on social justice – is ignored*." In other words, social policy development in post-1997 Hong Kong shows the "continuity" and "steadiness" of its subordinate role of social services/social welfare (Cheung, 2009). As Cheung (2009: 25, emphasis added) further explains, "Some public services had historically been developed and expanded not for the sake of any entrenched social policy values, *but as instrumentalist complements to the developmental agenda and related political objectives*. Welfare provisions had mostly been introduced not out of welfare ideology considerations . . . *but as a result of a fiscally and economically driven social development programme, in which case economic slowdown and recession could arguably cause a temporary readjustment, but still within the same logic*. Developmentalism is still the foundation of the East Asian public policy discourse." However, the realisation of social cohesion predominantly depends on whether policy actions can narrow the gaps between the haves and the have-nots, and eventually enhance people's life chances. Similarly, the findings of the charter are consistent with Mok's comparative work on social protection measures and social policy responses in East Asia after the 2008 global financial crisis in the conventional model of social protection, still placing recovery of economy first, than social welfare (Mok, 2011).

It is debatable how to identify an equitable contract that ensures sustainable livelihoods across the generations. The preceding analysis highlights several issues for further discussion and policy action in Hong Kong. Labour insecurity and income insecurity of the working population has limited their family resources and restricted them from participating in the normal activities available to the majority of people in a society. The Statutory Minimum Wage Ordinance has been implemented to protect the rights of the working poor but further actions are needed to close a loophole in the Employment Ordinance in Hong Kong (Oxfam Hong Kong, 2012). The increasing nuclearisation of families and changing family structure create significant pressure on the "sandwich generation" who have caring responsibilities for both their child(ren) and ageing parents, in terms of support and social care (Esping-Andersen, 2009b; Zhang and Goza, 2006). Although there is still interfamilial support in Hong Kong, official statistics show an increasing demand for care and support outside the family (Census and Statistics Department, 2009b, 2010b). Sustainable retirement protection for the older population has also become policy concern over the past decade (Hong Kong Council of Social Service, 2012a, 2012b). The foregoing discussion also indicates family effects on the life chances of the younger generation in Hong Kong. The equalising effect of formal education may be diminishing under the new 334 academic structure and the expansion of higher education in Hong Kong. The welfare mix, shifting responsibilities of welfare provision to individuals, family, market and the community will affect welfare distribution. Early and integrated policy interventions are needed, particularly for children in low-income families (Esping-Andersen, 2009a, 2009b).

Notes

1 The CSSA Scheme, which is mean-tested, provides a safety net for those who cannot support themselves financially. This scheme is designed to bring the income of those individuals and families up to a prescribed level to meet their basic needs.
2 Findings are drawn from the first stage of the study using focus group methods to produce new evidence on public perceptions of poverty and social exclusion in Hong Kong. The author would like to thank the Economic and Social Research Council (ESRC)/Research Grants Council (RGC) Joint Scheme, for funding the project "Poverty and Social Exclusion in Hong Kong" (Ref. no: RES-000-22-4400).
3 The Hong Kong Council of Social Service has commissioned a study of "Poverty, Deprivation and Social Exclusion in Hong Kong" (2012) in order to compare similarities and differences of living standards between the general population and particular target groups (including elderly people, people with disabilities and people receiving CSSA). Available at: http://www.poverty.org.hk/sites/default/files/ClientStudyReportRevised 120607_final.pdf (in Chinese).
4 "Ageing in Place" aims to allow older people to remain living in the community with which they are familiar for as long as they wish as long as there are formal and informal care and support services in the community (Chui, 2008).

References

Bonoli, G. (2006). "New Social Risks and the Politics of Post-industrial Social Policies", in K. Armingeon and G. Bonoli (eds), *The Politics of Post-industrial Welfare States: Adapting Post-war Social Policies to New Social Risks*. London: Routledge, pp. 3–26.

Buss, T. F. and Ahmed, U. (2011). "Social Equity and Development", in N. J. Johnson, and J. H. Svara (eds) *Justice for All: Promoting Social Equity in Public Administration*. Armonk, NY: M.E. Sharpe, pp. 56–75.

Census and Statistics Department (2001a). *Hong Kong Annual Digest of Statistics*. Hong Kong: Census and Statistics Department.

Census and Statistics Department (2001b). *Hong Kong Monthly Digest of Statistics*. (October) Hong Kong: Census and Statistics Department.

Census and Statistics Department (2004). *Hong Kong Monthly Digest of Statistics*. (October) Hong Kong: Census and Statistics Department.

Census and Statistics Department (2006). *Hong Kong Annual Digest of Statistics*. Hong Kong: Census and Statistics Department.

Census and Statistics Department (2007). *Hong Kong Monthly Digest of Statistics*. (October) Hong Kong: Census and Statistics Department.

Census and Statistics Department (2009a). *Hong Kong Monthly Digest of Statistics*. (October) Hong Kong: Census and Statistics Department.

Census and Statistics Department (2009b). *Thematic Household Survey Report No.40*. Hong Kong: Census and Statistics Department.

Census and Statistics Department (2010a). *Social Data Collected by the General House-hold Survey: Special Topics Report No. 52*. Hong Kong: Census and Statistics Department.

Census and Statistics Department (2010b). *Thematic Household Survey Report No.44*. Hong Kong: Census and Statistics Department.

Census and Statistics Department (2011a). *Hong Kong Annual Digest of Statistics*. Hong Kong: Census and Statistics Department.

Census and Statistics Department (2012a). *Hong Kong Monthly Digest of Statistics*. (April) Hong Kong: Census and Statistics Department.

Census and Statistics Department (2012b). *Hong Kong Monthly Digest of Statistics*. (October) Hong Kong: Census and Statistics Department.

Census and Statistics Department (2012c). *Special Report on Gross Domestic Product*. Hong Kong: Census and Statistics Department.

Census and Statistics Department (2012d). *Hong Kong 2011 Population Census – Thematic Report: Household Income Distribution in Hong Kong*. Hong Kong: Census and Statistics Department.

Census and Statistics Department (2012e). *Hong Kong Population Projections 2012–2041*. Hong Kong: Census and Statistics Department.

Chan, K. W. and Lee, J. (2010). "Rethinking the Social Development Approach in the Context of East Asia Social Welfare", *China Journal of Social Work*, 31(1): 19–33.

Chan, R. K. H. (2009). "Risk Discourse and Politics: Restructuring Welfare in Hong Kong", *Critical Social Policy*, 29(1): 24–52.

Cheung, A. B. L. (2009). "Interpreting East Asian Social Policy Development: Paradigm Shifts or Policy "Steadiness"? in K. H. Mok and R. Forrest (eds) *Changing Governance and Public Policy in East Asia*. London: Routledge, pp. 25–48.

Chiu, S. W. K. and Wong, S. L. (eds) (2011). *Hong Kong Divided? Structures of Social Inequality in the Twenty-First Century*. Hong Kong: Hong Kong Institute of Asia-Pacific Studies, Chinese University of Hong Kong.

Chui, E. (2008). "Ageing in Place in Hong Kong: Challenges and Opportunities in a Capitalist Chinese City", *Ageing International*, 32(3): 167–182.

Chui, E. W. T. and Ko, L. (2011). "Poverty and Social Exclusion of the Elderly", in S. W. K. Chiu and S. L. Wong (eds). *Hong Kong Divided? Structures of Social Inequality in the Twenty-First Century*. Hong Kong: Hong Kong Institute of Asia-Pacific Studies, Chinese University of Hong Kong, pp. 167–199.

Esping-Andersen, G. (2009a). "Ageing and Equity", in G. Esping-Andersen (ed.) *The Incomplete Revolution: Adapting to Women's New Roles*. Cambridge: Polity, pp. 145–166.

Esping-Andersen, G. (2009b). "Investing in Children and Equalizing Life Chances", in G. Esping-Andersen (ed.) *The Incomplete Revolution: Adapting to Women's New Roles*. Cambridge: Polity, pp. 111–144.

Fernandez, J. L. and Forder, J. (2010). *Ageing Societies: Challenges and Opportunities*. Available at: www.bupa.com/healthpulse/ageing.

Financial Secretary's Office (2011). *Indicators of Poverty – An Update for 2010*. Available at: www.lwb.gov.hk/eng/other_info/2010%20Poverty%20Indicators_Eng.pdf.

Gilbert, N. (2005). "Protection to Activation: The Apotheosis of Work", in P. Saunders (ed.) *Welfare to Work in Practice: Social Security and Participation in Economic and Social Life*. Aldershot: Ashgate, pp. 9–22.

Holliday, I. (2005). "East Asian Social Policy in the Wake of the Financial Crisis: Farewell to Productivism?", *Policy and Politics*, 33(1): 145–162.

Hong Kong Council of Social Service (2005). *A Statistical Profile of Low Income Households in Hong Kong*. Hong Kong: HKCSS (in Chinese).

Hong Kong Council of Social Service (2012a). *Poverty Data Analysis 2011*. Available at: http://www.poverty.org.hk/sites/default/files/Poverty_data_2011.pdf (in Chinese).

Hong Kong Council of Social Service (2012b). *Poverty in Figures (2000–2010)*. Available at: http://www.hkcss.org.hk/pra/research_report/PovertyStat_FullReport.pdf (in Chinese).

International Labour Organization (2010). *Global Employment Trends*. Geneva: ILO.

Izuhara, M. and Forrest, R. (2012). "Active Families: Familization, Housing and Welfare across Generations in East Asia", *Social Policy & Administration*. Available at: http://onlinelibrary.wiley.com/doi/10.1111/spol.12002/pdf.

Johnson, N. J. and Svara, J. H. (2011). "Social Equity in American Society and Public Administration", in N. J. Johnson and J. H. Svara (eds) *Justice for All: Promoting Social Equity in Public Administration*. Armonk, NY: M.E. Sharpe, pp. 3–25.

Lee, E. W. Y. (2005). "The Renegotiation of Social Pact in Hong Kong: Economic Globalization, Socioeconomic Change, and Local Politics, *Journal of Social Policy*, 16(1): 51–68.

Lee, E. W. Y. (2008). "Social Mobilization, Blame Avoidance and Welfare Restructuring in Hong Kong", in M. Sing (ed). *Politics and Government in Hong Kong: Crisis under Chinese Sovereignty*. London: Routledge, pp. 162–175.

Levitas, R., Pantazis, C., Fahmy, E., Gordon, D., Lloyd, E. and Patsios, D. (2007). *The Multi-dimensional Analysis of Social Exclusion*. Bristol: Department of Sociology and School for Social Policy, Townsend Centre for the International Study of Poverty and Bristol Institute for Public Affairs, University of Bristol.

Mok, K. H. (2011). "Right Diagnosis and Appropriate Treatment for the Global Financial Crisis?: Social Protection Measures and Social Policy Responses in East Asia", in G. J. Hwang (ed.) *New Welfare State in East Asia: Global Challenges and Restructuring*. Cheltenham: Edward Elgar, pp. 155–174.

Morgan, L. A. and Kunkel, S. R. (2011). "Politics, Government, and Aging in America", in L. A. Morgan and S. R. Kunkel (eds) *Aging, Society, and the Life Course* (4th ed.). New York: Springer, pp. 219–246.

OECD (2009a). *Employment Outlook 2009: Tackling the Jobs Crisis*. Paris: OECD.

OECD (2009b). *Helping Workers Weather the Economic Storm. Policy Brief, September*. Paris: OECD.

Oxfam Hong Kong (2012). *Before and After the Statutory Minimum Wage Ordinance in Hong Kong: Survey of Low-income Workers and their Families*. Hong Kong: Oxfam Hong Kong.

Phillipson, C. (2010). "Globalisation, Global Ageing and Intergenerational Change", in M. Izuhara (ed.) *Ageing and Intergenerational Relations: Family Reciprocity from a Global Perspective*. Bristol: Policy Press, pp. 13–28.

Powell, M. (2007). "The Mixed Economy of Welfare and the Social Division of Welfare", in M. Powell (ed.) *Understanding the Mixed Economy of Welfare*. Bristol: Policy Press, pp. 1–21.

Rafferty, A. and Wiggan, J. (2011). "Choice and Welfare Reform: Lone Parents' Decision Making around Paid Work and Family Life", *Journal of Social Policy*, 40(2): 275–293.

Singh, N. and Gilman, J. (1999). "Making Livelihoods more Sustainable", *International Social Science Journal*, 51(162): 539–545.

Standing, G. (2011). *The Precariat: The New Dangerous Class*. London: Bloomsbury.

Wilding, P. (2008). "Is the East Asian Welfare Model still Productive?", *Journal of Asian Public Policy*, 1(1): 18–31.

Williamson, J. B., McNammara, T. K. and Howling, S. A. (2003). "Generational Equity, Generational Interdependence, and the Framing of the Debate over Social Security Reform", *Journal of Sociology and Social Welfare*, 30(3): 3–14.

Wu, X. G. (2007). *Family Resources and Educational Stratification: The Case of Hong Kong, 1981–2001*. Population Studies Centre Research Report 07–624. Hong Kong: Division of Social Science, Hong Kong University of Science and Technology.

Zhang, Y. T. and Goza, F. W. (2006). "Who will Care for the Elderly in China? A Review of the Problems Caused by China's One-child Policy and their Potential Solutions", *Journal of Aging Studies*, 20(2): 151–164.

4 Economic insecurity and social protection for labour

The limitations of Hong Kong's adhocism during the financial crises

Kim-Ming Lee and Kam-Yee Law

Introduction

After decades of neoliberal globalisation, economic insecurity spreads around the globe and affects people of every walk of life. Rising economic inequality becomes an important concern for both advanced and developing countries. Nonetheless, political and business elites around the world never question the neoliberal agenda, despite the economic crises that happen every now and then. The year 2007 may mark the turning point of neoliberal globalisation. After the global financial tsunami kicked off from the burst of the sub-prime mortgage bubble in the United States in 2007, the global economy is facing an economic hardship never heard of since the Great Depression in the 1930s. Hong Kong, as a highly open economy, has also been severely damaged by the financial tsunami.

This chapter attempts to scrutinise how globalisation, especially financial globalisation, generates economic insecurity, and what roles social policies can play in protecting people against that insecurity. It further discusses how economic insecurity (especially in terms of unemployment) distributes unevenly in Hong Kong society. Our analysis indicates that even before the financial tsunami, Hong Kong was confronted with of the effects of economic downturn since the handover, and this brought significant impacts on all Hong Kong people's livelihoods, particularly the labour in the lower classes. This raises a serious question about whether the current social protection system adequately protects people against an increasingly risky global economic environment. By examining the social policy package adopted by the Hong Kong government in fighting against the financial tsunami (which is similar to what it did during the previous crises), we argue that there is lack of long-term strategies and commitments from the government in protecting Hong Kong workers against globalisation risks and economic insecurity. By drawing experiences from other countries, we suggest that active labour market policies (ALMPs) may be the social policy tools the government can use to reform the social protection system.

Financial globalisation, economic insecurity and social protection

The former chief executives of Hong Kong engaged in two major themes in the policy discourse in response to the challenges of globalisation: how to maintain Hong

Kong's economic competitiveness under globalisation, and how to help those negatively affected by globalisation. For instance, in his 2003 policy address, Tung Chee Hwa summarised the challenges: "In short, the advent of globalisation, the move towards a knowledge-based economy and the rapid rise in the competitiveness of our neighbours have posed obvious challenges to our traditional advantages and position . . . The community is suffering from the pains of economic adjustment, with rising unemployment and falling wages for many" (Hong Kong SAR Government, 2003: para. 9). Donald Tsang in his 2008–9 policy address emphasised the role of risk management in mitigating the negative effects of globalisation: "With globalisation, Hong Kong is even more exposed to external factors in areas such as the economy, finance, food safety and environmental protection . . . The Government's role is increasingly important and needs to be redefined . . . We should be ready to take decisive action to help stabilise the economy and rebuild people's confidence to ride out the difficulties" (Hong Kong SAR Government, 2008: para. 9).

These two themes within the Hong Kong globalisation policy discourse echo a recent academic debate about whether globalisation reduces the role of the state in providing social protection. The "efficiency hypothesis" argues that the welfare state is regarded as uncompetitive because of "increasing competition in international goods and services markets and the ability of the holders of capital to move money and production around the world in search of higher rates of return" (Garrett and Mitchell, 2001: 149–51). However, a competing "compensation hypothesis" argues that "globalisation may increase demands on governments to cushion market-generated inequality and insecurity by welfare state expansion" so as to maintain support for globalisation (Garrett and Mitchell, 2001: 152). Indeed, there are quite a number of researchers indicating that developed countries increase their welfare spending when their economies become more globalised (Burgoon, 2001; Cameron, 1978; Garrett, 1998; Rodrik, 1998). Thus, instead of retrenchment, welfare states show enormous resilience.

As radical economist Minsky (1992) argues, capitalist development is inherently unstable because over a period of good times, capitalist economies tend to move from a financial structure dominated by prudent economic units to a fragile financial structure occupied mostly by economic units engaged in speculative and excessively risk-taking finance. When an economy is filling up with more and more speculative financial units, asset bubbles (e.g. stock and real estate) are built up in an inflationary manner. Up to certain point, any event that makes the public or investors cast doubts on the "real" value of the assets may trigger debt deflation.[1] When debt deflations occur, financial intermediaries, like banks, will recall loans from, or refuse to rollover loans to, problematic borrowers because the value of the collateral has declined to an unacceptable level. Moreover, financial intermediaries become substantially risk-averse and are extremely reluctant to lend when debt deflation occurs. As a result, borrowers with cashflow shortfalls will be forced to sell their assets so as to either repay the existing debts or obtain operational capital. This leads to a further collapse of asset values and reinforces financial intermediaries' risk-averseness. If this vicious cycle cannot be broken, asset bubbles will finally burst and a financial crisis starts.

In accordance with Minsky's financial instability hypothesis, the International Labour Organisation (ILO) (2004: 28–9) remarks that while trade liberalisation promotes economic growth, financial liberalisation often leads to more economic instability and insecurity because "financial opening is fraught with risks that cannot easily be overcome by individual governments of developing countries". In his diagnosis of the financial tsunami, Krugman (2008a, 2008b, 2008c) uses the ideas of the international finance multiplier and the foreign trade multiplier to explain why the sub-prime mortgage crisis started in the US but spread to the rest of the world, even to those economies without financial intermediaries heavily invested in the US sub-prime market. Since financial globalisation allows the free flow of capital, both US overseas assets and foreign-owned US assets have increased tremendously since 1995. Once US asset prices decline, both US and foreign firms which own a lot of deflated US assets have to sell non-US assets so as to have a healthy balance sheet. This leads to a decline of non-US asset markets which have a lot of US foreign investment and/or a lot of local firms investing in the US asset market. This is the main reason why the Hong Kong and Singapore stock and real estate markets collapsed. For those economies, like China, with a relatively small proportion of foreign US investment and few local firms investing in the US asset market, their economies may be hurt by the declining market demands of those countries experiencing financial crisis, if their economies are export-led.

In sum, globalisation, especially financial globalisation, creates economic insecurity. Periodic crises have had real welfare impacts on people, and not just the poor. As Gunter and van der Hoeven (2004: 23–4) note, the insecurity is not evenly distributed in the population: "Many poor and disadvantaged people suffer a disproportional share of the increase in insecurity, largely because of market failures that prevent them properly balancing income and consumption" and "the absence of political action to counter the heightened risk and uncertainty". Providing economic security is not an individual matter, but also a government responsibility. Sound social protection that aims at reducing the vulnerability of people, especially the lower class labourers, to future crises are needed.

At the individual level, Rejda (1999: 2) defines economic security as "a state of mind or sense of well-being by which an individual is relatively certain that he or she can satisfy basic needs and wants, both present and future". For an economically secure person, his or her income must be continuous, otherwise his or her well-being may be disrupted and anxiety appears. In other words, the uncertainty of future income to meet needs is psychologically annoying and uncomfortable. For lower class labourers that have little earnings to save and invest, there are difficulties in accumulating enough resources to meet basic needs during an economic crisis. Thus, a public security system may be required to protect these people against unanticipated risks.

At the economic system level, Nesadurai (2006: 11) defines economic security under globalisation as "ensuring a low probability of damage to a set of three key economic values: (a) streams of income and consumption necessary for minimal human/family needs; (b) market integrity; and (c) distributive equity". Actually, the first component can be renamed as the social protection objective. Numerous social protection measures, like unemployment insurance, public pensions, social assistance and public health insurance, have been devised throughout the world to achieve this goal. Distributive equity is indeed one of the social objectives of the European welfare states. Nonetheless, with the rise of neoliberal ideology, both social protection and distributive equity are considered by numerous policy-makers as counterproductive. Neoliberals simply equate economic security with continuous economic growth, and argue that generous social protection and redistributive measures disrupt labour market operations to efficiently allocate human resources, create welfare dependence for benefit recipients, and choke the entrepreneurship and work motivation of the population. As a result, the global competitiveness of the economy declines and economic security at the system level cannot be guaranteed. By emphasising the primacy of the market, neoliberals fully embrace unrestrained economic globalisation, impose few regulations on market operations, keep redistributive social policies at bay, maintain minimal income transfer programmes for the most disadvantaged, and encourage the rest to economically secure themselves against risks through private means. The neoliberal agenda is described by Hacker (2006) as the "great risk shift": the shift of responsibility for managing economic risk from government and employers onto individuals and their families.

The global financial tsunami reveals the faults of neoliberal thinking. Market integrity does not simply mean market operations free of interference. Market integrity should be conceptualised as a market system that can enable individuals and firms to exploit economic opportunities legally and without fear (Nesadurai, 2006: 10). Fear is a psychological response to insecurity. As Minsky (1992) demonstrated, the global capitalist economy is inherently crisis-prone and not all people have sufficient resources (guaranteed future income, savings, investment, financial supports from family, relatives and friends) to survive an economic crisis, thus fear is inevitable, especially for lower class people. Kannan (2007) argues that a viable social protection system under globalisation should be comprised of: (1) basic social security that aims at helping those who are not able to access a minimum of resources to meet their economic and social requirements for a dignified life; and (2) social security for contingencies.

The Hong Kong situation: uneven distribution of risk to labour

Hong Kong has experienced a number of economic recessions since the 1990s: the brief economic downturn caused by former Governor under the British administration Chris Patten's democratic reform (1995),[2] the Asian financial crisis (1997–8), the recession caused by the burst of the dot-com bubble and the 9/11 terrorist attacks (2001), the SARS outbreak (2003) and the global financial tsunami (since 2007). Apart from the 1995 downturn, the recessions are directly or indirectly related to globalisation, which facilitates the free movement of capital, people, goods and services. As shown in Figure 4.1, one can easily observe the severity of economic instability after the handover. What are the consequences of the fluctuations for Hong Kong workers?

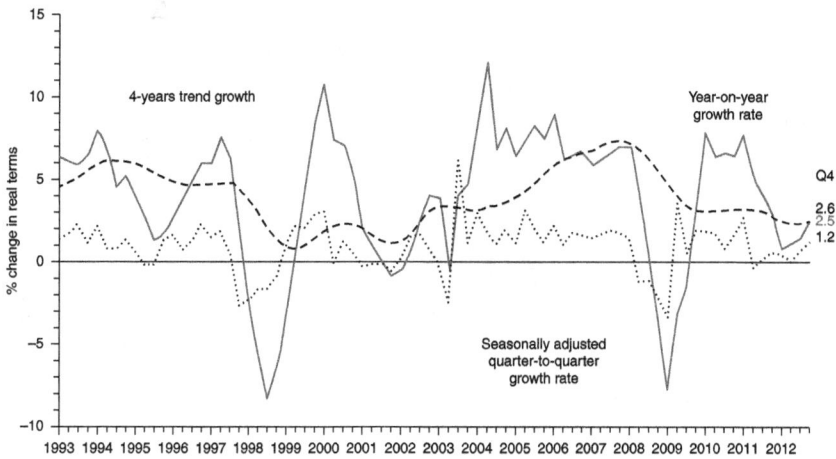

Figure 4.1 GDP growth rate of Hong Kong (1993–2012).

Source: Hong Kong SAR Government (2010a, 2013).

A commonly used objective indicator of economic insecurity is the unemployment rate because employment is the major source of household income. Losing a job may put a household into economic difficulty. Table 4.1a shows that the Hong Kong unemployment rates were below 4 per cent until 1997 when the Asian financial crisis occurred. From then on, the unemployment rate has remained high, until 2011. However, not all industries were confronted with the same level of unemployment risk: manufacturing and other low value-added industrial sectors (such as retail, accommodation and food services, and construction), have unemployment rates higher than the average (see Table 4.1b). This implies that the employment risk in these industries is higher than in other industries, no matter how the Hong Kong economy performs.

Surprisingly, although the financial sector has been severely hit by the crisis, the unemployment rate is still below average. The import/export and wholesale sectors also have a below-average unemployment rate, despite the dramatic drop in Hong Kong exports. The most unaffected sector is public administration and social service. This can be explained by the fact that its largest employer is the government, and services are mostly place-tied and protected by professional bodies (e.g. the Hong Kong Medical Association and the Hong Kong Social Workers Association) from foreign competition. In sum, the risks associated with globalisation are unevenly distributed among different industrial sectors.

Table 4.2 further indicates that economic risks are unevenly distributed among different occupations. The unemployment rates for managers, administrators, professionals and associate professionals are considerably lower than the average unemployment rate, while the low-skilled and manufacture-related workers are more likely to be unemployed. The facts suggest that appropriate skill and

Table 4.1a Unemployment rate by previous industry, 1991–2007* (%)

Period	Manufacturing	Construction	Wholesale, retail & import/ export trades, restaurants, hotels	Transport, storage & communications	Financing, insurance, real estate & business services	Community, social & personal services	Overall
1991	1.8	2.4[†]	1.9	1.8	1.2	0.8	1.8
1992	2.4	2.7	1.9	1.6	1.2	0.7	2.0
1993	2.4	2.8	1.9	1.2	1.1	0.8	2.0
1994	2.5	2.8	1.9	1.3	1.0	0.7	1.9
1995	4.2	5.7	3.1	2.4	1.4	1.1	3.2
1996	3.7	3.8	2.9	2.3	1.4	1.1	2.8
1997	2.9	2.9	2.3	2.1	1.2	0.9	2.2
1998	5.5	8.4	4.9	3.7	2.9	1.7	4.7
1999	7.1	12.5	6.4	5.3	3.3	2.2	6.2
2000	5.4	10.2	5.3	4.0	2.6	1.8	4.9
2001	5.3	10.8	5.5	4.3	3.0	2.1	5.1
2002	7.3	15.8	7.8	5.4	4.6	3.2	7.3
2003	7.7	19.0	8.2	6.5	5.2	3.5	7.9
2004	7.1	16.0	6.6	5.3	4.5	3.3	6.8
2005	6.3	13.0	5.5	4.8	3.5	2.6	5.6
2006	5.1	11.1	4.8	3.9	3.1	2.1	4.8
2007	4.5	8.4	4.1	3.3	2.5	1.9	4.0

Notes:

* Statistics are not reported for the "Others" category due to large sampling error.

   The above statistics are compiled based on the Hong Kong Standard Industrial Classification (HSIC) Version 1.1.

† The shaded cells show that the unemployment rate of that particular industry is above the overall unemployment rate.

Source: Census and Statistics Department (2009).

knowledge not only help people find a better job, but also reduce the unemployment risk in a turbulent global economy.

Different age groups have different unemployment risks, as shown in Table 4.3. Becker (1964) has argued that human capital is positively related to earnings and employment. Generally, age-wage profiles are in a concave shape, i.e. wages generally increase with age, then up to a certain age slow down and even decline. Wages increase because people make investments (education, on-the-job training and learning) in accumulating human capital. Wages increase slowly or even decline at the later life stage because the depreciation of their human capital outweighs their investment. Moreover, people with higher education have their initial earnings increased at a faster rate.

In a knowledge-based and rapidly changing global economy, one may expect that some skills and knowledge will "depreciate" in a very short period of time. This is why lifelong learning has become a motto nowadays. Indeed, people need lifelong learning for lifelong earnings. However, young people have difficulties in

Table 4.1b Unemployment rate by previous industry, 2008–2012* (%)

Period	Manufacturing	Construction	Import/export trade & wholesale	Retail, accommodation & food services	Transportation, storage, postal & courier services, information & communications	Financing & insurance, real estate, professional & business services	Public administration, social & personal services	All industries
2008	4.5[†]	6.7	2.6	5.0	3.0	2.4	1.3	3.5
2009	6.2	10.0	4.6	7.0	4.8	3.8	2.1	5.3
2010	4.7	6.9	4.1	5.8	3.8	3.4	1.7	4.3
2011	4.0	5.6	3.1	4.6	3.0	2.6	1.5	3.4
2012	4.0	4.9	2.8	4.3	2.8	2.6	1.4	3.3

Notes:

* Statistics are not reported for the "Others" category due to large sampling error.

The above statistics are compiled based on the Hong Kong Standard Industrial Classification (HSIC) Version 2.0 and the series has been backcasted to the quarter of January to March 2008. Statistics prior to 2008 have been compiled based on HSIC Version 1.1. Users may also download "HSIC Version 1.1-based statistics" for reference. For more details on the revision of HSIC, please refer to the feature article "Revision of Hong Kong Standard Industrial Classification" published in the November 2008 issue of the *Hong Kong Monthly Digest of Statistics*.

† The shaded cells show that the unemployment rate of that particular industry is above the overall unemployment rate.

Source: Census and Statistics Department (2013a).

Table 4.2 Unemployment rate by previous occupation, 1993–2012* (%)

Period	Managers & administrators	Professionals	Associate professionals	Clerks	Service workers & shop sales workers	Craft & related workers	Plant & machine operators & assemblers	Elementary occupations	Overall
1993	0.4	0.7	1.2	1.5	2.4§	2.5	2.0	1.8	2.0
1994	0.5	0.7	1.1	1.4	2.2	2.5	2.5	1.7	1.9
1995	1.1	0.7	1.7	2.2	3.9	4.8	3.5	3.0	3.2
1996	0.9	0.8	1.8	2.0	3.7	4.0	3.3	2.3	2.8
1997	0.8	0.6	1.3	1.8	3.0	2.8	2.3	2.2	2.2
1998	1.6	1.1	3.0	3.7	5.9	7.3	4.2	4.5	4.7
1999	2.3	1.5	3.4	4.3	7.7	10.9	6.0	6.1	6.2
2000	1.7	1.1	2.4	3.5	6.9	8.9	4.2	4.9	4.9
2001	1.8	1.8	2.9	3.7	6.6	9.3	4.6	5.3	5.1
2002	2.7	2.4	4.3	5.3	9.2	14.0	5.9	7.7	7.3
2003	2.4	2.4	4.3	5.4	10.3	16.1	7.1	8.7	7.9
2004	1.9	2.1	3.5	4.5	8.4	13.4	6.1	8.3	6.8
2005	1.9	1.8	2.8	4.0	6.9	10.7	5.0	6.7	5.6
2006	1.3	1.3	2.5	3.5	6.1	9.5	4.3	5.5	4.8
2007	1.2	1.4	2.3	3.2	5.0	6.9	3.2	4.7	4.0
2008	1.0	1.3	2.1	3.1	4.6	5.6	3.0	3.9	3.6
2009	2.1	2.2	3.6	4.9	6.5	8.7	4.8	4.9	5.3
2010	1.7	1.8	2.9	4.2	5.5	5.5	3.5	4.3	4.3
2011**	1.3	1.2	2.1	3.5	4.5†	4.9‡	2.2	3.5	3.4
2012	1.4	1.5	2.2	3.1	4.0	4.8	2.1	3.2	3.3

Notes:

* Statistics are not reported for the "Others" category due to large sampling error.

**The above statistics are compiled based on the International Standard Classification of Occupations 2008 (ISCO–08) while the series has been provided starting from the quarter of January to March 2011. Statistics prior to 2011 have been compiled based on ISCO–88. Users may also download "ISCO–88-based statistics" for reference.

† Starting from 2011, the classification "clerks" has been changed to "clerical support workers".

‡ Starting from 2011, the classification "service works and shop sales workers" has been changed to "service and sales workers".

§ The shaded cells show that the unemployment rate of that particular industry is above the overall unemployment rate.

Source: Census and Statistics Department (2010b, 2013b).

investing proper human capital stocks and they are easily dismissed because they lack sufficient experience. Older workers, whose human capital stocks have depreciated or become outmoded (maybe due to technological development, poor health or de-industrialisation) have greater unemployment risks than middle-aged workers, who may still continue to acquire new knowledge and skills.

Table 4.3 shows that young workers and older worker are higher unemployment risks. The age group 15–19 fares the worst, followed by the age group

Table 4.3 Unemployment rate by age, 1993–2012* (%)

Period	Age group						
	15–19	*20–29*	*30–39*	*40–49*	*50–59*	*60 and over*	*Overall*
1993	8.1[†]	2.7	1.3	1.3	1.8	1.2	2.0
1994	8.5	2.5	1.3	1.4	1.8	1.0	1.9
1995	12.7	4.0	2.3	2.7	3.2	1.7	3.2
1996	12.5	3.6	1.9	2.2	2.7	1.1	2.8
1997	10.0	2.8	1.6	1.7	2.2	1.0	2.2
1998	20.4	5.7	3.3	4.0	5.0	2.3	4.7
1999	26.8	7.5	4.3	5.3	7.2	3.5	6.2
2000	23.7	5.8	3.2	4.3	6.0	2.9	4.9
2001	23.5	6.2	3.5	4.6	5.4	2.7	5.1
2002	30.6	8.2	5.4	6.7	8.2	5.0	7.3
2003	30.2	8.7	6.0	7.4	9.3	4.6	7.9
2004	26.0	6.9	4.9	6.5	8.7	5.9	6.8
2005	21.9	6.2	3.8	5.3	6.9	3.9	5.6
2006	21.9	5.6	3.4	4.3	5.5	2.6	4.8
2007	19.8	4.6	2.9	3.5	4.6	2.5	4.0
2008	16.0	4.6	2.4	3.1	3.7	1.9	3.5
2009	21.8	7.2	3.9	4.6	5.3	3.0	5.3
2010	20.8	6.6	3.1	3.5	4.2	2.8	4.3
2011	15.8	5.3	2.5	2.7	3.3	2.0	3.4
2012	13.9	5.3	2.4	2.8	2.9	2.0	3.3

Notes:

* Statistics are not reported for the "Others" category due to large sampling error.

† The shaded cells show that the unemployment rate of that particular industry is above the overall unemployment rate.

Source: Census and Statistics Department (2010c, 2013c).

20–29, because of their relatively low human capital stocks. These young workers may still manage to make a living with family support. What is worrying is that even when they finally get a job, that job is usually a low-skilled one with limited chances for accumulating valuable work experience. They will face particular risks of long-term social and economic exclusion and induce high social costs. However, a social protection system accompanied with sound ALMPs may alleviate this problem.

The bigger problem is those low-skilled older workers (aged 50–59). Ho *et al.* (2000) find that unemployed workers aged above 45 tend to face a longer spell of unemployment, receive fewer job offers and expect lower future wages than their younger counterparts. Unemployed older workers have difficulties in finding a new job either due to negative cultural stereotypes (Chiu and Ngan, 1999) or their relatively higher wage and greater skill requirements (Heywood *et al.*, 1999). If these older workers were the only breadwinners, their families would be in severe economic destitution.

From our own qualitative research conducted in the spring and summer of 2009,[3] we found that casual, part-time, temporary and unstable jobs have been prevailing among low-income workers since 2000. Many more workers have been suffering continual and longer period of unemployment and under-employment. Due to the survival strategies of enterprises, they have been under-going "downward mobility" in their employment ladder, in the form of wage reduction, overdue wages or alterations in their contracts. Marginalised workers lacked labour protection such as insurance, maximum working hours or provident funds. Since most of the casual jobs are physical and labour-intensive, workers' health can be seriously undermined in a short period, especially in the case of middle-aged workers. During the previous economic downturn, social capital of marginalised workers played a crucial role as part of their their resilience. Heterogeneity in their social network was especially high. They heavily relied on it to connect with people of different social backgrounds, in order to gain informa-tion about available jobs (Lee and Wong, 2004). However, structural decline in various industries caused by the global financial tsunami during these years severely damaged the efficiency networks among low-income workers.

As revealed by the respondents in our case studies, the government's measures in relation to job-seeking and retraining failed to facilitate such workers success-fully re-engaging with the labour market. The government keeps emphasising that Hong Kong should be developing as a knowledge-based economy. Ironically, however, jobs offered by the Labour Department to jobseekers are mainly low-paid and unskilled. The Department is of very little use to middle-level and skilled labourers. Meanwhile, low-level and unskilled workers may be placed in less than desirable employment situations as mentioned above, and it is very difficult to achieve upward mobility thereafter. Most respondents in our case studies also revealed that the services provided by the Employees Retraining Board have no direct relevance for them in seeking reasonable employment, let alone assisting them in acquiring the necessary skills for upward mobility. Forcing the unem-ployed to re-enter the labour market by these means is simply forcing them into working poverty (Lee *et al.*, 2007).

Adhocism: the government's labour policy during the financial tsunami

Adhocism (thus "adhocracy") together with fancy rhetoric is the common tactic for the government in responding to social and political challenges without committing to any long-term strategy (Lee and Yue, 2001) and, by doing so, diluting accountability (Ma, 2006). Despite the rhetoric of "big market, small government", the Hong Kong government does have market-intervening policies to help people survive economic crises. However, the government ignores the structural/systemic nature of the crises and deals with each crisis in an ad hoc manner. The government merely adopts temporary measures without any inten-tion of devising a long-term strategy to tackle the increasing economic insecurity confronted by the people of Hong Kong.

The government seems to be repeating what it did after the Asian financial crisis: prioritising economic growth over social protection, known as "productivist welfare capitalism" (Holliday, 2000). After the handover, the government launched a number of economic policies to turn Hong Kong into an "Asian World City" (Pun and Lee, 2002). But the Asian financial crisis disrupted the whole economic plan and directed much energy of the Tung administration to dealing with the social suffering caused by the crisis. With the neoliberal belief that economic growth is the best way to enhance social welfare and that such growth can be attained through a low tax and low public expenditure regime, the economic and social policies adopted at that time were mostly concerned with restoring economic growth rather than ensuring sustainable livelihoods for people (Lee, 2005). Instead of establishing a better social protection system, the government began to re-commodify public services (e.g. health, education and housing) and contain the expansion of income-transfer programmes. The government adopted social authoritarianism and employed various rhetorical tactics and ideological controls to legitimate these blame-attracting policies (Lee, 2005).

Just before the financial tsunami, the Hong Kong economy was getting better. The government, under the leadership of Donald Tsang, was busy developing Hong Kong as a global financial centre and an economic powerhouse for China. With regard to social policy, the temporary relief measures launched during the SARS crisis were terminated. The term of the Commission on Poverty ended on 30 June 2007. However, the privatisation of public services and the cost containment of income-transfer programmes continues. The structural sources of the economic insecurity of lower-class labourers have not been dealt with under a neoliberal social protection system and an ad hoc social policy-making style. Hence their long-term capacity to recover from adverse outcomes and to build up resources to withstand another shock cannot be augmented. The booms of the stock and real estate markets in 2007 disguised the fact that lower-class labourers were not benefiting economically themselves. The brief economic growth before the burst just gave a breathing space for the poor to psychologically prepare for the next crisis.

The government again launched temporary relief measures to help people cope with the crisis. A temporary Task Force on Economic Challenges was set up in late 2008 to monitor and assess the impact of the financial crisis on Hong Kong's economy and identify ways to turn the crisis into business opportunities.[4] Nonetheless, the economic measures are relatively long-term, aiming at maintaining sustainable economic growth. But the social policy measures are short-term, targeted at temporary relief. In order to reduce the undesirable social consequences of unemployment, public works and infrastructure projects have been launched to create jobs (see Tables 4.4 and 4.5). Subsidised training, retraining and internship places have been created or increased temporarily. The government even openly urges Hong Kong firms not to lay off people so as to fulfil their social corporate responsibilities, despite the fact that this damages its non-interventionist image (e.g. *Sing Tao Daily News*, November 9, 2008; December 5, 2008; April 29, 2009).

The government has lessened its cost containment efforts on income-transfer programmes by increasing the rates and granting one additional month of payment

Table 4.4 Jobs created by the Hong Kong government in response to the financial tsunami

Department	Programme	Posts	Period
1. The HK Government and HK Housing Authority	• Expediting infrastructure projects	55,000	Not specified
2. HK Housing Authority	• In-flat inspection and repair under the Total Maintenance Scheme of some 20 estates	940	2 years
3. All departments	• Advancing recruitment of civil servants	7,700	Not specified
	• Creating temporary positions	4,000	Not specified
4. Buildings Department	• A territory-wide operation to remove 5,000 abandoned signboards	170	1 year
5. More than 20 statutory bodies	• Temporary jobs and internship	2,000	Not specified
6. Innovation and Technology Commission	• Small Entrepreneur Research Assistance Programme and Internship Programme	600	Not specified
7. Innovation and Technology Commission, Office of the Government Chief Information Officer and Tourism Commission	• Additional jobs mainly for university students	680	Not specified
8. Development Bureau	• A career expo on infrastructure to recruit about 1,000 professionals and technical personnel in government and non-government sectors	1,000	Not specified
	• To increase the approved allocation on minor works projects in 2009–10	1,600	Not specified
9. Home Affairs Bureau	• Development of a swimming pool complex in Tuen Mun and conversion of Yau Ma Tei Theatre into a Xiqu Activity Centre	500	Not specified
	• Redevelopment of the Hong Kong Sports Institute	1,000	Not specified
	• Construction and upgrading of various sports venues for the East Asian Games	1,000	Not specified
	• Improvement works for Mong Kok Stadium, construction of a public library and indoor recreation centre in Yuen Long and development of a swimming pool complex in Tuen Mun	1,000	Not specified
	• A project on improvement works for Mong Kok Stadium	200	Not specified
10. Transport and Housing Bureau	• Major railway and highway projects	40,000	Not specified
11. Environment Bureau	• The sludge treatment facilities	610	Not specified
	Total:	117,000	

Source: Hong Kong SAR Government, the Task Force on Economic Challenges (2009).

Table 4.5 Created jobs announced in the financial budget 2009/10 and 2010/11

Programme	Posts	Period
Financial budget 2009/10 (total: 17,760)		
Operation Building Bright campaign	10,000	2 years
Internship Programme for University Graduates	4,000	6–12 months
To assist organisers to host more attractive events in the areas of arts, culture and sports	2,800	3 years
To promote and organise community involvement activities under the theme of "Green, Cultural, Dynamic Games"	260	1 year
To conduct a one-year education programme to teach internet users, especially young students, how to use the internet appropriately and safely	500	1 year
To enhance energy efficiency of government buildings and public facilities	200	1 year
Financial budget 2010/11 (total: 500)		
A targeted employment programme (aged between 15 and 24 with low educational qualifications, who need special assistance because of emotional and behavioural problems or learning difficulties)	500	1 year

Source: Hong Kong SAR Government (2009, 2010b).

to the Comprehensive Social Security Assistance (CSSA) Scheme, Disability Allowance and the Old Age Allowance recipients. The government has also paid the basic rent for 700,000 public housing estate tenants for two months, and provided a one-off grant of $1,000 for each student receiving CSSA or student financial assistance to ease the financial burden on parents in the new school year.[5] Again, these measures are short-term and most of them will end when the financial tsunami recedes. It is uncertain whether these measures will have lasting effects in assisting the affected lower-class labourers to recover from adverse outcomes, not to say insure them against future economic risks.

This chapter is *not* arguing against short-term relief policies. These "reactive" measures *are* necessary for providing social protection against contingent events. However, as people's exposure to economic risks is rising under globalisation, the government needs to establish a basic social protection system as a "proactive" strategy to provide a vibrant but secure economic environment for all economic actors.

Active labour market policies as social protection tools

In the broadest sense, social protection programmes can serve four functions: protective, preventive, promotive and transformative (Davies and McGregor,

2009). The protective function is to provide immediate protection and relief from adverse outcomes. It is basically reactive in nature. The preventive function, both reactive and proactive, is to prevent adverse outcomes from happening, and once happened, to help people cope with the consequences. The promotive function is to promote resilience by increasing economic opportunities for people to diversify risks through various livelihood strategies. It is not only proactive but also contributes to social development (Midgley, 1995). Finally, the transformative function is about changing social relations to reduce exclusion. It proactively contributes to building a cohesive and harmonious society.

Within the ILO and among European countries, there is a debate about the role of ALMPs in providing social security within a flexible labour market environment. According to Auer *et al.* (2008), passive labour market policies include unemployment insurance, unemployment assistance and early retirement. They are mostly reactive in nature, merely serving protective and preventive functions. But ALMPs are proactive in the sense that they have promotive and transformative functions, potentially leading to a welfare regime in which efficiency and equity can both be pursued. The main thrust of ALMPs is to actively support labour market integration through demand-side measures (e.g. job creation in the form of public and community work programmes, employment subsidies, and enterprise creation and self-employment facilitation programmes) and supply-side measures (e.g. training and retraining, job matching, job search assistance, prospecting and registering vacancies, profiling and providing labour market information).

ALMPs serve the social protection function by ensuring everyone has a job. The basic idea is that "decent work is the best insurance against poverty" (Auer *et al.*, 2008: 21). If ALMPs fail to get a person a job, social assistance kicks in. Without ALMPs in Hong Kong, social assistance (i.e. CSSA) is the only way for the poor to survive the adverse outcomes of social risks. Because CSSA is a means-tested income-transfer programme, recipients are easily stigmatised by the government and society. ALMPs can serve as the first buffer against the invasion of economic risks generated by globalisation without imposing negative labels on participants. ALMPs also promote economic development by increasing the human capital stocks of Hong Kong and improving job matching. Moreover, well-designed ALMPs must address the issues of discrimination against older workers, ethnic groups and the disabled so that they can find a job and enhance their own capacity to survive economic risks. As a result, ALMPs indirectly promote social cohesion and improve social equity.

As Auer *et al.* (2008) argue, ALMPs are used in all regions of the world, though the way in which they are used, the financing methods, and the importance allocated to each type of ALMP, are different. In particular, ALMPs were enacted in some East Asian countries after the 1997 Asian financial crisis as policy responses to serious unemployment as well as inadequate earnings problems. Is it possible for Hong Kong to employ ALMPs? Indeed, many elements of ALMPs are present in Hong Kong, though they are not supposed to work as genuine labour market activation tools. With regard to the supply-side tools, for instance, the Employees Retraining Board sponsors numerous training and retraining programmes. The

Labour Department and Social Welfare Department provide limited job search assistance and job matching services.

Regarding the demand-side tools, the temporary internship programmes and employment subsidies used by the government during an economic crisis can be institutionalised as tools of ALMPs. Social enterprises and entrepreneurship are encouraged by the former chief executive, Donald Tsang, to deal with widening economic inequality, as highlighted in his policy address of 2007–8 (Hong Kong SAR Government, 2007, para. 71). The government also provides public work programmes, though they are not used as ALMP tools. Nonetheless, public work and infrastructure programmes are actively used as labour market tools to ease the severe unemployment problems created in an economic recession.

In addition, a number of anti-discrimination ordinances have been enacted. If properly implemented, they have great transformative potential for reducing the social exclusion of women, disabled people and ethnic minorities, thus enhancing their capacity to deal with economic insecurity. All in all, many potential ALMP measures are there, though they are fragmented: some are contracting to one another, some are temporary and some are of a very small scale. The biggest barrier to resolving these issues is whether the Hong Kong government has the determination to devise a package of ALMPs that can serve the four vital functions of a social protection system against globalisation risks.

However, as Wilding argues (2007), the Hong Kong government has a strong "economy first" ideology and anti-welfarist tradition – i.e. the brelief that anything more than basic social security will promote welfare dependency and destroy work incentives. It has stood firm against social policies that are seen as damaging to the economy. Both the former chief executives, Tung Chee-hwa and Donald Tsang, are faithful followers of this approach. When Hong Kong was still bearing the aftermath of the Asian financial crisis, Tung clearly declared in his policy address that the social policy under his administration "is complementary to the laissez-faire economic policy we follow" (Tung, 2000, para. 50).

Over the eight years of Tung's administration (1997–2005), the government issued 166 consultation papers across 18 policy areas, and not a single one was on labour policy. Tsang's administration (2005–2012) issued 131 policy consultation papers, and only one was on labour policy, concerning the statutory minimum wage, issued in a year after Hong Kong was stepping out from the hardship of the global financial tsunami (see Table 4.6). The priority of social protection for workers is obviously very low. In spite of the relief measures adopted by the government during the high tide of the global financial tsunami in 2009, the financial secretary John Tsang still asserted, at the same time, that the government should not be the main source of job creation during the period of job shortages, since taking that road would only damage the normal operation of the labour market.[6]

Although the lower-class workers' need for comprehensive ALMPs are known, initiatives to change established practices are not enforced, unless political pressure is exerted. When policy changes are needed, they are carried out with little enthusiasm, and only to meet political demands (Lindblom, 1959). This kind of

Table 4.6 Consultation papers issued by Hong Kong SAR government 1997–2012

Policy area	Tung Chee-hwa (1997–2005)		Donald Tsang (2005–12)		Total (1997–2012)	
	No.	*%*	*No.*	*%*	*No.*	*%*
Constitutional and electoral affairs	6	4%	20	15%	26	9%
Civil service	6	4%	1	1%	7	2%
Law and justice	16	10%	12	9%	28	9%
Security	7	4%	1	1%	8	3%
Commerce and economic development	5	3%	9	7%	14	5%
Public finance	5	3%	2	2%	7	2%
Financial services	17	10%	13	10%	30	10%
Information technology and broadcasting	43	26%	23	18%	66	22%
Labour	0	0%	1	1%	1	0%
Welfare	3	2%	0	0%	3	1%
Healthcare	6	4%	7	5%	13	4%
Housing	2	1%	4	3%	6	2%
Development	10	6%	8	6%	18	16%
Transport	0	0%	4	3%	4	1%
Home affairs	11	7%	7	5%	18	16%
Environment	8	5%	12	9%	20	7%
Food safety and environmental hygiene	5	3%	5	4%	10	3%
Education	16	10%	2	2%	18	6%
Total	*166*	*100%*	*131*	*100%*	*297*	*100%*

Source: Hong Kong SAR Government (2012), as cited in SynergyNet (2012: 10).

disjointed incrementalism, as argued by Tang (1998), was the basic approach to social policy-making during the British Hong Kong colonial age. However, ALMPs have not only been a low priority of the SAR governments' governance, but they also received very limited emphasis by other political parties. During the last legislation term (2008–2012), the Legislative Councillors moved 202 motions (which are not intended to have legislative effect), and, according to our judgement, only about six related to ALMPs (see Table 4.7). As the political party occupying the largest amount of seats in the Legislative Council, the Democratic Alliance for the Betterment and Progress issued more than 170 opinion documents and opinion surveys to the government during the last legislation term, but almost none of them relates to ALMPs. The Democratic Party, the biggest opposition party in Hong Kong, issued more than 80 opinion documents to the government during the same period, and only one of them advocated ALMPs (in terms

Table 4.7 Legislative councillors' motions related to ALMPs

Year(s)	Number of motions*	Concerns related to ALMPs
2008–9	53	**Ip Wai Ming:** assisting grassroots workers in counteracting economic adversities (4 February 2009)
2009–10	55	**Wong Kwok Kin:** enhancing employment support and creating employment opportunities (25 November 2009)
2010–11	60	**Pan Pey Chyou:** Work Incentive Transport Subsidy Scheme (10 November 2010)
		Tommy Cheung: promoting the relocation of departmental headquarters to the districts for creating employment (1 June 2011)
2011–12	34	**Cyd Ho:** improving further education and employment of sub-degree students (23 November 2011)
		Wong Sing Chi: comprehensively reviewing and perfecting the Work Incentive Transport Subsidy Scheme (30 November 2011)
Total	202	6

Note: *Motions not intended to have legislative effect

Source: Legislative Council (2009, 2010, 2011, 2012).

of the government's role in job creation).[7] Under such a light pressure from the political parties, it is not difficult to understand why the government has not taken ALMPs seriously. The stance of the government and the major political parties is probably in line with Hong Kong people's incongruous attitude towards social welfare: according to a survey conducted a few years after the Asian financial crisis, 42 per cent of respondents saw poverty as resulting from society not treating the poor fairly. Another survey conducted in 2006 found that 75.2 per cent of respondents disagreed with cutting social welfare. However, it also found that 69 per cent respondents believed that Hongkongers should rely on their own means in times of public budget austerity, and nearly half agreed that social welfare would make Hongkongers less willing to rely on their own means to take care of themselves. Wong *et al.* believe that there was a strong and prevailing anti-welfare sentiment and a commitment to individualism of 'pulling yourself up by your own bootstraps' in the society (2011: 261). Such a neoliberalist ethos is inextricably linked to the assumption that unemployment results from individual inadequacy and welfare dependency, and this ethos has dominated East Asian social policy-making for a very long time, including in Hong Kong (Chan, 2012).

Conclusion

We are all living in a risk society, but some social groups are more affected than others by the distribution and growth of risks. The disadvantaged have fewer opportunities to avoid risk because of their lack of resources compared with the advantaged (Beck, 1992). Globalisation creates risks, particularly contagious financial turmoil, through increasing interdependence among economies. As a result, even under the influences of neoliberal thinking, social spending in many countries has been increasing. Social protection provision becomes a paramount concern in social policy-making to ensure economic security, as the global economy becomes increasingly unstable and financial crises occur every now and then. Without social protection to help the vulnerable survive economic hardship, the ultimate legitimacy of the market system may be challenged because of its negative impacts. Indeed, economic security is not merely an economic problem, but also a political issue. To provide economic security to a society is a means of maintaining political stability and social harmony, but also a means of ensuring the legitimacy of government. Thus, Nesadurai (2006: 12) argues that "Economic security should constitute a central goal of economic governance rather than emerge on the political/policy agenda only when crises strike."

Unemployment is one of the major economic risks confronted by people, and has the capacity to seriously endanger the well-being of a household. In Hong Kong, the unemployment risks created by globalisation are unevenly distributed in terms of industrial sectors, occupational types and age. The disadvantaged groups suffer most in every economic crisis. However, the Hong Kong government simply relies on temporary measures to help them cope with the immediate adverse outcomes, without any intention or strategy for enhancing their capacity to recover from adversity and to withstand future risks. The Hong Kong government should take a proactive role in establishing a social protection system that can better deal with globalisation risks. Designing a package of ALMPs may be the first step to establish such a system because many potential ALMPs have been employed, though in a fragmented, unintentional and sometimes temporary way, by the government.

In his policy address of 2008–9, Donald Tsang emphasised "turning crises into opportunities" as a proper attitude towards the global financial tsunami. Davies and McGregor (2009: 2) also regard the crisis as a window of opportunity to seize for progressive social protection initiatives. They note that with strong political leadership the crisis may become "a key driver in the development of social protection schemes". Otherwise, it may "provoke political paralysis and the shrinkage of state protection which triggers a spiral of long-term decline" (Davies and McGregor, 2009: 2). Indeed, historically speaking, many countries have established a social protection system in response to political and/or economic crises.

For instance, the birth of the first social protection system in Germany is often attributed to Bismarck's attempt to stop the Socialist movement and to maintain political stability by buying off workers (Cutler and Johnson, 2004). In the USA, President Roosevelt set up a comprehensive social protection system in 1934 to alleviate the negative consequences of the Great Depression (Livingston, 2008). The social policy responses of affected countries towards the Asian financial crisis give further support to the importance of strengthening social protection systems as a way of alleviating the negative consequences of economic insecurity.

In response to the crisis, South Korea reformed its social protection system by scaling up the coverage and level of protection for its citizens (Shin, 2000). The ILO (2008: 15) points out that some countries such as Korea, Taiwan and Thailand have significantly expanded their social protection measures during the crisis, but other countries like Singapore, Malaysia, Indonesia and the Philippines have reacted with an emphasis on strengthening the values of self-reliance, family networks and economic growth, introducing temporary measures of social assistance. The ILO finds that the former countries "fared significantly better, both in terms of mitigating . . . rising poverty and unemployment and in terms of the speed with which they recovered from the crisis".

According to the ILO (2004: 4), economic insecurity "is about the capacity to cope with the adverse consequences of those risks and the capacity to recover from adverse outcomes". Ad hoc relief programmes are undeniably helpful to the poor when coping with economic crises, but they are no use in terms of enhancing their long-term capacity to recover from negative outcomes and to withstand another economic crisis. Continuous employment is one way to make the poor develop sufficient capacity to deal with an economic crisis. As a result, the ILO (2008: 16) stresses that the government should encourage enterprises to fulfil their social responsibilities, and ensure that "labour rules are respected and that the crisis does not become an excuse for firing people". As a more proactive strategy, the ILO (2008: 16) further argues that "the crisis can provide a unique opportunity for those countries that are still lacking proper social insurance systems to enact innovative policies and strengthen labour legislation". The objective of social policies of economic security is to establish a well-designed unemployment benefit system supplemented by public works programmes and ALMPs.

Fundamentally, Hong Kong also needs a review the productivist approach to social policy-making. As Chan argues (2012), many social problems in a risk society (like Hong Kong), such as unemployment, are the consequence of an over-concentration on economic growth. Labour policy tends to favour the managerial and professional sectors, while marginalising and under-valuing manual workers, thus contributing to the over-exploitation of the working class. A "confession" of the former chief executive Donald Tsang may be a good beginning of this fundamental review: appearing at a Legislative Council question-and-answer session for the last time in June 2012, he admitted his misjudgement in balancing economic and social developments: "I used to believe that different social stratums could enjoy the fruits of economic development as a result of the trickle-down effect. However, there were discrepancies between the theory and reality" (So, 2012).

Acknowledgements

The authors would like to thank the Department of Social Sciences at the Hong Kong Institute of Education for sponsoring the project, and the Hong Kong Catholic Commission for Labour Affairs, the Concerning CSSA Review Alliance and the Neighbourhood & Workers Service Centre, for kindly permitting us to use the data generated from the research project "Qualitative Research of the Unemployment

Conditions after the Financial Tsunami". The authors' thanks also goes to Ching-Yin Cheng, Matt Lui and Cody Kwong for their quality research support.

Notes

1 Debt deflation refers to "a situation that the collateral used to secure a loan, or another form of debt, decreases in value". Available at http://www.investopedia.com/terms/d/debtdeflation.asp.
2 Conventionally, an economic recession is defined by two consecutive quarters of negative economic growth as measured by a country's GDP. Thus, the 1995 economic downturn can be regarded as a recession, even though the nominal GDP growth rate is still impressive.
3 The project is hosted by the Jong Kong Catholic Commission for Labour Affairs, the Concerning CSSA Alliance and the Neighbourhood & Workers Service Centre. Two rounds of in-depth interviews were conducted with 12 cases during the period April–July 2009, while focus group discussion meetings were conducted in August 2009. They were referred by nine different social services agencies or civic NGOs.
4 HKSAR Government Press Release (12 November 2008), "LCQ5: Measures to tackle problems brought by the financial tsunami". Available at: http://www.info.gov.hk/gia/general/200811/12/P200811120158.htm.
5 HKSAR Government, "$16.8b in relief measures announced" (26 May 2009). Available at: http://news.gov.hk/en/category/businessandfinance/090526/html/090526en03003.htm.
6 HKSAR Government Press Release (26 May 2009), "FS speaks on new round of relief measures (1)". Available at: http://www.info.gov.hk/gia/general/200905/26/P200905260214.htm.
7 For the details of these documents and opinion surveys, see http://www.dab.org.hk/?st=19,20&t=1&mmode=ba, http://eng.dphk.org/.

References

Auer, P., Efendioğlu, Ü. and Leschke, J. (2008). *Active Labour Market Policies Around the World: Coping with the Consequences of Globalization* (2nd edn). Geneva: International Labour Office.

Beck, U. (1992). *Risk Society: Towards a New Modernity*. London: Sage.

Becker, G. S. (1964). *Human Capital: A Theoretical and Empirical Analysis, with Special Reference to Education*. New York: National Bureau of Economic Research.

Burgoon, B. (2001). "Globalization and Welfare Compensation: Disentangling the Ties that Bind", *International Organization*, 55(3): 509–551.

Cameron, D. (1978). "The Expansion of the Public Economy: A Comparative Analysis", *American Political Science Review*, 72(4): 1243–1261.

Census and Statistics Department (2009). *Unemployment Rate by Previous Industry, 1991–2/2009*. Available at: http://www.censtatd.gov.hk/FileManager/EN/HSICv11/TABLE009_HSICv1.1_E.xls.

Census and Statistics Department (2010a). *Unemployment Rate by Previous Industry, 1/2008–10/2010*. Available at: http://www.censtatd.gov.hk/hong_kong_statistics/statistical_tables/index.jsp?subjectID=2&tableID=009.

Census and Statistics Department (2010b). *Unemployment Rate by Previous Occupation, 1993–10/2010*. Available at: http://www.censtatd.gov.hk/showtableexcel2.jsp?tableID=010.

Census and Statistics Department (2010c). *Unemployment Rate by Age, 1993– 10/2010*. Available at: http://www.censtatd.gov.hk/showtableexcel2.jsp?tableID=011.

Census and Statistics Department (2013a). *Unemployment Rate by Previous Industry, 1/2008– 2/2013*. Available at: http://www.censtatd.gov.hk/showtableexcel2.jsp?tableID=010.

Census and Statistics Department (2013b). *Unemployment Rate by Previous Occupation, 1993–2/2013*. Available at: http://www.censtatd.gov.hk/hkstat/sub/sp200.jsp?subjectID =200&tableID=010&ID=0&productType=8.

Census and Statistics Department (2013c). *Unemployment Rate by Age, 1993–2/2013*. Available at: http://www.censtatd.gov.hk/showtableexcel2.jsp?tableID=011.

Chan, K. W. (2012). "Rethinking Flexible Welfare Strategy in Hong Kong: a New Direction for the East Asian Welfare Model?', *Journal of Asian Public Policy*, 5(1): 71–81.

Chiu, S. and Ngan, R. (1999). "Employment of Chinese Older Workers in Hong Kong: Cultural Myths, Discrimination and Opportunities", *Ageing International*, 25(3): 14–30.

Cutler, D. M. and Johnson, R. (2004). "The Birth and Growth of the Social Insurance State: Explaining Old Age and Medical Insurance across Countries", *Public Choice*, 120: 87–121.

Davies, M. and McGregor, J. A. (2009). "Social Protection Responses to the Financial Crisis: What do we Know?", *IDS in Focus Policy Briefing 7.4*. Brighton: IDS. Available at: http:// www.ids.ac.uk/download.cfm?objectid=3E8CC9CC-5056–8171-7B3BCA3FF00E8F81.

Garrett, G. (1998). *Partisan Politics in the Global Economy*. Cambridge: Cambridge University Press.

Garrett, G. and Mitchell, D. (2001). "Globalization, Government Spending and Taxation in the OECD", *European Journal of Political Research*, 39(2): 145–177.

Gunter, B. G. and van der Hoeven, R. (2004). "The Social Dimension of Globalization: A Review of the Literature", *International Labour Review*, 143(1/2): 7–43.

Hacker, J. S. (2006). *The Great Risk Shift: Why American Jobs, Families, Health Care And Retirement Aren't Secure – And How We Can Fight Back*. New York: Oxford University Press.

Heywood, J. S, Ho, L. S. and Wei, X. D. (1999). "The Determinants of Hiring Older Workers: Evidence from Hong Kong", *Industrial and Labor Relations Review*, 52(3): 444–459.

Ho, L. S., Wei, X. D. and Voon, J. P. (2000). "Are Older Workers Disadvantaged in the Hong Kong Labour Market?", *Asian Economic Journal*, 14(3): 283–300.

Holliday, I. (2000). "Productivist Welfare Capitalism: Social Policy in East Asia", *Political Studies*, 48(4): 706–723.

Hong Kong SAR Government (2003). *2003 Policy Address: Captialising on Our Advantages, Revitalising Our Economy*. Hong Kong: Hong Kong SAR Government. Available at: http://www.policyaddress.gov.hk/pa03/eng/speech_e.pdf.

Hong Kong SAR Government (2007). *2007–2008 Policy Address: A New Direction for Hong Kong*. Hong Kong: Hong Kong SAR Government. Available at: http://www.policyaddress.gov.hk/07–08/eng/docs/policy.pdf.

Hong Kong SAR Government (2008). *2008–2009 Policy Address: Embracing New Challenges*. Hong Kong: Hong Kong SAR Government. Available at: http://www.policyaddress.gov.hk/08–09/eng/docs/policy.pdf.

Hong Kong SAR Government (2009). *The Budget 2009–10*. Available at: http://www.budget.gov.hk/2009/eng/pdf/BudgetSpeech2009–10_e.pdf.

Hong Kong SAR Government (2010a). *Hong Kong Economy, Hong Kong Economic Trends: Gross Domestic Product and its Major Components*. Available at: http://www.hkeconomy.gov.hk/en/pdf/domestic.pdf.

Hong Kong SAR Government (2010b). *The Budget 2010–11*. Available at: http://www.budget.gov.hk/2010/eng/pdf/BudgetSpeech2010–11_e.pdf.

Hong Kong SAR Government (2013). *Hong Kong Economy, Hong Kong Economic Trends: Gross Domestic Product and its Major Components*. Available at: http://www.hkeconomy.gov.hk/en/pdf/domestic_ch.pdf.

Hong Kong SAR Government, the Task Force on Economic Challenges (2009). *Measures Adopted in Response to the Financial Tsunami*. Available at: http://www.fso.gov.hk/tfec/eng/doc/Measures%20Adopted%20by%20HK%20%28TFEC-INFO-03%29%20%28Eng%29.pdf.

International Labour Organization (ILO) (2004). *Economic Security for a Better World*. Geneva: International Labour Office.

International Labour Organization (ILO) (2008). *A Global Policy Package to Address the Global Crisis* (policy brief). Geneva: International Labour Office. Available at: http://www.ilo.org/public/libdoc/ilo/2008/108B09_307_engl.pdf.

Kannan, K. P. (2007). "Social Security in a Globalizing World", *International Social Security Review*, 60(2–3): 19–37.

Krugman, P. (2008a). *The International Finance Multiplier*. Available at: http://krugman.blogs.nytimes.com/2008/10/05/the-international-finance-multiplier.

Krugman, P. (2008b). *It's a Small World After All*. Available at: http://krugman.blogs.nytimes.com/2008/10/06/its-a-small-world-after-all.

Krugman, P. (2008c). "Cash for Trash." *The New York Times*, 21 September. Available at: http://www.nytimes.com/2008/09/22/opinion/22krugman.html.

Lee, E. W. Y. (2005). "The Renegotiation of the Social Pact in Hong Kong: Economic Globalisation, Socioeconomic Change, and Local Politics", *Journal of Social Policy*, 34(2): 293–310.

Lee, K. M. and Wong, H. (2004). "Marginalised Workers in Postindustrial Hong Kong", *The Journal of Comparative Asian Development*, 3(2): 249–80.

Lee, K. M. and Yue, W. C. (2001). "A Prolegomenon to the Study of the Role of Rhetoric in the Garbage-Can Policy Process: The Case of Hong Kong's Positive Non-Interventionism", *International Journal of Public Administration*, 24(9): 887–907.

Lee, K. M., Wong, H. and Law, K. Y. (2007). "Social Polarization and Poverty in a Global City: the Case of Hong Kong", *China Report*, 43(1): 1–30.

Legislative Council (2009). *Members' Motions 2008–2009*. Available at: http://www.legco.gov.hk/yr08–09/chinese/counmtg/motion/mot_0809.htmøptbl.

Legislative Council (2010). *Members' Motions 2009–2010*. Available at: http://www.legco.gov.hk/yr09–10/chinese/counmtg/motion/mot_0910.htmøptbl.

Legislative Council (2011). *Members' Motions 2010–2011*. Available at: http://www.legco.gov.hk/yr10–11/chinese/counmtg/motion/mot_1011.htmøptbl.

Legislative Council (2012). *Members' Motions 2011–2012*. Available at: http://www.legco.gov.hk/yr11–12/chinese/counmtg/motion/mot_1112.htmøptbl.

Lindblom, C. E. (1959). "The Science of 'Muddling Through' ", *Public Administration Review*, 19(2): 79–88.

Livingston, S. G. (2008). *U.S. Social Security: A Reference Handbook*. Santa Barbara, CA: ABC-CLIO.

Ma, N. (2006). "Committee Politics is a Political Regression", *Hong Kong Economic Journal*, 8 February: 18 (in Chinese).

Midgley, J. (1995). *Social Development: The Developmental Perspective in Social Welfare*. London: Sage.

Minsky, H. P. (1992, May). *The Financial Instability Hypothesis* (Working Paper No. 74). New York: The Jerome Levy Economics Institute of Bard College.

Nesadurai, H. E. S. (2006). "Conceptualising Economic Security in an Era of Globalisation: What does the East Asian Experience Reveal?", in H. E. S. Nesadurai (ed.) *Globalisation and Economic Security in East Asia: Governance and Institutions*. London: Routledge, pp. 3–22.

Pun, N. and Lee, K. M. (2002). "Locating Globalization: The Changing Role of the City-state in Post-handover Hong Kong", *The China Review*, 2(1): 1–28.

Rejda, G. E. (1999). *Social Insurance and Economic Security* (6th edn). Upper Saddle River, NJ: Prentice Hall.

Rodrik, D. (1998). "Why do More Open Economies have Bigger Governments?", *Journal of Political Economy*, 106(5): 997–1032.

Shin, D. M. (2000). "Financial Crisis and Social Security: The Paradox of the Republic of Korea", *International Social Security Review*, 53(3): 83–107.

Singtao Daily News (2008). "Matthew Cheung Urges Corporations not to Lay off People", 9 November: A06 (in Chinese).

Singtao Daily News (2008). Henry Tang Urges Employers not to Lay off Employees, 5 December: A18 (in Chinese).

Singtao Daily News (2009). "Donald Tsang: Don't Lay off People so Easily", 29 April: A12 (in Chinese).

So, P. (2012). "My Watershed Moment Came in 2008, *Tsang* Says", *South China Morning Post*, 15 June: CITY3.

SynergyNet (2012). *Review of the Government Performance of the HKSAR Government 2012*. Hong Kong: SynergyNet. Available at: http://www.synergynet.org.hk/pdf/201206102789_en.pdf.

Tang K. L. (1998). *Colonial State and Social Policy: Social Welfare Development in Hong Kong 1842–1997*. Lanham, MD: University Press of America.

Tung, C. H. (2000). *The Policy Address 2000: Serving the Community, Sharing Common Goals*. Hong Kong: Hong Kong SAR Government.

Wilding, P. (2007). "Social Policy", in W. M. Lam *et al.* (eds). *Contemporary Hong Kong Politics: Governance in the Post-1997 Era*. Hong Kong: Hong Kong University Press, pp. 205–221.

Wong, T. K. Y., Wan, P. S. and Law, K. W. K. (2011). "Public Perceptions of Income Inequality: Trends and Implications", in S. W. K. Chiu and S. L. Wong (eds) *Hong Kong Divided? Structures of Social Inequality in the Twenty-First Century*. Hong Kong: Hong Kong Institute of Asia-Pacific Studies, The Chinese University of Hong Kong, pp. 243–276.

5 Challenges for the developmental welfare regime in Taiwan

From authoritarianism to democratic governance

Yu-Fang Chang and Yeun-Wen Ku

Introduction

Taiwan as an economic miracle in the postwar era consisted of two elements. The first was its rapid economic growth that has transformed Taiwan's economy from agriculture to industry, from poor to well-off, and from less developed to developed. The second element was its fairly equal income distribution against the predictions of the Kuznets curve that inequality is expected to rise with economic growth before subsequently falling. In 1979, three scholars co-authored a book advocating Taiwan's development as a model of growth with equity (Fei *et al.*, 1979). However, this model is now under critical threat.

Along with increasing income inequality, the requirement of public efforts for a more equal society has become an important source of state legitimacy, especially under the democratisation movement after the 1990s. Welfare provision has ever been regarded as an important way to remedy negative impacts of inequality induced by market mechanisms, by which an even closer solidarity can be realised. Such argument underpins the necessity of state intervention into welfare using many social policy instruments ranging from means-tested to contributory/non-contributory benefits. While social spending was growing remarkably, official statistics showed poverty, unemployment, divorce, mental disease and child abuse (that all cause family crises) were all rising still. In particular, Taiwan has experienced the re-emergence of a poverty problem that was thought to be disappearing after remarkable economic growth in the postwar era.

In this chapter we look at poverty in the the developmental state in Taiwan, which faces the difficulty of fulfilling two contradictory desires – economic growth and social equity – simultaneously. The chapter aims to examine whether the economic miracle in the twentieth century will be sustainable in the new century.

The authoritarian state and developmentalism

The economic growth in the Asian Newly Industrialised Countries (hereafter cited as the Asian NICs) has attracted a lot of scholars' attention, exploring the dynamics behind this successful story. A developmental model is now becoming recognised, which emphasises the role and capacity of the state in managing conditions favouring production. Concepts, such as "governing market" (Wade, 1990), "disciplined market" (Amsden, 1989), and "guided market' " (White and Wade, 1988), have been widely used to refer to the relationship between the state and the market. As Castells states, "a state is developmental when it establishes as its principle of legitimacy, its ability to promote and sustain development, understanding by development the combination of steady high rates of economic growth and structural change in the productive system, both domestically and in its relationship to the international economy" (1992: 56).

Japan was first regarded as a developmental state by Johnson (1982). He explains how the Japanese government intervenes and organises state resources for the sake of economic development. Following Johnson's work, approximately between 1985–95, a plausible account of East Asian development was formed and named as "developmental state theory" to explain the cases of the four "tiger" economies (Amsden, 1985; Castells, 1992; Gold, 1986; Wade, 1990). The theme of the developmental state is based on three critical conditions: the developmental ideology or pressure for development; the capability of government for development; and its capacity for overcoming any possible reactions against development (Castells, 1992). "Capability of government" is the core by which public policies for development can be carried out effectively with the strength of state authority. However, such state capacity can be relatively limited by the other two conditions: "pressure for development" and "the capacity to overcome reaction against development". East Asia states have stood out against rising collective welfare demands within society, rather than responding to people's needs, in order to speed up the process of accumulation and development. Deyo (1989) interprets this situation as "labour subordination". Nevertheless, the high level of state capacity is crucial for the theme of the developmental state. So'rensen's study puts forward a controversial point that authoritarian regimes are more successful in achieving rapid economic growth because they are more capable of conducting radical reforms and curbing consumption to enhance accumulation (So'rensen, 1991).

To achieve fast economic growth, the social domain was underdeveloped with an incomplete social security system (Ku, 1995). So called "reluctant welfarism" is used by Midgley (1986: 234) to describe the fact that the East Asian states are reluctant to increase their roles in social welfare: "the four Asian NICs had been congruent with a marked reluctance on the part of [the] political elite to expand social programs. They have consistently affirmed their faith in the virtues of free enterprise, self-reliance and hard work and frequently declared an aversion to welfarism". For this reason, a plausible interpretation is exaggerated as being that the rapid economic growth in East Asia is because of its underdeveloped state welfare, and thus the state is capable of spending relatively more on matters directly linked to economic growth. MacPherson argues that four extreme methods of economic adjustment have been widely applied by the Asian NICs in response to changes in the world market: reduction in government expenditure, shifting resources from consumption to investment, adopting macro-economic policies in favour of international trade, and raising productivity levels through reliance on market mechanisms (MacPherson, 1992: 56). In contrast to MacPherson's point, Deyo argues that social and economic development goals are often compatible and closely linked under the development strategy of export-oriented industrialisation (EOI) – the basic model of development in the Asian NICs. EOI calls for more effective utilisation of human resources, such as low wages and compensation levels, high productivity and a low level of labour conflict. For the success of EOI there must be some social policies to maintain or reproduce human resources, particularly in the fields of education, health and housing. Furthermore, a low level of labour conflict relies on state intervention in wage negotiation and control over trade unions. Even if there are some different components of social policies in the Asian NICs, they all perform well in terms of enhancing labour productivity, encouraging enterprise training and subsidising wages in favour of economic growth (Deyo, 1992: 304–5).

In order to combine these two opposite views and search for a practical way of integrating economic and social policies in pursuit of general social welfare objectives, Midgley proposes the social development approach, which means "a process of planned social change designed to promote the well-being of the population as a whole in conjunction with a dynamic process of economic development" (1995: 25). He regards economic and social processes as equally important components of the development process. Social development cannot take place without economic development, and economic development is meaningless if it fails to bring about significant improvements in the well-being of the population as a whole. Midgley's points provide a very reflective idea, particularly his indicating that the state should not avoid a positive role in this process. However, to some extent he seems to oversimplify the constraints made upon by the global system, in which it is somehow beyond the nation state, and competition, conflict and contradiction within it are even more significant than cooperation and harmony.

Truly in the Asian NICs, we note a significant improvement of living conditions with the increasing incomes resulting from economic growth. Although there should be a dilemma of making choices between economic growth and social progress, some social programmes had been developed even earlier than the economic take-off in the Asian NICs, such as the Central Provident Fund in Singapore in 1953, the labour insurance scheme in Taiwan in 1950, and compensation for work injury in Hong Kong and Korea in 1953. In particular, we find the gradual but important expansion of state welfare in the Asian NICs in more recent decades (e.g. Holliday and Wilding, 2003).

From developmental state to developmental welfare regime in East Asia

Gradually, studies on East Asian welfare have been regarded by the international community of social welfare as an important field of comparative social policy. The regime aspect contains a great many publications, under Esping-Andersen's giant shadow (1990), that reveal the intention of promoting East Asian welfare studies in comparative social policy originally dominated by the experiences of

Western welfare states. However, it cannot be regarded as an effort to reject Esping-Andersen's theme but to expand his three types of welfare regime with a fourth, or more, even though it is also implying the fact that East Asia contains late-welfare-developed countries. Some detailed case studies open the development, such as Ku (1997a), who locates welfare in the context of Taiwanese capitalist development and sees how the capitalist world system, the state, ideology and social forces interweave to shape the particular regime in Taiwan, and Kwon (1999), who interprets institutional characteristics of the Korean welfare state with the politics of legitimation. Both authors have shown some different regime characteristics from Esping-Andersen's typologies but they are also reluctant to conclude the two cases as different regimes. On the contrary, some other authors, after browsing East Asia as a region, are more affirmative to name it the "oikonomic welfare state" (Jones, 1990), "productivist welfare capitalism" (Holliday, 2000) or "conservative" (Aspalter, 2001). In fact, Holliday (2000) moves further towards, in concept, the imagined fourth regime and provides a new idea for exploring the core components of East Asian welfare, though we still need to examine his constructing regimes with empirical data analysis. Nevertheless his phrase of "productivist", namely two central components of a growth-oriented state and subordinating all state policies to economic/industrial objectives, does have some echoes. For example, in his discussion of East Asian welfare, Gough (2004) also uses this phrase to signal the regime characteristics, which are absent in the other regions.

What features, then, does East Asian welfare share? Tang (2000: 139–40) demonstrates some common social policy strategies. First, East Asian states are keen to believe in that economic growth will raise incomes through real growth and that benefits will spread throughout the whole population. Second, the following defining characteristics of government are deemed essential to development: the relatively small share of social expenditure in total public spending; relatively small fiscal deficits; and flexibility in the labour market. Third, social security is primarily targeting politically important interest groups, which can result in unequal redistribution. Fourth, the states have generally been prodded into expanding social welfare by crises. Fifth, statutory social assistance programmes are established in all the tiger economies, but these programmes are smaller in scope and lower in level of benefits, compared to industrialised countries, and often with the effect of stigma. Sixth, the ideology of rejecting the expansion of social welfare comes from culture. Seventh, labour laws and related benefits have been paid much attention to rapid industrialisation and to minimising possible rebels in labour movements.

Even though it presents in different institutions and ways, Holliday and Wilding (2003: 161–70) point out that East Asian welfare is very much side by side in six dimensions: political purposes have always been primary; economic growth and full employment have been the main engines of welfare; productivist welfare has been the goal; welfarism has been shunned; the family has been accorded a key welfare function; and the states have been strong but limited. The main features of East Asian welfare can be summarised as follows:

- Economic development is the core value in state policy and possesses priority beyond social policy or income redistribution.
- As social policy is underdeveloped, public expenditure in welfare might not take a role as in Western countries, implying that low welfare expenditure should be regarded as a policy output rather than due to a need for low welfare expenditure.
- Lower welfare expenditure does not mean weak government since state intervention is strong in the field of development. Thus, East Asian countries should not be realised as large-scale private welfare/pension markets, as in the liberal welfare states.
- Families are required to and ought to take more welfare responsibility for individual members.
- Regarding the distribution of welfare, universalism is hardly found and the effects of welfare stratification are common in East Asian countries. Welfare has been primarily rendered to governmental employees such as civil servants, teachers and military servicemen.

We argue, theoretically, that East Asian welfare should be embedded in the contexts of the politico-economic development that have been identified as "state developmentalism" by many studies. Welfare is actually constrained by the East Asian developmental trajectory. By constructing a new set of 15 indicators for factor and cluster analysis of 20 countries with data from the 1980s and 1990s, Lee and Ku (2007) do find a new group formed by Taiwan and South Korea that cannot be included in Esping-Andersen's existing three regimes, while Japan switches between the three regime types. After conducting hierarchical cluster analysis, the branching plots shown in Figure 5.1 represent the degrees of similarity of these 20 country cases based on the 1990s data.

The branching plots indicate five groups in all: three major groups and another two groups scattered away from the main three. The three classic welfare regimes – social democratic, corporatist and liberal – early constitute the main groups. However the social democratic regime group included Belgium with four Scandinavia countries (Denmark, Sweden, Finland and Norway), though we should note that the relative distance between Belgium and the four Scandinavian countries was greater than between any of the latter. The second corporatist group includes Austria, Italy, France, Germany and Japan, but the relative distance between Japan and the other four classic corporatist countries is greater than the distance between any of the others. The third liberal group consists of Canada, the United States, Switzerland, Australia, the Netherlands and the United Kingdom, which has been moving away from social democracy since the experience of Thatcherism in the 1980s. Ireland and New Zealand seems to have become more or less independent cases. As shown in Figure 5.1, an East Asian welfare regime does indeed exist, but it is quite separate from the three classical groupings.

In short, South Korea and Taiwan have merged together to form a new, distant group apart from Esping-Andersen's *The Three Worlds of Welfare Capitalism*.

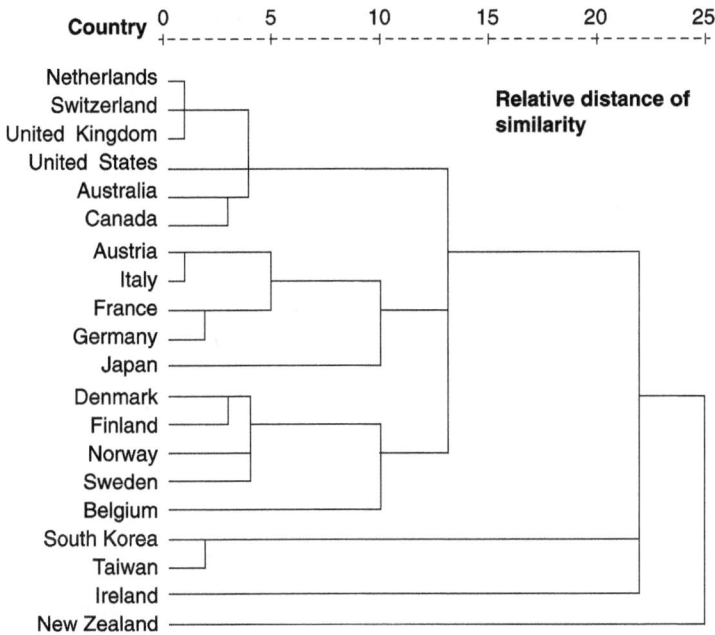

Figure 5.1 Welfare regimes in hierarchical cluster.

Source: Lee and Ku (2007)

These two East Asian country cases are not joined with other welfare groups until the relative distance reaches 20, but the relative distance between the two of them is quite short and close, strongly displaying their similarity in welfare regime. Moreover, since the three classical welfare regimes show themselves steady in this study, it is all the more significant for our case that there is a consistent welfare regime group discernible in East Asia, with reference to South Korea and Taiwan. This new welfare regime coincides with the theme of developmentalism as proposed by scholars such as Holliday (2000).

Even so, this finding raises a new question: where is Japan in this regime investigative study? Why is Japan not in the group of developmental welfare regimes, as might have been expected? What makes Japan different from South Korea and Taiwan with regard to welfare? To what extent does Japan's welfare development take in the "corporatist" and "developmental" factorial dimensions? To answer these questions, we might look at Figure 5.2 to find a possible explanation. In Figure 5.1, Japan is lined up with corporatist countries but we also find that there is a larger distance between Japan and the other members of this group. This finding suggests that Japan may better be described as having more "pro-corporatist" characteristics than typical corporatist ones. Figure 5.2 shows country features in both "corporatist" and "developmentalism" dimensions. With

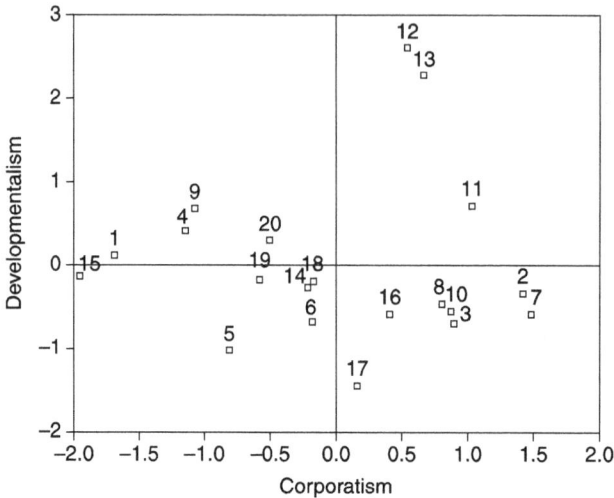

Country code
1. Australia 2. Austria 3. Belgium 4. Canada 5. Denmark 6. Finland 7. France 8. Germany
9. Ireland 10. Italy 11. Japan 12. South Korea 13.Taiwan 14. Netherlands 15. New Zealand
16. Norway 17. Sweden 18. Switzerland 19. United Kingdom 20. United States

Figure 5.2 Countries scattered along developmentalist and corporatist dimensions.

Source: Lee and Ku (2007)

"corporatist" as the X axis and "developmentalism" as the Y axis, Japan (country code 11), South Korea (country code 12), and Taiwan (country code 13) are all in the same quadrant, but we see that Japan is nearer to the X axis and farther from the Y axis than are the other two countries. A plausible explanation is that, in Japan, the "developmentalism" factor is weaker and the "corporatist" stronger. In other words, Japan is in between the corporatist group (Austria, Italy, France and Germany) and the East Asian group (Taiwan and South Korea). This explains why Japan is found to be among the corporatist countries with thick "developmental" features – or is indeed a hybrid case, as observed by Esping-Andersen (1997).

Some regime characteristics found particularly in the cases of Taiwan and South Korea are low/medium social security expenditure, high social investment, larger gender discrimination in salary, medium/high welfare stratification, high non-coverage rate of pension, high individual welfare loading and high family welfare responsibility. In comparison to the three regimes, the East Asian developmental welfare regime shows similarity in welfare stratification with the conservative, while the non-coverage of welfare entitlement is similar to the liberal. Similarity between the developmental welfare regime and the social democracy is rare.

Taiwan's developmental welfare regime in the postwar era

To understand Taiwan's development and, especially, the issue of how Taiwan transformed from a developing economy to a more advanced one, a more systematic exploration is required that doesn't just focus on the role of the state and its policy orientation. Policy is actually not emerging in a vacuum. Poverty reduction may be a product of economic transformation and development, intentionally and unintentionally, but it is also tied to social and political struggles around the organisation and distribution of resources, rights and statues that have shaped Taiwanese society remarkably in the past 60 years.

Following the success of economic development in East Asia, income distribution remains a relatively fair condition. In Taiwan's case, for instance, the gap of disposal income between top and bottom 20 per cent of households was less than five times during the 1970s and 1980s and therefore "economic growth with equity" has been said to characterise the experience of East Asian development as a "miracle".

Ku's comprehensive study on welfare capitalism in Taiwan traces Taiwan's development from 1895 to 1990, searching for dynamics among four factors: the capitalist world system, state structure, ideology and social structure (1997a). He finds, firstly, that the capitalist world system, as international politics, introduces Western welfare measures to Taiwan and gradually replaces traditional and informal care, on the one hand; as an intensively competitive global economic system, it sets limits on Taiwan's welfare development in order to speed up economic growth, on the other hand. In particular, Taiwan suffers from political isolation in the international community because of China's repression and economic growth has been the most important means to consolidate its links with the external world. Economic growth in Taiwan is mostly motivated by the competitiveness of its products in the world market. Taiwan cannot afford the cost of economic isolation, especially as it has been isolated politically as well. The limited resources are therefore poured into areas which would benefit economic growth, especially infrastructure in the economic domain, and public health and education in the social domain. This explains why the disadvantaged are neglected most.

Second, in order to stabilise the production relationship in favour of economic growth and particularly to repress possible disorder because of constrained working conditions, social control, rather than social welfare, is employed by the state and its bureaucrats. This explains why veterans, civil servants and military servicemen benefit most. Even though welfare programmes have been initiated and expanded to include more disadvantaged groups as the state faces political crisis, these efforts are limited to a piecemeal provision and are not allowed to consume too many national resources, as long as the existing social control is still in effect.

Third, education policy is preferred by the state for two reasons. Firstly, it can train necessary labour forces for production, and secondly, it is an important ideological means to "tame" people's minds. Hostility to the European-style welfare state is deliberately advocated by the Taiwanese state and its economic elite in order to legitimise their "economics first" policy, using exaggerated negative effects of social welfare on the economy, such as "A welfare state encourages people to be unemployed in order to claim benefits."

Finally, at the start of the 1980s, Taiwan's political isolation in the international community showed no signs of improvement, due to China's repression. However, its capitalist development had been maturing and had created a private sector strong enough to influence political power, particularly because the state needed the private sector to consolidate its links with the outside world through economic trade. Moreover, radical social movements were provoked to struggle against long-term social underdevelopment. Without support from abroad, the Taiwanese state found these developments difficult to suppress. A more democratic political environment and an institutional welfare system became important to win support from society. This explains why National Health Insurance was introduced (e.g. Wong, 2004).

In short, welfare was developing alongside the contradictions of capitalist development in Taiwan, either for economic growth or for political legitimacy. As the policy direction wandered between economy and welfare, public efforts in the social domain were not consistent with social expectations. Even if we take "the Golden Decade of Welfare Development" in the 1990s as an example, the social situation was still downwards in many aspects. Table 5.1 shows income distribution, tax burden and crime rates from 1985 to 1996. Although disposable income per household increased significantly, from NT$320,495 in 1985 to NT$826,378 in 1996, reflecting the economic performance of the Taiwanese state, social inequality also expanded faster than before. The ratio of the wealthiest to poorest quintile in Taiwan increased from 4.5 in 1985 to 5.38 in 1996. As social inequality expanded, it became increasingly difficult to satisfy people with the existing conditions, especially as there was a growing feeling of relative deprivation. Two social problems emerged.

The first was the rise of the crime rate from 317.3 cases in 100,000 population in 1985 to 933.4 in 1996, nearly three times higher (see Table 5.1). The most significant example of the crime problem was the so called "three heaviest criminal cases" in 1996 and 1997: eight officials and councillors of Taoyuan county, including the mayor, were murdered on the same day; a feminist leader of the Democratic Progressive Party (DPP) was raped and killed; and the only daughter of a famous actress was kidnapped and killed. In the three heaviest criminal cases only the kidnapping case was finally solved in November 1997 after a dramatic event in which the final surviving kidnapper held a diplomat and his family from South Africa hostage, bargaining with the police for a better trial. The domestic criminal case was not only becoming a diplomatic event and drawing attention internationally, but such a situation had never happened before, clearly demonstrating the incapacity of the government and the police to maintain social order. Many protests from the people were provoked and this forced reshuffle of the Cabinet. In particular, the other two cases are still deadlocked.

The second was the rise of social movements fighting for better social conditions. This induced uncertainty in production relations and slowed down the speed of capital accumulation, therefore causing complaints among capitalists. They asked the government to restore social order in favour of economic production. For example, a survey in 1990 found that 72 per cent of enterprises in Taiwan were dissatisfied with economic conditions, especially with social disorder and the labour movement. Also, 49.5 per cent of surveyed enterprises thought that the Kuomintang (KMT), the ruling party, should take responsibility for improving matters. Another survey of capitalists in the same year showed that the most critical problem in terms of economic growth in Taiwan was social disorder, which was forcing enterprises to leave the country (Wang, 1992: 12–13). A survey of public opinion in 1992 showed that the public thought the government did not pay enough attention to improving income distribution, especially due to corruption between politicians and businessmen, which damaged existing conditions in favour of economic growth. In addition, the public asked the government to do more to improve income distribution, through measures of education and social welfare in particular (The 21st Century Foundation, 1992, 1993).

Whatever the people and the capitalists asked for, the state was always at the core. Under democratisation, the Taiwanese state was no longer able to satisfy people with economic growth only. Social development was therefore an urgent and important policy for the legitimacy of the state in order to win support from society. For this reason, the KMT was forced to expand its welfare efforts in the face of competition from the opposition, the DPP.

Table 5.1 also shows an important feature of the Taiwanese political economy: the relatively low tax burden compared with the Western welfare states. In the past decade, the per capita tax burden as a percentage of income has remained around 20 per cent. This is deliberately created by the state to encourage investment, using

Table 5.1 Income distribution, tax burden and crime rates (1985–1996)

Year	Disposable income per household (NT$)	Ratio of wealthiest to poorest quintile	Gini-coefficient	Per capita tax burden as % of income	Crime rate in 100,000 population
1985	320,495	4.50	0.290	17.7	317.3
1986	341,728	4.60	0.296	16.5	481.4
1987	366,487	4.69	0.299	16.1	457.3
1988	410,483	4.85	0.303	17.8	445.8
1989	464,994	4.94	0.303	19.5	451.6
1990	520,147	5.18	0.312	21.9	453.6
1991	587,242	4.97	0.308	19.1	600.1
1992	639,696	5.24	0.312	20.4	674.5
1993	707,879	5.42	0.316	20.1	674.6
1994	769,755	5.38	0.318	20.0	577.7
1995	811,338	5.34	0.317	20.2	802.6
1996	826,378	5.38	0.317	18.2	933.4

Source: DGBAS, *Social Indicators in Taiwan*, various years.

three measures: establishing an economic infrastructure, tax rebates and financial assistance (Ku 1997a: 149–151). The expansion of state welfare could cause an increase in taxes but this is not the general public's preference, especially if the increase is drawn from income and goods and services taxes. Taxation on profits would, on the other hand, make the capitalists even more unhappy. Moreover, improvements in state welfare accompanied by increased taxes represents a growth of state interventionism in the market that is fundamentally in conflict with the development of deregulation at the global level, particularly the economic policy of the government since the 1980s.

As early as 1982, the eighth Four-Year Plan for economic development adopted economic liberalisation and internationalisation as new guiding principles, and gave greater emphasis to the functioning of market forces and price mechanisms. This policy integrated Taiwan's economy even further into capitalist development at the global level. In particular, negotiations in relation to the General Agreement on Tariffs and Trade (GATT) and with the The World Trade Organisation (WTO) also pressed Taiwan to open its domestic market and deregulate its economic controls. Under intensive economic competition, as well as in the face of the unacceptability of rigid repressive measures in terms of production relations and wage levels due to democratisation, the government turned to the task of strengthening and upgrading its basic infrastructure and developing technology-oriented industries, in order to encourage more private investment and to expand high value-added products for more profits. The Six-Year National Development Plan 1991–1996 was therefore proposed and implemented by the government in pursuit of four goals: raising national income, generating more resources for continued industrial growth, promoting balanced regional development and achieving living conditions of acceptable quality. This had an important effect on state finances. It meant that the government had to increase its expenditure on economic development and thus we can see the expansion of total government expenditure to gross domestic product (GDP) and the increasing burden of public debt in the early 1990s. However, the development of state welfare also required more public resources and this caused radical competition between governmental expenditure on economic growth and social welfare. As democratisation is further confirming since the beginning of the 2000s, the dilemma between economy and welfare has become even more complicated and difficult.

A fading economic miracle

The year 2000 was a historic watershed for Taiwanese politics. For the first time, the authoritarian ruling party, the KMT, lost its power in the presidential election and was replaced by the young opposition party, the DPP. As the strongest opposition party in the 1990s, the DPP was well known not only for its political argument for Taiwanese independence but also for its pro-welfare ideology, in contrast to the KMT's mainlanders' identity and economy-first philosophy. This shift was significantly shown in the DPP's White Paper on social welfare in 1993, proposing an idealist social democratic welfare state. The dominance of the DPP during

2000–8 signified a new era of Taiwanese democratisation, while it was also raising expectations for social reform. However, there was not a happy ending to this story. The failure of the DPP to solve worsening unemployment and working conditions brought the KMT back into power in the 2008 presidential election with a 58.5 per cent majority to the DPP candidate's 41.6 per cent. However, the new KMT government still needs to face the same challenges imposed by the changing economic climate at the global level.

The export-oriented development strategy adopted by the state has further opened up the economy to the rise and fall of world markets and global competition. Since the beginning of the 1990s, there has been a migrant movement of labour-intensive industries, which was the core source of Taiwanese economic growth in the 1970s and 1980s, to low labour cost areas, such as Southeast Asia and China. This movement has raised the unemployment rate and in turn increased pressures on state welfare. If the government pours more public resources into state welfare as a result, the shortage of money for economic development could be critical and inflict even greater damage on profit-making enterprises. Yet, if the government is unwilling to expand its welfare efforts, it could forfeit its position as the ruling power in the next election. The pressures of unemployment and low pay aggregate with an increasing flow of capital are a growing problem; therefore, a great difficulty looms (Ku, 1997b):

> In the process of globalisation, local labourers are not only competing with other labourers in the country, but also competing with foreign labourers for limited job opportunities. Having or having not jobs and the levels of wage will influence employees' subsistence and enterprises' profits directly. However, wage levels are very difficult to raise because of global competition. If the government should raise wages through social programs and statutes, they risk reducing job opportunities. Both high unemployment and low wages will greatly damage the legitimacy of the state . . . economic crisis will transform into a political crisis.

This difficulty did not improve even under a democratic government, which raises the question: why is Taiwan's economy so vulnerable under globalisation? This issue is closely linked to the transformation of Taiwan's economy in the past several decades. Table 5.2 shows the economic transformation in Taiwan from the mid-1960s to 2010. Taiwan has become a post-industrial economy in which over 77 per cent of the labour force are employees, implying that two typical risks in a capitalist society (i.e. unemployment and retirement) are now critical in Taiwan.

Figure 5.3 shows the general picture of Taiwanese economic changes since 1991, and the radical slump of the economic growth rate just after the DPP government came into power. The growth rate in 2002 seemed to be improving, but it was only a reaction to the radical recession in the preceding year, and it was also far lower than the economic performances before 2000. Along with poor economic growth, Taiwanese wealth, in terms of GDP per capita, was shrinking back to the

Table 5.2 Economic transformation in Taiwan by labour forces, 1966–2010 (%)

Year	Sector			Occupational status			
	Agriculture	Industry	Services	Employers	Self-employed	Unpaid family workers	Employees
1966	45.0	22.6	32.4	2.3	27.9	24.6	45.3
1971	35.1	29.9	35.0	2.9	25.9	18.5	52.7
1976	29.0	36.4	34.6	2.5	23.9	14.5	59.1
1981	18.8	42.4	38.8	4.5	20.8	10.4	64.3
1982	18.9	41.3	39.8	4.3	21.1	10.5	64.1
1983	18.6	41.2	40.2	4.0	21.1	11.1	63.8
1984	17.6	42.3	40.1	4.1	20.7	10.8	64.4
1985	17.5	41.6	41.0	4.3	20.8	10.8	64.1
1986	17.0	41.6	41.4	4.3	20.2	10.9	64.7
1987	15.3	42.8	42.0	4.3	19.2	9.9	66.7
1988	13.7	42.5	43.8	4.5	18.9	9.5	67.1
1989	12.9	42.1	45.0	4.6	18.8	9.2	67.4
1990	12.9	40.8	46.3	4.8	18.6	9.0	67.6
1991	13.0	39.9	47.1	5.1	18.6	9.1	67.1
1992	12.3	39.6	48.1	5.1	18.2	8.9	67.8
1993	11.5	39.1	49.4	5.2	17.6	8.5	68.7
1994	10.9	39.2	49.9	5.3	17.3	8.6	68.9
1995	10.6	38.7	50.7	5.3	17.0	8.5	69.2
1996	10.1	37.5	52.4	5.4	17.0	8.4	69.3
1997	9.6	38.2	52.3	5.5	16.5	8.0	70.0
1998	8.9	37.9	53.2	5.4	16.3	7.7	70.6
1999	8.3	37.2	54.5	5.5	16.2	7.7	70.6
2000	7.8	37.2	55.0	5.4	16.0	7.5	71.1
2001	7.5	36.0	56.5	5.2	15.8	7.3	71.7
2002	7.5	35.2	57.3	5.2	15.8	7.4	71.6
2003	7.3	34.8	57.9	5.2	15.5	7.3	72.1
2004	6.6	35.2	58.2	5.2	14.9	7.0	72.9
2005	5.9	36.4	57.7	5.1	14.5	6.7	73.8
2006	5.5	36.6	57.9	5.1	13.9	6.4	74.6
2007	5.3	36.8	58.0	5.1	13.6	6.2	75.1
2008	5.1	36.8	58.0	4.9	13.2	6.0	76.0
2009	5.3	35.9	58.9	4.6	13.0	5.7	76.8
2010	5.2	35.9	58.9	4.5	12.7	5.6	77.2

Source: DGBAS, *Social Indicators in Taiwan*, various years.

level of the mid-1990s. Once again, a similar situation happened in the 2008 financial crisis with a radical slump to a negative level that precisely demonstrated the serious impact of a global market, even when the government had changed to the KMT. Moreover, a recession was spreading and job opportunities were under threat (see Figure 5.4).

Following the economic recession, unemployment became a serious problem. In the early 1990s, the unemployment rate in Taiwan remained below 2 per cent,

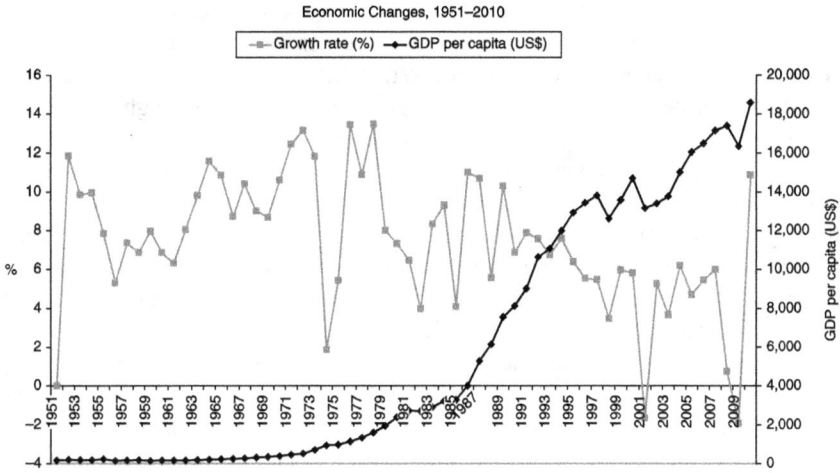

Figure 5.3 Economic changes in Taiwan (1951–2010).

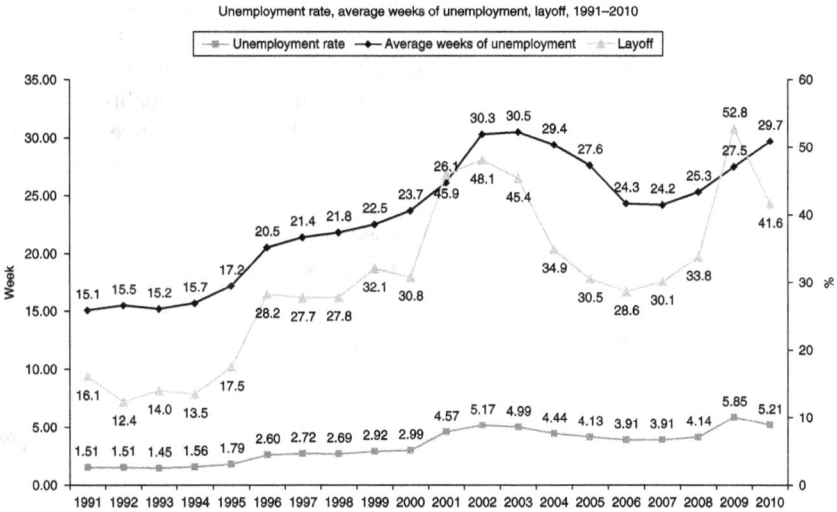

Figure 5.4 Employment changes (1991–2010).

but it increased significantly to over 5 per cent in 2002. Since then, unemployment has floated between 4 to 5 per cent and never returned to the level of the 1990s. The government was under pressure to initiate related policy measures, in which employment security became an important policy objective. Finally, unemployment insurance was enforced in 2002. Due to the radical change in the world economy, once again the unemployment rate increased to a historical high in 2009 of 5.85 per cent, implying that there was no possible way back to full employment. It should also be noted that the major reason for unemployment was not seasonal adjustments of the labour market; rather, it was massive layoffs from around 16 per cent in 1991 to nearly 50 per cent in 2002. Although layoffs did improve in the mid-2000s, they jumped again remarkably from 33.8 per cent to 52.8 per cent in just one year between 2008 and 2009, which signified the important impact made by the migrant movement of businesses at the global level, while the degree of difficulty of finding a new job was increasing. In 2002, the average time for an unemployed worker to move to a new job was over 30 weeks, compared to only 15 weeks in 1991. The 2008 crisis brought the average unemployment week almost back to the level in 2002 that forced the KMT government to launch many workfare programmes, such as the Employment Promotion Program (EPP) in 2009 that offered cash subsidies for those workers who would do temporary jobs and for employers who would hire unemployed workers (Chang, 2011).

These harsh conditions stimulated further social instability in Taiwan. Figure 5.5 demonstrates two related indicators. Because of job security and fair wage issues, conflicts between employers and employees increased from 1,810 cases in 1991 to 14,017 cases in 2002, and this figure has risen even higher since then. These conditions did not improve after the KMT took back power, and the numbers increased to 30,385 cases in 2009. Interestingly, during the same period, violent crimes did not increase correspondingly. After separate high peaks in 1996 and 2002, the government had learned how to maintain social order, not only through the police force but also through employment security and a fair quality of living. For example, in response to the financial crisis in 2008, the Executive Yuan (the highest administrative authority) in 2009 launched "Strengthening Social Security

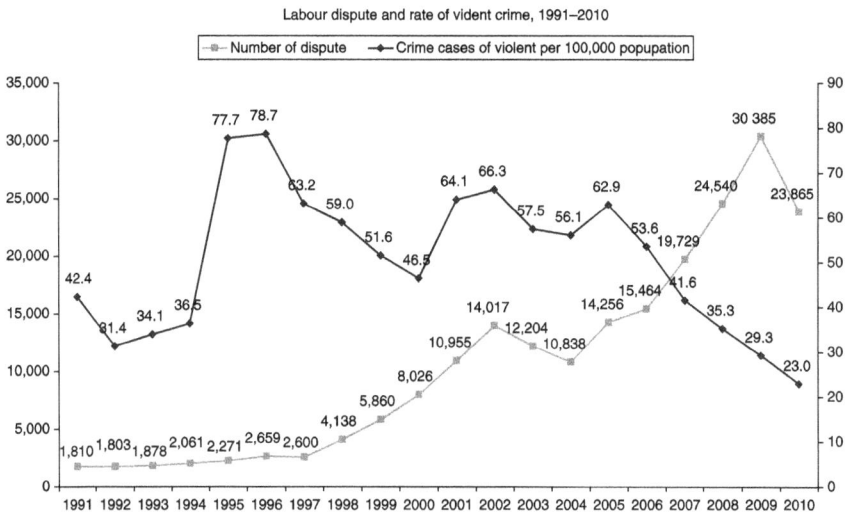

Figure 5.5 Selected indicators of social unrest (1991–2010).

Networks", defining welfare for the disadvantaged, suicide prevention, job opportunities, education and training for youth, and crime control as five major tasks of governmental policy. These measures somehow controlled the increase of labour disputes without risking an increase in crime that could lead to social unrest.

Because employees currently occupy about 77 per cent of the total labour force, they mostly rely on working wages as their major income. Unemployment and underemployment therefore present risks of income termination. Poverty follows insufficient income not just for the present generation but also for the next generation, especially if the current generation cannot afford the costs of food, education and health. A generation with a lower standard of education and a lack of skills will suffer most from the unemployment that will be passed down from generation to generation. The fear of unemployment and the poverty cycle is now common in Taiwan. A survey in 2002 showed that the people who regarded themselves as impoverished rose to 67 per cent, two times higher than those who did not feel the same previously (Ku, 2008). There are two different interpretations of why Taiwan cannot retain its economic growth with full employment. First, the government is performing poorly in attracting private investment, which is the main reason that businesses are moving out of the country, thereby leading to more requests for public investment in infrastructure, such as higher education and economic restructuring. Second, the focus is on global labour and the production division, which argues for a more liberal and deregulated economic policy (Ku, 2004).

The policy statement known as "Challenge 2008: National Development Plan (2002–2007)", published by the DPP government, clearly revealed its views on the aforementioned question. In its statement, the DPP government recognised three major challenges: (CEPD, 2002)

- **Global competition:** a growing intensive global competition for talent and capital that has significantly changed core production elements to quality, creation and speed, implying more flexible production and more investment in knowledge.
- **Mainland China's magnetic effect:** China is a strong competitor with cheap labour and land, and a vast market that has attracted many Taiwanese businesses and, in turn, made an impact on the increasing unemployment rate in Taiwan.
- **Historical burden:** including social problems left over from the period of the authoritarian regime and the democratic transition (e.g. "black gold" politics, rigid administrative and legal systems, and long accumulation of bad debts and financial burdens).

In short, the DPP blamed China and the KMT for its own failure, yet the DPP cannot acquire popular confidence, and this led to its failure in the 2008 presidential election. Interestingly, Taiwan has accumulated a lot of trade surplus from China, increasing remarkably from US$7 billion in 1991 to US$22 billion in 2002. However, during the same period, Taiwanese businesses have invested over US$24 billion in China, occupying about 70 per cent of the total outward foreign direct investment (FDI) in Taiwan, while the inflow of FDI in Taiwan was only US$17 billion. A tricky picture emerges. Taiwan has to rely on China's market for profits, but China is also regarded as the major competitor for Taiwanese private investment, as well as other foreign capital.

To restore Taiwan's competitiveness in the global economy, the DPP government promises more reforms in respect of finance and taxation and more investment in human capital and infrastructures. However, it is not as simple as that. The statement is indeed a hybrid of the above two interpretations. In order to cope with growing global competition, a more open and deregulated environment will encourage more private and foreign investment in Taiwan, but this could also risk an even speedier migration of Taiwanese businesses to China, on the one hand, and a great loss of government revenue, particularly if a tax credit was adopted as an incentive, on the other. The loss of government revenue will eventually reduce the necessary public resources for more investment. Furthermore, without more investment it is very difficult to restructure Taiwan's economy towards high value-added industries and therefore enhance Taiwan's competitiveness. This is a great dilemma which fundamentally changes the traditional explanation of East Asian development, especially regarding the role of the state in directing economic policy. The shortage of public funds eventually confined governmental policy choices and state capacity, especially as more necessary investments, such as human capital and infrastructure, were needed for improving national competitiveness, on the one hand, and more benefits were required to enhance the welfare image of the DPP government and its legitimacy on the other. The clash between the economy and welfare is growing day by day. The slogans of "We Want Jobs", "Anti-poverty", "Affordable Education" and so forth have become the main theme in every social movement.

Social inequality during the first term of the Ma Ying-jeou government

Interestingly, despite his pro-welfare image, President Chen Shui-bian did not publish any new social welfare policy guidelines in his first term between 2000–4. Only when the 2004 presidential campaign was looming and political pressures were aggregating, was the 2004 Social Welfare Policy Guideline finally announced. It claimed nine principles for social welfare under the DPP government:

- putting priority on people's well-being;
- including disadvantaged citizens;
- supporting different types of family;
- constructing sound welfare systems;
- investing in positive welfare measures;
- collaborating with central and local authorities;
- making public/private partnerships;
- delivering services to the most local;
- integrating service resources.

Frankly speaking, the 2004 Guideline included many new ideas such as positive welfare and social inclusion, into social policy in Taiwan, but it was not completely realised because President Chen Shui-bian was in deep trouble due to corruption. The Cabinet was reshuffled quite often during his second term and policies went as well. It is unsurprising that the result of the 2008 presidential election brought the KMT's President Ma Ying-jeou back to power with a 58.45 per cent vote majority. This did not mean the return of public confidence in the new government, and people are observing the KMT regime closely, looking for consistency between policy performance and public expectation.

Unfortunately in his first term President Ma Ying-jeou was not able to fulfil public expectations for social equity. Figure 5.6 shows the income gap between the top and bottom 20 per cent of households before and after public transfers. The income gap before public transfers was about five times, steadily increasing to about six times by the end of the 1990s, while a big increase happened in the beginning of the 2000s, from 6.57 times to 7.67 times in just one year and since then never back to below seven times. During the 1990s, the real income gap was well controlled below six times because of governmental public transfers. However, in the 2000s, the real income gap was still increasing, even though the government had made an effort to achieve a more equal income distribution. For instance, public transfers successfully reduced the income gap from 8.22 to 6.34 in 2009, at the peak of global financial crisis, implying the effectiveness of government efforts.

The reason why the government cannot do this more is closely linked to the poverty of the Taiwanese developmental state against economic tides at a global level. Generally, welfare and taxes are two fundamental policy instruments to remedy income distribution and achieve poverty reduction, especially for those disadvantaged population groups such as the elderly, children, women and minorities. Taxation is important not just for its effects on income distribution but also in

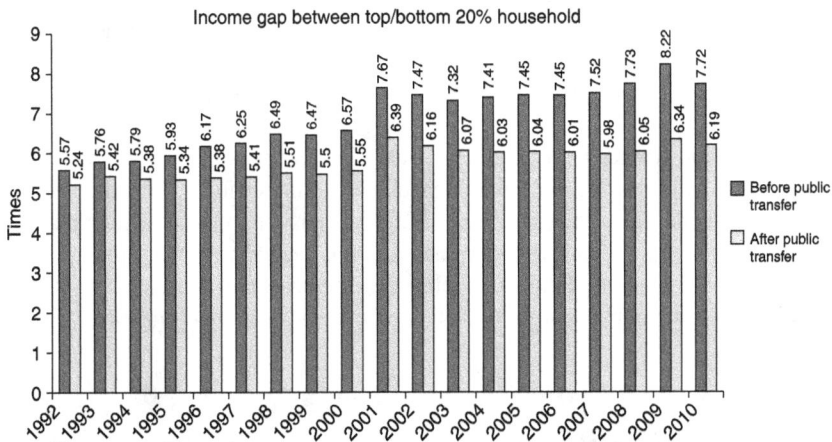

Figure 5.6 Income gap before and after public transfers (1991–2010).

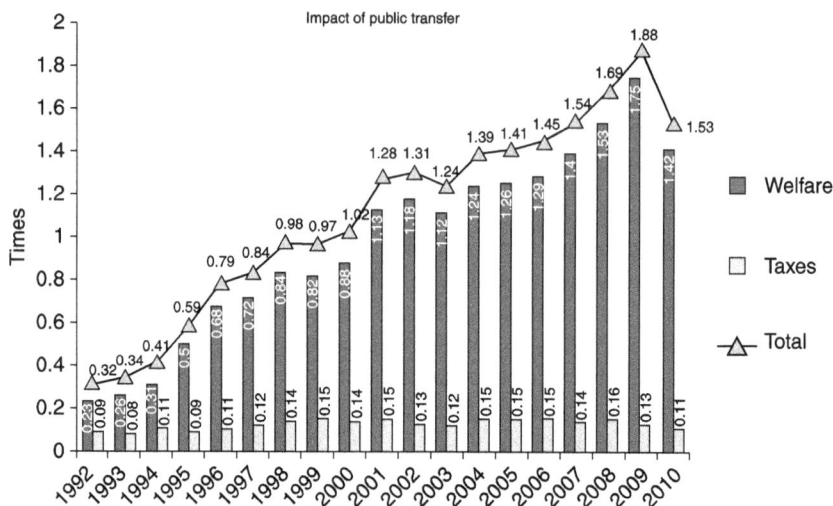

Figure 5.7 Impact of public transfers by welfare and taxes (1991–2010).

financing all governmental efforts, including welfare. Figure 5.7 shows the impact of public transfers made respectively by welfare and taxes from 1991 to 2010. We find, in the case of Taiwan, that welfare is indeed the major aspect of income distribution. For instance, in 2009, the government successfully reduced by 1.88 times the income gap, in which welfare contributed 1.75 times, equivalent to 93 per cent, compared to 0.13 times by taxes. In fact, taxes maintained minor role in income distribution during the 1990s and 2000s. There are two implications of this situation. First, without healthy financial support from taxation governmental welfare efforts will be limited and cannot last long; this explains partly why the government is not able to reduce the income gap further. However, second, we also observe that the government did expand its welfare efforts and the result is the remarkable increase in public debt in the past decade.

Such a situation did improve significantly and this forced President Ma Ying-jeou to claim equity of redistribution as key goal of social policy in Taiwan. His success, or not, would heavily influence public confidence in the government and the result of the presidential campaign in 2012. Interestingly, like the former President Chen Shui-bian, President Ma and his party did not pay enough attention to creating new social welfare policy until his second term was approaching. The 2012 Social Welfare Policy Guideline was therefore still being written during the election campaign and was finally announced just before polling day.

The 2012 Social Welfare Policy Guideline

Taiwan's presidential election in early 2012 came out in favour of President Ma Ying-jeou, with a majority of 51.6 per cent. However, there remain many challenges in his second term, especially the emerging issues of poverty and income inequality.

In August 2011 the DPP's presidential candidate Tsai Ing-wen published her overall policy statement for the coming decade. She proposed a sustainable social safety net as a response to a society at risk of demographic change, family dysfunction, natural disasters, unemployment and a working poor. The core elements of her policy include:

- pensions and long-term care for the coming of an aged society;
- women- and family-friendly policy to raise the fertility rate;
- a sound financial system of social insurance;
- health reform for a better quality of national health insurance;
- improvement of capacity for public health and disease control;
- an integrated public administration for service delivery;
- increasing manpower for social welfare;
- reducing income inequality between urban and rural households;
- enhancing transition from education to employment;
- constructing a new plural society with respect to differences;
- empowering youth and generational justice.

In reaction to the DPP's policy, President Ma Ying-jeou also published his policy statement entitled "Golden Decade" just a month later. He emphasised social justice as the main goal of his social policy, by improving income distribution and reducing social inequality, and measures related to the disadvantaged. There are six elements in President Ma's social policy:

- **fairly shared wealth:** improvement of income distribution to help everyone benefit from the fruits of economic development;
- **safety and health:** high quality of medical care to secure livelihoods;
- **assistance to children and elders:** enhancing care and education for children and long-term care services for the elderly;
- **social harmony:** respect for cultural difference, developing local economic activities and empowering aboriginal people to manage their own affairs;
- **housing justice:** residential assistance to needy people, adjusting the housing supply for a healthy property market;
- **gender equality:** combating gender discrimination.

If we check look at the detailed contents of both social policy statements in historical perspective, a very interesting convergence can be found. At the side of Tsai Ing-wen has held onto the pro-welfare position inherited from the first DPP's White Paper on social policy from 1993, but she has also mentioned more about the financial health of the social security system that that tended to be the main tone of the KMT. On the other hand, after suffering defeats in 2000 and 2004, the KMT has learned the importance of social welfare and therefore President Ma mentions more about justice and equality in his social policy. Finally, as the current president, Ma Ying-jeou is able to put forward the 2012 Social Welfare Policy Guideline to the government.

The 2012 Guideline states that the country's social welfare policy is based on the essence of the Constitution's protection of the basic human rights of citizens. In 2009, the International Covenant on Economic, Social and Cultural Rights and the International Covenant on Civil and Political Rights – two United Nations conventions passed by the Legislative Yuan and signed and ratified by the president – further facilitated the country's social welfare development and helped bring it in line with international standards, seeking to establish a social welfare system that is in keeping with the trends of the era and the needs of the people. Passively, it intends to eliminate the injustice existing in the society and to help the disadvantaged, looking to safeguard the basic living of all citizens and the happiness and harmony of families. Actively, it aims to highlight the values of mutual assistance and solidarity in the society and to shorten the gap between rich and poor, giving every generation a fair opportunity for development and allowing the fruits of economic growth to be shared by all citizens. Therefore, the government will uphold the basic spirit of the Constitution and international conventions on human rights, will regularly inspect the changes in social and economic environments and will promptly adjust the existing social welfare policy, holding "Towards a New Society of Equity, Inclusion, and Justice" as the vision of the guiding principles for social welfare policy for the centenary of ROC on Taiwan.

The primary emphasis of a new, equitable society lies in protecting underprivileged citizens and reducing social injustice. Besides supporting families to allow them to bear, rear, care for and educate children, the government should actively assist disadvantaged families to maintain their quality of life and to implement local services as the principle that takes precedence, enabling children, juveniles, the disabled and elders to receive care and protection in their families and communities. Additionally, after taking into consideration the most favourable benefits for the aforementioned population groups, the government should provide supplementary measures that tally with the personalised demands and individual needs of those served. For this purpose, the central and local governments should push forward social welfare as an integrated body with the central government planning and implementing national programmes and local governments being in charge of planning and enforcing region-adjusted schemes. The central government should assist actively in reducing the gap between urban and rural areas. The government should focus on safeguarding the basic living standards, well-being and dignity of citizens. Regarding services that the private sector is capable of providing, the government should promote public-private partnerships and should encourage collaborations with the private sector. Moreover, the government should be committed to creating non-profit organisations and to creating an environment for the development of social enterprises in order to provide better services for citizens.

A new society with inclusion at its heart aims to remove all institutional barriers and protect the rights of all citizens to participate in society. The government should intervene actively, preventing and eliminating all forms of discrimination, exploitation, abandonment, abuse, harm and injustice that citizens may possibly encounter as a result of their differences in age, gender, race, religion, sexual inclination, physical and mental status, marriage, socio-economic status and geographical environment, to avoid social exclusion. Also, the government should respect differences across cultures, building a friendly and tolerant social environment for family patterns consisting of different sexual inclinations, races, marital relationships, and family sizes and structures. To achieve the above-mentioned objectives, the government should integrate relevant departments, such as those concerned with social welfare, health and medical care, civil affairs, household registration, labour affairs, education, agriculture, judicature, construction and indigenous people, strengthening cross-departmental integration and performance management, to better provide whole-person, whole-course, all-round services so as to enhance the efficiency of resource utilisation.

A new society with justice provides all citizens with equal opportunities for development, regards the well-being of citizens as a priority and proposes actively coping strategies in response to the needs of citizens facing rapid political, economic and social change. In particular, it puts an emphasis on *active* welfare, facilitating steady economic and income growth through society investing in and accumulating human capital, subsequently improving the quality of life of all citizens and maintaining social solidarity and cohesion. Therefore, the various measures of social welfare should each fulfil its function, and a sound preventive system should be constructed in response to the risks of life, maintaining the dignity of citizens with social assistance and allowances, preserving the basic economic security of citizens with social insurance, improving families' quality of living with welfare services, sustaining the well-being of citizens and the quality of manpower with health care, stabilising the income security of and social participation by citizens with employment, and assisting citizens in settling down locally and living peacefully and contentedly with housing assistance and community building. Furthermore, in anticipation of the sustainable development of social welfare, it must also be committed to the balancing of finance for social welfare, the integration of real-time information systems, the strengthening of social work and health manpower, the advancement of educational training, the innovation of research and development, and the establishment of science indicators.

Is the Taiwanese developmental welfare regime sustainable?

In contrast to liberalist explanations of economic development in terms of relying on market mechanisms, the developmentalist strategy focuses on those elements in society seen as crucial for economic development. Several elements have been generally identified, including educational attainment, physical infrastructure, corporate governance, competition and economic openness, political stability, and flexible labour markets. There are also other elements which might be better defined as social capital, in particular, interpersonal trust, social cohesion, association and cooperation (Mkandawire, 2004: 9). To some extent, positive state intervention is very important to those elements in the social domain. Therefore, social policy is no longer regarded as pure consumption by developmentalist scholars. For instance, Kwon argues that "economic development requires social policy" (2005: 5). All such public efforts require healthy financial sustainability, yet we observe that the financial capacity of the Taiwanese developmental state has been declining sharply. This is especially significant because, as we learned from the previous section, the DPP government was forced to cut taxes and to expand welfare programmes.

Table 5.3 demonstrates the relative changes between governmental revenue and debt. Economic growth brought a significant increase of governmental revenue and therefore enhanced state capacity for policy practice. However, tax credit initiatives adopted by the government to stimulate export-led economic growth have gradually had a negative impact on governmental financial health: the gap between revenue and expenditure was increasing and public debts were aggregating, from an average 8.8 per cent of GDP in the 1970s to 38.6 per cent in 2004. The foregoing discussion showed that the democratisation movement did not help Taiwan to escape from such a dilemma. The DPP government was still insisting on tax cuts and welfare increases that damaged the financial sustainability of the government and therefore constrained policy implementation in the future. People's confidence in the DPP government was declining sharply because it was not able to realise promised social reform, and poverty and inequality were worsening during its dominance. But this does not mean the return of public confidence in the KMT government. People want not just a clean government but also a capable government, which is actually the main theme behind the developmental state. Consistency between policy performance and public expectation will be crucial in determining people's trust or distrust, and the results of the next election. As long as financial health cannot be restored, the sustainability of the Taiwanese developmental welfare regime will be put on an uncertain ground.

Table 5.3 Government revenue and debt

	1950s Average	1960s Average	1970s Average	1980s Average	1990s Average	2004
GDP	129.1	668.0	2,701.5	7,094.2	9,847.9	10,279.8
Annual growth rate	14.2	20.3	11.9	8.9	1.6	4.3
Revenue	25.7	160.5	640.0	1,606.1	1,945.1	2,023.0
Annual growth rate	16.0	21.6	12.4	5.7	1.5	−2.7
% of GDP	19.9	24.0	23.7	22.6	19.8	19.7
Expenditure	25.9	154.3	674.5	1,836.1	2,303.0	2,369.0
Annual growth rate	14.7	21.8	12.4	6.8	2.7	−2.6
% of GDP	20.0	23.1	25.0	25.9	23.4	23.0
Surplus (+) or deficit (−)	−2	61	−345	−2,300	−3,579	−3,460
% of GDP	−0.1	0.9	−1.3	−3.2	−3.6	−3.4
Public debts	. . .	. . .	238.1	1,619.1	3,433.2	3,970.9
% of GDP	. . .	. . .	8.8	22.8	34.9	38.6

Unit: NT$ billion (%)

Conclusion

Taiwan has long been regarded as a model for economic growth with equity. Up to the 1990s, nearly all indicators showed significant improvement in every aspect. However, this did not last long and, especially after the 1990s, economic growth slowed down, and this was combined with higher unemployment and stagnation of incomes.

We also reviewed the trends in income inequality. The main finding is that, after significant improvement prior to the 1980s, it has been very difficult to maintain similar improvement trends. The claims for social reform have created huge pressures on the government. With democratic elections, how to acquire both economic growth and social equality has become the greatest challenge for the state and the measure of its legitimacy. The KMT government did not pay much attention to this and the result was its failure in 2000. The succeeding DPP government did increase welfare expenditure but could not prevent the trends of inequality.

We also pointed out the vulnerability of Taiwan's current social policy that fails to satisfy the expectations of the middle classes. Full employment and a massive number of small and medium-sized businesses contributed to wealth and income equality in Taiwan, but were no longer sustainable after the 1990s. The former is threatened by globalisation, capital mobility and international labour division, while the latter is likely to decrease because of the governmental policy towards liberalisation that encourages merger and acquisition for the sake of competitiveness. Eventually the income gap widened, especially after the 1990s. The government tried to narrow this gap with more welfare provision, but its effect was critically restrained by the financial health of the government itself.

As long as the miracle of growth with equity is fading, the question whether the Taiwanese developmental welfare regime can be sustainable has become a theoretical issue, meaning that we need to re-examine the interpretation of a developmental state in the new globalised and democratic era. The country and its society have continued to face challenges. The sustainment of national competitiveness under globalisation, the changes in employment patterns, the opportunities brought by industry transformation, the generational justice issues resulting from population ageing and a low birth rate, the gradual diversification in family patterns, and the expanding wealth gap have all led to an increasing sense of concern among the youth and middle classes of Taiwan of falling into poverty, and this constitutes the new challenge in Taiwan's current social development.

Democratisation in Taiwan has changed the state-led and top-down process of policy-making and required more open participation from varied stakeholders such as interest groups and political parties. The legitimacy of the government, therefore, is not just based on its capacity to implement policy but also on public confidence in its being accountable to its citizens. Unfortunately, neither are as much in evidence as they might be.

It is a new era of Taiwan's democratisation, implying a great opportunity for President Ma and his party to bring the people new hope. With a good social welfare policy, the challenge is the ability to make it happen.

References

Amsden, A. (1989). *Asia's Next Giant: South Korea and Late Industrialization*. New York: Oxford University Press.

Aspalter, C. (2001). *Conservative Welfare State Systems in East Asia*. Westport, CT: Praeger.

Castells, M. (1992). "Four Asian Tigers With a Dragon Head: A Comparative Analysis of the State, Economy, and Society in the Asian Pacific Rim", in R. P. Appelbaum and J. Henderson (eds) *States and Development in the Asian Pacific Rim*. Newbury Park, CA: Sage, pp. 33–70.

CEPD (Council for Economic Planning and Development) (2002). *Challenge 2002: National Development Plan (2002–2007)*. Taipei: CEPD.

Chang, C. F. (2011). "Workfare in Taiwan: From Social Assistance to Unemployment Absorber", in C. K. Chan and K. Ngok (eds) *Welfare Reform in East Asia: Towards Workfare*. New York: Routledge, pp. 78–99.

Deyo, F. C. (1989). *Beneath the Miracle: Labor Subordination in the New Asian Industrialism*. Berkeley, CA: University of California Press.

Deyo, F. C. (1992). "The Political Economy of Social Policy Formation: East Asia's Newly Industrialized Countries", in R. P. Appelbaum and J. Henderson (eds) *States and Development in the Asian Pacific Rim*, pp. 289–306. Newbury Park, CA: Sage.

Esping-Andersen, G. (1990). *The Three Worlds of Welfare Capitalism*. Cambridge: Polity.

Esping-Andersen, G. (1997). "Hybrid or Unique? The Japanese Welfare State Between Europe and America", *Journal of European Social Policy*, 7(3): 179–189.

Fei, J. C. H., Ranis, G. and Kuo, S. W. Y. (1979). *Growth with Equity: The Taiwan Case*. New York: Oxford University Press.

Gold, T. (1986). *State and Society in the Taiwan Miracle*. New York: M. E. Sharpe.

Gough, I. (2004). "East Asia: the Limits of Productivist Regimes", in I. Gough and G. Wood (eds) *Insecurity and Welfare Regimes in Asia, Africa and Latin America: Social Policy in Development Contexts*. Cambridge: Cambridge University Press, pp. 169–201.

Holliday, I. (2000). "Productivist Welfare Capitalism: Social Policy in East Asia", *Political Studies*, 48(4): 706–723.

Holliday, I. and Wilding, P. (eds) (2003). *Welfare Capitalism in East Asia: Social Policy in the Tiger Economies*. Basingstoke: Palgrave Macmillan.

Johnson, C. (1982). *MITI and the Japanese Miracle: The Growth of Industrial Policy, 1925–1975*. Stanford, CA: Stanford University Press.

Jones, C. (1990). "Hong Kong, Singapore, South Korea and Taiwan: Oikonomic Welfare States", *Government and Opposition*, 25(3): 446–462.

Ku, Y. W. (1995). "The Development of State Welfare in the Asian NICs with Special Reference to Taiwan", *Social Policy and Administration*, 29(4): 345–364.

Ku, Y. W. (1997a). *Welfare Capitalism in Taiwan: State, Economy and Social Policy*. Basingstoke: Macmillan.

Ku, Y. W. (1997b). "The Welfare State under the Trend of Privatization: A Challenge", *Community Development Journal (Quarterly)*, 80: 70–78 (in Chinese).

Ku, Y. W. (2004). "Is There a Way Out? Global Competition and Social Reform in Taiwan", *Social Policy and Society*, 3(3): 311–320.

Ku, Y. W. (2008). *Back to the Basic: Reconstructing Social Safety Net in Taiwan*. Taipei: Health, Welfare and Environment Foundation (in Chinese).

Kwon, H. J. (1999). *The Welfare State in Korea: The Politics of Legitimation*. Basingstoke: Macmillan.

Kwon, H. J. (2005). "An Overview of the Study: the Developmental Welfare State and Policy Reforms in East Asia", in H. J. Kwon (ed.) *Transforming the Developmental Welfare State in East Asia*. Basingstoke: Palgrave Macmillan, pp. 1–20.

Lee, Y. J. and Ku, Y. W. (2007). "East Asian Welfare Regimes: Testing the Hypothesis of the Developmental Welfare State", *Social Policy & Administration*, 41(2): 197–212.

MacPherson. S. (1992). "Social Policy and Economic Change in the Asia Pacific Region", *Social Policy and Administration*, 26(1): 55–61.

Midgley, J. (1986). "Industrialization and Welfare: The Case of the Four Little Tigers", *Social Policy and Administration*, 20(3): 225–238.

Midgley, J. (1995). *Social Development: The Developmental Perspective in Social Welfare*. Thousand Oaks, CA: Sage.

Mkandawire, T. (2004). "Social Policy in a Development Context: Introduction", in T. Mkandawire (ed.) *Social Policy in a Development Context*. Basingstoke: Palgrave Macmillan, pp. 1–20.

So'rensen, G. (1991). *Democracy, Dictatorship and Development: Economic Development in Selected Regimes of the Third World*. London: Macmillan.

Tang, K. L. (2000). *Social Welfare Development in East Asia*. Basingstoke: Palgrave Macmillan.

The 21st Century Foundation (1992). *A Survey of Public Opinion on Social Conditions in Taiwan, 1992*. Taipei: The 21st Century Foundation (in Chinese).

The 21st Century Foundation (1993). *A Survey of Public Opinion on Economic Conditions in Taiwan, 1992*. Taipei: The 21st Century Foundation (in Chinese).

Wade, R. (1990). *Governing the Market: Economic Theory and the Role of Government in East Asian Industrialization*. Princeton, NJ: Princeton University Press.

Wang, J. H. (1992). "Private Capital and Political Transition in Taiwan", paper presented at the Conference on the State and Society in the process of Taiwan's Democratization. Taipei, 7–8 March 1992 (in Chinese).

White, G. and Wade, R. (1988). 'Development States and Markets in East Asia: An Introduction', in G. White (ed.) *Developmental States in East Asia*. Basingstoke: Macmillan, pp. 1–29.

Wong, J. (2004). *Healthy Democracies: Welfare Politics in Taiwan and South Korea*. Ithaca, NY: Cornell University Press.

6 Bringing the state back in

The development of Chinese social policy in China in the Hu-Wen Era

Kinglun Ngok

Introduction

Social policies in post-Mao China have changed dramatically in order to enhance market competition, increase economic efficiency and accelerate economic growth. Under the guideline of "efficiency first, equity second", the post-Mao Chinese leaders began to embrace a new set of market-led policies, such as the creation of a private market, the privatisation of state enterprises, the marketisation of public services and the withdrawal of welfare subsidies. The retreat of the state from areas of education, health, housing, and so on, represents a major departure from the socialist social policy regime practised in Mao's China. Different conceptualisations have been developed to describe these changes in China's social policy, such as "marketisation of social welfare" (Guan, 2000), "socialisation of social welfare and services" and "individualisation of social rights" (Wong, 2002). Such changes have brought about negative impacts on the basic livelihood of low-income citizens, mainly unemployed urban people, migrant workers and peasants. The neglect of the basic needs of the ordinary people has invited much social unrest. A social crisis behind the economic prosperity occurred in China (Wang *et al.*, 2002), and strong appeal to social justice was made by intellectuals. The time for policy change had come at the turn of the new century.

The leadership succession in 2002–3 opened a "policy window" for urgent social policy changes (Breslin, 2008). The succession of the new generation of political leadership led by Hu Jintao and Wen Jiabao facilitated the policy change. The outbreak of the Severe Acute Respiratory Syndrome (SARS) epidemic in early 2003 was a trigging event, and also provided an opportunity for the Chinese policy-makers to rethink the role of social policy in China's market transition. The lessons from the SARS crisis made Hu and Wen really recognise the steep price China had paid for its rapid economic growth. After the SARS crisis, the newly-formed leadership sought to formulate a new set of ideas on Chinese development, such as "putting people first", "harmonious society" and "service-oriented government", which opened a new page for Chinese social policy development.

Within such a favourable policy context, social policy, or "people's livelihood policy" in official jargon, has become the core work of the government in China since 2003 as an array of social policy initiatives has been launched. While many old social programmes have expanded their coverage, especially the social insurance programmes, a number of new social policy programmes have been launched, which make China's social policy regime beyond the occupation-based social insurance model. Accordingly, the overall social expenditure has increased considerably. It is safe to draw the conclusion that a rapid expansion of social policy has taken place in China in the first decade of the new century. This chapter outlines the trajectory of the changes in China's social policy in the post-Mao era. The core of the chapter is to examine the new developments of social policy and social spending in China since 2003 which indicate a rapid expansion of social policy, especially during the Hu-Wen era. It argues that a process of "bringing the state back in" is taking place in China's social policy expansion.

Rolling back the state role: Chinese social policy in the market transition

Before the economic reform, China established a state-led socialist welfare system based on the public ownership of the means of production and the planned economy so as to develop an egalitarian society. Based on the socialist ideology of collectivism and equality (Wong, 1998), the state monopolised the provision of welfare and services. Market and private enterprises were eliminated. The key providers of the state-led welfare system were communes in rural areas and work units (*danweis*), especially the state-owned enterprises in cities (Leung and Nann, 1995).

Although Mao's socialist welfare regime was characterised by the rural-urban divide and a low level of welfare provision, it provided a basic social protection for both workers and farmers (Leung and Nann, 1995). However, the socialist welfare system suffered from the low productivity and backward economy resulting from Mao's leftist development strategy. Although the government was responsible for people's welfare, the poor economy could not afford a decent living standard for the people.

Given the economic backwardness and poor economic performance in Mao's era, the post-Mao leadership, led by Deng Xiaoping, shifted the focus onto economic growth reather than the class struggle in 1978, when the reform and open-door policy was launched. In order to improve the dire economic performance and provide Chinese people with enough food, Deng Xiaoping decided to give up the traditional socialist planned economy and introduce the market mechanism.

The post-Mao economic reform started in the rural areas in the late 1970s when the Household Responsibility System (HRS) was introduced to stimulate farmers' work incentives. The old commune system was eventually dismantled in the mid-1980s. With the initial success of rural economic reform, the Chinese government extended the reforms to the cities in the mid-1980s, and the state-owned enterprises (SOEs) became the main target. By the mid-1980s, many SOEs were facing increasing competition from non-state enterprises. In order to make SOEs more competitive in a market-orientated economy, the government tried to reform the rigid employment and wage system practised in SOEs. The most significant break with the old employment system was, undoubtedly, the introduction of labour contracts in 1986. This indicated that the government had broken the previous promise of full employment to socialist workers. As a result of contract-based employment policy, Chinese workers had to cope with unemployment again after three decades of job security in a communist economy (Chan *et al.*, 2008).

From the early 1990s, reforms aimed to transform SOEs into modern enterprises compatible with the requirements of a market economy. Social welfare programmes such as pensions, housing, health care and education were gradually separated from the commercial activities of SOEs. In other words, SOEs were no longer to provide generous packages of welfare and benefits to their employees.

Meanwhile, in order to pursue economic growth, the Chinese government formulated a guideline of "efficiency first, equity second". After the Tiananmen Incident in 1989 and the collapse of communist regimes in the Soviet Union and Eastern Europe in the early 1990s, the pursuit of economic growth turned into "GDPism" (economic growth worship) in China as economic prosperity became the key source of the legitimacy of the Communist Party. As a result, economic development measured by the GDP growth rate became the paramount policy goal of the Chinese government. Since then, the state has focused on GDP growth and has ignored its role in ensuring all people benefit from economic prosperity.

To support the reforms of SOEs and minimise the fiscal burden of the state, the government took many measures to reduce welfare expenses, minimise the welfare commitments of SOEs and privatise public services. Public money for public services, such as education and health care was reduced gradually. To finance public services, government departments, SOEs and service providers in the public sectors were encouraged to make use of market mechanisms in service provision. As a result, marketisation became trendy in the main sectors of the public services (Wong and Flynn, 2001). The market-oriented economic reforms and marketisation of public services brought about uncertainties and risks to hundreds of thousands of people, especially those worked in the SOEs. However, there were no well-organised and comprehensive policies for tackling the negative social consequences brought about by the economic reforms. From a social policy perspective, the market-oriented economic reforms restructured China's social policy framework and dismantled the state-led socialist welfare system (Chan *et al.*, 2008).

With the retreat of the government from various policy areas such as education, health, housing, and so on, low-income citizens, mainly unemployed urban people, rural-urban migrant workers and peasants, could not afford to pay for housing, education or health care services. Patients without money were rejected by the hospitals; students with economic hardship were not allowed to go to schools and universities. Such miserable stories have attracted wide media coverage in China since the mid-1990s. Property prices are so high that only a small number of rich people can buy. Increasing expenditure on education, health care and housing has put great financial pressure on ordinary Chinese people. The phrase "new three mountains" (*xin sanzuo dashan*) was coined to indicate the heavy financial burden carried by Chinese citizens in the basic service sectors of education, health care and housing. The grievances of those who have lost ground as a result of the economic reform process have led to widespread civil unrest in China.

The outbreak of the SARS epidemic in early 2003 functioned as a trigger for change. Drawing on the lessons from the SARS crisis, the leadership under Hu Jintao and Wen Jiabao realised that China's relatively wasteful, investment-led, high cost and polluting method of economic growth must be changed. On 17 June 2003, Premier Wen put forth for the first time the idea of "comprehensive, coordinated and sustainable development" at a national symposium on public health. On 28 July, at the National Meeting on Fighting SARS, President Hu called for a new outlook on development aimed at making it coordinated, integrated and sustainable. On 1 October, when he delivered a speech at the National Day reception, Premier Wen said: "The most important revelation of the campaign of anti-SARS for us is that we must persist in the principle of balance and coordination, and maintain the coordinated development between economy and society, between cities and villages, and among regions; must persist in the principle of people-centeredness, and increase the living standards of both materials and culture and the health standard of the people; must persist in the harmony between human being and nature, and achieve sustainable development; must persist in reform and innovation, and push the common progress of socialist material civilisation, political civilisation and spiritual civilisation" (quoted in Hu and Jin 2004). As a result, some new policy ideas, such as "putting people first", "harmonious society" and "service-oriented government" have been formulated. In line with this new direction, more and more social policies have been made and implemented by the central government.

Bringing the state back in: social policy expansion since 2003

The year 2003 was critical for social policy development in China. For the purpose of building up a harmonious society, social policy, or "people's livelihood policy" in Chinese official jargon, has become the core work of the government and an array of social policy initiatives has been launched since 2003 (see Table 6.1). By analysing the Work Report of the Central Government from 2004 to 2012, it is realised that the government has paid much more attention to the subject of "people's livelihood", or "people's wellbeing", and more social policy areas have gained their places at the top of the government agenda. While many old social programmes have expanded their coverage, especially the social insurance programmes, a number of new social policy initiatives have been launched, which take China's social policy regime beyond an occupation-based social insurance model. Accordingly, overall social expenditure has increased considerably.

Some salient features of this round of social policy expansion can be identified. First, peasants who had been excluded by the urban-biased social policy regime in China for a long time have benefited from the rural social policy reforms. Under

Table 6.1 Social policy expansion in China since 2003

Policy area	New policy initiatives
Health care	• Contributory health insurance for urban residents • New type of rural cooperative medical system for farmers
Social security	• Contributory old age insurance for both urban and rural residents who are not employees • Minimum living standards security system for both urban and rural residents • "Five Guarantees" system based on budgetary fund
Employment	• Active employment policy, especially for college graduates and migrant workers • Employment services for migrant workers • Implementing of the Labour Contract Law and Employment Promotion Law in 2008
Education	• Free compulsory education for all children
Housing	• Building welfare housing for urban low-income families

Unit: 100 million yuan.

the policy strategy of building a new socialist countryside, the central government has made policy efforts to promote social development in rural areas, and especially to increase the income of peasants since 2003. As a result of a reform of rural taxes and fees, the agricultural tax was completely rescinded throughout the country in 2006. Meanwhile, the central government has dramatically increased its budget expenditure for agriculture, rural areas and farmers. The Minimum Living Standards Security System (MLSS) was extended to the rural population in 2007. The New Agricultural Cooperative Medical System was established in 2003 and covers almost all peasants in villages. A new type of pension insurance for rural residents has been in progress since 2009. Children in rural areas have been entitled to nine-years of free compulsory education since 2007.

Second, the social inclusion of migrant workers has been further strengthened. The urban social insurance schemes have been extended to cover migrant workers. Labour education services for the children of migrant workers have become a top priority in the education policy agenda.

Third, the central government's budget on social policy expenditure has been further expanded. In 2011, two-thirds of the central budget was invested in people's livelihoods. Lastly, the social work profession has been developed. Until the beginning of the 2000s, the social work profession and social work services did not exist in China. Nowadays, social work has been recognised as a profession and social workers have become an important force in social service provision. Based on these new developments, it is safe to draw the conclusion that a rapid expansion of social policy has taken place in China in the first decade of the new century. Social policy development in China will be further elaborated as follows.

Employment policy

Being the most populous country, management of employment has been a long-term challenge faced by the Chinese government. Some positive changes have been made in the Chinese labour policy regime for migrant workers since 2003. On 18 January 2006, the State Council reclassified migrant workers as part of the Chinese industrial working class and pledged that prejudice against peasant workers would be gradually dispelled in the process of building a unified labour market of equal competition between urban dwellers and farmers (State Council of the People's Republic of China, 2006). The government would try to remove obstacles restricting rural migrant workers in urban and inter-regional employment. In order to help farmers to adapt better to the competitive market environment, the government promised to provide peasant workers with vocational training and public employ-ment services (State Council of the People's Republic of China, 2006). In fact, some new labour policies were adopted to take care of migrant workers. For example, migrant workers were allowed to join official trade unions, and qualify for public employment services and government-sponsored vocational training programmes. In some cities, migrant workers were even given the status of "new citizens".

On 30 August 2007, China enacted the Employment Promotion Law. The Law prohibits discrimination against job-seekers on the basis of their ethnicity, race, gender, religious belief, age or physical disability. By enhancing the skills of workers, it requires governments above the county level to support vocational training and employers to provide "pre-employment training, on-the-job training and re-employment training". In addition, government-run employment service agencies have to provide free services for job-seekers.

In view of the plight of workers and the huge complaints about employers' mistreating workers, the Chinese government enacted the Labour Contract Law in June 2007, which was effective from January 2008. The Labour Contract Law, which consists of eight chapters and 98 articles, became effective 1 January 2008, and is considered to be the most significant change in China's labour policy since the implementation of the Labour Law in 1995. It aims to further standardise labour contracts in favour of employees and to facilitate their implementation. Specifically, the Law is intended to establish sound standards for labour contracts, the use of temporary workers, and severance payment. It makes mandatory the use of written contracts and strongly discourages short fixed-term contracts. The Law also strengthens the role of workers' organisations, such as unions and workers' congresses in labour relations as it stipulates that employers must submit proposed workplace rules or changes concerning salary, work allotment, hours, insurance, safety and holidays to the workers' congress for discussion (Ngok, 2008).

Education policy

When the economic reform was launched in the late 1970s, the post-Mao Chinese leaders realised that education was the essential tool for China's economic modernisation. Against this backdrop, "education serves the economy", a new principle of education policy, was established (Ngok, 2007). Under this new policy principle, the Chinese government was increasingly concerned with the role of education in improving China's economic competitiveness and its place in the regional and global markets. This pragmatic orientation opens the way for the government to reshape its role in education and readjust its education policy.

Since the late 1980s, education at various levels became increasingly a paid service. Although the Chinese government decided to implement nine-year compulsory education nationwide in the mid-1980s, it was not totally free. Parents had to pay high tuition fees for their children in compulsory education. The great change happened in the higher education sector in the 1990s when the state decided to marketise higher education. To gain access to higher education, students and their families had to share the costs by paying tuition fees. As there was no clear mechanism of fee-charge, the tuition fees for higher education rose very rapidly. As tuition fees have been soaring since the late 1990s, to some extent access to higher education is denied to many students from low-income families.

Since 2003, the issue of unequal education opportunities began to gain a place on the agenda of the central government, and some new initiatives have been made to promote educational equality between cities and villages and between regions. In 2004, the central government decided to reduce and waive the tuition fees and miscellaneous school fees of students in the poor regions who were receiving compulsory education. In 2005, such a policy was extended to poor students in the whole western region of China. In 2006, a new Law on Compulsory Education was enacted, which stipulates that China's compulsory education is free for students. In 2006, the central government decided to waive the tuition and miscellaneous school fees of compulsory education for all rural students in the whole western region and some middle regions, and declared that tuition fees for all rural students would be waived within two years. In 2007, the State Council made rural compulsory education really free in China. In 2008, free compulsory education was extended to the whole country. As a result, a free compulsory education system has been realised in China.

Education for migrant children has been a critical challenge in China in the reform era. Due to continuous urbanisation and industrialisation, numerous peasants move into the cities for work. For many years, the migrant workers have found it difficult to find schools for their children as they left their hometown and moved to cities. In September 2003, the State Council required that receiving cities should provide migrant children with compulsory education. Local governments should provide financial subsidies to the schools which enrolled a huge number of migrant students. Meanwhile, financial support would be offered to private schools specifically for migrant children (General Office of the State Council, 2003). Since 2003, many cities opened their state schools to migrant workers' children.

Health care policy

Free health care services for urban workers and employees in public sectors were regarded as an important element of the socialist welfare system in Mao's China.

However, the old health care system became a heavy burden for the SOEs and the government. Many SOEs found it difficult to finance the free health care services for their employees. As the central government failed to work out a nationwide health care reform strategy, local governments and enterprises had to develop their own measures to cope with the funding shortage in health care since the 1980s. In 1994, the central government proposed a medical insurance scheme that included a social pooling fund and a personal account for workers of SOEs. In 1998, the medical insurance system was extended to cover workers from all kinds of enterprises.

In rural areas, due to the dismantling of the People's Communes, the old rural cooperative medical system lost its economic basis, and was phased out in the 1980s. Most rural clinics became private practices. With the demise of the co-operative medical system, the majority of Chinese farmers were unable to access basic treatment.

After the SARS crisis in 2003, the Chinese government started to strengthen its public health system so as to improve its preventive capacity against large-scale infectious diseases and other public health crises. Meanwhile, the pilot reform of the urban medical system was launched. By 2005, a three-tier disease prevention and control system with three levels of government of province, city and county was basically established. In 2006, the state began develop and build the rural health service system, develop full force urban community services and deepen the reform of the health care system overall. In 2007, China began to build up a risk-sharing health care insurance scheme for urban residents who were not covered by the employment-based health care insurance scheme.

Meanwhile, a new type of rural medical cooperative system was also developed. In October 2002, the central government decided to establish a new type of cooperative medical scheme in rural areas. In June 2003, the pilot work on establishing such a scheme was started throughout the country. This is a voluntary scheme for farmers. The financial resources are from the subsidies provided by both central and local governments and the premiums paid by farmers. In 2008, the new type of rural medical cooperative scheme was practised nationwide.

A breakthrough in China's health care policy occurred in April 2009 when a new policy document on health care system reform was unveiled by the central government. The government recognised that basic health care services were public goods and admitted its responsibilities in providing basic health care for citizens. The document declares that the government role in "formulating policies and plans, raising funds, providing service, and supervising" must be strengthened in order to ensure the fairness and equity of the service. It was the first time in the history of China that the government promised to ensure fair and affordable health services for all 1.3 billion citizens. According to the document, China will have a basic health-care system that can provide "safe, effective, convenient and affordable" health services to urban and rural residents in 2020 (State Council of the People's Republic of China, 2009). Meanwhile, the State Council announced an investment plan of 850 billion *yuan* (124 billion US dollars) for health care reform in three years from 2009.

Currently, China has established three key social health insurance systems: a new rural cooperative medical system for farmers, a basic health insurance system for urban workers and another for urban residents. By the end of 2011, these three basic social medical insurance systems had covered 1.3 billion people, with a coverage rate of more than 95 per cent. A grassroots-level, a health care service covering both urban and rural areas has been established. This is historic progress in China. It is safe to say that China is moving towards universal health insurance coverage.

Social security

Before the economic reform, Chinese people were dependent mainly on communes and *danweis* for social security. With the demise of the commune system and the dismantling of the *danwei* system, the majority of Chinese lost their grounds for social security. In order to establish a social security system suitable for the market economy, the Chinese government decided to establish a social-insurance-based social security system for social risks such as old age, unemployment and work injury and accidents, beginning the mid-1980s. However, the emerging social insurance system was proven inadequate and inefficient to cope with the mounting unemployment and urban poverty caused by the reform of SOEs and eventually so many people were excluded from social protection that this posed a threat to social stability. From the mid-1990s to the early 2000s, more than 20 million workers in SOEs were made redundant and released from the production process. These workers were named *xiagang* (laid-off) workers (Wong and Ngok, 2006). Many urban people fell into poverty even though they were employed or received their pension or other benefits. The size of the new urban poor in China was estimated variously (based on different methods), as ranging from 12 million to 30 million (Leung, 2006). The majority of the new poor included retirees, the unemployed, laid-off employees and even current employees from SOEs, for whom benefits or wages could not be delivered on time or sufficiently (Ministry of Civil Affairs, 2002), which became a source of social instability.

To pacify the laid-off workers and poor retirees, the government strengthened efforts to improve the existing social insurance schemes for retirees and workers in SOEs such as old-age pensions, unemployment benefits and medical insurance. Nevertheless, the newly-emerging social insurance system failed to protect the mounting number of unemployed and laid-off workers. Under these circumstances, it was urgent for the government to restructure the traditional social relief system and set up an alternative welfare mechanism to address the financial needs of the new poor. The MLSS has been implemented throughout the country since the mid-1990s.

In the 1990s, China's social security policy focused on the basic living guarantee for laid-off workers and the establishment of multi-tier old age insurance for urban workers. Since the end of the decade, the MLSS has become one of the key social security systems in China. In 2005, the government began to explore how to establish the MLSS in rural areas. In late 2005, the State Council issued a decision to improve the basic old age insurance system for the urban staff and employees. The decision aimed to extend the coverage of the basic old age insurance system, gradually substantiate the individual accounts of the insurers, and achieve the shift from the "pay-as-you-go" system to the partial accumulation system. In 2006, a new regulation on the rural "five-guarantee" system was issued by the State Council, and a new funding mechanism based on governmental budgeting for the five-guarantee system was introduced. In 2008, new policies were implemented to encourage peasant workers, workers in non-state sectors and those in informal sectors to join the social insurance schemes.

Of these developments, the most important was the establishment of the MLSS scheme all over the country. Known as an anti-poverty scheme, the MLSS was first introduced in Shanghai in 1993. In 1999, the MLSS was established in all cities and towns throughout the country. However, the beneficiaries were limited. The first decade of the new century has witnessed a rapid growth of the urban MLSS. In 1999, only 2.65 million of urban poor people benefited from MLSS. This figure soared to 22.46 million in 2003. Since then, the total urban beneficiaries of the MLSS remain about 23 million. In December 2006, the central government decided to extend the MLSS to all rural areas in 2007. With strong policy pressure from the central government, the rural MLSS was set up nationwide within one year. While only 3.67 million poor peasants benefited from the MLSS, this figure rose to 47.6 million in 2009 (Ministry of Civil Affairs of People's Republic of China, 2010).

After having established the MLSS nationwide, the central government became more active in addressing the medical, educational and housing needs of poor people. In 2003, the rural medical aid system began to be established in China. In 2004, the government started to set up an educational assistance system. In 2005, the urban medical assistance system began to take shape. Currently, China has established a social assistance policy framework which consists of the MLSS for both urban and rural residents, the "five guarantees" scheme for the poorest rural residents, emergency aid for the victims of natural disasters, aid for homeless people in urban areas, and some special programmes to supplement the MLSS, such as educational aid, medical aid and a housing allowance. Even legal aid is regarded as an integral part of the social assistance system in China (Ngok, 2010).

Housing policy

In the Mao era, a state-led housing system was developed in urban China, in which the government took the lead role in building, allocating and maintaining housing. The role of the private market was heavily constrained and eliminated in principle. Housing reform started from the early 1980s with the purpose of reducing the burden of housing provision of the SOEs and local governments. The basic approach to housing reform was to re-establish housing as a commodity and introduce the principle of marketisation in housing provision. The main reform measures included rent increases, the sale of new housing at cost price, selling rental housing to sitting tenants at a discounted price and monetisation of housing (Wang and Murie, 1999).

For nearly two decades, the state and SOEs stopped being the main providers of housing, and individuals relied more on the market than on the state and employers to acquire housing. To make workers to share the burden of housing provision, a Housing Provident Fund system was introduced in 1994, which required contributions from both employers and employees to meet housing needs. Although the government created the policy to provide economic and comfortable housing for low- and middle-income families, local governments were reluctant to do so. Since the mid-1990s, with the marketisation of housing provision and the booming property market in China, house prices have increased rapidly, and more and more people are not able to afford decent housing (Lee, 2000).

Although the housing reform policy launched in 1998 proposed a multi-tiered housing provision framework composed of commercial housing, affordable housing and public rental housing, in fact, local governments still paid less attention to the provision of affordable housing and public rental housing for the middle- and low-income families. Social housing as an important public service has not been realised by the Chinese government. It is safe to say that only real estate policy rather than social housing policy existed in China before 2006. The shortage of public housing provision and the speculation in the property market resulted in the irrational high price of housing. Many people complained about the unaffordable housing. Since 2006, housing demand from middle- and low-income families has become the core target of housing policy. In the 2006 *Government Work Report*, social housing policy was separated from real estate policy, and the government vowed to build up a sound public rental housing system to satisfy the needs of low-income families. In August 2008, the State Council issued the document titled *Opinions on Solving Difficulties in Housing for Low-income Families in Urban Areas*, and proclaimed that providing public housing for low-income families was "an important duty of government public services" (State Council of the People's Republic of China, 2007). According to the 2008 *Government Work Report*, a housing guaranteeing system would be established over the next five years.

Reorienting public money towards social equity: increasing social spending since 2003

To recognise the actual purposes and goals of policies, it is important to look into which items receive most of the investment from government (Wang, 2004). Theoretically, public policy and public budgets are two key governing instruments. To ensure effective governance, these two instruments should be combined and coordinated. However, policy process and budget process are always separated from each other. Such a phenomenon exists both in developed and developing countries (Ma and Hou, 2005). This means some policies will fail because of insufficient money.

The separation of policy process and budget process is distinct in China, especially in social policy areas as the government has a strong economic growth orientation. This has resulted in symbolic policy implementation in some social policy areas. For instance, the Public Rental Housing Scheme was introduced as one of the three major forms of housing provision in 1998 when the central government dismantled the in-kind welfare housing provision system and provided a cash allowance instead. However, there had been no specific stipulation about the financial resources for policy implementation. As a result, the Public Rental Housing Scheme was poorly implemented and subject to local leaders' preferences. By the end of 2002, there were only several thousand public rental flats available in the entire country, which provided shelter to only 7 per cent of the target groups (Li and Sun, 2002).

As more and more social policies have been formulated and implemented, since 2003, social policy oriented budgeting is taking shape in China. Under the policy guideline of "scientific development", the Chinese government began to shift its expenditure emphasis to social policy and more public funding has been appropriated to social purposes. As shown in the work reports of the central government since 2003, the Chinese government has gradually started to integrate policy-making and budgeting processes. More and more social policies are accompanied by fiscal resources. As a result, the share of social policy expenditure in the total public expenditure and its ratio to GDP has increased. For instance, in the 2008 *Government Work Report*, every social policy statement includes not only policy goals, as usual, but also the corresponding financial arrangements. In addition, the responsibilities of central and local government are defined clearly in the report. In terms of the absolute number, public social spending has increased remarkably since 2003. In 2003, government spending on employment and social security, education and health accounted for 4.69 per cent of GDP, and this ratio rose to 6.60 per cent in 2010 (Ministry of Finance of the People's Republic of China, 2011a). Meanwhile, the central government began to take more fiscal responsibility in funding social policies (see Figure 6.1). The foregoing discussion shows that social policy oriented budgeting is taking shape in China.

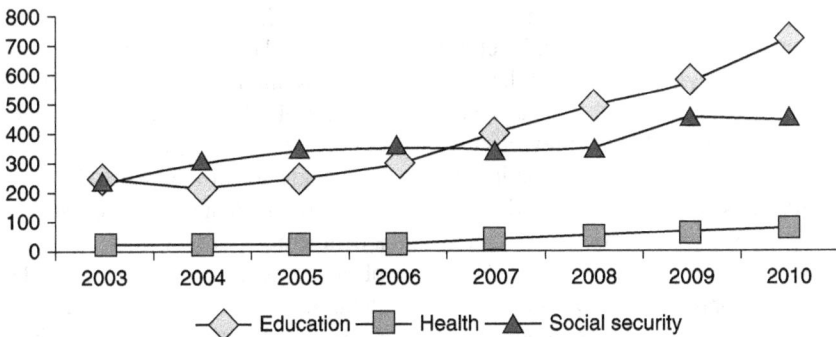

Figure 6.1 The central government investment in major social policy areas (2003–2010).

Source: The statistics of 2003 to 2009 are from *China Finance Yearbook* (2004–2010). The statistics of 2010 are from Ministry of Finance of the People's Republic of China (2011b)

Conclusion

In the context of market transition, China's social policy has been experiencing dramatic changes. Mao's state-dominated social policy regime began to fade away in the early 1980s, and finally disappeared in the 1990s. Instead, a market-dominated new social policy regime was developed under the policy guideline of "efficiency first, equity second". The privatisation of SOEs and the declining role of the state in welfare financing and provision have brought about adverse impacts on ordinary people, especially low-income citizens. With the advent of the new century, along with the new leadership of Hu and Wen, a quite fundamental policy change has emerged in China which indicates that the state has started to reposition its role in public welfare and social justice. Such a policy reorientation was hailed as the "coming of the era of social policy" in China.

Many reasons contribute to this policy reorientation. First, the negative social consequences brought about by the all-out development strategy in the reform era led to wide public complaints, even social unrest. Second, the outbreak of the SARS epidemic functioned as a trigger for the Chinese government and society to revisit the economic growth model practised in the Chinese market transition. Third, the succession of political leadership opened a "policy window" for urgent policy changes. The new leadership led by Hu and Wen needed policy changes to consolidate their authority and legitimacy. Following this thread of thought, a set of new ideas, such as "scientific outlook of development", building a "harmonious society" and developing a "service-oriented government" was formulated. By formulating the ambitious goal of building a socialist, harmonious society, the new leadership demarcated themselves from their predecessors (Ngok, 2009). Finally, after about three decades of rapid economic growth, China has accumulated a significant pool of wealth which enhances the financial capacity of the Chinese government to provide more welfare and benefits to its people.

The coming of the social policy era in China is desirable for the Chinese people, especially those who have contributed to China's economic miracle but not benefited from it. China has just opened the door to a the new era. The positive changes in Chinese social policy that occurred in the Hu-Wen administration are not the result of a strong social welfare movement or a labour movement existing in a strong civil society. To a large extent, they are the responses made by the Chinese leadership to the social crisis brought about by the all-out development approach practised in the previous two decades. Their aims are to alleviate social problems and social dissatisfaction, rather than tackle social inequality. In other words, these changes are related to the imperative to maintain social and political stability. Without a strong civil society and a democratic polity, China's new era of social policy may suffer. Whether the emphasis on social policy and a people-oriented approach in improving people's livelihoods is still subject to further research, since the Chinese government has changed its leadership in March 2013. With a strong need for social stability, social protection may still be adopted as policy tool by the new administration to promote social harmony in the near future.

References

Breslin, S. (2008). "Do Leaders Matter? Chinese Politics, Leadership Transition and the 17th Party Congress", *Contemporary Politics*, 14(2): 215–231.

Chan, C. K., Ngok, K. L. and Phillips, D. (2008). *Social Policy in China: Development and Well-being*. Bristol: Policy Press.

China Fina nce Yearbook (2004–2010). Beijing: China Financial & Economic Publishing House (in Chinese).

General Office of the State Council (2003). *Notice on the Improvement of the Living and Working Conditions of Peasant Workers* (in Chinese).

Guan, X. P. (2000). "China's Social Policy: Reform and Development in the Context of Marketisation and Globalization", *Social Policy & Administration*, 34(1): 115–130.

Hu, L. H. and Jin, Z. (2004). *An Interpretation of the Scientific Oulook on Development*. Beijing: Yanjiu Press.

Lee, J. (2000). "From Welfare Housing to Home Ownership: The Dilemma of China's Housing Reform", *Housing Studies*, 15(1): 61–76.

Leung, J. (2006). "The Emergence of Social Assistance in China", *International Journal of Social Welfare*, 15: 188–198.

Leung, J. and Nann, R. (1995). *Authority and Benevolence: Social Welfare in China*, Hong Kong: The Chinese University Press.

Li, B. and Sun, Y. B. (2002). "Social Rental Housing System not Established in more than Half Major Cities in China", *China Construction*, 7 August 7.

Ma, J. and Hou Y. L. (2005). "From Budgetary Process to Policy Process: a Case Study of Two Chinese Provinces", *Comparative Economic and Social Systems*, 5: 64–72.

Ministry of Civil Affairs of the People's Republic of China (2010). *China Civil Affairs' Statistical Yearbook 2010*. Beijing: China Statistics Press.

Ministry of Civil Affairs (2002). *The Statistical Bulletin of the Development of Civil Affairs Undertakings in 2001*. Available at: http://www.mca.gov.cn/article/zwgk/tjsj/ (in Chinese).

Ministry of Finance of the People's Republic of China (2011a). *Finance Yearbook of China 2011*. Beijing: China Financial & Economic Publishing House (in Chinese).

Ministry of Finance of the People's Republic of China (2011b). *Report on the Central and Local Governments Budget Implementation Situation and the Central and Local Govern-ments Draft Budget*. Available at: http://www.gov.cn/2011lh/content_1826493.htm (in Chinese).

Ngok, K. L. (2007). "Chinese Education Policy in the Context of Decentralization and Marketisation: Evolution and Implications", *Asia Pacific Education Review*, 8(1): 142–157.

Ngok, K. L. (2008). "The Changes of Chinese Labour Policy and Labour Legislation in the Context of Market Transition", *International Labour and Working-Class History*, 73: 45–64.

Ngok, K. L. (2009). "State Capacity, Policy Learning and Policy Paradigm Shift: The Case of the Institutionalization of the 'Theory of Scientific Development' in China", *Korean Journal of Policy Studies*, 24(2): 1–23.

Ngok, K. L. (2010). "Social Assistance Policy and Its Impact on Social Development in China: The Case of the Minimum Living Standard Scheme (MLSS)", *China Journal of Social Work*, 1: 35–52.

State Council of the People's Republic of China (2006). *The Resolutions of the CCP Central Committee on Major Issues Regarding the Building of a Harmonious Socialist*

Society. Available at: http://news.xinhuanet.com/politics/2006–10/18/content_5218639. htm (in Chinese).

State Council of the People's Republic of China (2007). *Opinions on Solving Difficulties in Housing for Low-income Families in Urban Areas*. Available at: http://www.gov.cn/ zwgk/2007–08/13/content_714481.htm (in Chinese).

State Council of the People's Republic of China (2009). *Opinions on Deepening the Reform of Medical Hygiene System*. Available at: http://www.gov.cn/test/2009–04/08/ content_1280069.htm (in Chinese).

Wang, S. G. (2004). "The Changes Accord with Public Opinion: Observing Policy Adjustment of Chinese Government from the Flow of Financial Fund", *Strategy and Management*, N2: 51–60 (in Chinese).

Wang, S. G., Hu, A. G., and Ding, Y. Z. (2002). "The Social Crisis Behind the Economic Prosperity" [*Jingji Fanrong Beihou de Shehui Weiji, Strategy and Management*, 3: 26–33 (in Chinese).

Wang, Y. P. I. and Murie, A. (1999). *Housing Policy and Practice in China*. New York: Macmillan.

Wong, L. (1998). *Marginalization and Social Welfare in China*. London: Routledge.

Wong, L. (2002). "Individualization of Social Rights in China", in S. Sargeson (ed.) *Collective Goods, Collective Futures in Asia*. London: Routledge, pp. 162–178.

Wong, L. and Flynn, N. (eds) (2001). *The Market in Chinese Social Policy*, London: Palgrave.

Wong, L. and Ngok, K. L. (2006). "Social Policy between Plan and Market: 'Xiagang' (Off-Duty Employment) and the Policy of the Re-employment Service Centers in China", *Social Policy and Administration*, 40(2): 158–173.

7 Asserting the "public" in welfare provision

A study of resident evaluation and expectation of social services in Guangzhou, China

Ka Ho Mok and Genghua Huang

Introduction

China's welfare system has been a typical "residual welfare regime", which did not manifest too many flaws in the planned economy era. However, the economic reform and market-oriented transformations in recent decades have shaken the original well-balanced "residual" and "needs" pattern. The decline of the "work unit system" has led to two consequences. First, it has radically transformed the social and economic structures which gave rise to increased and diversified needs of social welfare. Second, the government is pressed to shoulder more responsibility for social welfare provision. This chapter adopts a case study approach to examine changing social welfare needs and expectations in Guangzhou, a relatively developed city in Southern China. Based upon our field interviews conducted in Guangzhou, together with policy, documentary and secondary data analysis, the chapter examines how Guangzhou residents evaluate the social service and social welfare provision provided by the government. More specifically, the chapter also reports on the welfare expectations of Guangzhou residents through focus group discussions.

Policy context and research questions

American policy expert Glazer (1986) divided social welfare into two types. The first is to provide welfare services for all people on the grounds of absolute and universal rights. The second is to offer selective, remedial welfare services where they are most needed, this usually being identified by household survey. To many scholars studying Chinese social welfare (e.g. Leung and Nann, 1996; Wang, 2009; Wong, 2001), China's welfare system belongs to the second type, "remedial social welfare", with a much narrower conception of welfare as compared to the first type. "Remedial social welfare" did not fare too badly in the planned economy era, when the state monopolised all important social resources including wealth and goods, and significantly determined urban people's living conditions and their career development. In such a highly organised, integrated, centralised and unitary social structure, every urban worker's basic living security and social welfare was taken care of by his or her work unit (*danwei*). This is what we call the "work unit system" (Lu, 1989) and also what Walder (1986) refers as "organised dependence" in China. Under the leadership of Chairman Mao Zedong during the earlier years after the foundation of the People's Republic of China, the state implemented the "life-long employment system" in urban areas and established town workers' employment security. In 1951 China issued "Labour insurance regulations", requiring that the units should provide comprehensive welfare for their workers. Therefore, In Mao's period, China's social welfare was based on the "life-long employment system", and supported by the units. Due to the differences between different units, this system divided and segmented China's social welfare system. Nevertheless, it effectively shared the responsibility of social welfare provision with the state. While the social security of the majority of urban people was taken care of by their units, the state only attended to those being left out of the unit system and those who were not sufficiently supported by the units (the number of the former was relatively small; the latter's living difficulties were mainly inflicted by natural disasters and poverty). The state could therefore focus on the macro regulation of unit operations and their personnel arrangements. It is against such a context that the welfare services offered by the state were remedial and narrow in nature (Leung and Nann, 1996: 182–183). At that time, the cooperation of the state and unit system in offering welfare services successfully maintained social stability, resolved many social problems such as inflation, unemployment, crime, etc., and secured people's living standards. All of these welfare arrangements were regarded as the embodiment of the socialist system's superiority (Leung and Nann, 1996: 182–183).

However, the market-oriented economic reforms and transformations in the late 1970s and early 1980s radically altered the well balanced structure of the "residual" and "needs" pattern. According to Kapstein and Mandelbaum (1997), in the process of market transition, the old social security system or social safety network was falling apart, leading to the decline of living standards for socially vulnerable groups. Enterprises, under the guidance of an "efficiency first" philosophy and oriented to the objectives of economic production (especially after the full implementation of the national labour contract in 1986), were no longer the guarantors of their workers' welfare provision, but were only the contractors, assuming "limited" protection responsibilities. It is against this wider market transition context that we have witnessed large-scale reforms of state-owned enterprises in China mainland, and this has deprived a large number of laid-off and unemployed workers, forced to become independent from the "organised dependence" under the traditional welfare arrangements provided by their work units (Wong *et al.*, 2002). The Chinese government, therefore, had to undertake more responsibility for social welfare relief due to the weakened security functions of the units. As a consequence, the call to "bring the state back in" become increasingly louder (Painter and Mok, 2010).

In view of the above changes, the Chinese government has begun to establish a set of social welfare systems which aim to salvage and relieve the poor. These systems include a minimum standard of living, health care security, education assistance, housing security, employment assistance and judicial assistance. However, as China's social welfare is not grounded on a sound and well-resourced public finance base, the limited state resources that can be allocated to social welfare have constrained its development. Although disadvantaged groups have expected improved living conditions in recent years, they are still socially marginalised (Wong, 2001: 223–225). This is partly because the Chinese government does not believe that China can effectively address poverty and unequal distribution of wealth by modelling itself on the Western welfare state model. An article published in the party press *People's Daily* in the 1990s stated that "the fundamental objective of the newly-established social security system of China is to improve productivity . . . we should not offer too much welfare . . . we should maintain the protection of basic living standards in a manner that suits our country" (*Renmin Ribao*, 1995). Even when we have seen more measures being adopted by the government to improve social service delivery and social protection for Chinese citizens, it seems that the current Chinese social welfare system still has a strong remedial feature in terms of social protection.

Like other East Asian countries, China's economic and social transformation has accelerated since the Asian financial crisis in 1997. Social issues such as the grim situation of employment, inflation, an ageing population and a declining birth rate have led to the Chinese people's growing and diversified needs for basic social welfare, social security and protection. Some scholars have already pointed out that the current social welfare system in China not meet the basic needs of the people. The new problems under the new circumstances generate new expectations for the new role of the state in providing social welfare and social protection (Haggard and Kaufman, 2008; Walker and Wong, 2005). The social welfare system for Chinese residents now needs effective re-evaluation once again.

Research methods

This study is primarily concerned with how urban residents in Guangzhou perceive their welfare needs and how they evaluate the municipal government's welfare policies or social protection measures in addressing those needs. The major focus of the present research is closely related to how Guangzhou citizens assess their welfare needs regarding the minimum standard of living, health care security, housing security and the education service. In terms of research methods, firstly, we conducted literature and policy analysis of the government's strategies, priorities and preferences in the above policy areas. Secondly, we conducted in-depth interviews[1] with related experts to understand their views and opinions on the welfare system and policy measures of Guangzhou in particular, and of China in general. Thirdly, we conducted focus group discussions with the urban residents in Guangzhou. In this qualitative study, "purposive sampling" is deployed rather than "random sampling" (Kuzel, 1992; Morse, 1989). Since the number of respondents or target samples is quite large in our research, we adopted a purposive sampling method to select residents to participate in the focus group discussions, which would enhance the credibility of the research (Patton, 1990).

Therefore, our research followed the "funnel principle" to narrow down the range of sample selection from the urban area to the streets. The focus group discussions consisted of urban residents of various age groups, different occupations (e.g. students, fresh graduates, unemployed persons, laid-off SOE workers, retirees, etc.), different family backgrounds (e.g. low-income households, single-parent families, etc.) and socio-economic characteristics. We conducted the focus group interviews in three different communities in Guangzhou (see Table 7.1). Apart from the qualitative data collected from interviews and focus group discussions, we also collected and analysed the data from government and from some research institutions to bolster our arguments. As Rossman and Wilson (1984) pointed out, the two kinds of data can complement each other through triangulation, and enhance the analysis. We therefore adopt such an approach for data collection.

Major findings

Social welfare is a broad concept and covers a very wide range of aspects. Due to the length of this chapter, we have only selected a few major aspects, namely, the system of the minimum living standard guarantee, health care security, particularly related to social insurance, housing, and education provision.

Minimum standard of living

Generally speaking, the low-income people are the ones in urgent need of social welfare (Gu, 2008: 4). Therefore, the household survey that helps identify this group of people is the foundation of the social welfare system. Meanwhile, because the system of the Minimum Living Standard Guarantee is often associated with some other relief programmes, the implementation of the system is the core of the construction of the social safety net and the key to ensuring that disadvantaged people can enjoy their social welfare rights. However, based on the overall social welfare values and the features of the social welfare system, China's system of Minimum Living Standard Guarantee still focuses on the "minimum" level (Wang, 1999) and places its attention on the "survival" level (Yang, 2004). In 1995, Guangzhou established the system of minimum standard of living for urban

Table 7.1 Focus group discussion arrangements

Focus group	Time	Place	Group size	Interviewees
A	6.11.2010	*Changgang Street*	16	Residents of *Changgang* Street (A1-A16)
B	17.7.2010	*Haizhuang* Social worker's office	10	Residents of *Tongfu* Street (B1-B10)
C	30.12.2010	*Jingtai* Street Office	15	Residents of *Jingtai* Street (C1-C15)

residents and has adjusted the standard level six times since then. From 1995 to 2011, the standard level has increased from 200 yuan per person per month to 480 yuan per person per month.[2] To determine whether the standard is high or low, we usually compare it with the local residents' average income (Gu, 2008: 7). In 2008, for instance, the minimum standard of living in Guangzhou was 365 yuan per person per month (that is 4,380 yuan per person per year), while the residents' annual per capita disposable income was 25,316.72 yuan (Statistics Bureau of Guangzhou Municipality, 2008). Thus, the minimum standard of living was equivalent to 17.3 per cent of local residents' annual per capita disposable income in that year. Some local and foreign social policy literature set the level of 30 per cent of residents' median[3] income as the "extreme poverty line", 40 per cent as the "severe poverty line", 50 per cent as the "moderate poverty line" and 60 per cent as the "near poverty line". According to this international academic standard (Behrendt, 2002; Gu, 2008:7; Smeeding and Phillips, 2001), we can say that the families receiving allowances in Guangzhou are still living under extreme poverty conditions.

In recent years, as elsewhere in China, Guangzhou's price levels have continued to rise and inflation is expected to stay strong. In 2008, Guangzhou's annual urban consumer price index increased by 5.9 per cent (Statistics Bureau of Guangzhou Municipality and Guangzhou Investigation Team of National Bureau of Statistics, 2011). Realising the pressure of inflation on the living standards of low households, which are more sensitive to price fluctuations than other groups, in December 2010, Guangzhou promulgated "The Pilot Scheme of the Adjustment of the Minimum Living Standard Guarantee in Guangzhou" and established a "linkage growth mechanism" that adapts the standard of "minimum living" to price fluctuations. However, the scheme sets quite rigorous starting conditions for the "growth mechanism", that is, only when "the price index of low-income consumers rises to a certain level (4 per cent or more) and lasts for six months" will the adjustment mechanism be launched. That means the adjustment of the standard of "minimum living" will always lag behind the changes in prices and consumption. Our interviewee C4 (female, 42 years old) is a single mother with a son in junior high school and they were receiving the minimum living standard guarantee in Jingtai Street. In the face of price inflation, the minimum living standard guarantee obviously could not meet their basic needs. C4 said, "The allowances we received were only more than a hundred yuan at the beginning stage, which could barely help us. Later, it rose to more than five hundred yuan, and now there is 603 yuan. But the changes cannot match the rises in price levels. When the allowance level began to rise, I felt very happy. However, the price levels rose even faster. My son is now growing up, who needs to eat more meat, so I have to let him have my share as well"[4] (C4, interview records).

The reasons that many families have become low-income households are complex and complicated, such as their members suffering from physical disabilities or chronic illnesses, the increasing burden of children's education, and so forth. To them, the relief offered by the minimum living standard guarantee is obviously not enough. In recent years, Guangzhou has promulgated and implemented a series of supporting measures such as medical aid and students' aid to further support such families. However, these relief measures that set strict limitations for the amount of allowances and have rigorous application procedures still cannot cater to the special difficulties of some low-income households. Interviewee B6 (female, 44 years old) has a son who has had heart disease since a very young age. She said, "[My son] did a heart surgery. At the same when he was in hospital, the government had just begun to launch the student health insurance programme. Therefore, the insurance was covered by [the] Bureau of Civil Affairs of Guangzhou Municipality. However, when my son left the hospital, I went to [the] Bureau of Social Security of Guangzhou Municipality to apply for its insurance, the officer turned me down and explained that the insurance policy did not cover the period in which my son was in hospital. The policy took effect on July 1st while my son already left hospital on June 22. So we could not get even a penny of subsidy." She added, "We turned to the neighbour-hood committee for help, then it sought help from the Civil Affairs Bureau, and they just replenished us 1,000 yuan. They said they have already done their best." She said, "Our family now owes more than 50,000 yuan for the cost of surgery. The few hundred yuan we received from the government could do nothing to alleviate our living burdens" (B6, interview records). In fact, according to a survey in 2009, the degree of dissatisfaction towards "government policies for the vulnerable groups" in Guangzhou was 32.6 per cent, an increase of 8.8 per cent compared to 2008 (Guangzhou Social Facts and Public Opinions Research Center, 2010a: 288). Our field interviews and observations confirm the results of this survey, providing more details of the living difficulties of Guangzhou urban residents.

Health care services

Economists Kornai and Eggleston once pointed out that "Compared with anything else, health, survival and the relief of physical pain possess unparalleled unique values" (Kornai and Eggleston, 2003) Disease not only deprives people of the ability to work and thus cuts down their opportunities and incomes, but it also sends many well-heeled families into poverty. Therefore, health care security is one of the most important aspects of social welfare. In China, the health care security system needs great improvements in many aspects. According to the World Health Organisation's evaluation of performance of the health care system of 191 countries, China was ranked the 144th (aibai.com, 2001). Since then, Guangzhou has begun to extend its coverage as the priority objective in improving the health care security system. Apart from promoting health care security to urban workers, Guangzhou has also issued specific policies that will expand the basic health care security coverage to the people employed in a flexible manner, the rural-to-urban residents, and non-Guangzhou household registered employees in various ways. By the end of 2010, the number of people participating in health care security in Guangzhou was 6.784 million, among which the number of retirees was 809,000 (Statistics Bureau of Guangzhou Municipality and Guangzhou Investigation Team of National Bureau of Statistics, 2011). A recent random sample survey of 1,001 residents from 12 districts of Guangzhou revealed that the percentage of people who have participated in "medical social insurance" programmes was 53 per cent

(Guangzhou Social Facts and Public Opinions Research Center, 2010b: 282). The rate of health care security coverage in Guangzhou is among the highest in China.

The financial model of medical institutions in China is a combination of government resource allocation and business operations. This mechanism, established in the planned economy era, has now undergone significant changes amidst the marketisation of public service provision and delivery. With the reduction of government resource allocation, medical institutions have to enlarge their commercial operations to seek more revenue in order to cover their costs and maintain service quality. Nowadays, the main source of funding for medical institutions comes solely from business operations, while the government resource allocation only takes up a small share (Liang and Zhao, 2007). This will inevitably lead to a rise in medical fees. Further worsening the situation is the lack of cost efficiency mechanisms and incentives in medical institutions, which makes the rise of medical costs hard to control (Zuo and Hu, 2001). According to a recent survey, 80 per cent of Guangzhou residents thought that medical expenses were "too high" or "high" (Guangzhou Social Facts and Public Opinions Research Center, 2010b). Although Guangzhou has adopted effective efforts in promoting the rate of medical security coverage, the benefits of these efforts have been offset by the excessive medical costs, and thus have, ironically, reduced public satisfaction with the health services. A survey of public opinion on Guangzhou social insurance status in 2009 revealed that 54.1 per cent of the public thought that the medical insurance was little or even no help in relieving the financial burden of people suffering from "serious illnesses", while 56 per cent of the public thought that it was little or no help in relieving the financial burden of people suffering from "minor illnesses" (Guangzhou Social Facts and Public Opinions Research Center, 2010c: 311–312).

In addition to the increase in medical costs, another challenge facing China's health system is a change in demography. Due to the decline in the birth rate and the enhanced life expectancy level, the total number and the proportion of elderly people in China is increasing. Usually, the elderly is one of the most physically vulnerable groups with many of them suffering from hypertension, diabetes and other chronic diseases. They are in strong and urgent need of medical security. Interviewee A12 (Male, 70 years old), a hypertension patient, said that, "I have to spend 700–800 yuan a month on medical check-up and medicines while I receive only 100 yuan subsidies a month and 300 yuan reimbursement for health care security. There is a very large gap between them" (A12, interview records). To the elderly population which regards health care security as the most important element of social welfare, the current scope of health care security is not sufficient. As interviewee A16 (female, 78 years old), a resident of the Chang Gang Street, said, "If we (old people) got sick, the medical spending would be uncontrollable" (A16, interview records).

Housing services

Famous social welfare scholar Marshall once said that housing is one of the six social rights of citizens in modern society, since it has a direct impact on the welfare of citizens (Marshall, 1975). Excessive housing spending will make people poor, so housing security is an important safeguard against poverty for disadvantaged groups (Ritakallio, 2003: 81–101). In the planned economy era, the government in China acted like "parents", allocating housing and providing housing security for urban residents. From the late 1970s, the government began to reform the housing system along the lines of marketisation and monetisation. The pressure to supply housing, and government spending on housing, were thus reduced. The reform was marked by neoliberal ideas which gave away the power of the government to the market (Zhu, 2007). With less government subsidy for housing after the reform, the people had to venture into the real estate market to buy their houses. However, due to weak macro control of housing prices by the government, house prices have been soaring in recent years to a level beyond many people's financial capabilities. "Home ownership" has become an expensive luxury rather than a basic and easily accessible living necessity. For example, in October 2010, in 10 districts in Guangzhou, the average price of primary housing has exceeded 15,000 yuan per square metre (CHINANEWS.COM, 2010), while the per capita disposable income of urban residents in Guangzhou in the same year was only 30,658 yuan (Statistics Bureau of Guangzhou Municipality and Guangzhou Investigation Team of National Bureau of Statistics, 2011). Which means an average person can only afford two square metres of local residential area with his/her whole year's disposable income.

Similarly, other studies point out that the beneficiaries of housing reform are usually the people with higher political and social status who are dominating many institutional resources, rather than those at the bottom level of society. There is little evidence that market-oriented reforms can lessen social stratification (Logan *et al.*, 1999). The disadvantaged people under the old welfare housing system are still at a disadvantage in the real estate market. In this regard, housing welfare or housing security provided by the government should be given more emphasis in relation to this group of people, which is very large. In Guangzhou, the housing security system comprises economic and suitable houses, lower-rent houses, price-limited houses, and so on. However, the threshold of application for housing security is "high" (see Tables 7.2 and 7.3), and the scope of potential recipients of housing welfare is narrow. Such strict or harsh application requirements have created a large group of people called the "sandwich layer", who cannot receive the government's housing security nor are they able to purchase private houses by themselves.

In the face of rising house prices, even university graduates, who are usually regarded as the potential middle class, have to surrender to the harsh reality. In the late 1990s, China increased the level of college enrollment. As a consequence, the number of college graduates has increased every year and made job competition fiercer. According to the Chinese Academy of Social Sciences, the monthly salary of college graduates declined from 2006 to 2009. In 2009, the average monthly salary of college graduates was 2,703 yuan (NETEASE, 2010). The vast majority of college graduates are unable to purchase property in the private market, and it is quite difficult for them to meet the rigorous application requirements for low-rent houses or economic and suitable houses. These students are the typical

Table 7.2 Application requirements for low-rent houses in Guangzhou

Family member (person)	Monthly disposable income of the family (yuan)	Annual disposable income of the family (yuan)	Per capita living space (m²)	Quota of applicant's household net worth (10,000 yuan)
1	640	7,680	<10	7
2	1,280	15,360	<10	14
3	1,920	23,040	<10	21
≥4	2,560	30,720	<10	26

Table 7.3 Application requirements for economic and suitable houses in Guangzhou

Family member (person)	Monthly disposable income of the family (yuan)	Annual disposable income of the family (yuan)	Per capita disposable annual income (yuan)	Per capita living space (m²)	Quota of applicant's household net worth (10,000 yuan)
1	1,524	18,287		<10	11
2	3,048	36,574		<10	22
3	4,572	54,861	18,287	<10	33
≥4	6,096	73,148		<10	44

"sandwich layer". Interviewee B5 (female, 23 years old) graduated from college in 2009 and is now working in an NGO in Guangzhou with a monthly salary of more than 2,000 yuan. She sees housing as the biggest living problem. She said, "I think we (the young people) are the most suffering group. We are not only unable to afford housing but also not eligible for low-rent houses" (B5, interview records). Her colleague and our interviewee B4 (female, 24 years old) is also a university graduate, who is very frustrated about the housing problem. She said, "We are forced to face the housing problem especially after marriage, don't we? Although the government has introduced a number of policies about economic and suitable houses, the application requirements are extremely harsh for us. And even if my future husband and I will be eligible for applying [for] the economic houses, I think we may not be able to buy it, because I know that we have to pay a large sum of money beforehand" (B4, interview records).

Besides housing prices, citizenship rights also affect the urban residents' eligibility for applying for government-subsidised housing. Like many other areas in China, Guangzhou's low-rent houses and economic and suitable houses are only offered to the urban residents with local household registration; non-permanent urban residents are excluded. Although the housing fund serves as an important part of housing security and covers almost all of the economic organisations or units, the benefit ratio the citizens can enjoy is dependent on the employer units' payment (Zhu, 2009: 236). As Zhu points out, "China's housing security system is neither universal and non-occupational nor entirely related to one's income level. It is indeed related to one's identity and his/her working unit. It is a social exclusion with Chinese characteristics" (Zhu, 2009: 236).

Education provision

We found through our investigations into education that Guangdong Province has carried out a full implementation of "free compulsory education" in the urban and rural areas since 2008, but educational expenses are still one of the three heaviest financial burdens on the family. Though the latest policy has attempted to stop schools from charging tuition fees and the cost of books and supplies for primary and junior secondary students, the reality reveals that a large sum of "contribution money" or "sponsorship fees" is charged among almost all schools in the Guangzhou urban area (A7, interview records). Meanwhile, our interviewees also reported to us that "schools would also come up with a lot of items to collect fees, such as school uniforms, lunches and even [a] 'nap fee' if you sleep at noon at school. At weekends, you also have to pay [a] 'cramming fee' for the weekend's supplementary lessons" (B1, interview records). Under the one child policy context, parents in the mainland are very keen to invest in their children's education, which has inevitably led to a sharp rise in the collection of education fees in the kindergarten stage. One respondent told us during the field interview that "now the tuition in the kindergartens needs several hundred yuan a month while some 'famous' kindergartens even charge ... more than 10,000 yuan a year" (B5, interview records). At present, the call for the extension of "free compulsory education" to the coverage of the kindergarten and high school stages is very strong in Guangzhou. According to a survey carried in 2008 by the Statistics Bureau of Guangzhou Municipality, "the pressure of education expenses" has become the second major factor in the decline of household living standards in Guangzhou, which is only second to the "prices inflation" (Huang and Le, 2009: 231).

Discussion and conclusion: is China's current welfare model durable?

The changing welfare needs and expectations emerging from China mainland have clearly driven the Chinese government to rethink how to manage such accelerated welfare needs during the rapid market transition. Realising the old welfare arrangements along the line of privatisation and marketisation of social welfare/social policy are unproductive for the promotion of social harmony and political stability (Mok and Ku, 2010), the Chinese government has tried to bring the "public" back into social service delivery and social policy-making (Painter and Mok, 2010). Like many other newly industrialising economies in East Asia, China is also regarded as a "productivist" welfare regime, in which social policies and social welfare are subordinated to the logic of economic development and productivity growth (Holliday, 2005: 148). The Chinese government has been a reluctant welfare provider in the post-Mao era, trying to make use of market forces to resolve people's welfare and social needs through the adoption of privatisation strategies (Shi and Mok, 2012). The top priority of this welfare regime is to foster social investment rather than to promote social protection (Gough, 2004:190). However, as Holliday argues, social policies under a productivist welfare regime are not insignificant, rather they are essential to nurturing productive workers, maintaining social and political stability, and ensuring the smooth operation of the labour market (Holliday, 2005: 148).

Adopting the guidance of "economic efficiency first" and also the ideas of residual welfare, like many other East Asian countries or regions, China has maintained low social welfare spending during the transitional period. The state only provided basic protection and necessary "residual" services for the poorest and most disadvantaged groups. Since the economic reform, the state-owned enterprises and work units have gradually abandoned their responsibilities of providing working security and social welfare, while the state has not fully taken up those responsibilities. Such power has been gradually transformed to the market, evident in the adoption of welfare programmes such as social insurance. However, without a sound and comprehensive blueprint for the development of social insurance, the government's premature withdrawal from social security has led to immediate harm being caused to the most needy. Wong also maintains that there is a great gap between social insurance and relief, and this gap should not continue to exist and needs to be bridged (Wong, 2001).

This study has reviewed the current welfare system in Guangzhou, following the logic of "supporting the poor and relieving the needy". Policy priorities are always given to people in the worst plight. Yet in the face of rapid economic, social and demographic changes, policy-makers have had to be alert to the living difficulties facing the general public as well, especially in the areas of medical, educational and housing services. Although the Guangzhou Municipal Government has taken certain measures to address the changing needs of their residents in the past few years, without major changes in the underlying policy philosophy, the outcomes of such measures tend to be piecemeal and limited. Nowadays, some experts are advocating a social policy based upon needs assessment of welfare benefit recipients, or evidence-based conditions in order to address the imbalance between social welfare provision and social policy. Cook, from the United Nations Research Institute for Social Development, maintains that China's social policies must better respond to the needs of society and also keep consistent with China's system of truth. In addition, the provision of social welfare in China should be based on the specific needs of certain groups (Cook, 2001). However, neither academia nor government has yet arrived at a consensus concerning the issue of how to formulate the content of policies based on needs assessment and how to define the relationship between needs assessment and the institutional framework.

In view of welfare regionalism, coupled with the growing concerns of citizens in regard to variations in terms of social protection across different parts of China, the central government and local governments should work hand in hand to improve social welfare provision and social protection for the people (Mok and Wu, 2013). One question remains unanswered: is the current welfare model adopted by the Chinese government durable enough in a long run to manage people's heightened welfare expectations and to handle complex and negative social consequences resulting from rapid social, economic and demographic changes? The answer is still open for further research.

Based on the above analysis, we conclude that the Chinese government is under tremendous and continued pressure to improve not only people's economic circumstances but also to provide for sustainable livelihoods and sustainable development in the future. Whether the government has the capacity to search for new governance methods in managing changing welfare and social needs appropriately and strategically to maintain social harmony and political stability is a crucial question in asserting the legitimacy of the ruling party in China.

Acknowledgements

The authors thank the Hong Kong Institute of Education for providing research funding, and some of the data in this chapter are derived from the project RG25/2009–2010R. The chapter is a revised version of "The Changing Social Welfare Needs and Expectations in China's Market Transition: A Study of Resident Evaluation and Expectation of Social Services in Guangzhou", by Ka Ho Mok and Genghua Huang, *Journal of Current Chinese Affairs*, 2013.

Notes

1 Expert interviews were conducted on 10 June 2010 in Sun Yat-Sen University, Guangzhou. Participants of the interview and discussion included Chinese and foreign experts and scholars on social policy, education policy, social security, health policy, political sociology, public administration, studies of policy and so on.
2 Changes in the standard of "minimum living" in Guangzhou are as follows: 200 yuan in 1995, 240 yuan in 1997, 300 yuan in 1999, 330 yuan in 2005, 365 yuan in 2008, 410 yuan in 2010 and 480 yuan in 2011.
3 If the sample size is large enough, the overall median and mean will be very close. They can be regarded as equivalents.
4 All interviews were conducted in Chinese. The English transcripts were translated by the authors.

References

Aibai.com (2001). "China's health care level ranked the 144th in the world". Available at: http://www.aibai.com/infoview.php?id=520 (May 19, 2001) (in Chinese).
Behrendt, C. (2002). *At the Margins of the Welfare State: Social Assistance and the Alleviation of Poverty in Germany, Sweden and the United Kingdom*. Aldershot: Ashgate.
CHINANEWS.COM (2010). "Compared to the same period, the average price of primary housing has increased by 50 per cent, and has exceeded 15,000 yuan per square meter in Guangzhou". Available at: http://www.chinanews.com/estate/2010/11–19/2667325. shtml (November 19, 2010) (in Chinese).

Cook, S. (2001). "The social policy based upon needs: research and analysis framework". Available at: http://www.cass.net.cn/file/20100323261999.html (in Chinese).

Glazer, N. (1986). "Welfare and 'Welfare' in America", in R. Rose and R. Shiratori (eds) *The Welfare State, East and West*. Oxford: Oxford University Press.

Gough, I. (2004). "East Asia: The Limits of Productivist Regimes", in I. Gough and G. Wood (eds) *Insecurity and Welfare Regimes in Asia, Africa and Latin America*. Cambridge: Cambridge University Press, pp. 169–201.

Gu, X. (2008). *The Institution Construction of Social Safety Net in China*. Hangzhou: Zhengjiang University Press (in Chinese).

Guangzhou Social Facts and Public Opinions Research Center (2010a). "Public Appraise on Guangzhou Society and Economy Development in 2009", in Y.W. Tang and J. T. Li (eds) *Annual Report on Social Development of Guangzhou in China (2010)*. Beijing: Social Sciences Academic Press, pp. 284–297 (in Chinese).

Guangzhou Social Facts and Public Opinions Research Center (2010b). "A Survey on Public Appraise of Guangzhou Medical Industry Service in 2009", in Y.W. Tang and J. T. Li (eds) *Annual Report on Social Development of Guangzhou in China (2010)*. Beijing: Social Sciences Academic Press, pp. 274–283 (in Chinese).

Guangzhou Social Facts and Public Opinions Research Center (2010c). "A Survey on Public Appraise of Guangzhou Social Insurance in 2009", in Y.W. Tang and J.T. Li (eds) *Annual Report on Social Development of Guangzhou in China (2010)*. Beijing: Social Sciences Academic Press, pp. 298–318 (in Chinese).

Haggard, S. and Kaufman, R. R. (2008). *Development, Democracy and Welfare States: Latin America, East Asia and Eastern Europe*. Princeton, NJ: Princeton University Press.

Holliday, I. (2005). "East Asian Social Policy in the Wake of the Financial Crisis: Farewell to Productivism?", *Policy and Politics*, 33(1): 145–162.

Huang, Y. L. and Le, J. (2009). "An Investigation Report about Resident Evaluation on the Quality of Life in Guangzhou", in Y. W. Tang and J. T. Li (eds) *Annual Report on Social Development of Guangzhou in China (2009)*. Beijing: Social Sciences Academic Press, pp. 230–239 (in Chinese).

Kapstein, E. B. and Mandelbaum, M. (1997). *Sustaining the Transition: The Social Safety Net in Postcommunist Europe*. New York: The Council on Foreign Relations.

Kornai, J. and Eggleston, K. (2003). *Welfare, Choice and Solidarity in Transition: Reforming the health sector in Eastern Europe*. Beijing: Citic Publishing House (in Chinese).

Kuzel, A. J. (1992). "Sampling in Qualitative inquiry", in B. F. Crabtree and W. L. Miller (eds) *Doing Qualitative Research* (2nd edn) Newbury Park, CA: Sage, pp. 33–46.

Leung, C. B. and Nann, R. (1996). *Authority and Benevolence: Social Welfare in China*. Hong Kong: The Chinese University Press (in Chinese).

Liang, H. and Zhao, D. Y. (2007). "Analysis of the Reform of the Fundamental Medical Insurance System in China", *Fudan Journal (Social Sciences)*, 1: 123–131 (in Chinese).

Logan, J. R., Bian, Y. J. and Bian, F. Q. (1999). "Housing Inequality in Urban China in the 1990s", *International Journal of Urban and Regional Research*, 23(1): 7–25.

Lu, F. (1989). "Unit: A Special Form of Social Organization", *Journal of China Social Science*, 1: 71–88 (in Chinese).

Marshall, T. H. (1975). *Social policy* (4th edn). London: Hutchsinon.

Mok, K. H. and Ku, Y. W. (eds) (2010). *Social Cohesion in Greater China: Challenges for Social Policy and Governance*. London: Imperial College Press.

Mok, K. H. and Wu, X. F. (2013). "Dual Decentralization in China's Transitional Economy: Welfare Regionalism and Policy Implications for Central-Local Relationship", *Policy & Society*, 32(1): 61–75.

Morse, J. M. (ed.) (1989). *Qualitative Nursing Research: A Contemporary Dialogue*. Newbury Park, CA: Sage.

NETEASE (2010). "Chinese Academy of Social Sciences: college graduates' actual salaries drop considerably". Available at: http://news.163.com/10/1216/09/6O12O9FL00014AEE. html (December, 16 2010) (in Chinese).

Painter, M. and Mok, K. H. (2010). "Reasserting the Public in Public Service Delivery: The De-privatization and De-marketization of Education in China", in M. Ramesh, E. Araral Jr and X. Wu (eds) *Reasserting the Public in Public Services*. London: Routledge.

Patton, M. Q. (1990). *Qualitative Education and Research Methods* (2nd edn). Newbury Park, CA: Sage.

Renmin ribao [People's Daily] (1995): 29 July (in Chinese).

Ritakallio, V. M. (2003). "The Importance of Housing Costs in Cross-national Comparisons of Welfare (State) Outcomes", *International Social Security Review*, 56(2): 81–101.

Rossman, G. B. and Wilson, B. L. (1984). "Number and Words: Combining Qualitative and Qualitative Methods in a Single Large Scale Evaluation Study", *Evaluation Review*, 9(5): 627–643.

Shi, S. J. and Mok, K. H. (2012). "Pension Privatisation in Greater China: Institutional Patterns and Policy Outcomes", *International Journal of Social Welfare*, 21(S1): S30–S45.

Smeeding, T. M. and Phillips, K. R. (2001). "Social Protection for the Poor in the Developed World", in N. Lusting (ed.) *Shielding the poor: Social Protection in the Developing World*. Washington, DC: Brookings Institution Press, pp. 267–308.

Statistics Bureau of Guangzhou Municipality (2008). Conditions of Per Capita Cash Income and Expenditure of Urban Households (2008)", *Guangzhou Statistical Information Network*. Available at: http://data.gzstats.gov.cn/gzStat1/chaxun/njsj.jsp (in Chinese).

Statistics Bureau of Guangzhou Municipality and Guangzhou Investigation Team of National Bureau of Statistics (2011). "2010 Guangzhou National Economic and Social Development Statistical Bulletin", *Guangzhou Statistical Information Network*. Available at: http:// www.gzstats.gov.cn/tjfx/gztjfs/201104/t20110411_24947.htm (in Chinese).

Walder, A. (1986). *Communist Neo-traditionalism: Work and Authority in Chinese Industry*. Berkeley, CA: University of California Press.

Walker, A. and Wong, C. K. (eds) (2005). *East Asian Welfare Regimes in Transition*. Bristol: Policy Press.

Wang, H. (1999). "The Institutionalization Creation of Chinese Urban Social Relief", in D. Q. Xu (ed.) *Social Security Reform in China*. Beijing: Economic Science Press, pp. 666–676 (in Chinese).

Wang, S.B. (2009). "Building an Appropriate Universal-type Social Welfare System in China", *Journal of Peking University (Humanities and Social Sciences)*, 3: 58–65 (in Chinese).

Wong, L. (2001). *Marginalization and Social Welfare in China*. Hong Kong: The Commercial Press (in Chinese).

Wong, L., Mok, K. H. and Lee, G. (2002). "The Challenges of Global Capitalism: Unemployment and State Workers' Reactions and Responses in Post-Reform China", *International Journal of Human Resource Management*, 13(3): 339–415.

Yang, L. X. (2004). "A Review of Urban Minimum Living Standard Program in China: Problems and Policy Options", *Population Science of china*, 3: 71–80 (in Chinese).

Zhu, Y. P. (2007). "Housing Problems and Housing Policy Paradigm Shift in China", in K. L. Ngok and W. Q. Guo (eds) *Chinese Public Policy Review* (Vol. 1). Shanghai: Shanghai Renmin Press, pp. 62–76 (in Chinese).

Zhu, Y. P. (2009). "Chinese Housing Policy paradigm: Review and Prospect", in K. L. Ngok (ed.) *The Construction of Social Security System in China: Review and Prospect*. Shanghai: Shanghai East Publishing Center, pp. 219–242 (in Chinese).

Zuo, X. J. and Hu, S. Y. (2001). "Urban Health Insurance System Reform in China: Role of the Government and the Market", *Social Sciences in China*, 5: 201–11 (in Chinese).

8 Social Policy in the Macao Special Administrative Region of China

A case of regulatory welfare regime

Dicky W. L. Lai

Introduction

From 1990 onwards, the debate over welfare regimes has revolved around Esping-Andersen's (1990, 1997) three worlds of welfare capitalism, comprising the liberal, the conservative-corporatist and the social democratic welfare regime. However, Esping-Andersen's welfare regimes have been criticised for only being applicable to "those capitalist states so strongly affected by their social policy" and have been deemed irrelevant to those states whose social policy is largely subordinate to other policies (Holliday, 2000: 708). Moreover, commentators point out that the basic features of welfare systems in East Asia are largely different from their counterparts in the West (Goodman and Peng, 1996; Kwon, 1997; White and Goodman, 1998). An increasing body of literature is emerging which suggests that the East Asian tiger economies, namely, South Korea, Taiwan, Hong Kong and Singapore, have distinct welfare models. These models include the East Asian social welfare regime of Goodman and Peng (1996), the Confucian welfare state of Jones (1993), the liberal and the conservative welfare models of Ramesh (2004), the conservative regime of Aspalter (2006), the productivist welfare regime of Holliday and Wilding (2003) and the developmental welfare state of Kwon (2005). Among these models, Kwon's welfare developmentalism is the most substantial as its existence has been reconfirmed by Lee and Ku's (2007) study.

Although Macao is located in East Asia, the city's current welfare model has not been explained by any of the East Asian welfare models reviewed above. This chapter sets out to fill such a long-standing research gap by identifying the specific features of Macao's social policy that typify its welfare regime. It also examines the extent to which those prominent welfare models can explain Macao's current welfare model. Because of the limitation of space, the scope of analysis of this study focuses only the social security and housing policies of Macao.

The city of Macao, dubbed the "Las Vegas of the East", is located on the south-east coast of China to the west of the Pearl River Delta. Macao's population was estimated to be 552,503 in 2011, and around 92 per cent of the inhabitants were of Chinese nationality (Macao Statistics and Census Service, 2012c). However, imported workers constituted a significant proportion of the population, and they numbered 94,028 as of December 2011 (Macao Statistics and Census Service, 2012a), which accounted for 17 per cent of the total population.

Before 1999, Macao was administrated by the Portuguese for over 170 years in political terms. On 20 December 1999, the People's Republic of China resumed the exercise of its sovereignty over Macao and proclaimed that the Macao Special Administrative Region (MSAR) was established. The MSAR has a limited democracy without universal suffrage for election of the chief cxecutive (CE) who is the authorised head of the MSAR government. Members of the Legislative Assembly (LA), which is the law-making body, are chosen through a combination of direct election, indirect election and appointment by the CE. The low level of democracy is largely attributed to the fact that the Macao Basic Law does not provide that both the CE and the LA will be ultimately elected by universal suffrage.

Since the early 2000s, Macao has witnessed robust economic growth and enjoyed a tourism and gambling boom. In 2010, its GDP per capita was US$51,214 and the unemployment rate was 2.8 per cent (Macao Statistics and Census Service, 2011b). Since the gambling industry has been the major source of Macao's economic development, direct taxes from the sector constituted an average of 70.8 per cent of the government's total revenue during the period 2008–10 (Macao Statistics and Census Service, 2011b). In other words, public and social services of the MSAR government are mainly financed from tax revenue from gambling.

This introductory section is followed by a brief description of the social welfare system of Macao. The third section is a discussion of two central but contradictory functions of social policy that define the uniqueness of a welfare regime. The fourth section comprises a discussion of the modifying effect of social policy and an examination on the modification impact of Macao's social policy on its capitalist social structure from an international perspective. The fifth section discusses in detail the regulatory role of social policy in maintaining the functioning of capitalism. The sixth section outlines the development of the city's social security and housing policies in the 2000s. This historical account is followed by an analysis of the regulatory roles of these policies in maintaining the development of the capitalist system of Macao. This chapter is concluded by suggesting the idea of a regulatory welfare regime and by explaining the major contributions of this study to the debate and discussion of welfare regimes.

Social policy in Macao

Like East Asian tiger economies, the MSAR government offers a range of welfare provisions to address social needs. The government implements a 15-year free education policy covering kindergarten to higher secondary schooling. In addition, eligible low-income families are entitled to receive a range of means-tested subsidies related to students' essential expenses, such as tuition subsidy and stationery subsidy. In the case of health care provision, Macao has one public hospital and several district health centres. Although the health centres provide a variety of free, universal primary health care services, the public hospital offers free services only for several social groups such as children, the elderly, the poor and cancer patients. In recent years, the Macao government has implemented a health care voucher scheme to subsidise medical services in private clinics. As far as personal welfare services is concerned, non-governmental organisations (NGOs) are the major provider of the services which are heavily subsidized by public funding. In addition to financing and monitoring the services provided by NGOs, government departments provide a range of services related to certain statutory duties, including medical social services, services for families experiencing domestic violence, and services for offenders and prisoners.

Macao's social security system consists of four types of programme. The first type is social insurance that is a contributory scheme for all citizens. The second is social assistance whose beneficiaries are confined to the deprived groups. Thirdly, the MSAR government provides social allowance payments for the elderly and disabled people. Fourthly, the government implements a temporary wage subsidy scheme for low-paid employees. In regard to housing policy, the government has four major forms of provision. The first is low-rent social housing units for low-income households with means-tested assessment. The second is a temporary rental allowance for households that are on a waiting list for social housing. Thirdly, the government implements a home ownership scheme under which the housing units are sold at prices much lower than their market value. Finally, the government provides two forms of support, a mortgage interest subsidy and a guaranteed house loan, which assist the eligible households to purchase housing flats in the property market.

The two contradictory functions of social policy

In the literature, it is acknowledged that social policy has two contradictory functions with respect to its effect on the social structure of capitalism. The first one can be understood as a *modifying function*, implying that social policy reforms part of the capitalist social structure or alters the basic operation of capitalism on the basis of socialist principles. Marshall (1981: 111) argues that the central role of social policy is "to supersede the market by taking goods and services out of it, or in some way to control and modify its operations so as to produce a result which it would not have produced of itself". In his view, the extension of social rights gives rise to "an invasion of contract by status, the subordination of market price to social justice, the replacement of the free bargain by the declaration of rights" (Marshall, 1950: 68). Briggs (2006: 16) notes that "a welfare state is a state in which organised power is deliberately used in an effort to modify the play of market forces".

In contrast, a group of commentators are sceptical of the achievement of social policy in reforming capitalism or altering its basic social structure in a fundamental way. Their central argument is that social policy is destined for "social and political control over the working class" in order to prevent their revolutionary action, the guarantee of interests of capital and the smooth functioning of capitalism (Midgley, 1997: 105). In other words, they argue for the *regulatory function* of social policy. In discussing the origin of the welfare state, Saville (1983: 13) asserts that certain provisions of social welfare are necessary for industrial capitalism "to work at full stretch". As Offe (1984: 154) notes, social policy is actually "a device to stabilise, rather than a step in the transformation of, capitalist society". Ginsburg's (1979: 2) assertion is that the main function of the welfare state is "fundamentally concerned with the maintenance and reproduction of capitalist social relations". According to Jones and Novak (1999: 140), various forms of welfare provision are important attempts "to secure the social relationships and ideologies that justified enduring poverty and inequality".

In fact, the modifying and regulatory functions of social policy coexist, although their natures are completely contradictory. While social policy modifies the capitalist social structure by promoting social equality, curtailing market dominance over individuals and empowering labourers against the coercion of their employers, the provisions of social welfare play an important part in securing the functioning of capitalism by resolving class conflicts, reproducing labour power and maintaining the core ethos of the market economy. As Gough (1979, 1983) notes, social policy performs the functions of accumulation, reproduction and legitimisation to secure the processes of capital accumulation, and, meanwhile, it brings detrimental effects on these processes because of its decommodifying impact and the utilisation of part of the resources available for reproducing capital. Offe (1984: 92, 147) argues that social policy plays a significant part in the "transformation of non-wage-labourers into wage-labourers" but also leads to a process of decommodification through which a certain degree of disincentive to investment and work is created. His well-known conclusion is that "while capitalism cannot coexist with, neither can it exist without, the welfare state" (Offe, 1984: 153).

Given the coexistence of the modifying and regulatory functions of social policy, the performance of these two functions plays a crucial role in defining the uniqueness of a welfare regime. Accordingly, we can identify two welfare regimes whose basic features of social policy are completely opposite. One of them has a strong modification effect on its capitalism social structure while the regulatory role of its social policy is less emphasised. Conversely, the other one is marked by a strong regulatory role of its social policy and its modification impact on the capitalist social structure is relatively less significant. As a result, the modification and regulatory effects of social policy can be used as two conclusive criteria for identifying the uniqueness of a welfare regime.

The modification impact on capitalist social structure

There are three important dimensions within the capitalist social structure on which social policy has a modifying impact: the decommodification of people, the promotion of personal autonomy and the abatement of class divisions. The important contribution of social policy to the decommodification of people has been widely acknowledged (see Marshall, 1963; Offe, 1984). Esping-Andersen notes that social policy plays an important role in combating the process of commodification of labourers by undermining the dominance of the market system. In his work, decommodification denotes the extent to which social policy makes people capable of obtaining "a socially acceptable standard of living independently of market participation" (Esping-Andersen, 1990: 37).

Secondly, personal autonomy refers to "the ability to make informed choices about what should be done and how to go about doing it" (Doyal and Gough, 1991: 53–54). It is argued that a range of welfare provisions play a significant role in guaranteeing the autonomy of individuals by offering a choice between working in paid jobs and depending on welfare payments (Goodin *et al.*, 1999). Thirdly, Marshall (1950) notes that the extension of social rights has altered the entire structure of the social inequality of capitalism by guaranteeing that people of different strata are all protected under the same social security plan, receiving the same package of social services, and having the right to enjoy common amenities. In Briggs' (2006: 16) view, the achievement of the welfare state with respect to the abatement of class divisions is that "all citizens without distinction of status or class are offered the best standards available in relation to a certain agreed range of social services".

Lai (2013) uses the concepts of decommodification of people, autonomy promotion and class abatement as measurement tools to compare the modification impact of social policy between Macao and six welfare states, which are the representatives of prominent welfare models in the West and East Asia. These welfare models include the social democratic regime, the conservative regime, the liberal regime, the South European regime, the Australasian workfare state and the (inclusive) developmental welfare state. The overall modification impact of social policy, which is measured with 10 indicators related to the provisions of social security, education and health care, and labour legislation, is expressed as an overall modification score. A higher overall modification score means a stronger modification impact.

The results of comparison with respect to the modification impact of the seven states are reported in Table 8.1. It shows that Macao, with an overall modification score of –1.99, achieved the poorest performance in modifying the capitalist social structure through its social policy. Macao was followed by the USA, which

Table 8.1 The modification effects of social policy on the capitalist social structure

Welfare regime	Representative case	Overall modification score
Social democratic	Sweden	0.70
Conservative	Germany	0.27
Liberal	USA	–1.76
Australasian workfare state	Australia	–0.46
South European	Italy	–0.08
Inclusive developmental welfare state	Korea	–1.01
	Macao	–1.99

Source: Lai (2013)

scored –1.76. Macao's score was also significantly lower than those of the other welfare states. Korea ranked fifth and scored –1.01, which was nearly half Macao's score in absolute value. This reveals that Macao does not appear to fit with the (inclusive) developmental welfare state in view of the difference in the modification impact between Macao and Korea. Lai's (2013) conclusion is that Macao should be identified as a distinct welfare regime.

The regulatory effect on a capitalist system

Lai (2008) suggests that the regulatory effect of social policy in particular can be achieved in three distinctive ways: disciplinisation, legitimisation and reproduction. Disciplinisation is the process in which people's minds and behaviours are controlled or shaped in accordance with the logic of market economy. At its heart is reinforcing work discipline and simultaneously penalising welfare dependence. Legitimisation refers to the process in which the capitalist social structure as a whole can be legitimised and, equally, political loyalty to the capitalist state can be secured. In capitalist societies, it is absolutely necessary for states to maintain the social stability that is an essential prerequisite for economic development and to sustain political legitimacy for perpetuating a pro-capitalist regime. Reproduction denotes the process of reproducing labour power to meet the requirements of perpetuating capitalism. In concrete terms, it includes a range of education, technical training and vocational retraining for both existing labourers and potential workforce in order that they are qualified to meet market demands.

The development of Macao's social policy in the 2000s

Expansion of social security provisions

Before the establishment of MSAR, Macao's social security system comprised two major programmes: the Social Security Fund (SSF) and Financial Assistance (FA). The SSF, which was introduced in 1990, is the major pillar of the city's social security system. It is funded triply by general revenue and contributions from both employees and employers. Since the SSF's monthly flat-rate contributions are extremely low (US$1.90 for employees and US$3.80 for employers in 2011), the major source of its income is from the government's allocation. The SSF offers a wide range of benefits to protect its members against different kinds of social contingency but their payment levels are low. For example, payment levels of Old-age Pension and Unemployment Benefit under the SSF were equivalent to 18.2 per cent and 19.1 per cent respectively of Macao's median wage in 2011 (Macao Statistics and Census Service, 2012b).

In response to the increasingly deteriorating employment conditions in Macao, the Portuguese government established an Assistance and Encouragement Scheme for the Local Unemployed with Special Difficulties (generally named the "Fifty Million Fund") under SSF in 1998, and then introduced Unemployment Relief (UR) in 1999. In the first few years after Macao's return to China, the MSAR government continued to expand the provisions for the unemployed population. In February 2001, the government introduced a social literacy course that was designed as a three-month education programme on basic literacy skills and civic knowledge for the unemployed. In 2002, the government launched a Four Hundred Million Fund for Vocational Training (FHMF) that was aimed at offering intensive vocational training for 4,000 unemployed persons. Two years later, the government initiated an Allowance for Supportive Training for Employment (ASTE) to replace the social literacy courses which had been blamed for their ineffectiveness in equipping trainees with job skills and for creating a problem of welfare dependency. The courses under the ASTE were more directly vocational training compared with the social literacy courses, and their main target was unemployed persons who had previously enrolled in the social literacy courses or their family members (Lai, 2009). As Macao's economy has performed very satisfactorily since the mid-2000s, these supportive programmes for the unemployed were almost terminated.

The MSAR government introduced the Old Age Allowance (OAA) in 2005, with the aim of showing the community's care for and promoting the virtue of respect for the elderly (Macao SAR Government, 2005). This allowance is provided to all Macao's citizens aged 65 or above. The OAA's payment was 1,200 patacas on a year term when it was introduced, and the rate was raised to 6,000 patacas in 2012.

Since the first quarter of 2008, the MSAR government has provided the Temporary Income Supplement (TIS) that is paid to full-time employees aged 40 or above whose average monthly income is less than an income threshold. The payment of the supplement is calculated as the difference between the income threshold and the employee's actual income. The income threshold was raised from 4,000 to 4,400 patacas in 2011 (Macao SAR Government, 2011a). The threshold can be regarded as a poverty line for the working poor despite the fact that the government has not established an official poverty line as such.

In 2010, the MSAR government introduced a non-mandatory Central Provident Fund (CPF), and opened an individual saving account under the scheme for all Macao's permanent citizens aged 22 or above. At the same time, the government deposited a sum of US$1,245 as "seed money" in all the CPF accounts (Macao SAR Government, 2009). Since then, the government has annually deposited a sum of money in all the accounts. Both of the government's allocations in 2011 and 2012 were the same amount of US$747. However, at the time of writing, the government has still not made any policy on the implementation of the CPF, such as regulations on contribution and fund management. In other words, the CPF has not performed its primary function of old-age financial security.

From limited to considerable scales of housing intervention

In the 2000s, there were two distinctive stages of the development of housing policy in Macao. The first stage, five years after Macao's return to China, was marked by a restricted scale of housing intervention of the MSAR government.

Before 1999, the Portuguese government had three main categories of social intervention in the area of housing. The first category was the provision of social housing for low-income families, a programme which could be traced back to the late 1920s. The second was the Home Ownership Scheme (HOS) which was introduced in 1984 and under which housing units are sold to families on a waiting list at prices much lower than their market value (Lai, 2009). Thirdly, the government has offered a 10-year mortgage loan interest subsidy (generally named the "Four Per Cent Interest Rate Subsidy") since 1996, with the purpose of "helping first-time buyers of private housing" (Chiang, 2005: 150). The provision of the Four Per Cent Interest Rate Subsidy came to an end in 2002.

In the first half decade of its administration, the MSAR government almost suspended the construction of public housing, including social housing and the HOS housing. Table 8.2 shows that the government only provided 1,197 and 62 units of the HOS housing and social housing respectively between 2001 and 2005. In these years, the total supply of public housing units was only equal to 7.4 per cent of the provisions in the period of 1991–2000. Because of such a low supply of public housing, there were 12,786 families on the waiting list for the HOS housing and 6,610 families waiting for the social housing as of May 2007 (Macao Housing Bureau, 2007). The government had two reasons for the suspension of public housing project. First, there was an oversupply of private housing flats in Macao. Second, the social demand for the HOS housing was inadequate, illustrated by the fact that a batch of the HOS housing units in 2003 was slow selling (Macao Housing Bureau, 2012).

The years after 2005 were the second stage of the development of housing policy in Macao. In this stage, the MSAR government played a more active role in providing public housing and other kinds of housing assistance. In 2005, the CE announced that the government would "build around 4,000 public housing flats within three years, and pursue the goal of building at least 6,000 flats within five years" (Macao Chief Executive, 2005: 27). Two years later, the government reaffirmed the position that it should try its utmost to meet citizens' housing needs in the context of the rapid development of Macao. The CE further made a greater promise that, in the following five years, 8,000–9,000 social housing units would be built and 10,000 public flats would be provided for sale (*Macao Daily News*,

Table 8.2 Provision of public housing units in Macao

	HOS housing	*Social housing*	*Total public housing units*
1971–80	/	270	270
1981–90	8,141	3,158	11,299
1991–2000	14,612	2,431	17,043
2001–10	1,565	2,213	3,778
(2001–5)	(1197)	(62)	(1259)
Total	24,318	8,072	32,390

Source: Macao Statistics and Census Service (2009, 2011b)

4 April 2007). This is known as 'the promise of 19,000 public housing units'. As at mid-2012, some of the public housing units had been sold or rented for the eligible families, and the rest were under construction.

Since September 2008, the MSAR government has provided a rental allowance for those eligible families on the waiting list for social housing, in order to relieve their heavy burden of housing expenses. There were two categories of monthly payment of the allowance when it was introduced: US$93 for 1- to 2-person families and US$137 for families with three or more members (Macao SAR Government, 2008). The payment levels were regularly revised, and they increased to US$156 and US$236 in 2011 (Macao SAR Government, 2011b).

In addition to the rental allowance which is targeted at low-income families, the MSAR government launched two supportive schemes for the purchase of private housing in 2009. First, the Home Purchase Loan Subsidy Scheme (HPLSS) provided a subsidy for the interest on mortgage repayments for private flats, like the previous Four Per Cent Interest Rate Subsidy. Second, the Home Purchase Guaranteed Loan Scheme (HPGLS), accompanied by the HPLSS, provided a credit protection of a maximum of 20 per cent of the housing price (Macao Housing Bureau, 2010). Their introduction is largely attributed to soaring housing prices in the private market over the second half of the 2000s. As the CE (Macao Chief Executive 2008: 23) noted, these two schemes working together were expected to "ease citizens" from the pressure of making a down payment for buying a new home, and the ensuing interest burden.

The regulatory functions of Macao's social policy

Economic and political contexts of the MSAR

From the mid-1970s to 1993, Macao experienced a "golden age" of economic development. The manufacturing sector was the locomotive of economic growth before the 1990s (Huang and Zheng, 1994). The sector fell into decline in the 1990s and has been replaced by the tourism and gambling industry as the key economic sector (Huang, 1999). Despite this, Macao's economic prosperity did not last beyond 1993. The GDP growth rate fell sharply from 30.9 per cent in 1992 to a negative 4.4 per cent in 1999, while the unemployment rate rose from 2.2 per cent to 6.3 per cent. The slowdown, coinciding with the Asian economic crisis, was mainly caused by the sluggish growth of commodity exports, the decline of construction and real estate due to the bursting of the bubble economy, and the stagnation of tourism following a decline in visitors from Hong Kong (Maruya, 1999). In the first three years of the 2000s, Macao's unemployment problem persisted and its unemployment rates were all over 6.0 per cent during this time (see Table 8.3).

Since 2002, the MSAR government has adopted a successful economic strategy: the gambling and tourism industry has been assigned the role of chief locomotive of economic growth (Macao Chief Executive, 2001). The MSAR government employed an open bid for three casino concessions in 2002. In the end, Sociedade de Jogos de Macau (SJM), Wynn Resorts (Macau) and the Galaxy Casino Company were the three winning concessionaires. The SJM was chaired by a local casino tycoon, Stanley Ho, who had held the gambling monopoly since the 1960s. While Wynn Resorts was owned by an American businessman, the Galaxy Casino Company was joint-owned by an American entertainment corporation and a Hong Kong property development company. These three concessionaires promised in their tenders that they would make investment of at least a total of US$2.18 billion in Macao (Macao Government Information Bureau, 2003). The huge sums of money caused an immediate and rapid expansion of casino, hotel and construction businesses, which in turn created abundant job vacancies in these sectors.

The Chinese central government's "facilitated individual travel" (FIT) policy introduced in 2003 was another driving force for Macao's economic growth. This policy provided a convenient way for the mainland's residents to travel and shop in Macao (Macao Government Information Bureau, 2004). It led to an immediate expansion of visitors from the mainland, playing a major role in fuelling the recovery of Macao's tourism in the second half of 2003 in spite of the outbreak of SARS in the East Asian region (Macao Chief Executive, 2003).

The MSAR government's liberation of the gambling industry working together with the FIT policy brought about a rapid and dramatic rebound of the economy. Table 8.3 shows that, from 2003 to 2008, all the GDP growth rates exceeded 10 per cent, and, in particular, the economy expanded by over 20 per cent in 2004,

Table 8.3 Macao's GDP growth rate and unemployment rate

	Nominal GDP growth rate (%)	*Unemployment rate (%)*
1991	15.8	/
1992	30.9	2.2
1993	14.8	2.1
1994	11.5	2.5
1995	12.1	3.6
1996	1.6	4.2
1997	0.4	3.2
1998	−7.1	4.6
1999	−4.4	6.3
2000	2.7	6.8
2001	1.4	6.4
2002	7.6	6.3
2003	12.9	6.0
2004	29.4	4.9
2005	14.8	4.1
2006	23.4	3.8
2007	24.5	3.1
2008	14.5	3.0
2009	2.4	3.6
2010	32.9	2.8

Source: Macao Statistics and Census Service (2011a, 2012d)

2006 and 2007. In the meantime, the unemployment rate fell steady from 6.8 per cent in 2000 to 3.0 per cent in 2008.

It is important to highlight the fact that the liberation of the gambling industry in Macao has resulted in a process of internationalisation of the economy, which is characterised by an expansion of foreign direct investment and a greater participation of multinational enterprises in the economy (Mishra, 1999). However, this does not imply that the MSAR government's capacity to manage the economy has diminished seriously or that its policy-making has been increasingly constrained by foreign investors. The government still has strict control over the workings of the gambling sector. For instance, the number of gambling tables that the concessionaires open in their casinos is controlled by the government.

In contrast to the prosperity of the tourism and gambling sector, the prospects for the manufacturing sector caused the MSAR government considerable concern. The government believed that the abolition of the global trading and quota system in textiles and garments in 2005 would have a negative impact on the exports of textile and garment products and cause massive unemployment in the sector. As the Secretary for Economy and Finance noted, "[a]pproaching 2005, the harmful impact of the abolition of the garments quota system on textile and garment industry and the related sectors [was] gradually coming up" (Macao SAR Government, 2001: 3).

Unlike most of the capitalist economies in the West, Macao's economy was not seriously hit by the global financial crisis of 2008–9. The city only experienced a slow growth of GDP and its unemployment rates were all below 4 per cent in 2008 and 2009.[1] Unexpectedly, the economy rebounded vigorously after the crisis. Macao's GDP grew by 32.9 per cent and the employment rate dropped rapidly to 2.8 per cent in 2010 (see Table 8.3).

However, the outstanding economic development of Macao since the early 2000s was accompanied by an escalation of housing prices. Table 8.4 shows that

Table 8.4 Average transaction price of residential units per square metre in Macao

Year	Average price (patacas)
2002	6,261
2003	6,377
2004	8,259
2005	11,621
2006	13,881
2007	20,729
2008	23,316
2009	23,235
2010	31,016

Note: The exchange rate of the US dollar to patacas is 1:8.034

Source: Macao Statistics and Census Service (2004, 2011a)

the average transaction price of residential units rose considerably from 6,261 patacas in 2002 to 23,316 patacas per square metre in 2008, an increase of 272 per cent. During the period of the global financial crisis, housing prices only had a short-term stagnation, and then experienced a significant rebound from 2009 to 2010 at a rate of 33.5 per cent.

Since the mid-1980s, the importation of foreign workers has been a controversial issue in Macao, incessantly igniting class conflict between capitalists and workers and, occasionally, posing a legitimacy problem for the government. Immediately after Macao's return to China, social grievances arising from unemployment continued to be focused on the issue of labour importation. There were several vigorous struggles against labour importation in mid-2000. In particular, three protest marches became violent confrontations between the protestors and the police, resulting in injuries to protesting workers and police officers, suspension of business in the city's busiest street and a serious threat to social stability. It was evident that the MSAR government was faced with a serious legitimacy problem and Macao society experienced severe social disorder. The depth of the sense of shock that these confrontations produced can be seen in the CE's comment that Macao society had not experienced this kind of intensive confrontation over the past 34 years (Lai, 2008).

The legitimacy problem of the MSAR government appeared to improve steadily from 2001. This was largely attributed to the recovery of Macao's economy and the consequent rapid improvement in employment conditions. As shown in Table 8.5, the rating of the CE rose from 70.9 in 2000 to 84.7 in 2004, while the proportion of people who were satisfied with the MSAR government's performance increased from 64 to 76 per cent.

Nevertheless, the MSAR government's popularity started to decline from 2005. Table 8.5 shows that the CE's rating fell to a bottom of 59.8 in 2007. While the

Table 8.5 Macao people's appraisals of the chief executive and the performance of the Macao SAR government

	1999	2000	2001	2002	2003	2004	2005	2006	2007	2008	2009
Rating of the CE	72.7	70.9	73.7	75.8	79.1	84.7	78.8	69.3	59.8	63.3	60.1
Satisfaction rate of the government's performance (%)	41	64	54	64	72	76	68	53	34.1	43.8	51.6
Dissatisfaction rate of the government's performance (%)	26	8	8	4	5	2	5	9	21.8	17.9	14.2

Source: Public Opinion Program of the University of Hong Kong (2007, 2009a, 2009b, 2010)

Table 8.6 Incidence of sizable protest marches in Macao (2003–2009)

Year	Number of protest marches involving 100 or more people
2003	0
2004	0
2005	5
2006	9
2007	12
2008	10
2009	5

Source: Macao Daily News (2003–2009)

satisfaction rate of the government dropped to 34.1 per cent, the proportion of people who were dissatisfied with the government's performance rose to 21.8 per cent in the same year. From 2007 onwards, the government's legitimacy problem showed a moderate improvement as a whole. For example, the government's satisfaction rate climbed to 51.6 per cent in 2009 despite the slight rise in the CE's rating.

Furthermore, the incidence of large-scale protest marches, defined as those events involving at least 100 protestors, was also indicative of the level of public dissatisfaction with the MSAR government's administration. There were no large-scale protest marches between 2003 and 2004, and their frequenciy rose to 9 in 2006, 12 in 2007 and then 10 in 2008 (see Table 8.6). The most frequent issues raised by the protestors included: settlement of adult children from the mainland in Macao; importation of labour and illegal workers; bureaucratic corruption; expansion of public housing provision; improvement in people's livelihood; and traffic problems (Lai, 2009).

In fact, the MSAR government was alerted to the problems of both its own legitimacy and significant social instability. As a consequence, "Building a Harmonious Society" was a central theme of the CE's policy address in 2007. As he noted, "we must prevent and ease social problems in a timely fashion, before demands accumulate . . . we must meet citizens' needs and expectations as far as possible. Only when people in all sectors are generally satisfied with overall aspects of social life can a complete, genuine, and sustainable social harmony be achieved" (Macao Chief Executive, 2006: 26).

There were four factors contributing significantly to the government's loss of political legitimacy. First, the MSAR government was deeply distrusted as regards its impartiality and incorruptibility since the disclosure of the bribery case of Ao Man Long, the former Secretary for Transport and Public Works. His case was widely believed to be only the tip of the iceberg in the whole government with respect to the problem of corruption. Secondly, there was a prevailing under-standing among the genral public that Macao's robust economic growth did not bring about a fair distribution of wealth among different social classes. It was widely perceived that the fruits of the economic boom mostly rested in the hands of the well-off. Thirdly, despite the low unemployment level, the government was blamed for its inability to safeguard local workers' rights and interests affected by the importation of massive numbers of foreign workers and employment of illegal workers. Finally, the government was seriously criticised as being unable to contain housing prices and rents and also for its inadequate provision of public housing to meet the enormous social needs (Lai, 2009).

The regulatory roles of social security policy

In the first few years of the MSAR government's administration, Lai (2010) points out that the policy initiatives of the SSF performed different regulatory roles in terms of social policy. The social literacy courses were expected to perform the function of legitimisation as they were launched against the background of uncontrollable social disorder caused by severe unemployment and a serious social discontent over the labour importation policy. As the Director of Labour Affairs evaluated, "the social literacy courses provided the SAR government a three-year period of stability so that it could consider and handle the issue of liberation of the gambling industry and the transformation of the STDM's employees. Their role in maintaining social stability could not be replaced by any other policies" (*Macao Daily News*, 20 January 2004).

The primary concern of the FHMF was to reproduce labour power in response to new demands for skilled workers resulting from Macao's economic transformation. In addition, the scheme was expected to prevent massive unemployment, which was caused by the abolition of the garments quota system, by enabling manufacturing workers to take jobs in other industrial sectors (Lai, 2010). As the CE explained, the FHMF aimed to arm trainees "with rich knowledge and stronger competitiveness to get or change jobs" and help them "to gain employment in tourism, services and other industries" (Macao Chief Executive, 2001: 26).

When Macao's economy had a sustainable rally and the MSAR government's political popularity improved steadily, the government introduced the ASTE to enforce work discipline by forcing social security recipients into work and tackling the problem of welfare dependence created by the social literacy courses (Lai, 2010). In other words, the scheme was expected to perform the function of disciplinisation. The Director of Labour Affairs explained that the primary purpose of the ASTE was to serve as a transitional arrangement to encourage trainees to re-engage in the labour market (*Macao Daily News*, 1 October 2004).

The expansion of Macao's social security provision in the second half of the 2000s, including the introductions of the TIS and the CPF, can be regarded as a strategy of legitimisation. As a result of its political popularity declining successively, it was necessary for the MSAR government to expand social security provision with the purpose of easing public discontent and maintaining social stability. In particular, the TIS and the CPF had more specific political functions that needed to be achieved apart from improving the economic security of the people. The problem of the working poor aroused a lot of public concern between

2007 and 2008 as low-income employees increased to a significant number. Social organisations and trade unions constantly asked for the minimum wage and provision of an income supplement to relieve the financial hardship of low-paid employees. The minimum wage was strongly opposed by employers as this policy would lead to a rise in their labour costs. Therefore it is not surprising that the government strived to release the political pressure arising from the problem of the working poor by introducing the TIS, which guarantees a minimum level of income for employees in the private sector (Lai, 2010).[2]

Two years after the introduction of the TIS, the Director of Labour Affairs evaluated that the scheme had more advantages than the minimum wage, which had been implemented in neighbouring cities. According to his explanation, the scheme could provide a basic level of income protection for employees, but had no impact on labour costs of middle and small enterprises. In addition, certain groups of workers whose competitiveness was relatively low had not lost their jobs after the scheme was implemented (*Macao Daily News*, 23 July 2010).

The significant political function of the CPF was that its introduction was a strategic response to labour's campaign for long-service payments when the Bill on General Regulations of Labour Relations was discussed and voted on in the Legislative Assembly. The long-service payment, which would increase the labour costs of employers, was eventually excluded from the new labour laws. Instead of the scheme, the MSAR government introduced the CPF to address the need for retirement protection of the working population. As the Secretary for Economy and Finance noted, the long-service payment was ineffective in providing adequate protection for elderly employees and their retirement protection should be strengthened by the reform of the social security system (including the introduction of the CPF) (Lai, 2010).

The regulatory role of the housing policy

It is noted earlier that the housing problem was one of the sources from which public dissatisfaction with the MSAR government's administration arose. In a survey conducted at the end of 2007, 23.9 per cent of the respondents chose "housing problem" to be the most pressing problem to be handled by the MSAR government in the following year, putting it at the top of the list (Public Opinion Programme of the University of Hong Kong, 2009a). The same survey in 2008 shows that 'housing problem', which followed "economic problem", was the second most pressing problem (Public Opinion Programme of the University of Hong Kong, 2009b). The same survey in 2009 indicates that "housing problem" went back to the top of the list, as 44.5 per cent of respondents wished the government to give first priority to the problem in 2010 (Public Opinion Programme of the University of Hong Kong, 2010). In fact, the MSAR government fully understood the political implication of this policy issue and responded that: ". . . local citizens are facing new difficulties about the cost of buying and renting housing. The MSAR Government is paying a high degree of attention to this issue; and we will work to draft new housing policies as soon as possible, on the basis of swift, comprehensive and objective evaluation" (Macao Chief Executive, 2005: 16).

Faced with a strong public expectation that it should make an effort to tackle the housing problem, the MSAR government announced two large-scale projects for public housing in 2005 and 2007. These housing projects were expected to perform the function of partially easing the government's legitimacy problem and maintaining social harmony. As the CE (2007: 19) noted, "Adequate housing and employment are the expectations of all Macao citizens, and achieving both is among the major tasks of building a harmonious society . . . Many residents face housing pressure, and are worried about the future. The MSAR Government is very concerned about this issue, and will try every means to resolve the problem."

Nevertheless, the government's public housing projects could not immediately provide a large number of housing units within one or two years. As political demand for its intervention in housing affairs was increasingly strong, it was impossible for the government to be hands-off, only looking forward the completion of the 19,000 public housing units. In addition, house prices had a significant rally immediately after the global financial crisis. As a result, the MSAR government was obliged to implement different measures to assist people of different classes to meet their housing needs in the market. While the temporary rental allowance aims to relieve the financial burden of rent expense on low-income families, the HPLSS and the HPGLS together assisted a batch of relatively better-off people to buy their houses in the private market. In conclusion, it is clear that the change of housing policy in the second half of the 2000s was largely driven by the government's intent of legitimisation. Even the third-term chief executive who took office in December 2009 highlighted the impact of housing problems on social harmony. As he noted, "Improving living conditions of low-income groups is an important bread-and-butter issue . . . The MSAR government will expedite construction of public housing. This is significant for improving people's livelihood and enhancing harmony in society. The construction of more public housing estates is a priority of our administration in this year, as well as in coming years" (Macao Chief Executive, 2010: 5).

Conclusion

This chapter started with a discussion of two contradictory functions of social policy in relation to its effect on the capitalist social structure – modifying and regulatory functions. It has been argued that the performance of these two basic functions of social policy defines the uniqueness of a welfare regime. In regard to the welfare regime of Macao, it has been shown that the modification impact of social policy on its capitalist social structure has been much weaker than that of the prominent welfare models. The historical account of Macao's social security and housing policies demonstrates that these two policies were expected to perform different regulatory functions for maintaining the development of the city's capitalist system: restoring the government's political legitimacy, maintaining social stability, reproducing labour power and maintaining labour discipline. In short, Macao's welfare regime is characterised by the low modification impact and the strong regulatory role of social policy. Therefore, it is suggested that Macao should be understood as a prototype of a *regulatory welfare regime*. This welfare regime is marked by a low level of the modification impact of social policy and a dominant role of social policy in securing the functioning of the capitalist system.

The idea of a regulatory welfare regime probably offers a new approach to studying welfare regimes in the East Asian region. The major characteristics of such a regime have been identified with specific reference to the modification impact and the regulatory role of social policy. Since the modifying and regulatory effects are two fundamental functions of social policy, it is argued that the construction of welfare models based on these two criteria is closely related to the very basic features of welfare states. The idea of a regulatory welfare regime probably offers a new approach to studying welfare regimes in the East Asian region. The major characteristics of the regime are identified with specific reference to the modification impact and the regulatory role of social policy. Since the modifying and regulatory effects are two fundamental functions of social policy, it is argued that the construction of welfare models based on these two criteria is closely related to the very basic feature of welfare states. When we study Scandinavian countries with this framework, we probably identify another welfare regime which has the strongest modification impact and plays a less dominant regulatory role in social policy, a sharp contrast to Macao's regulatory welfare regime.

Given that Macao's regulatory welfare regime is empirically supported, it is worth exploring whether Hong Kong is a "fit" with this regime. Macao and Hong Kong share similar political and social backgrounds, as the latter is widely known as a society with huge social inequalities and restricted development of social rights. Some scholars have identified the role of Hong Kong's social policy in promoting economic development or securing the market economy (Chan, 2003; Yu, 1996). It is probably the case that, similarly, Hong Kong's social policy has a relatively weak modification impact and performs effectively the function of regulating the development of its capitalist system.

There is little doubt that many social problems are rooted in the basic structure of capitalism, such as social inequalities, poverty and so forth. It is obvious that the dominance of the market system is a structural obstacle to social development in advanced capitalist economies. When the regulatory role of social policy is largely emphasised in the government's policy-making, it cannot be expected that people's welfare needs will be fully addressed. In Macao, for example, the beneficial rates of social security schemes are low and the problem of inadequate housing is still prevailing. Therefore, Macao society should strive for a social policy with a stronger modification effect on its capitalist social structure, in order to combat the prevailing social problems and promote social development. That is to say, social policy should play a more prominent role in freeing people from market dominance, promoting a greater degree of social equality and strengthening people's ability to make choices about their lifestyles and goals.

It is also interesting to note the effects of internationalisation on the making of social policy in Macao. Unlike the liberal welfare regimes' policy reforms following economic globalisation, namely the strategies of privatisation, marketisation and targeting (Esping-Andersen, 2007), the MSAR government expanded remarkably its intervention in the areas of social security and housing over its first decade of administration. As noted earlier, the inflow of foreign capital into the gambling industry and the related services sector was one of the driving forces for Macao's rapid economic development. This led to a sustained growth in public revenues and thus the MSAR government had adequate financial resources to expand the provision of social welfare, without imposing a higher tax burden on the business sector. It is unlikely that the government's policy-making was constrained by the external forces of the international of economy. Rather, the historical account has shown that the domestic political economy, i.e. the needs for regulation of Macao's capitalist system, still played a crucial role in shaping the development of social policy in the city. The conclusions drawn from this chapter are consistent with Mok and Ramesh's in Chapter 2, in that the MSAR has not had fundamental change in its social welfare model. But whether this model can sustain in the future is still an open question.

Notes

1 In fact, the major impact of the global financial crisis was a suspension of American investment projects in hotels and casinos. The most striking case was the Las Vegas Sands Corporation's suspension of the construction sites of two hotel projects owing to "problems in the credit markets" (*The Macau Post Daily*, 14 November 2008). However, the suspension did not significantly hit the economy and employment conditions of Macao even for a medium period of time.

2 Apart from the TIS, the government also established the minimum wage for those workers who were employed by contractors as cleaners or security guards in the public sector. The extra labour costs generated from this measure were solely financed by public funding.

References

Aspalter, C. (2006). "The East Asian Welfare Model", *International Journal of Social Welfare*, 15: 290–301.

Briggs, A. (2006). "The Welfare State in Historical Perspective", in C. Pierson and F. G. Castles (eds) *The Welfare State Reader* (2nd edn). Cambridge: Polity, pp. 16–29.

Chan, C. K. (2003). "Protecting the Ageing Poor or Strengthening the Market Economy: The Case of the Hong Kong Mandatory Provident Fund", *International Journal of Social Welfare*, 12: 123–131.

Chiang, C. M. (2005). "Government Intervention in Housing: The Case of Macao", *Housing Studies*, 20(1): 149–155.

Doyal, L. and Gough, I. (1991). *A Theory of Human Need*. Basingstoke: Macmillan.

Esping-Andersen, G. (1990). *The Three Worlds of Welfare Capitalism*. Cambridge: Polity Press.

Esping-Andersen, G. (1997). "Hybrid or Unique?: The Japanese Welfare State Between Europe and America", *Journal of European Social Policy*, 7(3): 179–189.

Esping-Andersen, G. (2007). "The Sustainability of Welfare States into the 21st Century", in R. Vij (ed.) *Globalization and Welfare: A Critical Reader*. Basingstoke: Palgrave Macmillan, pp. 50–59.

Ginsburg, N. (1979). *Class, Capital and Social Policy*. London: Macmillan.

Goodin, R. E., Headey, B., Muffels, R. and Dirven, H. J. (1999). *The Real Worlds of Welfare Capitalism*. Cambridge: Cambridge University Press.

Goodman, R. and Peng, I. (1996). "The East Asian Welfare States: Peripatetic Learning, Adaptive Change, and Nation-Building", in G. Esping-Andersen (ed.) *Welfare States in Transition: National Adaptations in Global Economics*. London: Sage, pp. 192–224.

Gough, I. (1979). *The Political Economy of the Welfare State*. London: Macmillan.

Gough, I. (1983). "Thatcherism and the Welfare State", in S. Hall and M. Jacques (eds) *The Politics of Thatcherism*. London: Lawrence & Wishart in association with Marxism Today, pp. 148–168.

Holliday, I. (2000). "Productivist Welfare Capitalism: Social Policy in East Asia", *Political Studies*, 48: 706–723.

Holliday, I. and Wilding, P. (2003). "Conclusion", in I. Holliday and P. Wilding (eds) *Welfare Capitalism in East Asia: Social Policy in the Tiger Economies*. New York: Palgrave Macmillan, pp. 161–182.

Huang, H. (1999). *Macao's Economy*. Beijing: Xin Hua Chu Ban She (in Chinese).

Huang, Q. and Zheng, W. (1994). *An Economic History of Macau*. Macao: The Macao Foundation (in Chinese).

Jones, C. (1993). "The Pacific Challenge: Confucian Welfare States", in C. Jones (ed.) *New Perspectives on the Welfare State in Europe*. London: Routledge, pp. 198–217.

Jones, C. and Novak, T. (1999). *Poverty, Welfare and the Disciplinary State*. London: Routledge.

Kwon, H. J. (1997). "Beyond European Welfare Regimes: Comparative Perspectives on East Asian Welfare Systems", *Journal of Social Policy*, 26(4): 476–484.

Kwon, H. J. (2005). "An Overview of the Study: The Developmental Welfare State and Policy Reforms in East Asia", in H. J. Kwon (ed.) *Transforming the Developmental Welfare State in East Asia*. New York: Palgrave Macmillan, pp. 1–23.

Lai, D. (2010). "The Political Economy of Social Security Development in Macao", *China Journal of Social Work*, 3(1): 65–81.

Lai, D. W. L. (2013). "Macao's Welfare Model: An Extreme World of Welfare Capitalism?", *International Social Work* (forthcoming).

Lai, W. L. D. (2008). "The Regulatory Role of Social Policy: Macao's Social Security Development", *Journal of Contemporary Asia*, 38(3): 373–394.

Lai, W. L. D. (2009). *Macao's Social Welfare Model: A Prototype of a Regulatory Regime*. Hong Kong: The University of Hong Kong.

Lee, Y. J. and Ku, Y. W. (2007). "East Asian Welfare Regimes: Testing the Hypothesis of the Developmental Welfare State", *Social Policy and Administration*, 41(2): 197–212.

Macao Chief Executive (2001). *Policy Address for the Fiscal Year 2002 of the Government of the Macao Special Administrative Region of the People's Republic of China*. Macao: Macao Special Administrative Region Government.

Macao Chief Executive (2003). *Policy Address for the Fiscal Year 2004 of the Government of the Macao Special Administrative Region of the People's Republic of China*. Macao: Macao Special Administrative Region Government.

Macao Chief Executive (2005). *Policy Address for the Fiscal Year 2006 of the Government of the Macao Special Administrative Region of the People's Republic of China*. Macao: Macao Special Administrative Region Government.

Macao Chief Executive (2006). *Policy Address for the Fiscal Year 2007 of the Macao Special Administrative Region of the People's Republic of China*. Macao: Macao Special Administrative Region Government.

Macao Chief Executive (2007). *Policy Address for the Fiscal Year 2008 of the Macao Special Administrative Region of the People's Republic of China*. Macao: Macao Special Administrative Region Government.

Macao Chief Executive (2008). *Policy Address for the Fiscal Year 2009 of the Government of the Macao Special Administrative Region of the People's Republic of China*. Macao: Macao Special Administrative Region Government.

Macao Chief Executive (2010). *Policy Address for the Fiscal Year 2010 of the Macao Special Administrative Region of the People's Republic of China*. Macao: Macao Special Administrative Region Government.

Macao Daily News (2004, 20 January). "Maintain social stability in order to buy time for the SAR government, Director of Labour Affairs: social literacy courses are good despite some criticisms", p. A03 (in Chinese).

Macao Daily News (2004, 1 October). "Macau Unemployment Population Survey in Progress. Director of Labour Affairs: not expand retaining courses", p. B10 (in Chinese).

Macao Daily News (2007, 4 April). "20,000 Flats will be Built in Five Years, Immigration by Housing Purchase Stopped, Age Eligible for Social Insurance Reduced to 60. Chief Executive Wants to Reduce Public Grievance", p. A06 (in Chinese).

Macao Daily News (2010, 23 July). "Director of Labour Affairs: Temporary Income Supplement Better than Minimum Wage, Urge Workers to Report Employers Who abuse the System", p. B02 (in Chinese).

Macao Government Information Bureau (2003). *Macao Yearbook 2003*. Macao: Macao Special Administrative Region Government.

Macao Government Information Bureau (2004). *Macao Yearbook 2004*. Macao: Macao Special Administrative Region Government.

Macao Housing Bureau (2007). *Consultation Paper on Amendments of the Laws Related to Public Housing*.

Macao Housing Bureau (2010). *Home Purchase Guaranteed Loan Scheme*. Available at: http://www.ihm.gov.mo/en/page/index.php?id=26.

Macao Housing Bureau (2012). *Consultation Paper on the Development of Public Housing Policy (2011–2020)*.

Macao SAR Government (2001). *Minutes of the Legislative Assembly, Group 1, Vol. II–10*. Macao: Macao Legislative Assembly.

Macao SAR Government (2005). *Administrative Law No. 12/2005*.

Macao SAR Government (2008). *Administrative Law No. 23/2008*.

Macao SAR Government (2009). *Administrative Law No. 31/2009*.

Macao SAR Government (2011a). *Administrative Law No. 7/2011*.

Macao SAR Government (2011b). *Administrative Law No. 32/2011*.

Macao Statistics and Census Service (2004). *Yearbook of Statistics 2003*.

Macao Statistics and Census Service (2009). *Construction Statistics 2008*.

Macao Statistics and Census Service (2011a). "Time Series Database". Available at: http://www.dsec.gov.mo/TimeSeriesDatabase.aspx.

Macao Statistics and Census Service (2011b). *Yearbook of Statistics 2010*.

Macao Statistics and Census Service (2012a). *Employment Survey 4th Quarter 2011*.

Macao Statistics and Census Service (2012b). *Employment Survey 2011*.

Macao Statistics and Census Service (2012c). *Global Results of Census 2011*.

Macao Statistics and Census Service (2012d). *Gross Domestic Product 2011*.

Marshall, T. H. (1950). *Citizenship and Social Class*. Cambridge: University Press.

Marshall, T. H. (1963). *Sociology at the Crossroads and Other Essays*. London: Heinemann.

Marshall, T. H. (1981). *The Right to Welfare and Other Essays*. London: Heinemann.

Maruya, T. (1999). "Macroeconomy: Past, Present, and Prospects", in J. A. Berlie (ed.) *Macao 2000*. Oxford: Oxford University Press, pp. 123–144.

Midgley, J. (1997). *Social Welfare in Global Context*. Thousand Oaks, CA: Sage.

Mishra, R. (1999). *Globalization and the Welfare State*. Cheltenham: Edward Elgar.

Offe, C. (1984). *Contradictions of the Welfare State*. Cambridge, MA: MIT Press.

Public Opinion Programme of the University of Hong Kong (2007). *HKU POP SITE releases the latest popularity figures of Macau CE Edmund Ho and the Macau SAR Government*. Available at: http://hkupop.hku.hk (in Chinese).

Public Opinion Programme of the University of Hong Kong (2009a). *Macau Tracking Survey 2007 – Frequency Tables*. Available at: http://hkupop.hku.hk (in Chinese).

Public Opinion Programme of the University of Hong Kong (2009b). *Macau Tracking Survey 2008 – Frequency Tables*. Available at: http://hkupop.hku.hk (in Chinese).

Public Opinion Programme of the University of Hong Kong (2010). *Macau Tracking Survey 2009 – Frequency Tables*. Available at: http://hkupop.hku.hk (in Chinese).

Ramesh, M. (2004). *Social Policy in East and Southeast Asia*. London: RoutledgeCurzon.

Saville, J. (1983). "The Origin of the Welfare State", in M. Loney, D. Boswell and J. Clarke (eds) *Social Policy and Social Welfare*. Milton Keynes: Open University Press.

The Macau Post Daily (2008, 14 November). "Venetian axes 9,000 imported workers, mothballs two sites 2,000 local employees awaiting relocation within company", p. P01.

White, G. and Goodman, R. (1998). "Welfare Orientalism and the Search for an East Asian Welfare Model", in R. Goodman, W. Gordon and H. J. Kwon (eds) *The East Asian Welfare Model: Welfare Orientalism and the State*. London: Routledge, pp. 3–24.

Yu, S. W. K. (1996). "The Nature of Social Services in Hong Kong", *International Social Work*, 39(4): 411–430.

9 Old age care concerns and state–society relations in China

Public anxiety and state paternalism

Lijun Chen and Dali L. Yang

Introduction

A revolution in rising expectations is happening in China. For more than three decades China has enjoyed a remarkable period of hyper-growth and this growth has helped the Chinese ruling elite enjoy an extraordinary level of public support (Shi 2001; Tang 2005). Against the background of the global economic crisis and continuing Chinese economic buoyancy, it is no surprise that the Chinese public continues to show such support for the country's direction of development (see Figure 9.1). According to a tracking opinion survey conducted by Horizon Research Consultancy Group, one of China's leading independent survey organisations, the percentage of respondents who said they approved of China's direction of development (as well as the country's economic situation, not shown here) has been at nearly 80 per cent between 2004 and 2010, dipping only slightly in 2010.

Yet the same survey series shows strikingly different results when the respondents were asked to indicate their sense of happiness. As can be seen from Figure 9.2, the percentage of respondents who said they were happy has steadily declined from just under 80 per cent in 2004 to under 50 per cent in 2010, even while China's overall economic performance has held steady. We hold it that these contrasting numbers suggest rising expectations. Again and again, Chinese officials have pushed for growth and rushed the completion of projects ahead of time for political reasons; such efforts, such as the drive to build the world's largest high-speed rail network, have often had undesirable side-effects and sometimes dire consequences. Indeed, in a time of unparalleled prosperity, growing numbers of Chinese have become disenchanted with the undesirable side-effects of China's hyper-growth, including high income inequality, corruption and environmental degradation. Following a deadly train crash near Wenzhou on 23 July 2011, Tong Dahuan (童大焕), a columnist for the *Oriental Daily*, captured the sentiment of the nation with a tweet:

> Oh China, may you please slow down your pace and pause your flying feet; wait for your people, wait for your soul, wait for your morality, wait for your conscience! Don't let the trains derail, don't make the bridges collapse, don't turn the roads into traps, don't allow the houses become ones of danger. Go a

bit slower, let every life have freedom and dignity, let no one be left behind by "the era", and make every one reach the final destination safely![1]

More generally, the writer Yan Lianke (阎连科) has conveyed the sense of uncertainty a growing number of Chinese have felt:

> [I am] fearful, but don't know why and of what, this is the feeling in my heart and that of many others. The powerful are fearful, so are the powerless; those who have jobs are fearful, so are the jobless; the poor are fearful, so are the rich; the elderly are fearful, so are the children. The whole society and everyone are enveloped in fear, but nobody knows why, this is the true state of the psychology and plight of today's Chinese.[2]

It turned out the sense of fear and uncertainty that Mr Yan wrote about was not misplaced. Only a few months later, Mr Yan himself became the victim of harassment and possible eviction in Beijing when his house suddenly faced demolition.[3]

One of the growing challenges and anxieties facing Chinese families and the country as a whole is how to take care of the old. The State Council plan for the aged (2011–2015) notes that China has entered a period of accelerated population ageing. According to official figures, the number of people at or above 60 is expected to grow from 178 million in 2011 to 221 million in 2015, an average increase of 8.6 million per year. As a result, the percentage of the population accounted for by seniors at or above the age of 60 will increase from 13.3 per cent in 2011 to 16 per cent in 2015.[4] Having confronted China's surging population with the world's most extensive system of coercive family planning, the Chinese

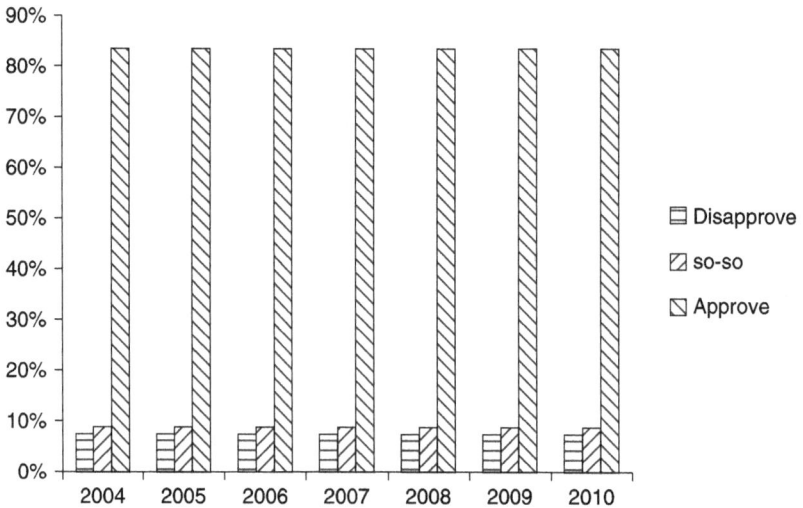

Figure 9.1 Percentage of respondents approving of the developmental direction in China.

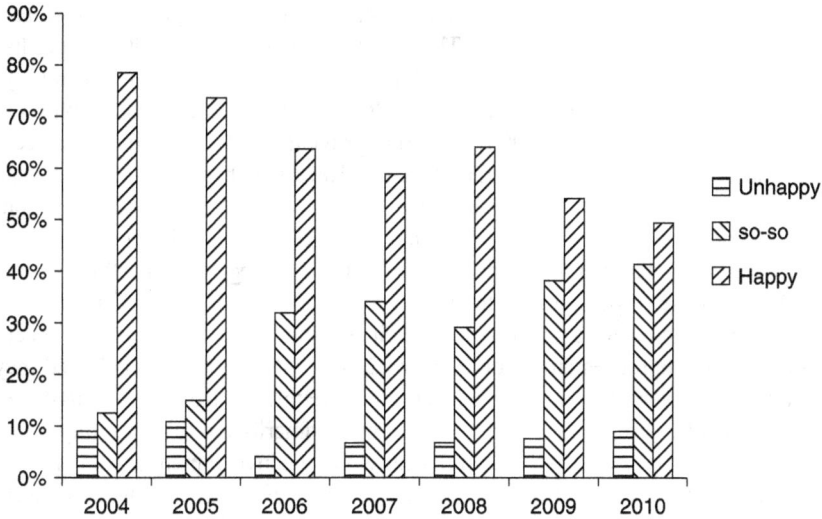

Figure 9.2 Percentage of respondents feeling happy or unhappy in various years.

government now faces the daunting consequence of that policy, namely to provide for the retirement and old age care of a growing proportion of the national population.[5]

There is currently no systematic examination of the patterns and temporal evolution of concerns about financial dependence in old age and old age in general for Chinese residents. In this study, we seek to fill this lacuna through an analysis of a multi-year sample survey of urban and rural residents in China. In doing so, our analyses will not only help us understand changing public attitudes toward old age care in China but will also provide a useful lens through which we can better understand public attitudes about the role of the state and thus state–society relations.

Context and literature review

As more and more societies age, scholars have paid increasing attention to the study of ageing anxiety, that is, people's fears or concerns about getting older and having adequate old age care. Using data from a 1994 survey of 1,200 US adults, Lynch (2000) found that those with better education, higher income, better health and more knowledge about the ageing process had significantly less ageing anxiety. A major concern for most people is financial dependence, i.e., fears of being unable to support oneself in old age or pay for health care costs. A more recent study of a survey sample of American baby boomers also finds that people with better education and income and in good health show less anxiety about ageing than those who are poor, less educated and in ill health (Yan *et al.* 2011).

National economic conditions have a direct impact on people's income and wealth and thus the level of public concern about care in old age often fluctuates with national economic conditions. The Great Recession in the United States has caused severe financial distress to many households because of soaring unemployment, negative home equity and investment losses. It has also dealt major blows to pensions and prompted calls for reforms to improve the viability of the social security system. It is thus no surprise that the Great Recession has induced widespread anxiety about retirement. According to a Gallup study, the percentage of non-retired Americans who believe they will have enough money to live comfortably in retirement plummeted from 59 per cent in 2004 to 41 per cent in 2009 (Gallup 2009). For those respondents in the 50–62 age bracket with formal employment, more than half indicated a desire to delay their retirement. Partly because of concern about inadequate retirement income, over 22 per cent of US adults believed they would need to work part-time in their retirement (Hurd and Rohwedder 2010).

Traditionally care of the elderly in China was primarily the responsibility of the extended family in both urban and rural areas with little involvement or support from the government. Following the Communist takeover of power and the subsequent push to promote a centrally planned economy, the individual in urban areas was soon enmeshed into state-controlled work units such as state-owned enterprises (SOEs) and collective enterprises that offered employment as well as health care and retirement benefits (Walder 1986). Rural areas were under the thrall of communes and production brigades that offered far less social welfare than in urban areas.

The introduction of market-oriented reforms in the post-Mao era has brought both growing prosperity and greater uncertainty. Most importantly, the urban state enterprise sector has gone through massive restructuring in response to competition from foreign and non-state firms. Millions of former SOE employees lost their jobs as well as the health care and retirement benefits that were tied to those jobs (Gold *et al.* 2009). Since the late 1990s, facing rising discontent among laid-off former SOE workers, the Chinese government has sought to offer some measure of social protection, including unemployment benefits and a minimum livelihood guarantee (*zuidi shenghuo baozhang*).

Meanwhile, to provide for the retirement benefits for the large number of retirees from existing and reorganised SOEs and the retirement needs of employees from the flourishing non-state sector, local governments throughout China, under the guidance from the central government, have adopted a new basic retirement insurance (*jiben yanglao baoxian*) system composed of a "social pool" with funds paid by employers and government subsidies and an "individual account" from employee salary deductions and employer matching funds (Frazier 2010). By the end of first decade of this century, the retirement insurance funds in many provinces had been centralised at the provincial level, and cover employees of both the state and private sectors. Meanwhile, through a separate civil service pension system, employees of government agencies and affiliated public institutions can enjoy more pension payments than workers in the enterprise sector. Between 2009–2011, the central government began to vigorously promote a retirement scheme for rural residents and those urban residents not covered under existing pension or social insurance systems. With individual contributions and government supplements, this social insurance scheme would guarantee those aged 60 or above a monthly payment of no less than 55 yuan per month (in both rural and urban areas). Premier Wen Jiabao vowed that the system would be extended to cover the entire country by the end of his term in 2012.

Even with the recent developments to extend coverage to previously neglected populations, the weaknesses and deficiencies of the existing arrangements are also glaring. The various urban area-based retirement benefit systems are fragmented along municipal lines and portability remains a forlorn hope. The urban retirement insurance programmes cover most urban workers and retirees, but the participation rate is much lower among migrant workers due to their job instability and portability concerns (Jackson *et al.* 2009). Facing the legacy cost of large number of SOE retirees and limited investment channels for appreciation, the social insurance funds in many regions are seriously underfunded and it is not unusual for some local authorities to "borrow" funds from personal retirement accounts to meet current payout needs (Ye 2011). According to the *2011 Report on the Development of China's Retirement Pension*, the retirement insurance systems in 15 provinces are unable to meet current liabilities from current contributions. The shortfall of as much as 67.9 billion yuan has to be covered by local and central government subsidies (Xia 2011). The situation will only worsen over time in the absence of significant reforms.

China's rapid demographic transition to an ageing society is expected to add further to the strains facing the current system of retirement and elderly care. According to the 2000 China census, those over 65 years accounted for 8.9 per cent of the entire population then, but this rate is predicted to rise to over 20 per cent in 2030, matching that of the United States (Jackson *et al.* 2009). The shrinking size of the household means that traditional family support for the elderly is simply not going to be tenable. Rapid urbanisation has compounded such strains. Over 200 million rural residents have migrated to urban areas in search of work and better income, often leaving behind their elderly parents in the countryside fending for themselves (Liu 2010).

Yet, as the Chinese economy has soared and living standards have increased, expectations about retirement have also risen. According to a 2010 survey by HSBC of over 1,000 urban working adults in China, over 80 per cent of the respondents thought they would be better off in retirement than their parents' generation (HSBC Insurance China 2011). Meeting the growing public expectations about retirement for a rising tide of retirees could seriously dent the government's finances and strain state–society relations. Under the rubric of improving the people's livelihood, the Chinese leadership, as noted above, has committed to provide universal access to a modicum of social insurance, including for rural residents. Yet such modest payments may not have served to ease public concerns about having adequate provision for retirement and elderly care and may paradoxically activate fears among a subgroup of the population about the growing costs of retirement and old age care.

Considering the concerted efforts by Chinese central and local governments in establishing more inclusive pension and health care schemes in recent years and the importance of such schemes not only in providing a decent quality of life for retirees but also in helping to preserve social peace, it is useful to examine the patterns of public concern about old age care and the implications such patterns may hold for public policy and state–society relations.

Survey description and research questions

Administered annually since 2000, the Chinese Residents' Life Quality Index Survey, conducted by the independent survey research organisation Horizon Research Consultancy, aims to collect information on people's perception of various aspects of their lives and their opinions on social and economic policy issues. Each year, about 20 locations, including cities, small towns and rural villages, are selected throughout China and, with some exceptions, most locations are included from year to year. Then a sample of households is selected from the survey locations through a multi-stage cluster sampling method, and an adult respondent from 18 to 60 years old is selected randomly from the sample household.

Figure 9.3 shows the survey locations from 2005 to 2010 on a map of China. Even though the survey locations were not selected randomly, they nonetheless come from different parts of the country, including major coastal cities such as

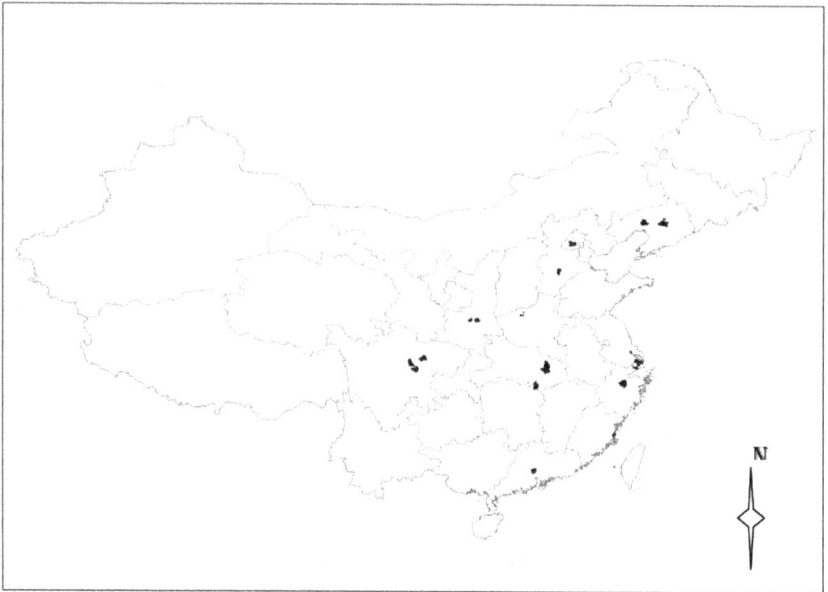

Figure 9.3 Locations of Horizon surveys from 2005 to 2010 shown on a map of China

Note: The highlighted areas are counties and urban districts where the surveys are conducted. In cities, only their central districts (two or more) are covered in the surveys; in counties, the surveys cover the town where the county government seat is located and several rural villages.

Guangzhou and Shanghai, small towns and rural areas.[6] Because of the different sampling ratios (i.e. proportion of population selected in the sample) of the survey locations, statistical weights are generated to make each sample representative of the population of all survey locations. Further weighting is applied to the urban and rural samples separately to make them more representative of the national distribution of the population in rural and urban areas.

By analysing the Horizon survey data, we expect to address several research questions in this study. First, what is the proportion of Chinese residents who are concerned about their care in old age? Second, how does the level of concern vary systematically among people with different demographic characteristics and socio-economic status? Third, what is the temporal trend in the proportion of concerned residents? Fourth, does the trend differ among people of different demographic and social characteristics? On the basis of answers to these questions, we hope to probe the larger implications for Chinese governance and state–society relations.

Data and methods

From 2005 to 2010, the Horizon survey included two questions that gauged respondents' concerns about care in old age: (a) Are you concerned about the issue of "who will care for you when you are old"?; (b) Are you concerned about the expenses or costs of caring for you in old age?[7] The respondents could choose from one of four possible responses: (1) very worried, (2) relatively worried, (3) not very worried, and (4) not worried at all; they could also volunteer the answer "so-so", which became the de facto "neutral category".[8] In this study we collapse the five responses into three categories, "worried", "so-so" and "not worried", but it is worthwhile to note that few respondents answered that they were "very worried" or "not worried at all". Less than 4 per cent of observations in each year have missing or invalid answers and these are excluded from the analysis. To make the findings representative of the national population, all descriptive and statistical analysis is weighted by the proportional weights provided in the survey data.

We include the following personal and socio-economic characteristics in our analysis: respondent's age, gender, education, urban or rural residency, household income and occupation. A respondent's education can be at one of five levels: primary school or lower, middle school, high school or vocational school, two-year college, college or above. Household income includes monetary and in-kind incomes of all household members per month. Besides differences in urban/rural residency, we also classify urban residents into those in cities (large metropolitan areas with a population of over 1 million) and those in towns (mostly the urban centre of a county or county-level city, where the county government operates). The classification of occupations is more fraught and Chinese sociologists have in recent years made strenuous efforts to better measure stratification through occupation (e.g., Li 2005). Based on our understanding of occupational prestige in China, we group occupations into seven categories: (1) high and mid-level government administrators, corporate owners and managers, and high-level professionals; (2) government and corporate employees, office clerks and general professionals; (3) manual workers/labourers, and sales clerks; (4) self-employed small proprietors or vendors; (5) retirees; (6) farmers; and (7) students, unemployed or not working.

Table 9.1 shows the weighted distribution of the covariates included in the study for each year from 2005 to 2010. Even though the period covered in this study is for five years only, the numbers indicate significant temporal variations that reflect the breakneck speed of China's development. In step with the rise in per capita income in China, we note that the weighted proportion of respondents with less than 1,000 yuan of monthly household income has decreased dramatically, while the proportions of higher income categories have increased. The level of education has also increased and the weighted proportion of respondents with a primary school education or less has significantly decreased, while the proportion with a high school education has increased. Rapid urbanisation driven by rural-to-urban migration continues to reshape the rural–urban demographic landscape; between 2005 and 2010, the proportion of residents living in cities increased from 37 to 46 per cent while the proportion living in rural areas has dropped from 63 to 54 per cent.

Findings on concerns about cost of old age care

We now examine the data on respondents' concerns about care in old age. Figure 9.4 clearly indicates that the weighted proportion of respondents who are worried about old age care arrangements (i.e., who care for me?) has nearly doubled from 24 per cent in 2005 to 46 per cent in 2010 ($\chi2=441$, $df=1$, $p<.0001$), and the proportion concerned about the cost of old age care has risen from 27 per cent in 2005 to 43 per cent in 2010 ($\chi2=236$, $df=1$, $p<.0001$). Considering that per capita incomes have generally increased during this period, the rising concern about old age care is especially noteworthy. Interestingly, the proportions of respondents worried about caregiver availability in old age and the cost of old age care closely track each other for the period covered by the survey and are highly correlated.[9] Given such similarity, we focus our attention on concerns about the cost of old age care first.

As we prepare to further dissect the survey data, we expect that, with their superior pension coverage and other forms of social insurance, urban residents in general and government employees in particular should be less concerned about financial dependence in old age. By the same logic, those with higher socioeconomic status, including higher household income and more schooling, should be less worried about care in old age. We also expect that young people would be less worried about old age care because for them the shadow of the future is more distant.

As an initial step in our analysis, Table 9.2 presents, for the years of 2005, 2008 and 2010, the weighted proportions of respondents in different categories of covariates who are worried about the cost of old age care. First, we note the

Table 9.1 Weighted percentage of respondents for different covariates in each year

Covariate	Category	Year of survey						
		2005	2006	2007	2008	2009	2010	Total
Gender	Male	48%	49%	48%	49%	49%	49%	49%
	Female	52%	51%	52%	51%	51%	51%	51%
Age	18 thru 30	26%	24%	21%	22%	25%	28%	25%
	31 thru 40	28%	27%	29%	28%	26%	26%	27%
	41 thru 50	25%	28%	31%	28%	28%	27%	28%
	51 thru 60	21%	20%	19%	22%	21%	19%	20%
Education	Primary school or less	23%	21%	22%	21%	18%	15%	20%
	Middle school	43%	43%	39%	44%	43%	40%	42%
	High school/vocational school	23%	26%	27%	25%	28%	31%	27%
	Two-year college (*dazhuan*)	7%	7%	8%	7%	8%	10%	8%
	College graduate or above	4%	4%	3%	3%	3%	4%	4%
Region	City	24%	24%	24%	24%	24%	25%	24%
	Small town	13%	13%	13%	19%	20%	21%	17%
	Rural village	63%	63%	63%	57%	55%	54%	59%
Urban/rural	Urban	37%	37%	37%	43%	45%	46%	41%
	Rural	63%	63%	63%	57%	55%	54%	59%
Occupation	High-level administrator, manager and professional	3%	4%	4%	6%	5%	5%	4%
	Ordinary government and corporate employee, clerk, professional	12%	13%	8%	9%	8%	10%	10%
	Manual worker, sales personnel, peasant labourer	8%	13%	16%	18%	23%	23%	17%
	Self-employed small proprietor and vendor	16%	12%	13%	16%	21%	24%	17%
	Retiree	5%	4%	4%	3%	3%	3%	3%
	Farmer	38%	43%	46%	44%	34%	26%	38%
	Not working, jobless, student	19%	11%	10%	5%	7%	8%	10%
Family Income	Less than 1,000 yuan	48%	37%	30%	29%	30%	23%	33%
	1,001 to 3,000 yuan	33%	44%	48%	46%	40%	38%	41%
	3,001 to 5,000 yuan	8%	12%	15%	16%	18%	20%	15%
	Over 5,000 yuan	11%	7%	7%	8%	12%	19%	11%
Total		**100%**	**100%**	**100%**	**100%**	**100%**	**100%**	**100%**

Note: Except for gender, Chi-square tests indicate significant differences ($p < 0.05$) in the distribution of the covariates for the different years.

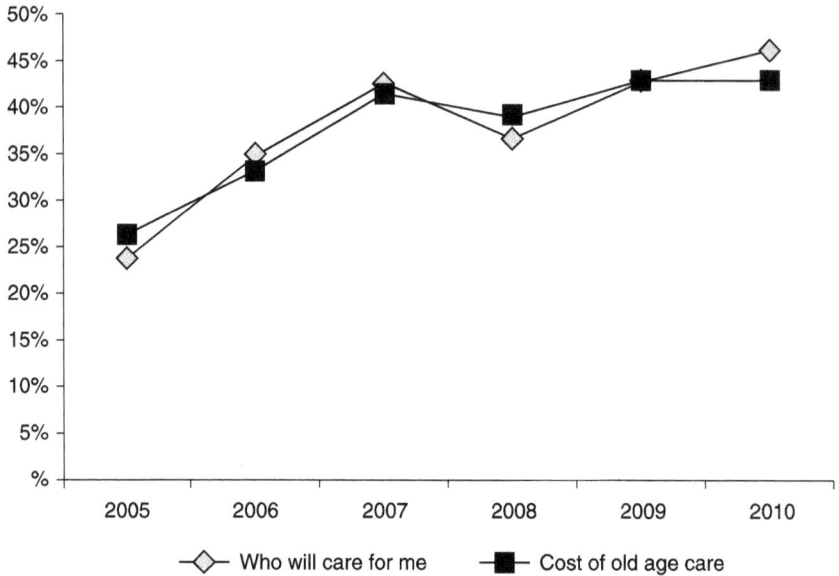

Figure 9.4 Weighted percentage of respondents worried about old age care and its cost in China.

Note: The percentage for 2007 is higher than 2006 and 2008 partly because respondents are not allowed to answer "so-so" as in other years. Therefore, some respondents who may answer "so-so" are forced to answer "worried", thus increasing its percentage.

substantial increase in the level of concern about the cost of old age care for respondents in all categories of each covariate, including people with high family income and education. Second, with a few exceptions, chi-square tests confirm a significant association between the covariates and respondents' concerns about old age care in each of the three years.

In both 2005 and 2010, a higher proportion of women than of men expressed concern. The association of age with concerns about old age care is significant but not linear. Among the age groups, less than one third of respondents younger than 30 showed concern about old age care; those in their 40s are the most worried, with nearly half claiming to be worried in 2010.

In general socio-economic indicators are correlated with expressed concerns about old age care as expected, with more of those with the least education and more of those with lower income showing worries about old age care in comparison with those with higher education and higher income. Yet it appears that government policies have reshaped public attitudes. For 2005 and 2008, a much higher proportion of those with the lowest household income express concern but with greater government efforts to promote basic social insurance such as the minimum livelihood guarantee, the percentage of respondents in the lowest

Table 9.2 Weighted percentage of respondents worried about old age care by personal characteristics

Covariate	Category	2005	2008	2010	p value
Gender	Male	25%	39%	40%	.010/.711/<.001
	Female	28%	40%	45%	
Age	18 thru 30	16%	32%	33%	<.001/<.001/<.001
	31 thru 40	31%	39%	47%	
	41 thru 50	29%	44%	49%	
	51 thru 60	31%	40%	43%	
Education	Primary school or less	35%	45%	47%	<.001/<.001/<.001
	Middle school	26%	41%	46%	
	High school/vocational school	25%	36%	40%	
	Two-year college (dazhuan)	21%	29%	35%	
	College graduate or above	10%	22%	36%	
Region	City	28%	38%	50%	<.001/<.001/<.001
	Small town	19%	33%	42%	
	Rural village	28%	42%	40%	
Urban/rural	Urban	25%	36%	46%	.069/<.001/<.001
	Rural	28%	42%	40%	
Occupation	High-level administrator, manager, and professional	13%	31%	35%	<.001/<.001/<.052
	Ordinary government and corporate employee, clerk, professional	21%	29%	43%	
	Manual worker, sales personnel, peasant labourer	21%	38%	45%	
	Self-employed small proprietor and vendor	18%	35%	45%	
	Retiree	27%	30%	37%	
	Farmer	33%	45%	44%	
	Not working, jobless, student	28%	41%	38%	
Family Income	Less than 1,000 yuan	34%	44%	31%	<.001/<.001/<.001
	1,001 to 3,000 yuan	24%	42%	52%	
	3,001 to 5,000 yuan	13%	29%	44%	
	Over 5,000 yuan	16%	27%	37%	
Total		**27%**	**36%**	**43%**	

Note: The p values are from Pearson chi-square tests (two-sided) of association of each covariate with whether worried or not about old age care for each year. The three p values are for 2005, 2008 and 2010 respectively.

personal income bracket showing concern declined between 2008 and 2010. In contrast, a growing proportion of those in higher income brackets have become worried.

In terms of professions, it is not surprising that relatively fewer of those serving in senior civil servant positions and company management, with their superior government pensions and retirement benefits, indicated they were concerned about old age care. In contrast, 43–45 per cent of all other working groups showed concern in the 2010 survey.

Interestingly, contrary to our expectations, the association of urban and rural residence with concerns about old age care is not so obvious. In 2005 and 2008, residents in small towns were the least worried about old age care, while a similar proportion of residents in big cities and rural areas were worried about old age care. However, reflecting the rising cost of living in big cities, a larger proportion of residents in big cities expressed concern about the cost of old age care than rural dwellers in 2010 (see Figure 9.5). In fact, while only 28 per cent of urban and rural residents expressed concerns in 2005, half of the urbanites were worried in 2010 compared to 40 per cent for rural residents.

Following the preliminary analysis above, we now present, in Table 9.3, the results of binary logistic regression models on respondents' concerns about the cost of care in old age for 2005, 2008 and 2010. In this exercise, the dependent variable is a dichotomous variable having either the value of "worried about old age care" (set at "1") or " 'so-so' and 'not worried' " (set at "0"). The independent variables include age, education, household income, residence and occupation. Because occupations in China are heavily correlated with urban/rural locations

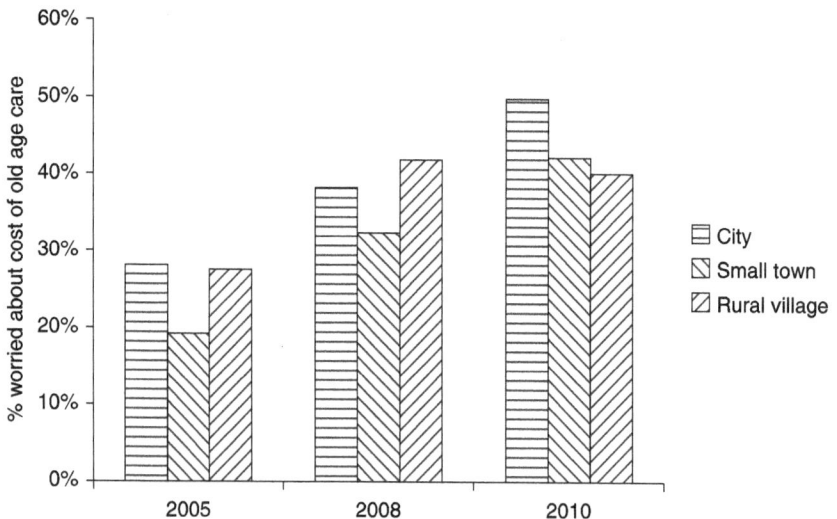

Figure 9.5 Weighted percentage of respondents worried about the cost of care in old age by residence.

Table 9.3 Binary logistic regression: concern about care in old age in China for the years 2005, 2008 and 2010

Variable	2005 B	S.E.	Sig.	2008 B	S.E.	Sig.	2010 B	S.E.	Sig.
Gender: male vs. female	-.091	.077	.238	.038	.070	.583	-.140	.066	.034
Age: over 50			.000			.001			.000
Lowest thru 30	-.581	.129	.000	-.133	.114	.246	-.300	.108	.006
31 thru 40	.175	.108	.104	.071	.101	.481	.251	.102	.014
41 thru 50	.072	.110	.512	.252	.099	.011	.293	.100	.003
Education: college			.000			.002			.000
Primary school or less	1.134	.290	.000	.814	.261	.002	.553	.201	.006
Middle school	.812	.279	.004	.669	.247	.007	.417	.179	.020
High/vocational school	.807	.277	.004	.454	.245	.064	.012	.175	.944
Two-ear college (*dazhuan*)	.822	.303	.007	.268	.270	.322	-.146	.194	.453
Household income: over 5,000 yuan			.000			.000			.000
Less than 1,000 yuan	1.388	.169	.000	.725	.163	.000	-.018	.126	.884
1,001 to 3,000 yuan	.646	.154	.000	.605	.149	.000	.834	.106	.000
3,001 to 5,000 yuan	-.189	.214	.377	.025	.160	.875	.368	.107	.001
Residence: rural			.000			.000			.000
City	.957	.125	.000	.435	.111	.000	.804	.105	.000
Town	.325	.142	.023	-.079	.102	.436	.112	.090	.216
Constant	-2.969	.334	.000	-1.724	.293	.000	-1.147	.219	.000
N	3929			3650			4090		
-2 log likelihood	4234			4769			5285		
Cox & Snell R Square	0.067			0.031			0.068		

Note: The model shows the log odds of being "worried about old age care" as one category (=1) versus "'not worried and so-so'" as the other category (=0).

(farmers by definition are rural while retirees, administrators and managers are urban residents), inclusion of both occupation and residence in the models will cause collinearity problems for estimation and interpretation. Therefore, we run two sets of logistic regression models, one including urban/rural residence and the other controlling for occupation.

Table 9.3 shows the results of the logistic regression model with the residence variable included. All variables but gender are significantly associated with the likelihood of concern about the cost of old age care in all three years. Gender is statistically significant only in 2010, with females more likely to be worried about old age care than males. The effect for age is consistent in all three years: those in the under-30 cohort are less worried about old age care but those in the 41–50 cohort are more likely than the 50-plus group to be worried about old age care in 2008 and 2010. Consistent with Table 9.2, the increases in the coefficients for the two middle age cohorts (31–40 and 41–50) from 2005 to 2010 indicate growing levels of concern about old age care for these two age groups relative to those over 50 years old.

With the college-educated as the base category, we find that those with a middle school education or lower are more likely to be worried than those with a college degree. However, unlike in 2005, for 2008 and 2010 there is no significant difference in the likelihood of concern about old age care between those with a college degree and those with a high school or two-year college diploma. Instead, there are similar proportions of people among the three groups who are worried.

It is not surprising that those with lower levels of household income are generally more likely to be worried about the cost of care in old age than those with higher income levels. What is noteworthy, however, is that in 2010 those in the lowest household income group are no more worried than those with 5,000-plus yuan of income per month. The increases in the coefficients for the two middle-income household groups from 2005 to 2010 reveal heightened levels of concern for middle-income households relative to those from wealthy households.

In what appears to be a commentary on the paradox of development and notably the rising costs of urban life, residents of big cities are more likely to show worries about old age care than rural residents. In contrast, the results for 2008 and 2010 (in contrast to 2005) suggest dwellers of towns can enjoy a good measure of urban life without becoming more worried about old age care than rural residents. When occupation is included in the logistic regression model instead of urban and rural residence, the results show that occupation is significantly associated with concerns about the cost of old age care in year 2005 only but not for 2008 and 2010. Thus the heightened level of concern by farmers (as shown in Table 9.2) is mostly captured by their generally lower income and education compared to the other occupations.

Concerns about caregiver availability in old age care

As we noted earlier, the two indicators for concerns about care in old age, caregiver availability and cost of care, are highly correlated. People who are worried about caregiver availability are likely to be worried about the cost of care. Those who are worried about the availability of family caregivers in old age also tend to have financial concerns. If outside caregivers and nursing facilities are easily accessible and affordable, most people would not be concerned about whether family members are around to care for them. As a result, the proportions of people worried about the cost of care and caregiver availability are similar for each year and have increased in sync from 2005 to 2010. We also find that the results of bivariate analysis and logistic regression models are largely similar for the two indicators.

Yet there is one major difference that we would like to point out. While in 2005 the proportion of people worried about caregiver availability was three percentage points lower than the proportion of people worried about the cost of care (24 per cent vs. 27 per cent), the trend was reversed in 2010, when more people became worried about caregiver availability than the cost of care (46 per cent vs. 43 per cent) (see Figure 9.4). This six percentage points swing in five years shows that caregiver availability has in recent years become more salient than the cost of care in people's concerns about care in old age and this development applies equally to urban/rural residence, different age groups and different levels of education. The growing concern about caregiver availability reflects China's demographic transition from an economy with a virtually unlimited supply of cheap labour to one facing increasing difficulties for the manufacturing and service sectors to recruit enough workers even with increasing pay (Yang 2005). The relatively low pay and status of those who provide care for the elderly compared with those who help with newborns (月嫂) has discouraged potential providers from becoming caregivers for the elderly.

Most likely and most preferred care arrangement in old age

Another angle for us to look at old age care in China is to examine respondents' responses to questions concerning what are the most likely vs. most preferred types of care arrangement when they get old. Figures 9.6 and 9.7 show, for the 2008–2010 period, the weighted percentages of people choosing each of six types of care arrangement.

As the figures show, the most preferred option for more than half of the respondents is living at home to be cared for by adult children or other relatives. The next most popular care type, for about 10 per cent of the respondents, is living in nursing homes established by the civil affairs agencies (government). Another 10 per cent of respondents choose to depend on themselves. Only less than 5 per cent of respondents prefer commercially-operated nursing homes.

We note that the percentage distribution of respondents for the most likely and the most preferred care types are very similar. In fact, a cross-tabulation indicates that a large majority of respondents select the same care arrangement type as both the most likely and most preferred. Yet there is an important difference. The percentage of respondents who prefer staying at home is less than the percentage who says staying at home is their most likely option. In contrast, more

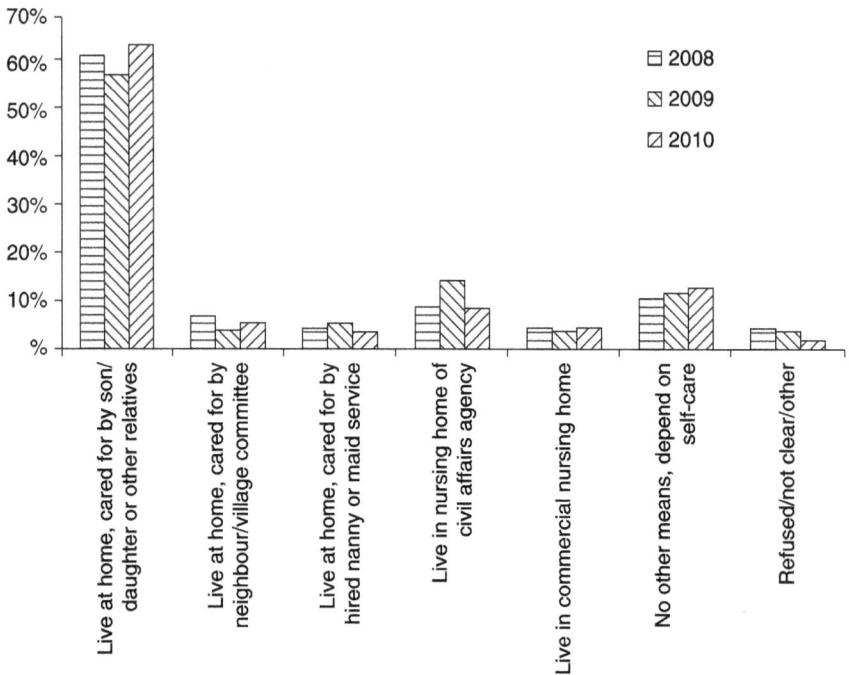

Figure 9.6 Weighted proportions of respondents in their most likely types of care arrangement in 2008, 2009 and 2010.

respondents prefer living in nursing homes set up by the civil affairs agencies than
think such a care option is likely. This discrepancy points to greater demand for
government-provided nursing facilities than is available.

As China's demographic transition to an ageing society accelerates and the
burdens of caring for the elderly become more prominent, it is likely that the
public desire for government-supported facilities will see further increases.
Meanwhile, China's leaders also appear to recognise both the growing needs of
the elderly and the public desire for government-supported facilities. According
to a Ministry of Civil Affairs official, under a State Council initiative for the
Twelfth Five-year Plan period (2011–2015), the number of beds for elderly care
is to increase by 3 million to reach 30 beds per 1,000 elderly people, doubling the
current capacity.[10] Local authorities such as Beijing and Jiangsu have begun to
subsidise the training of elder-care providers and to provide government aid for
building facilities on a per-bed basis.[11]

Summary and discussion

Our study has revealed that in the last few years, an increasing number of Chinese
people have become worried about their care arrangements in old age and the cost

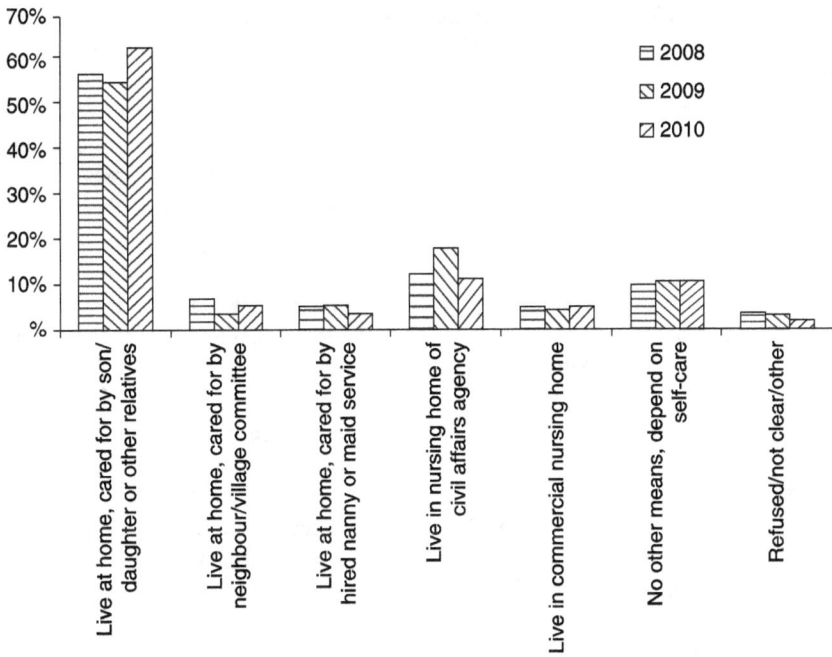

Figure 9.7 Weighted proportions of respondents in their most preferred types of care arrangement in 2008, 2009 and 2010.

of care. From 2005 to 2010, the proportion of residents worried about the cost of old age care increased from 27 to 43 per cent. Moreover, the increase is across the board and for people of all age groups and at different education and income levels. Those in their thirties and forties are more likely to be worried about care in old age than either younger or older people. Socio-economic status also makes a difference and residents with lower education and incomes tend to be more concerned. Yet, contrary to our expectations, residents of big cities are found to be more concerned about old age care than rural residents in 2010.

Considering the fact that people's household and personal incomes have generally increased amid China's extraordinary economic boom, their heightened level of concern about old age care is remarkable. While there may be multiple reasons for the increasing concern about the cost of old age care, one important and proximate cause is their perceived or relative deterioration of personal economic conditions and life quality in a period of national economic boom. In other words, there is a yearning gap between expectations for the country and for oneself. The Party has used the media to extol the nation's achievements but by so doing it also raises the people's expectations. Yet the average person knows well his or her own economic conditions.

In spite of the general increase of nominal personal income, the proportion of respondents who characterised their personal economic conditions as "good" has decreased from 35 per cent in 2004 to 29 per cent in 2010. The proportions of people who think their living standard will improve in the next year have dropped from 80 per cent in 2005 to 43 per cent in 2010. Indeed, nearly half of the respondents (47 per cent) in 2010 claimed to be under severe financial/economic strain, particularly due to inflation and the resulting increase in living costs, and a majority of the respondents were pessimistic about the prospect of their living standards getting better. Since the perceived change in economic conditions and living standards are correlated with people's concern with old age care, it is no surprise that concerns about old age care should increase with the decline in self-perceived personal economic conditions. As noted at the beginning of this chapter, it appears that these growing worries have contributed to a significant decline in the proportion of respondents who feel "happy".

The growing concern about the cost of old age care is further exacerbated by the inadequacies in the current retirement benefit systems. With its rapid demographic transformation, traditional ways of elderly care through the extended family will simply not be viable in China. At the same time, economic reforms have fundamentally undermined the previous state work-unit-centred welfare system. In response to pressure from dismissed SOE workers, the Chinese government has revamped the retirement system where the work unit (i.e. public employers) provides pensions and medical insurance in favour of a national social insurance system by pooling insurance funds from all employers and employees. Despite its uneven implementation, many cities and provinces have made the transition to a regionally centralised social insurance system where all retirees, including those laid off by reorganised or bankrupt firms, can draw a pension from the pooled insurance fund. With rapid economic growth in the last decade, the Chinese government has been able to expand the coverage of the social insurance system to the non-state sector and increase the pension payment to retirees.

According to the 2010 Horizon survey data, 37 per cent of Chinese residents regard the pensions from government or work unit as the most dependable source of income for care in old age, higher than the percentage of residents (35 per cent) who would depend on their children or other relatives for care in old age. In big cities, over half of the residents (54 per cent) regard government or work unit pensions as the most dependable source of retirement income compared to 30 and 32 per cent respectively for town and rural residents (see Figure 9.8). The higher proportions for city residents reflects the paternalistic nature of the state–society relationship in urban areas under which the state is expected to provide the needed social insurance and pensions for its citizens. On the other hand, township and rural residents have received very limited social insurance benefits from the government, thus their lower dependence on state or employer's pensions for retirement income. According to a 2011 report by HSBC, compared to most advanced or developing countries, a higher proportion of Chinese urban residents claim that they will rely on a government pension as a major source of retirement income (HSBC Insurance China, 2011).

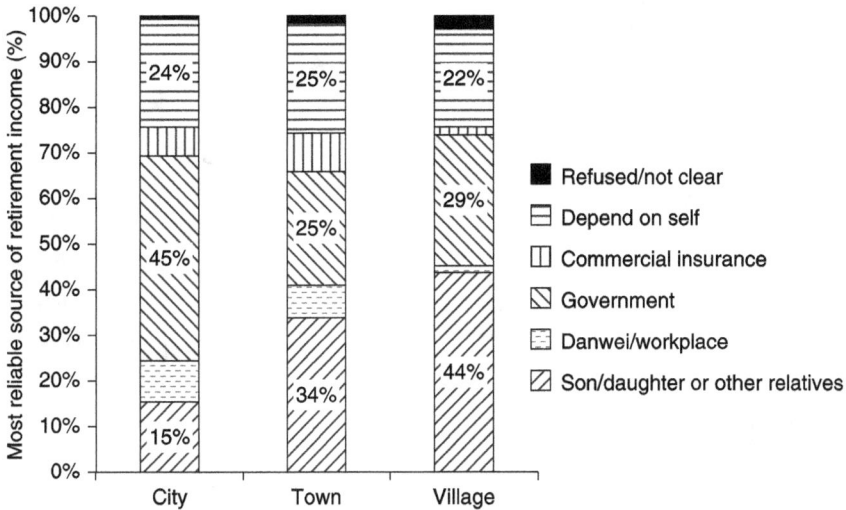

Figure 9.8 Most reliable source of retirement income identified by percentage of respondents in cities, towns and villages in 2010 (weighted percentage).

Yet at the same time people's satisfaction level with social insurance benefits (mostly medical insurance and pensions) they receive from the government or their employers dropped precipitously in 2010. Figure 9.9 indicates that the proportion of people satisfied with their social insurance benefits has risen from 43 per cent in 2005 to 47 per cent in 2009, but dropped to 34 per cent in 2010. For residents of big cities, the proportions satisfied with social insurance provision have dropped from 61 per cent in 2009 to 46 per cent in 2010. For rural residents, the corresponding proportions are much lower, at 41 per cent in 2009 and 28 per cent in 2010. The growing dependence on and declining satisfaction with the social insurance system suggests growing pressure on the Chinese government to play a paternalistic role in helping provide for social insurance and elderly care. However, the rapidly increasing ranks of the elderly and the rising cost of caring for them have already started to put a strain on the financial resources of local governments (Xia 2011). This means the Chinese government will need to find new revenue sources for meeting pension liabilities and the costs of more generalised social insurance, including (probably) the option of increasing the retirement age. Failure to address the growing needs for welfare may fuel further public discontent (Ye 2011).

As we mentioned earlier, the fragmentation of the retirement insurance system among different provinces and cities and the resulting portability impasse have effectively excluded many migrant workers from the system. This has caused further social inequity besides the separate and more generous civil service

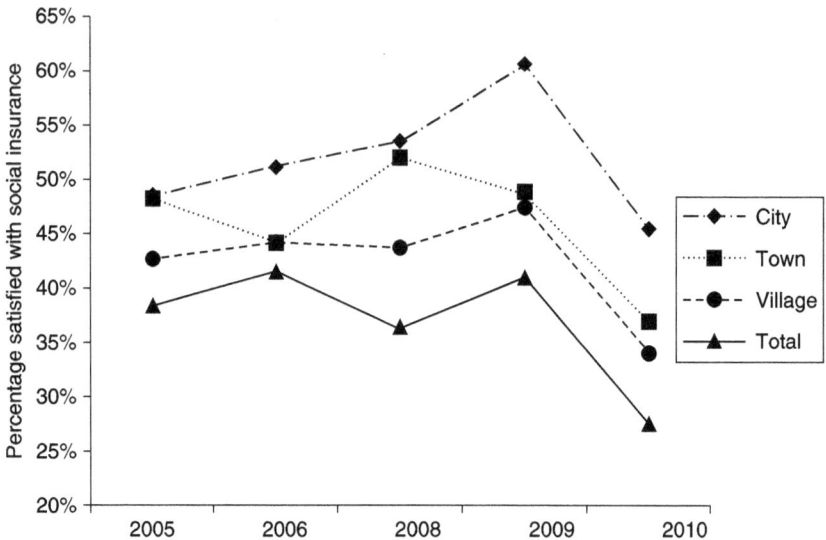

Figure 9.9 Weighted percentage of residents in three types of region who are satisfied with their social insurance benefits from government or employer.

Note: The percentages for 2007 are not shown because the question on social insurance satisfaction has only two categories instead of three for the other years.

retirement pension scheme (Yuan 2011). Understandably migrant workers who work mostly in the private sector are disenchanted with the government and have high levels of concern about old age care (see Table 9.2). With the instalment of Xi Jinping and Li Keqiang as president and premier, there is an indication that redressing the inadequacies of the fragmented social insurance arrangements has risen to the top of the policy agenda. It is still too soon to know whether the proposed measures for reform, which have percolated in policy circles for many years and include nationalising the system along the lines of the US social security system, will be adopted and implemented.

Conclusion

A good measure of the moral character of any society is how it takes care of that society's weakest, from the young to the old, as well as the disabled. To the extent that China's official policies to coercively limit population growth have aggravated population ageing and undermined the foundations of family-based care for the elderly, it seems natural that Chinese society would demand greater efforts by the Chinese government, with its command of vast economic resources, to do more to help provide for the rapid expansion of China's elderly ranks. China's government policies to expand coverage of the social security system and to boost investments in care for the elderly are steps in the right direction but such steps appear to have fallen short of public expectations so far. Yet at the same time, the growing government liabilities to provide social insurance and other welfare benefits may serve as some form of constraint on the Chinese Leviathan. Thus, as Chinese society ages rapidly, the provision of decent care for the elderly will pose a significant challenge to China's state–society relationship and will likely help reshape China's evolving social contract.

Acknowledgements

The authors thank Horizon Research Consultancy for allowing us to use the data from the Residents' Life Quality Index Survey. We gratefully acknowledge the financial support from the Confucius Institute and the Social Sciences Division of the University of Chicago. The authors also thank Jingsheng Zhu and Jiaqiang Chen for their comments on an early version of this chapter. The chapter is a revised version of "Old Age Care Concerns and State–Society Relations in China: Public Anxiety and State Paternalism", by Lijun Chen and Dali L. Yang, 2012. Reprinted by permission of the *Journal of Asian Public Policy*.

Notes

1 Tong Dahuan, "China, please walk slowly" (*Zhongguo, qingni manxie zou*), July 24, 2011. Available at: http://blog.qq.com/qzone/622007901/1311574820.htm (accessed 20 December 2011). On the crash, see Jamil Anderlini, "China Failed to Heed Rail Safety Warnings," *Financial Times*, 26 July 2011. Available at: http://www.ft.com/intl/cms/s/0/bbd56722-b78c-11e0-b95d-00144feabdc0.html#axzz1fx6mvAqO.
2 Yan Lianke. Available at: http://weibo.com/2056049087, 18 August 2011.
3 Andrew Jacobs, "Harassment and Evictions Bedevil Even China's Well-Off", *New York Times*, 27 October 2011. Available at: http://www.nytimes.com/2011/10/28/world/asia/harassment-and-house-evictions-bedevil-even-chinas-well-off.html.
4 "The 12th Five-year Plan on the Development of Elderly Care in China" (*Zhongguo laoling shiye fazhan shi'erwu guihua*), 17 September 2011. Available at: http://www.gov.cn/zwgk/2011–09/23/content_1954782.htm.
5 See Huang and Yang (2003) for a detailed analysis of the evolution of the birth control policy and its implementation in China. We recognise that the population planning policy is only one of many factors that have caused China's demographic transition, as described by Hussain (2002) and Greenhalgh and Winckler (2005).
6 We note that no regions where the ethnic minorities are concentrated are included, although these minority regions only account for a small proportion of the national population.
7 The original Chinese questions are: "老了之后，由谁来照料自己的生活 (不涉及到经济问题)？" and "您对于自己的养老费用 (或今后的养老费用) 感到忧虑吗？"
8 In 2007 "so-so" was excluded as a possible response category.
9 The Pearson correlations between the two variables (with three responses) for concerns about old age care are 0.74, 0.81 and 0.72 respectively for 2006, 2008 and 2010.
10 Wei Mingyan, "The Civil Affairs Ministry: 3 Million Beds to be Added for Elderly Care in Five Years, Doubling the Current Number" (*Minzhengbu: wunian ni zen yanglao chuangwei 300 wan zhang, bi muqian fanyifan*), *New Capital Newspaper* (*xinjingbao*), 9 December 2011. Available at: http://news.sohu.com/20111209/n328402099.shtml.

11 Ibid.
12 "Human Resources and Social Security Ministry: Reform of Dual-Track Pension System is under Top-Down Design" (*Renshebu: yanglaojin shuangguizhi zhen zai jinxing dingcen sheji*), Xinhua News, 5 March 2013. Available at: http://news. xinhuanet.com/yuqing/2013–03/05/c_124416883.htm.

References

Frazier, M. W. (2010). *Socialist Insecurity: Pensions and the Politics of Uneven Development in China*. Ithaca, NY: Cornell University Press.

Gallup (2009). *Americans Increasingly Concerned About Retirement Income: Expected reliance on 401(k) plans shows major drop from last year*. Available at: http://www. gallup.com/poll/117703/americans-increasingly-concerned-retirement-income.aspx.

Gold, T. B., Hurst, W., Won, J. and Li, Q. (2009). *Laid-off Workers in a Workers' State: Unemployment with Chinese Characteristics*. New York: Palgrave Macmillan.

Greenhalgh, S. and Winckler, E. A. (2005). *Governing China's Population: From Leninist to Neoliberal Biopolitics*. Stanford, CA: Stanford University Press.

HSBC Insurance China (2011). *HSBC Global Survey Report on the Future of Retirement: The Power of Planning*. Available at: http://www.hsbcinsurance.com.cn/1/ PA_1_083Q9FFKG80E20RA9Q00000000/content/jv_pws/bank_insurance/images/ communication_BANC_2.pdf.

Huang, Y. and Yang, D. L. (2003). "Population Control and State Coercion in China", in B. Naughton and D. L. Yang (eds) *Holding China Together: Diversity and National Integration in the Post-Deng Era*. New York: Cambridge University Press.

Hurd, M. and Rohwedder, S. (2010). *The Effects of the Economic Crisis on the Older Population*. University of Michigan Retirement Research Center working paper, WP 2010–231. Available at: http://www.mrrc.isr.umich.edu/publications/papers/pdf/wp231. pdf.

Hussain, A. (2002). "Demographic Transition in China and Its Implications", *World Development*, 30(10): 1823–1834.

Jackson, R., Nakashima, K. and Howe, N. (2009). *China's Long March to Retirement Reform: The Graying of the Middle Kingdom Revisited*. CSIS Report 22 April 2009. Available at: http://csis.org/publication/chinas-long-march-retirement-reform.

Li, C. (2005). "Prestige Stratification in Contemporary China: Occupational Prestige Measures and Socioeconomic Index", *Sociological Research*, 2: 74–102.

Liu, X. (2010). *Elderly Care Insurance for Rural Residents in China: Theory and Practice*. Beijing: Science Press.

Lynch, S. M. (2000). "Measurement and Prediction of Aging Society", *Research on Aging*, 2 (5): 533–558.

Shi, T. (2001). "Cultural Values and Political Trust: A Comparison of the People's Republic of China and Taiwan", *Comparative Politics*, 33(4): 401–419.

Tang, W. (2005). *Public Opinion and Political Change in China*. Stanford, CA: Stanford University Press.

Walder, A. G. (1986). *Communist Neo-Traditionalism: Work and Authority in Chinese Industry*. Berkeley, CA: University of California Press.

Xia, M. (2011). "China's Retirement Pension Reform Can Learn from European Debt Crisis: *2011 Report on the Development of China's Retirement Pension*, officially published", *China Social Science Bulletin*, 249, 21 December.

Yan, T., Silverstein, M. and Wilber, K. H. (2011). "Does Race/Ethnicity Affect Aging Anxiety in American Baby Boomers?", *Research on Aging*, 33(4): 361–378.

Yang, D. L. (2005). "China's Looming Labor Shortage", *Far Eastern Economic Review*, Jan/Feb: 18–24.

Ye, L. (2011). "Demographic Transition, Developmentalism and Social Security in China", *Social Policy & Administration*, 45(6): 678–693.

Yuan, X. (2011). "Rectify the Social Construction of Income Inequality for the Elderly", *China Social Science Bulletin*, 198, 21 June.

10 Public–private pension mix and its governance

Japan and Taiwan compared

Chung-Yang Yeh and Shih-Jiunn Shi

Introduction

Over the past decades, pension privatisation has been a central issue in comparative studies of the welfare state because pensions have become the predominant social insurance programmes of almost all OECD countries and other newly industrialising countries (Béland and Shinkawa, 2007; Häusermann, 2010; Orenstein, 2008; Rein and Schmähl, 2004; Vangunsteren and Rein, 1985). Countries with earning-related public pension schemes tend to restrict the role of the private sector in pension provision regarding multi-pillar pension systems (Vangunsteren and Rein, 1985). In a multi-pillar system, universal flat-rate public pension schemes provide minimum economic security while private pensions play a more crucial role than public pensions but require more state regulation for implementation (Ebbinghaus and Gronwald, 2011; Leisering, 2010; Myles and Pierson, 2001).

In contrast to the European reform experiences, pension reforms in East Asia have gained unusual momentum with the broadened coverage of current pension schemes and increased levels of pension benefits to provide basic income security for all citizens. Rapid population ageing and globalisation have placed substantial financial pressures on the current pension systems, rendering pension privatisation a suitable option in future reform repertoires. The pension systems of Japan and South Korea, which are traditionally based on the social insurance principle, have a long history of incorporating private pensions on top of public pensions at the beginning of welfare state development (Estévez-Abe, 2008; Yi, 2007). This distances them from European social insurance states where occupational pensions play a minor role in pension provision (Bonoli and Shinkawa, 2005). By contrast, Taiwan is a latecomer in this respect, and initiated occupational pension schemes in the mid-1980s, and subsequently reformed them in 2004 from defined-benefit to defined-contribution schemes. East Asian countries have redefined the boundary between public and private responsibilities for old-age security, and recalibrated their governance modes in the changing political-economic and demographic contexts.

Recent research has demonstrated that the paths towards a public-private pension mix and governance modes are embedded in specific welfare production regimes (Ebbinghaus and Gronwald, 2011; Ebbinghaus and Wiß, 2011; Rein and

Turner, 2004), and the influences of globalisation on pension systems are also filtered by national-specific institutions (Huber and Stephens, 2001; Swank, 2002). However, except for Japan, the nexus between pension policy and capitalist production in other East Asian countries has not been investigated (Choi, 2008). Conventionally conceived as the developmental welfare states, East Asian countries have used specific approaches towards modernisation and created distinctive welfare systems that differ from their Western counterparts. Japan has well-developed occupational and private pension schemes embedded in the Keiretsu-dominated (corporate conglomerate) welfare production regime, which provides opportunities for private insurance companies and the possibility of contract-out for the second-tier occupational pension schemes. By contrast, in Taiwan, the limited role of private companies as providers of occupational pensions is mainly the result of the economic structures in which small and medium enterprises (SMEs) constitute the majority of businesses that are sensitive to high non-wage labour costs. This difference is crucial to the role of the state in the dimension of governing pension mix, because strong occupational pensions in Japan require regulation of the pension funds and financial markets, whereas in Taiwan the state remains the main public pension provider and is hesitant to shift financial responsibility of old-age security onto private pensions.

In the contexts of East Asian welfare capitalism, the differences in the public-private pension mix in East Asia are more significant than previously assumed. Taiwan and Japan are selected as two contrasting cases in the models of pension privatisation and pension governance. It is against this context that the present chapter sets out to compare pension mix in Japan and Taiwan. This comparison should reveal crucial features of the political economy in East Asian pension reform experiences, which may influence the evolutionary paths of pension institutions in this region. Further investigation of the political and economic structures is essential to identifying the intricacies of state activities in merging public and private welfare provision in old-age security.

Political economy of pension reforms in East Asia

Social policy in East Asian countries used to play a subsidiary role in overall developments before the 1990s. The state deliberately maintained social expenditures at a low level and provided social security only to privileged groups, such as the military, civil servants and teachers. By contrast, workers in private enterprises had moderate social benefits; other population groups such as farmers and self-employed people were excluded from social security schemes. Pension systems in this region were mostly fragmentally structured to include specific occupational groups, with considerable variety in entitlements among the various schemes. The preoccupation with economic "catch-up" at the expense of social welfare has led scholars to label East Asian countries as "developmental" welfare states (Kwon, 2005; Lee and Ku, 2007). Family welfare, status-segregated social insurance systems and corporate occupational plans for core workers are crucial in East Asian welfare states (Goodman *et al.*, 1998; Gough, 2000; Kwon, 1997).

Although the developmental welfare state thesis offers an explanation of the reason why social policy was underdeveloped in East Asia, the various manners in which private welfare functioned in the respective architectures of social provision remain unclear (Holliday, 2000; Holliday and Wilding, 2003; Pempel, 2002; Tang, 2000). The preoccupation with public social provision has obscured the hidden domain of private welfare regarding active state regulations (Kim, 2010). The developmental state thesis neglected the differences within the East Asian region because of its aim to identify an East Asian welfare regime by focusing on similarities (Pempel, 2002). The cross-national variation in economic systems has been largely ignored because of the emphasis on the manner in which social policy is embedded in capitalist production (Holliday, 2000; Lee and Ku, 2003). Although recent studies have been consistent in this regard and explored the specific historical evolution of welfare regimes in several countries, such as Japan, South Korea and Taiwan) (Choi, 2009; Lee, 2011), the issue of cross-national variation in the public-private pension mix within East Asia remains underexplored.

The varieties of capitalism approach (VoC) provides theoretical insights to comprehend the changing public–private mix in East Asian pension reforms. The VoC emphasises the complementary institutional coupling between welfare regimes and capitalist production, and highlights the influences of capitalist structures and business on social policy development (Ebbinghaus and Manow, 2001; Iversen, 2005; Manow, 2001b; Schröder, 2009). Two models of capitalism stand out, that is, liberal market economies (LMEs) and coordinated market economies (CMEs) that emanate from the ideas of elective affinities and institutional complementarity, as follows: "within a given country, different aspects of the welfare state 'fit' together and 'fit' with different aspects of the production regimes" (Huber and Stephens, 2001: 109). Maintaining the regime-specific institutional complementarities implies that the LMEs are compatible with the liberal welfare state regime, whereas the CMEs fit with the conservative and social democratic welfare regimes.

Pension policy is linked to capitalist production in two ways. It can be used to solve the dilemma of skill formation between employers and employees as a crucial policy instrument of human resource management. According to Iversen (2005), the type of social protection schemes is closely related to the degree of skill specificity. Economies that rely on low-portability skill types, such as industry- or company-specific skills, tend to provide higher levels of social protection for employment and unemployment to enhance the likelihood of specific skill formation. In this respect, a defined-benefit (DB) pension scheme with back-loaded final-pay formulas may be used by economies that rely on industrial- or company-specific skills, because it provides strong incentives for the workers to invest in low-portability skill types, and sustains their efforts to achieve high career-end salaries. By contrast, in countries where general skill formation prevails, employers do not have sufficient incentives to extract the loyalty of employees with replaceable skills. Therefore, a defined-contribution (DC) pension scheme is often used because it can effectively reduce the costs of corporate pension schemes by shifting the risk to employees (Conrad, 2011; Dulebohn *et al.*, 2009). This implies that a DB pension scheme is preferable as a policy instrument of skill formation in Japan, because firm-specific skill is crucial to its economic structure (Busemeyer, 2009; Estévez-Abe *et al.*, 2001). The economy in Taiwan is known for the domination of SMEs that have relatively short corporate lives, and lack sufficient financial resources to sustain DB pension schemes. This specific capitalist structure as characterised by high labour mobility tends to favour the formation of general skills, and prefers DC pension schemes as the main financial method.

The other linkage between pension policy and capitalist production is the financial system. Jackson and Vitols (2001) contend that policy choice and institutional design affect the supply side of national savings, and the regulations of private pension shape the manner in which financial capitals are channelled into capital markets. This aspect is crucial for the developmental state in East Asia, because financial systems often function as an effective conduit for the state to channel financial resources into particular strategic sectors (Choi, 2009; Woo-Cumings, 1999). Apart from other financial sources (such as foreign venture capital), pension funds are often regarded as one of the essential sources of working capital for both government and private companies (Choi, 2009; Estévez-Abe, 2001; Manow, 2001a, 2001c). This is vital in CMEs in which capital is not dominated by the stock market, but is credit based. In Japan, the financial capital of pension funds, from public pension or private pension, is often redirected into strategic sectors. A strong link exists between pension policy (financial system) and industrial development. However, the pattern differs in Taiwan. Although state-owned and party-owned enterprises can receive preferential treatment from financial institutions, SMEs must rely on family or informal curb market loans. Public and private pension schemes have not been mobilised for capital accumulation in Taiwan.

This institutional complementarity entails the issue of financial regulation and pension governance. The multitude of pension fund assets reflects the differences in the design and operation of various pension systems (Ebbinghaus and Wiß, 2011). Prevailing private pensions tend to play a vital role in both old-age security and financial regulation to achieve the goals of the state. The combination of public and private pensions is often more complex than the simple purpose of income protection for senior citizens.

The different logic of institutional coherence between pension policy and capitalist production is not only about how institutions work together, but also about reform paths, argued by the VoC (Ebbinghaus and Gronwald, 2011; Huber and Stephens, 2001; Manow, 2001a; Myles and Pierson, 2001). Without sudden crash, institutional reform cannot contradict to the existing path, as the institutional coherence is forged. Economic integration, arguably, has caused the loss of autonomy of states to tax and finance social protection. Constrained by institutional contexts, yet we can expect that the reform paths of pension systems in Japan and Taiwan would be different in the age of new socio-economic environment.

The following discussion of the Japanese and Taiwanese cases advances the understanding of the transformations of the public–private mix in the respective pension systems, and presents an analysis of the link between the economic system and pension policy. The comparative study of the two contrasting cases helps identify the specific political and economic contexts that have shaped the role of private pensions in both old-age security and industrial development.

Japan

Social protection in Japan served as a policy instrument to manage the political problem of coordination (Thelen and Kume, 2006) and a part of the overall developmental strategy (Takahashi, 1974, cited in Manow, 2001c). The function of the pension system in Japan was to collect funding that offered patient capital to key industries through the Ministry of Finance (MoF) (Choi, 2009; Manow, 2001c; Park, 2004).[1] Conversely, it was also institutionalised to address labour scarcity, particularly in the pre-war period (Manow, 2001c; Shinkawa and Pempel, 1996), and most importantly, to solve economic coordination of skill formation (Estévez-Abe, 2001, 2008). These institutional legacies have shaped the public–private pension mix and its governance, and the trajectory of subsequent pension reforms.

The institutionalisation of public–private pension mix before the 2000s

Japan is considered a hybrid regime that combines occupationally fragmented public pension schemes based on a social insurance principle, and well-developed corporate pension schemes (Esping-Andersen, 1997). Three corporate pension schemes were used before the introduction of the two new corporate pension laws in 2001.[2] The Retirement Allowance (RA), a DB plan, was initiated in 1905 at the firm level, followed by nationwide legislation in 1936, and subsequently merged into the Employee's Pension Insurance of 1944 (Kimura, 1997). In 1952, the government provided tax deductions on RA, and offered substantial incentives for employers to introduce corporate pension schemes and provide lump-sum retirement payments. Initially, it was implemented to manage the problem of the collective dilemma of skill formation and as book reserves for financial mobilisation (Conrad, 2012; Estévez-Abe, 2008).

The private pension system in Japan underwent formal institutionalisation in the post-war period with two private pension schemes, including Tax-Qualified Pension Schemes (TQPSs) and Employee Pension Funds (EPFs).[3] The TQPSs were introduced in 1962 and allowed firms with more than 15 employees to set up corporate pension funds, with tax exemptions for their contributions to the funds and capital gains. The government, under the Liberal Democratic Party, mandated the life insurance industry to manage all TQPSs. The EPFs were introduced in

1965 as a new 'opting out' scheme of EPI. This scheme turned part of public pensions into occupational pensions (Estévez-Abe, 2008). The initial purpose of the EPFs was to set up a pension fund as working capital. However, the pension funds, by law, were managed by life insurance companies or trust banks.

The TQPSs and EPFs constituted two prominent private pension schemes for the creation of patient capital. Before the 1990s, the financial market was restricted under the supervision of the MoF, which offered the life insurance industry exclusive access to a market with enormous growth potential, under the condition to comply with the investment priorities set by the government (Estévez-Abe, 2001). In this manner, the pension funds were channelled into vital industries, such as electricity, steel, maritime and coal, through the Japan Development Bank and the Export-Import Bank of Japan (Park, 2004; Shinkawa and Pempel, 1996; Vogel, 2006). In addition, statutory regulations also protected the life insurance industry from market speculations, further consolidating the stable long-term investments of the welfare funds. Park (2004) identified two features of the private pension system in Japan. First, the state controlled the pension funds, indicating that the problem of pension investment returns and pension liabilities was beyond the control of firms. Second, the longstanding book reserve system ensured that pension liabilities could be managed as an off-balance-sheet by the old corporate accounting system. Although book reserve plans were used for capital accumulation, these funds were managed by the trust banks and life insurance companies, which provided insurance companies with a unique opportunity to become the most influential shareholders of the large banks in Japan (Estévez-Abe, 2001). The preferential status granted the banks considerable freedom to concentrate on creating patient capital through this cross-shareholding mechanism. This particular institutional combination of pension and financial systems with the state regulation of pension funds contributed to the consolidation of a banking-based finanical system and a stable stockholding pattern (Estévez-Abe, 2001).

Furthermore, firm-specific skills are crucial to the Japanese skill formation system (Busemeyer, 2009; Thelen, 2004). Therefore, DB pension schemes play a vital role in binding the employees to the firms and enhancing the coorperation of workers. The RA, TQPSs and EPFs are DB pensions, and effectively play this role. However, the hiring-to-retirement pensions and occupational welfare policies created an internal labour market and led to strong segmentalism and dualism in the labour market and welfare state (Busemeyer, 2009). Thus, substantial public pensions were prevented because of the predominance of corporate pensions.

Public pensions in Japan consist of three components: Mutual Pension Schemes (MPSs), Employee's Pension Insurance (EPI) and National Pension Insurance (NPI). The Japanese government instituted public pension schemes for civil servants and the military in the late nineteenth century, and employees in state-owned enterprises in the early twentieth century, which were revised to become MPSs. The EPI was instituted during the war, mainly for private employees. The NPI was introduced in 1961 to include those who had been excluded from the EPI and MPSs. The public pension system in Japan was a partially funded system, with the funds from the NPI and EPI transferred to the Trust Fund Bureau and overseen by the MoF. These funds, including pension and postal saving funds, were directed to strategic industries or construction of infrastructure through the Fiscal Investment Loan Programme.[4] Returns on the pension fund investments were a lower priority than the industrialisation-related activities (Park, 2004). This link has been the prominent nexus between the public pension scheme and economic development in Japan.

In summary, the Japanese pension system was governed as economically oriented, but state-led (Leisering, 2010). Public pension schemes were constituted beyond the goal of retirement income security, and further devised as a policy instrument to mobilise financial resources for key strategic industries during the industrialisation period. This instrumental character was more pronounced in non-state pension schemes that managed the problem of economic coordination and skill formation, and worked as patient capital to support enterprises through inter-locking shareholdings. The assets accumulated from pension funds were internalised and organisationally embedded into the Japanese political economic regime (Jackson and Vitols, 2001).

The new era of public–private pension mix

Japan encountered several internal and external challenges in the 1990s. The transformation of demographic structure, with an increase in the percentage of the ageing population, and a decline of the fertility rate, resulted in the increasing financial burden of the public pension system. The economic crisis in the 1990s undermined the fiscal capacities of providing corporate pension schemes. Externally, globalisation exerted pressures on the Japanese welfare state towards liberalisation, particularly regarding occupational welfare. A substantial influence was the introduction of the new International Accounting System in 2001, which stipulated that the future obligation of the corporate pension schemes must be included in corporate accounting under the Project Benefit Obligation (Katsumata, 2004; Vogel, 2006). Under this new regulation, the book-reserve pension schemes that provided firms with patient capital and reinforced solidarity of *keiretsu* ties to foster industrial development became considerable liabilities in the balance sheets of companies. This initiative raised concerns about corporate performance because of its direct negative effects. Consequently, it strengthened the incentive to focus on pension returns rather than hold cross-holdings (Park, 2004).

An immediate effect of these changes was the increase in the financial burdens of the pension system. Since the 1980s, the Japanese government successively introduced pension reforms to reduce financial burdens, such as the increase in retirement age and the introduction of the macroeconomic factor. With respect to corporate pension schemes, the Japanese government loosened its regulation of EPFs by reducing the officially required rate of return from 5.5 to 4.5 per cent, and reducing the amount of fund reserves (Shinkawa, 2005). However, these initiatives were insufficient to ameliorate the financial problem of public and private pension schemes. The number of TQPSs and EPFS did not decline considerably. Hence, further radical reforms were required.

Two new corporate pension schemes introduced in 2001, including the Defined-Contribution Corporate Pension Plan Act (DC plan) and the Defined-Benefit Corporate Pension Plan Act (DB plan), had substantial effects on the public-private pension mix. The DB plan included two types of pension scheme: the contract type plan and the fund type plan. The contract type plan was similar to the TQPSs and replaced them in 2012. It required employers to maintain assets at specific levels, although they may be transferred easily to other plans. By contrast, the fund type plan attempted to replace the EPFs; however, it only applied to firms with more than 300 employees. By introducing the hybrid/cash-balance model, the risk and responsibility of pension management was reduced, while the benefit levels depended on the performance of the investment and the minimum benefits remained guaranteed (Shinkawa, 2005).

Despite concern about the effects on income security after retirement, the government launched a DC plan in 2001 to transfer the responsibility of pension management from the employers to the employees and provide full portability of pension assets to deregulate the financial markets and revitalise the stock market (Katsumata, 2004; Shinkawa, 2005). The plan, described as the "Japanese 401k plan", included the corporate type pension and the individual type pension. The individual type pension is designed for insured category No. 1 (self-employed) and those insured under EPI who are less than 60 years of age and excluded by other corporate pension plans. The total contributions are borne by the insured. The National Pension Fund Federation administers the provision of the individual type pension benefits. By contrast, the corporate type pension is provided for the insured of category No. 2, who are mainly covered by the EPI, yet whose contributions are paid for by their employers. In 2010, a total of 3,705 corporate type pension plans were initiated to cover the total number of insured employees (approximately 3.7 million). Obviously, the financial risk is shifted from corporations to individuals, regardless of the types of DC pension plan. However, the contract-out pension schemes enhanced the power of individuals in the selection of pension fund investments, and increased the stakes for any of their choices. Meanwhile, it has weakened the function of the corporate pension system as internal patient capital, which functions now as a supplementary retirement income security for retired people.

The role of DB pension plans is more important than that of DC pension plans in the Japanese corporate pension system, because Japanese firms require the former as a policy instrument to solve the problem of firm-specific skill formation, which is regarded as the main source of their comparative institutional advantage in the global market (Conrad, 2011, 2012; Estévez-Abe, 2008; Estévez-Abe *et al.*, 2001; Vogel, 2006). Vogel (2006) points out that Japanese firms did not support a pension cut as pensions help to maintain labour-management cooperation and provide a critical source of patient capital. However, this leads to the dualisation of social protection: core workers with specific skills are covered by DB pension plans, while marginalised workers in the small firms or services sector usually rely on less generous DC pension plans (Peng, 2012). Figure 10.1 shows the current constitution of the Japanese pension system.

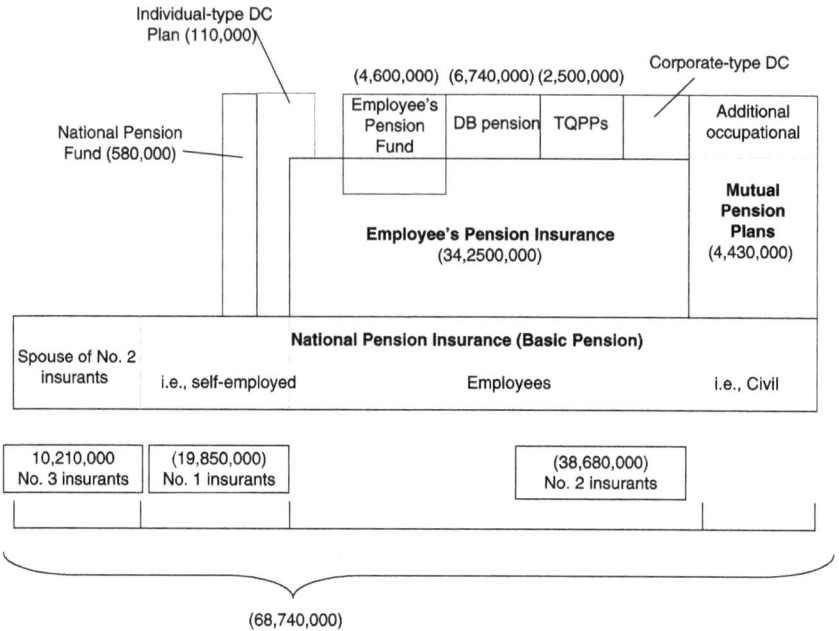

Figure 10.1 Pension system in Japan (the number in brackets means the number of scheme members).

Source: Ministry of Health, Labour and Welfare.

Although the influences of globalisation on the Japanese financial system and corporate governance are significant, through the enforcement of the new International Accounting System (Vogel, 2006) and the DC pension schemes are popular under the worldwide wave of neoliberalism, DB pension schemes dominate the Japanese pension system (see Table 10.1) because of its particular structure of capitalist production, within which comparative institutional advantages are derived from firm-specific skills. Consequently, Japanese firms require DB pension plans as part of human resource management to solve the dilemma of skill formation in the core sectors, even though the importance of DC pension schemes is increasing. However, this precipitates the aforementioned dualisation of the pension system (Peng, 2012).

Yet, paradoxically, the deregulation of the financial market has led to the rise of socially oriented pension governance in Japan. Instead of implementing neoliberal pension governance with an emphasis on the market-based financial regime or uncoordinated regulatory regime, the Japanese reform experiences have resulted in a welfare market in which the government has used the financial market and non-state welfare provisions as a specific object of social policy regulation (Leisering, 2010). During the reforms of non-state pension schemes, economic goals (as part of economic developmental strategy) have been replaced by social goals (as objects of social policy). The current non-state pension schemes in Japan are regarded as a supplementary pension system rather than a policy instrument to facilitate economic development, even though DB pensions continue to play a crucial role in skill formation. The state plays a more vital role in the regulation of non-state pension schemes through state regulation of the operation of pension funds. Although neoliberalism has influenced the Japanese pension system, its effect is filtered by the Japanese economic structure.

Table 10.1 Indicators of major Japanese occupational pension plans

Name of plan	Nature of plan	Year	Number of plans		Number of members (million)	Amount of assets (trillion yen)
Employee Pension Fund (EPF)	DB	1968	305		1.28	0.015
		1978	945		5.44	2.54
		1988	1,194		7.65	17.16
		1998	1,858		12.00	53.3
		2003	1,357		8.35	48.6
		2008	617		4.39	16.1
		2009	608		4.31	18.3
		2010	588		4.30	17.6
Tax-Qualified Pension Schemes (TQPSs)	DB	1963	161		0.04	–
		1968	34,737		2.35	0.078
		1978	57,001		4.90	1.63
		1988	74,423		8.21	9.43
		1997	88,312		10.43	19.15
		1998	85,047		10.30	20.0
		2003	59,162		7.78	20.7
		2008	25,441		3.49	–
		2009	17,184		2.50	–
		2010	8,051		1.26	–
DB Pension Plans	DB		Contract-type DB plan	Fund-type DB plan		
		2002	15	0	0.03	–
		2005	834	596	3.84	21.7
		2008	4,395	611	5.70	–
		2009	6,797	610	6.47	–
		2010	9,436	608	7.27	–
Corporate DC Plan	DC	2001	70		0.088	–
		2005	1,866		1.733	22.8
		2008	3,043		3.110	–
		2009	3,301		3.404	–
		2010	3,705		3.713	–

Source: Pension Fund Association (http://www.pfa.or.jp/); Ministry of Health, Labour and Welfare (http://www.mhlw.go.jp/); Conrad (2012: Table 1).

Taiwan

Welfare developments in Taiwan after World War II were influenced by the tension between the state and society. As a regime émigré, the Kuomintang was eager to consolidate its political rule over the native Taiwanese civil society. The authoritarian Kuomintang regime enforced martial law to tighten military and political control, and successively established generous social insurance schemes for specific groups, such as military servicemen, civil servants and teachers, to ensure their political loyalties (Ku, 1997; Lin, 2005; Lin, 1994; Wong, 2004: 43–61). Social policy exhibited an instrumental characteristic, that is, the regime intentionally devised social security institutions targeted at certain pivotal occupational groups in exchange for their political support. Public old-age security was the privilege of certain occupational groups, whereas the majority of the population had insufficient support from the state. Labour Insurance was established in March 1950 to cover the workers in enterprises with at least 20 employees. By 1953, the Labour Insurance programme was extended to small firms with over 10 employees and fishermen, and to those working in smaller firms with less than 10 employees on a voluntary basis. As the single social insurance bearer for the workers, Labour Insurance provided a package of benefits for work injury, old age, medical care, disability, death and maternity. In the same year, the Military Servicemen Insurance Programme was introduced, followed by the introduction of the Government Employee Insurance Programme in 1958.[5] Apart from the social insurance schemes for these occupational groups, the state did not address the requirements of the remainder of the population (such as the farmers and the unemployed). Old-age security was the responsibility of the individuals and their families.

The institutionalisation of public pensions before the 1990s[6]

Before the 1990s, pension provision was the sole responsibility of the public, and occupational pensions have long been an unfamiliar concept in Taiwan's pension system. The dominant role of public old-age security systems originated from the dual industrial structures of Taiwan in the post-war era, with the Kuomintang regime controlling and protecting the business of large state-owned enterprises in upstream industrial sectors, while leaving the downstream sectors to the SMEs, mostly established by indigenous Taiwanese people (Wu, 2004). Exposure to international competition has compelled the SMEs to swiftly react to turbulence in the markets, training them to evolve as the main thrust of Taiwan's economic growth since the 1970s. The demand for flexible business operations and strict cost control led the SMEs to resist any additional labour costs, especially those associated with the establishment of pension schemes within the corporate structures. Occupational pension schemes were generally underdeveloped within such industrial structures, even less with the introduction of funded social pension insurance (Choi, 2008). The lack of interest in the accumulated social insurance funds was also attributed to the various methods of corporate finance, as state-owned banks strategically favoured large state-owned enterprises, pressing the disadvantaged SMEs to secure funding through informal conduits of financial loans (Lee and Chen, 2011). There was little imperative for the state to mobilise additional funding capital through social insurance because state-owned banks already played this role.

This dual industrial structure fitted the dual corporate welfare system, as employees in large state-owned enterprises had generous fringe benefits granted by the state. Because the statutory regulations endowed these firms with the monopolistic status in crucial upstream fields (like petro-chemistry, electricity and public transport), they had abundant financial resources to reward their workers with occupational pensions, even in the absence of relevant statutory guidelines. This preferential status of employees in large state-owned enterprises was unmatched by their colleagues in private SMEs, which prioritised flexible competitiveness and cost containment. Under these circumstances, workers of SMEs could barely expect occupational pensions, and the only option for them remained the modest old-age benefits as stipulated by the Labour Insurance.

Moreover, before the 1990s, public pensions played such a predominant role that little room remained for the growth of private pensions. This is clearly shown in the earlier pension reforms that focused only on the gradual expansion of the Labour Insurance programme without paying much attention to the role of occupational pensions. Since its inception, the Labour Insurance programme has undergone several revisions to adjust the eligibility criteria and improve benefits. In the 1980s, workers in small firms (more than five employees) gained access to the programme, and the government increased subsidies for the monthly contribution of self-employed people from 30 to 40 per cent. In 1984, the government further promulgated the Labour Standard Act as an amendment to the programme. The complicated part was the regulation that required employers to make contributions for their employees to accumulate occupationasl pensions upon retirement. However, this new labour legislation did not improve much of the old-age security for the workers (Control Yuan, 2002; Council of Economic Planning and Development, 2000). To earn those entitlements, the employees had to work in the same company for at least 25 years, or 15 years when reaching the age of 55. This was a considerable obstacle for most workers because the majority of their employers were medium and small firms that operated for an average period of 12 years (Wu, 1997). The lack of any possibility for the portability of the entitlement to occupational pensions further disadvantaged the workers in case of employment changes. The targeted groups were initially confined to the manufacturing industry; even in this case, the problem of non-compliance prevailed because of the failure of the government to enforce the regulation effectively. This regulatory gap resulted in further political reforms that led to a series of new legislations to create a more comprehensive pension system.

Recalibrating the public-private pension mix and governance in the new era

The democratisation process essentially altered the nature of pension politics in the 1990s. Although the KMT remained the ruling party during this period, its main opposition, the Democratic Progressive Party (DPP), gradually rose to political prominence and created competitive pressure for the KMT to renew its pension policy (Fu, 2000; Lin, 2005). Pension politics has been complicated by the participation of diverse political and social interest groups, leading to a protracted process for over a decade (Shi, 2010; Tsai, 2008). The main concerns related to the lack of basic public pensions for the marginalised population groups, such as farmers, the unemployed and housewives, and adequate institutional design to provide old-age security for all workers. During the policy-making process, almost all conceivable institutional frameworks were discussed, including the fusion of all current pension schemes as a universal pension insurance programme, a defined-benefit basic pension design in which the overall pension expenses would be funded solely by tax revenues, and the establishment of defined-contribution individual accounts instead of the current pension insurance programmes (Council of Economic Planning and Development, 2000; Tsai, 2008). The ideational contestations behind the various policy proposals revealed diverse, yet contradictory, approaches towards the public-private mix for old-age security, that is, whether the state should bear the financial responsibility, or whether the individuals should be responsible for their own old-age security without any wealth redistribution and risk sharing among different population groups.

The National Social Welfare Conference held in May 2002 marked a turning point, in that the social activist groups garnered support for an institutional design in favour of social solidarity. During the session, almost all participants from the social activist groups and academia unequivocally criticised the option of individual accounts, and advocated social insurance as the suitable option for sustaining old-age security. This created an impetus towards social insurance, with the remaining question concerned about whether the current pension insurance schemes for various occupational groups should (could) be integrated as a universal scheme. To maintain the transitional cost as low as possible, the government envisaged the establishment of a separate social insurance scheme only for those excluded from any current pension schemes.

With the idea of establishing a separate pension insurance scheme solely for these population groups taking hold, the ensuing political efforts brought the draft proposal of introducing a National Pension Insurance programme into the legislature, and finally won wide support to become a statutory law in July 2007. Although the new scheme was entitled "National Pension Insurance", it covered only peasants and socially disadvantaged groups.[7] The new pension scheme set the contribution rate at 6 per cent, and scheduled its successive rise in the following years. The insured people shared 60 per cent of the payable contributions, and the government subsidised the remaining 40 per cent. However, the insured person was entitled to a minimum pension benefit of NT$3000, regardless of the term selected by the beneficiary.[8]

Meanwhile, the revision of the Labour Standard Act to ameliorate the prospect of old-age security for the workers has received equal recognition. Political discussions were concerned with the question of how to revise it towards a more feasible framework, as well as the proportion of the financial responsibility between employers and employees (Yeh, 2006). After several months of disputes, the government introduced the new supplementary pension scheme (Labour Pension Act) in June 2004. The new regulation stipulates that all employers must transfer 6 per cent (or more) of the monthly payrolls of each employee into an individual pension account to be managed by the Bureau of Labour Insurance (Council of Labour Affairs, 2004). In addition to the mandatory employer contributions, workers may voluntarily make contributions of another 6 per cent of their monthly payrolls to their accounts, with corresponding tax concessions made for these contributions. During the policy-making process of the Labour Pension Act, however, the issue of globalisation did not play any explicit role. The only probable factor might be the transition from defined-benefit to defined-contribution out of the consideration to promote labour market flexibility (Yeh, 2006). Figure 10.2 shows the current constitution of the Taiwanese pension system.

The new supplementary pension scheme has improved the prospect of old-age security for workers as the individual account is now portable with a change of occupation, and a minimum pension is guaranteed. However, there was also the ambiguous character of pension privatisation in Taiwan. The 2004 reform to introduce individual accounts is only practised in the social insurance schemes for

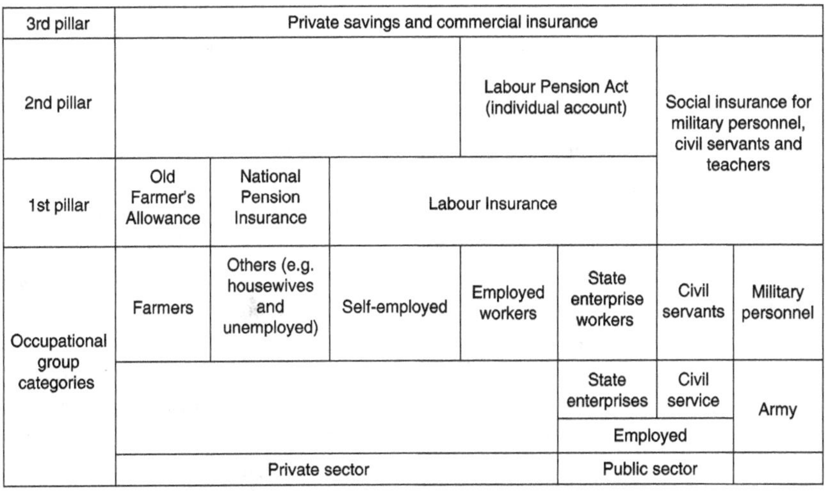

3rd pillar	Private savings and commercial insurance						
2nd pillar			Labour Pension Act (individual account)			Social insurance for military personnel, civil servants and teachers	
1st pillar	Old Farmer's Allowance	National Pension Insurance	Labour Insurance				
Occupational group categories	Farmers	Others (e.g. housewives and unemployed)	Self-employed	Employed workers	State enterprise workers	Civil servants	Military personnel
					State enterprises	Civil service	Army
					Employed		
	Private sector				Public sector		

Figure 10.2 Pension system in Taiwan.

Source: Compiled by authors

the workers, whereas the schemes for the other occupational groups (such as National Pension Insurance and the Farmers Insurance) remain unchanged. Even for the working population, public social insurance schemes function as the major bearer of their well-being, including income security in their old age. Moreover, although the Labour Insurance scheme incorporates the individual account as the second tier of old-age security, the government plays a dominant role, with the Labour Insurance Bureau acting as the exclusive administrator and custodian of the scheme. The government will close the gap with public finance should any investment loss occur. After decade-long pension reforms, the responsibility for old-age security in Taiwan still rests with public pensions, implying heavy burdens of the state in view of the ageing population. The subsequent theme of pension politics may change the manner in which to empower the role of private pensions.

Conclusion

East Asian welfare states have long been regarded as the prototype of intransigent developmentalism. Features of low social expenditures and the emphasis on family and individual responsibility were commonly associated with the political quest to "catch-up" in modernisation. In this regard, social policy has exhibited a strong productivist character that depressed consumptive welfare requirements in favour of economic growth. However, the preceding analysis indicates that, although the developmental state thesis captured the gist of East Asian welfare states, it did not sufficiently address the specific national diversity in welfare provision, particularly by private agencies. The lopsided stress on low public social expenditures has led to the negligence of private welfare where state involvements are equally active (Kim, 2010). Perceiving this hidden aspect of state regulation is crucial to understanding the developments of social welfare in this region. Related literature on East Asian welfare states indicated the strong regulatory role of the state in welfare provision; however, they failed to explore various roles of the state in diverse dimensions, especially in the private domain (Goodman *et al.*, 1998; Kwon, 2005; Lee and Ku, 2007).

The interplay of the public-private pension mix is of particular interest to the state in its efforts to weave a safety net for old-age security. Although Japan and Taiwan were regarded as two East Asian societies with similar institutional features in social protection, the manner in which public and private pensions are managed demonstrates considerable differences. The institutionalisation of non-state pension schemes in Japan was initially implemented to manage the problem of economic coordination, such as skill formation, and as patient capital for long-term investment in key industries. Non-state pension schemes served as a part of the economic developmental strategy. This state-led development encountered pressures to deregulate the financial markets in the era of globalisation, leading to new modes of governance that regarded non-state pension schemes more from the viewpoint of old-age security than economic development. This has substantial implications for state activities in financial markets because the main goal is to include pension markets in the overall regulatory framework of old-age security.

By contrast, private pensions in Taiwan played a minor role in the post-war era. The authoritarian regime concentrated key resources and capital in state-owned enterprises in upstream sectors, resulting in the emergence of SMEs in downstream sectors, which have become the major body of the Taiwanese economy. In such a dual economy, private pensions did not rise to political and economic prominence because large industries in key sectors secured the funding through bank loans, as dictated (and owned) by the government. The disadvantaged SMEs learned to manage on their own when encountering fierce international competition. Under these circumstances, both government and employers had insufficient incentives to encourage the growth of private pensions because this option yielded few economic gains and administrative burdens. Moreover, providing old-age security to the workers of SMEs, and all workers in general, was not a political imperative until democratisation unleashed a strong demand for this direction. Even at this stage, the new pension politics since the 1990s demonstrates a statist approach that emphasises the expansion of public pension schemes and encourages the incremental growth of occupational pensions.

The comparative study of Japanese and Taiwanese approaches toward pension provision in this chapter has highlighted a crucial aspect of welfare state transformation in East Asia, particularly regarding the manner in which the state recalibrates the scope and extent of its regulation in the interplay of public and private welfare provision. The rationales and directions of recent pension reforms in East Asia can be further understood only by considering the historical contexts of political and economic structures. In the quest to "modernise" pension systems in response to the foreseeable demographic pressure, Japan has an effective leverage to construct a multi-pillar pension system with its fully fledged occupational pension schemes. By contrast, the predominant industrial structures and the instinctive statist doctrine in Taiwan may limit the extent of future private pension provision, as public pensions still assume greater responsibilities for old-age security. However, with the impending demographic ageing and fiscal constraints in the near future, it becomes likely that the next pension reforms will introduce state regulation in favour of occupational pensions and private savings.

Notes

1 In post-war Japan, Postal Saving and Postal Life Insurance were two policy instruments for channelling financial resources to strategic industries to stimulate economic growth.
2 In 1991, the Japanese government launched the National Pension Fund that benefited population groups such as peasants or the self-employed who remained excluded from any corporate pension schemes. Because of its subsidiary features, the following analysis sets aside discussion of this scheme.
3 The EPFs is open to large firms with more than 1,000 employees, aiming to reduce the financial burdens of employers.
4 Two public banks, the Japan Development Bank and Exported, were founded in the 1950s, serving as key institutions in the developmental strategy to steer capital into key industries.

5 These two social insurance schemes also covered major risks as the Labour Insurance programme, albeit with much more lavish benefit levels.
6 The following analysis is a revised version of previous article written by Shi (2010).
7 Yet, this policy direction was reversed again in 2008 by the KMT's president Ying-jeou Ma, who decoupled the allowances for elderly peasants from the National Pension Insurance to quench their anger at possible benefit cutbacks.
8 The calculation of pension benefits would be based on two methods: either a basic pension of NT$3000 + number of pensionable years × monthly contribution × 0.55 per cent; or a pension benefit calculated in accordance with the number of pensionable years x monthly contribution x 1.1 per cent. The insured person could choose the better one of the two calculation terms.

References

Béland, D. and Shinkawa, T. (2007). "Public and Private Policy Change: Pension Reform in Four Countries", *Policy Studies Journal*, 35(3): 349–371.

Bonoli, G. and Shinkawa, T. (2005). "Population Ageing and the Logics of Pension Reform in Western Europe, East Asia and North America", in G. Bonoli and T. Shinkawa (eds) *Ageing and Pension Reform Around the World: Evidence from Eleven Countries*. Cheltenham: Edward Elgar, pp. 1–23.

Busemeyer, M. R. (2009). "Asset Specificity, Institutional Complementarities and the Variety of Skill Regimes in Coordinated Market Economies", *Socio-Economic Review*, 7(3): 375–406.

Choi, Y. J. (2008). "Pension Policy and Politics in East Asia", *Policy and Politics*, 36(1): 127–144.

Choi, Y. J. (2009). "From Developmental Regimes to Post-developmental Regimes: Business and Pension Reforms in Japan, South Korea and Taiwan", in K. H. Mok and R. Forrest (eds) *Changing Governance and Public Policy in East Asia*. London: Routledge, pp. 206–227.

Conrad, H. (2011). "Change and Continuity in Japanese Compensation Practices: The Case of Occupational Pensions since the Early 2000s", *International Journal of Human Resource Management*, 22(15): 3051–3067.

Conrad, H. (2012). "Economic System and Welfare Regime Dynamics in Japan Since the Early 2000s – The Case of Occupational Pensions", *Journal of Social Policy*, 41(1): 119–140.

Control Yuan (2002). *Investigation Report on the Examination of Social Welfare Institutions in Taiwan*. Taipei (in Chinese).

Council of Economic Planning and Development (2000). *A Briefing on the Individual Accounts of the National Pension Insurance and Tax-funded Balance Funds*. Taipei (in Chinese).

Council of Labour Affairs (2004). *A Briefing on the Labour Pension Act*. Taipei (in Chinese).

Dulebohn, J. H., Molloy, J. C., Pichler, S. M. and Murray, B. (2009). "Employee Benefits: Literature Review and Emerging Issues", *Human Resource Management Review*, 19(2): 86–103.

Ebbinghaus, B. and Gronwald, M. (2011). "The Changing Public–Private Pension Mix in Europe: From Path Dependence to Path Departure", in B. Ebbinghaus (ed.) *The Varieties of Pension Governance: Pension Privatization in Europe*. Oxford: Oxford University Press, pp. 23–53.

Ebbinghaus, B. and Manow, P. (2001). "Introduction: Studying Varieties of Welfare Capitalism", in B. Ebbinghaus and P. Manow (eds) *Comparing Welfare Capitalism: Social Policy and Political Economy in Europe, Japan and the USA*. London: Routledge, pp. 1–24.

Ebbinghaus, B. and Wiß, T. (2011). "The Governance and Regulation of Private Pensions in Europe", in B. Ebbinghaus (ed.) *The Varieties of Pension Governance: Pension Privatization in Europe*. Oxford: Oxford University Press, pp. 351–383.

Esping-Andersen, G. (1997). "Hybrid or Unique?: The Japanese Welfare State Between Europe and America", *Journal of European Social Policy*, 7(3): 179–189.

Estévez-Abe, M. (2001). "The Forgotten Link: The Financial Regulation of Japanese Pension Funds in Comprative Perspective", in B. Ebbinghaus and P. Manow (eds) *Comparing Welfare Capitalism: Social Policy and Political Economy in Europe, Japan and the USA*. London: Routledge, pp. 190–214.

Estévez-Abe, M. (2008). *Welfare and Capitalism in Postwar Japan*. Cambridge: Cambridge University Press.

Estévez-Abe, M., Iversen, T. and Soskice, D. (2001). "Social Protection and the Formation of Skills: A Reinterpretation of the Welfare State", in P. Hall and D. Soskice (eds) *Varieties of Capitalism: The Institutional Foundations of Comparative Advantage*. Oxford: Oxford University Press, pp. 145–183.

Fu, L. Y. (2000). "Old-age Pensions, Party Competition, and Elections", in M. Hsiao and K. M. Lin (eds) *Social Welfare Movements in Taiwan*. Taipei: Juliu Press, pp. 231–256 (in Chinese).

Goodman, R., White, G. and Kwon, H. J. (eds) (1998). *The East Asian Welfare Model: Welfare Orientalism and the State*. London: Routledge.

Gough, I. (2000). "Globalisation and Regional Welfare Regimes: the East Asian Case", *Global Social Policy*, 1(2): 163–189.

Häusermann, S. (2010). *The Politics of Welfare State in Continental Europe: Modernization in Hard Times*. Cambridge: Cambridge University Press.

Holliday, I. (2000). "Productivist Welfare Capitalism: Social Policy in East Asia", *Political Studies*, 48(4): 706–723.

Holliday, I. and Wilding, P. (2003). "Welfare Capitalism in the Tiger Economies of East and Southeast Asia", in I. Holliday and P. Wilding (eds) *Welfare Capitalism in East Asia: Social Policy in the Tiger Economies*. Basingstoke: Palgrave, pp. 1–17.

Huber, E. and Stephens, J. D. (2001). "Welfare State and Production Regime in the Era of Retrenchment", in P. Pierson (ed.) *The New Politics of the Welfare State*. Oxford: Oxford University Press, pp. 107–145.

Iversen, T. (2005). *Capitalism, Democracy, and Welfare*. Cambridge: Cambridge University Press.

Jackson, G. and Vitols, S. (2001). "Between Financial Commitment, Market Liquidity and Corporate Governance: Occupational Pensions in Britian, Germany, Japan and the USA", in B. Ebbinghaus and P. Manow (eds) *Comparing Welfare Capitalism: Social Policy and Political Economy in Europe, Japan and the USA*. London: Routledge, pp. 171–189.

Katsumata, Y. K. (2004). "The Relationship between the Role of the Corporate Pension and the Public Pension Plan in Japan", in M. Rein and W. Schmähl (eds) *Rethinking the Welfare State: The Political Economy of Pension Reform*. Cheltenham: Edward Elgar, pp. 56–80.

Kim, P. H. (2010). "The East Asian Welfare State Debate and Surrogate Social Policy: an Exploratory Study on Japan and South Korea", *Socio-Economic Review*, 8(3): 411–435.

Kimura, Y. (1997). "The Role of the Japanese Company in Compesating Income Loss after Retirement", in M. Rein and E. Wadensjö (eds) *Enterprise and the Welfare State*. Cheltenham: Edward Elgar, pp. 195–219.

Ku, Y. W. (1997). *Welfare Capitalism in Taiwan: State, Economy and Social Policy*. Basingstoke: Macmillan.

Kwon, H. J. (1997). "Beyond European Welfare Regimes: Comparative Perspectives on East Asian Welfare Systems", *Journal of Social Policy*, 26(4): 467–484.

Kwon, H. J. (2005). "An Overview of the Study: The Developmental Welfare State and Policy Reforms in East Asia", in H. J. Kwon (ed.) *Transforming the Developmental Welfare State in East Asia*. Basingstoke: Palgrave, pp. 1–23.

Lee, S. Y. (2011). "The Evolution of Welfare Production Regimes in East Asian: A Comparative Study of Korea, Japan, and Taiwan", *Korean Journal of Policy Studies*, 26(1): 49–57.

Lee, Y. J. and Ku, Y. W. (2003). "Another Welfare World? A Preliminary Examination of the Developmental Welfare Regime In East Asia", *Taiwan Journal of Sociology*, 31: 189–241.

Lee, Y. J. and Ku, Y. W. (2007). "East Asian Welfare Regimes: Testing the Hypothesis of the Developmental Welfare State", *Social Policy and Administration*, 41(2): 197–212.

Lee, Z. R. and Chen, C. Y. (2011). "Restoration: 1952–1961", in J. H. Wong and J. T. Wen (eds) *A Hundred Years of Enterprises and Industries*. Taipei: Chuliu, pp. 68–91 (in Chinese).

Leisering, L. (2010). "From Redistribution to Regulation: Regulating Private Old-Age Pensions as a New Challenge in Ageing Societies", in M. Hyde and J. Dixon (eds) *Comparing How Various Nations Administer Retirement Income: Essays on Social Security, Privatisation, and Inter-Generational Covenants*. Lewiston: The Edwin Mellen Press, pp. 213–236.

Lin, C. W. (2005). "Pension Reform in Taiwan: The Old and the New Politics of Welfare", in G. Bonoli and T. Shinkawa (eds) *Ageing and Pension Reform Around the World: Evidence from Eleven Countries*. Cheltenham: Edward Elgar, pp. 182–207.

Lin, W. I. (1994). *Welfare States: Historical and Comparative Analysis*. Taipei: Juliu Press (in Chinese).

Manow, P. (2001a). *Globalization, Corporate Finance, and Coordinated Capitalism: Pension Finance in Germany and Japan*. MPIFG Working Paper.

Manow, P. (2001b). *Social Protection, Capitalist Production: The Bismarckian Welfare State and the German Political Economy from the 1880s to the 1990s*. Konstanz: University of Konstanz.

Manow, P. (2001c). "Welfare State Building and Coordinated Capitalism in Japan and Germany", in W. Streeck and K. Yamamura (eds) *The Origins of Nonliberal Capitalism: Germany and Japan in Comparison*. Ithaca, NY: Cornell University Press, pp. 94–120.

Myles, J. and Pierson, P. (2001). "The Comparative Political Economy of Pension Reform", in P. Pierson (ed.) *The New Politics of the Welfare State*. Oxford: Oxford University Press, pp. 305–333.

Orenstein, M. A. (2008). *Privatizing Pensions: The Transnational Campaign for Social Security Reform*. Princeton, NJ: Princeton University Press.

Park, G. (2004). "The Political-Economic Dimension of Pensions: The Case of Japan", *Governance*, 17(4): 549–572.

Pempel, T. J. (2002). "Labor Exclusion and Privatized Welfare: Two Keys to Asian Capitalist Development", in E. Huber (ed.) *Models of Capitalism: Lessons for Latin America*. University Park, PA: The Pennsylvania State University Press, pp. 277–300.

Peng, I. (2012). "Economic Dualization in Japan and South Korea", in P. Emmenegger, S. Hausermann, B. Palier and M. Seeleib-Kaiser (eds) *The Age of Dualization: The Changing Face of Inequality in Deindustrializing Societies*. Oxford: Oxford University Press, pp. 226–249.

Rein, M. and Schmähl, W. (eds) (2004). *Rethinking the Welfare State: The Political Economy of Pension Reform*. Cheltenham: Edward Elgar.

Rein, M. and Turner, J. (2004). "How Societies Mix Public and Private Spheres in their Pension Systems", in M. Rein, and W. Schmähl (eds) *Rethinking the Welfare State: The Political Economy of Pension Reform*. Cheltenham: Edward Elgar, pp. 251–293.

Schröder, M. (2009). "Integrating Welfare and Production Typologies: How Refinements of the Varieties of Capitalism Approach call for a Combination of Welfare Typologies", *Journal of Social Policy*, 38(1): 19–43.

Shi, S. J. (2010). "The Fragmentation of the Old-Age Security System: The Politics of Pension Reform in Taiwan", in K. H. Mok and Y. W. Ku (eds) *Social Cohesion in Greater China: Challenges for Social Policy and Governance*. Singapore: World Scientific Publishing, pp. 339–371.

Shinkawa, T. (2005). "The Politics of Pension Reform in Japan: Institutional Legacies, Credit-claiming and Blame Avoidance", in G. Bonoli and T. Shinkawa (eds) *Ageing and Pension Reform Around the World: Evidence from Eleven Countries*. Cheltenham: Edward Elgar, pp. 157–181.

Shinkawa, T. and Pempel, T. J. (1996). "Occupational Welfare and the Japanese Experience", in M. Shalev (ed.) *The Privatization of Social Policy? Occupational Welfare and the Welfare State in America, Scandinavia and Japan*. Basinstoke: Macmillan, pp. 280–326.

Swank, D. (2002). *Global Capital, Political Institutions, and Policy Change in Developed Welfare State*. Cambridge: Cambridge University Press.

Tang, K. L. (2000). *Social Welfare Development in East Asia*. New York: St Martin's Press.

Thelen, K. (2004). *How Institutions Evolve: The Political Economy of Skills in Germany, Britain, the United States, and Japan*. Cambridge: Cambridge University Press.

Thelen, K. and Kume, I. (2006). "Coordination as a Political Problem in Coordinated Market Economies", *Governance*, 19(1): 11–42.

Tsai, Y. C. (2008). *Ideas, Interests, and Institutions: The Politics of National Pension Programme in Taiwan*. MA thesis, Department of Sociology, National Taiwan University (in Chinese).

Vangunsteren, H. and Rein, M. (1985). "The Dialectic of Public and Private Pensions", *Journal of Social Policy*, 14(2): 129–149.

Vogel, S. K. (2006). *Japan Remodeled: How Government and Industry are Reforming*. Ithaca, NY: Cornell University Press.

Wong, J. (2004). *Healthy Democracies: Welfare Politics in Taiwan and South Korea*. Ithaca, NY: Cornell University Press.

Woo-Cumings, M. (1999). "Introduction: Chalmers Johnson and the Politics of Nationalism and Development", in M. Woo-Cumings (ed.) *The Developmental State*. Ithaca, NY: Cornell University Press, pp. 1–31.

Wu, M. J. (1997). "Analysis of Future Reforms on Occupation Pension Institutions in Taiwan", *Social Policy and Social Work*, 1(2): 137–186 (in Chinese).

Wu, Y. P. (2004). "Rethinking the Taiwanese Developmental State", *China Quarterly*, 177: 91–114.

Yeh, S. Y. (2006). *The Comparison between "National Pension Law" and "Labour Retirement Pension System" in the Legislative Process from the Polity-centered Perspective.* MA thesis, Graduate Institute of Political Economy, National Chengkung University (in Chinese).

Yi, I. (2007). *The Politics of Occupational Welfare in Korea.* Fukuoka: Hana-Syoin.

11 Poverty reduction, welfare provision and social security challenges in China in the context of fiscal reform and the 12th Five-year Plan

Emile Kok-Kheng Yeoh and Susie Yieng-Ping Ling

Introduction

Since the 1994 "tax sharing" reform, while about equal shares have been generally observed in terms of total volume of government revenue at the level of the central government and that of the local provincial governments, the comparison between revenues and expenditures shows that practically every local provincial government annually had registered a budget deficit in relation to the central government's budget surplus (Gao, 2007: 188–189). The extent of the deficit has been huge, especially in those local governments in the western part of the country, and this has greatly constrained local governments' ability to take care of anything in excess of their very basic fiscal expenditure responsibilities, hence making the central government obliged to take up social welfare responsibilities even at the local level, especially health care (Gao, 2007). Going back to the details of "tax sharing", the fiscal reform in 1994, at least in the short term, has been seen to result in centralisation or recentralisation after the large extent of decentralisation during the earlier reform period. As a result, the Chinese central state's fiscal power has been greatly strengthened in relation to local government (*difang*) in terms of the division of taxes. "Tax sharing" (*fenshuizhi*) divided the taxes into the central taxes, local taxes and shared taxes. This chapter critically examines poverty reduction, welfare provision and social security challenges in china against the policy context of finical reform after the 12th Five-year Plan.

1994 fiscal reform's implications for decentralisation and local social security

Through the tax system reform, income sources were stabilised, tax sources concentrated and types of taxes with higher potential increased – though most of these are classified as central state's fixed revenue or shared revenue of the central and local governments (and among the taxes, the largest one is the enterprise value added tax which is designated as a shared tax, of which 75 per cent goes to central government and 25 per cent per cent to local government). Local sources of revenue are almost all those small and medium taxes with unstable and scattered tax bases, those which are difficult to collect and administer, or with high cost of collection. Through such division, the proportion of central government revenue has increased rapidly, changing the central-to-local ratio from 3:7 to 6:4. During the following decade (mid 1990s to mid 2000s), this level was maintained, but the central to local ratio of public expenditure over the same period remained at 3:7.[1] The 1994 reform represented the second phase of reform-era China's fiscal decentralisation. From the year 1978, when reform began, until today, public expenditure decentralisation has been consistent throughout, but decentralisation of revenue has experienced two stages of, first, decentralisation, and then (re-)centralisation. The first stage was between 1978 and 1993, and during that period local governments were not only given a higher degree of autonomy in terms of public expenditure but were also allowed considerabe revenue autonomy. As the growth of local government revenue had been greater than that of the central government and hence the decentralisation of fiscal revenue had been increasing, the central government's financial risk had been increasing too. In this context, tax sharing reform was implemented in 1994 and fiscal revenue centralisation had begun. The second stage is the tax sharing system reform since 1994. By adjusting the division of tax revenue, the central government, has since rapidly increased the proportion revenue accrued to itself. At the same time, the central government's transfer payments also increased rapidly (Wang *et al.*, 2010). What is the implication of the change for poverty reduction and narrowing the income gap?

Evolution of social security and poverty alleviation

The evolution of modern China's social security system since the establishment of the People's Republic has generally been divided into four historical stages: (1) the 1951–66 period of founding and development; (2) the 1967–77 period of stagnation or retrogression; (3) the 1978–85 period of adjustment and recovery; and (4) the period of reform and innovation since 1986 (Tang, 2008: 144). However, China's social security reform has been described as an exercise from scratch, and in the drive to accelerate the effective construction of a social security system, the policy implementation has in general been top-down in the form of the enforcement of rules and regulations at various tiers of local government and government departments, rather than through nationwide legislation (Yin, 2008: 269). Nevertheless, whether the initiative came directly from the central government or stemmed from the localities' practical necessities, the establishment of a social security system guaranteeing a minimum standard of living, and health care especially as a priority target for the setting up of an adequate rural social security system, is closely linked to poverty reduction efforts, in particular in the hardcore poverty areas (Tang, 2008: 333).

According to statistics on China's rural incidence of poverty, poverty reduction after the beginning of the "reform and opening up" policy can also be divided into two phases. With the "reform and opening up" policy, China's poverty problem has been greatly ameliorated, with the incidence of poverty declining rapidly.

However, from 1987 to 1993, the incidence of poverty has been fluctuating at above 10 per cent. Since 1994, the incidence of poverty has experienced a more significant decline, dropping rapidly to about 3 per cent and at the same time entering a period of relative stability. Putting these together with China's fiscal decentralisation, it can be seen that the complete fiscal decentralisation since 1978 has seemingly brought about about a rapid decline in the rural incidence of poverty, stabilising at 10 per cent, and the partial fiscal decentralisation since 1994 has led to the rural incidence of poverty stabilising at 3 per cent. Therefore, China's practice of fiscal decentralisation has in a way seemed to provide a foundation for the positive performance of poverty reduction policies (Wang *et al.*, 2010).

China's poverty reduction policies can be largely grouped into three categories: (1) developmental poverty reduction policies; (2) social security policies; and (3) pro-peasant policies. In terms of developmental poverty reduction, policies for rural areas have been population relocation and work-replacing subsidies in poor counties (1985); fiscal development investment (1986); soft loans, technological poverty reduction and social poverty reduction in poor areas (1986); compulsory education in the western region (1995); microcredit in poor areas (1996); whole-village development (2001); retraining of the labour force in poor counties (2004); industrialisation in poor areas (2004); and the western region's "two-basic" campaign (2004). Developmental poverty reduction policies for urban areas have been in the form of re-employment (*xiagang*[2]) (1995). Social security policies for rural areas have included the "Five Guarantees System" (*wubaohu*) (era of people's communes; rural three-destitution population – those with no land, no job and no social security protection); rural medical assistance (2002); rural low-income security; and rural hardcore poverty assistance (2003). Social security policies for urban areas are childbirth insurance (urban female employees, 1988); unemployment insurance for employees of urban enterprises and organisations (1993); old-age insurance for employees of urban enterprises (1995); urban low-income security for poor urban families (1997); medical insurance for urban work unit employees (1998); and work injury insurance for employees of urban enterprises (2003). Among the pro-peasant policies (for rural areas) are the one-fee reform for rural primary and secondary schools (2001); adjustment of distribution planning of primary and secondary schools (2001); compensation for efficiency of forest habitat (2001); defarming-reforestation and defarming-degreasing and grassland-forest-restoration (2002); food, seed and fertiliser subsidies for food-producing areas (2003); new cooperative medical service for rural populations (2003); reform of rural taxes and fees (2004); and rural compulsory education reform (2006).[3] China's focused poverty reduction policies began in the mid-1980s in the rural areas, while urban poverty only received attention from the mid-1990s with the emergence of the problems of urban unemployment – partly as a result of state-owned enterprise (SOE) reform and the related issue of *xiagang*. On the other hand, with the disintegration of the people's commune (*renmin gongshe*) system, provision of certain basic social services and securities such as basic medical services further deteriorated.[4] In line with the differentials in government financial strength and the gap in urban-rural levels of development, different policies and institutional arrangements have been followed in poverty reduction in urban and rural areas. The focus of rural poverty reduction is to promote the economic growth of poor areas and the income growth of the poor (the developmental approach to poverty reduction), whereas the focus of urban poverty reduction has been to provide basic social security (i.e. implementing the system of minimum living security and various systems of compulsory social insurance).[5]

The 17th Party Congress declared the target and mission of "a goal, an expansion, two enhancements" of poverty alleviation (i.e. to basically eliminate absolute poverty by the year 2020), to expand the development support effort for the old revolutionary base areas, ethnic minority areas, frontier areas and poverty areas, and to enhance the level of poverty alleviation and gradually increase the standard of poverty alleviation. This is in recognition that the country's rural poor population is still very large, and the gap between their per capita income and the national rural per capita income is still widening, showing that the growing developmental disparity between the poverty-stricken areas and other areas has not been fundamentally reversed. Yan points out that China's rural Gini coefficient has always been higher than in urban areas, implying that the intra-rural income disparity is fuelled by the expansion of the national income disparity, while the urban-rural income disparity is the main cause of the continuous expansion of the national income gap – in fact, the 20 per cent urban highest income group's income is shown to be 5.5 times the income of the 20 per cent urban lowest income group, whereas the 20 per cent rural highest income groups income is 7.3 times the income of the 20 per cent rural lowest income group (Yan, 2010: 177–179). The poverty level of the absolute poor remains severe, and there are many poor people living in places with harsh natural conditions. Chen (2006) shows that among China's 592 poor counties, 366 are in the western region and 258 of these are in remote mountain counties, occupying about 70 per cent of the western mountain counties. Most of these poor counties are distributed over six major areas of fragile ecology – the Inner Mongolian plateau's south-eastern border area (which suffers from desertification), the *Huangtu* plateau's gully area (which suffers from severe soil erosion), the environmentally deteriorating mountainous areas of the *Qin Ba* region, the ecologically endangered hilly areas of the karst plateau, the sealed-off mountain and valley areas of the *Hengduan* range, and the severely cold mountain areas of the western deserts. Being ecologically fragile and sensitive, all these are areas are extremely short of resources and are extremely poor environments for human habitation (Chen, 2006: 176–177). Due to weak self-development capacity, the rate of returning to poverty in these areas is still relatively high, especially in the case of falling back to poverty due to natural calamities.

Developmental approach to rural poverty alleviation and social assistance during the earlier Five-year Plan periods

According to the mid-term evaluation results of "China's Rural Poverty Alleviation and Development (2001–2010)" framework, five years since its implementation the poverty population with inadequate food and shelter has been reduced from 29.27 million to 23.65 million (i.e. a reduction of 5.62 million), while the low-income poor population has been reduced from 61.02 million to 40.67 million (i.e. a reduction of 20.35 million). At the same time, there has also been a relatively substantial improvement in production and living conditions in poor areas, and significant progress in various social undertakings. In 2005, when the World Bank president visited China, he commented that since 1980 China's out-of-poverty population accounted for 75 per cent of all developing countries' out-of-poverty populations, and this was a striking fact that made China's achievements in poverty reduction particularly remarkable. However, at the same time, data also shows that the rate of poverty reduction in China has apparently been slowing down. While the average annual reduction in rural poverty was 13.7 million in the 1980s, the average annual number reduction during the 1990s was 6.2 million. Moving into the twenty-first century, the average was 1.5 million (Gong, 2009). During the implementation of rural developmental approach to poverty reduction in the past, China's central government and local governments invested a large amount of funds, while some international organisations, civil organisations and other organisations were also involved in funding. During the past two decades, the central government's poverty reduction fiscal investment in production sectors amounted to more than 150 billion yuan (i.e. 2 per cent–3 per cent of the central government expenditure), while the government's financial organisations released more than 160 billion yuan in funds for poverty assistance loans.[7] The central government has invested more than 10 billion yuan in the poor regions to promote social development capital in the education and health sectors. At the same time, local governments' poverty assistance investments have amounted to more than 70 billion yuan and those from the various international organisations and social organisations are estimated to be over 100 billion yuan.

From the early 1980s, there were three main sources for central government's poverty assistance investment. The first is the "*San Xi*"[8] construction capital (1983): this development fund increased in 1986 and a new poverty assistance fund was added in 1997. The second is the funding for the "work for subsidies" (i.e. work instead of subsidies) programme (1985). The third is the poverty assistance soft loans (i.e. discounted government loans), managed by the China Agricultural Bank since 1986. These three poverty assistance tools came to a cumulative amount of 322.8 billion yuan from 1986 to 2005 at current prices, including soft loans of 167.1 billion yuan, "work for subsidies" of 83.4 billion yuan and fiscal development funds of 72.3 billion yuan.[9] The structure of the three types of poverty assistance funding shows that most of the time more than half of it has been in soft loans, making these the main source of poverty assistance funding. Other than the poverty assistance soft loans managed by the China Agricultural Bank, there are some other types of small-scale loan available for poor regions, including loans for the revolution base areas, ethnic minority areas and remote areas provided by the China People's Bank in 1984; the general normal interest poverty assistance loans began by the China Agricultural Bank (also in 1984); loans for the pastoral regions provided by the China Agricultural

Bank (1988) and loans for county enterprises for the government-designated poverty counties provided by the China People's Bank and the Industrial and Commercial Bank (1988). The World Bank's estimates, however, show that despite these efforts, whether in accordance with the poverty line of China's statistical bureau or its low-income definition, or the poverty line of US$1 per day per head, the proportion of rural poor in relation to the total poor of the country was above 99 per cent. Even if one includes the shifting rural population in urban areas as part of the urban poor, the rural poor still make up 91 per cent of the national total.[10] An expanding income gap has always been a major negative result of China's "economic reform and opening up" policy, and the urban-rural income gap and inter-regional income disparity play a very important part in explaining the overall income gap of the country. The urban-rural income gap and inter-regional income disparity are indeed widening, and this is to a certain extent related to the institution of economic decentralisation. The relationship between the urban-rural income gap and economic/fiscal decentralisation can be explained by local governments' priority of developing cities and implementing economic policy incentives which are biased towards cities (Wang *et al.*, 2006).

Economists have observed the substantial influence of four major factors on the formation of the huge urban–rural income gap: (1) the government's price control on agricultural and agri-based products; (2) the unreasonable tax burden the rural people are subjected to; (3) the urban-rural labour market segmentation and the closure of the urban labour market; and (4) the discriminatory nature of social welfare and social security. All four can be seen as manifestations of urban bias in terms of economic policy (Wang *et al.*, 2006). Furthermore, due to the prevalent poverty in rural areas, the type of poverty reduction by assistance areas that focuses, in urban areas, on income subsidies is not feasible in rural areas. A major reason for the unfeasibility of a comprehensive social security system in rural areas is the financial capacity of the local governments as well as these governments' administrative capability, including technical and institutional problems suhc as the identification of the beneficiary families and individuals in rural areas. Furthermore, after more than two decades of developmental poverty reduction, the problem of identifying poor populations has only been resolved very recently.[11] On the other hand, it should be noted that China's urban poverty is a social problem that began to be apparent only in the 1990s, when the reforms in economic institutions (especially SOEs) led to large-scale *xiagang*, unemployment and living difficulties.

The incidence of poverty rose by 10 per cent during 1995–9, and the poverty differential rose by 36 per cent.[12] China's government has since implemented urban anti-poverty policies to tackle the increasingly serious urban poverty problem, with the construction of an urban anti-poverty system that focuses on an urban social security system guaranteeing a minimum standard of living. Four phases can be delineated through which this system in general has evolved. The first is the trial phase from 1993 to the first half of 1997, beginning in Shanghai and extending to some other coastal cities. Shanghai implemented a social security system guaranteeing a minimum standard of living in June 1993, at a monthly income per capita of 120 yuan.[13] The system moved into the formation phase from 1997 to the first half of 2001 with the government issuing a formal declaration of the construction of a nationwide urban social security system guaranteeing a minimum standard of living and clearly stated the building of such a system under the 9th Five-year Plan. One feature of the policy was to let each local government fix its own security line, instead of following a standard national line. This pioneering "Shanghai model" – comprising the aforesaid urban social security system guaranteeing a minimum standard of living in 1993, a similar programme in 1994 for rural areas, the nation's first provincial government/ province-level municipality social assistance regulations in 1996, social insurance for workers from outside Shanghai in 2002 and the nation's first ever social insurance system for townships in 2003 – has provided a good legal institutional experience for other localities and has been confirmed by the central government for gradual nationwide implementation (Yin, 2008: 269–270).

In 1999, the central government allocated 400 million yuan to subsidise the regions experiencing economic difficulties, and this increased to 800 million yuan in 2000. Moving into the third phase of implementation from the second half of 2001 to 2002, the number of beneficiaries of this policy rapidly climbed from 4.02 million to 20.64 million.[14] Because of the acceleration in SOE reform, problems of *xiagang* personnel and their families have become increasingly apparent, and led to social instability. Hence, in August 2001, the government decided to add 1.5 billion[15] yuan onto the basic budgeted 800 million yuan to further strengthen the social security system guaranteeing a minimum standard of living. The budget for this increased to 4 billion yuan by early 2002, which meant that the central government had taken up the major part of the funding for this system. Moving into the fourth phase of consolidation, the number of beneficiaries stabilised at the 2003 level. However, the central government's budget funding for this continued to increase even after 2003, with an increment of 1 billion yuan annually, from 9.2 billion yuan in 2003 to 11.2 billion yuan by 2005.[16]

After 2002, social assistance under this system had extended to medical assistance, employment assistance, educational assistance and lodging assistance. On the other hand, with the rapid economic growth and acceleration in urbanisation, a massive number of rural people were leaving for urban areas to look for employment opportunities. The number of such rural-to-urban migrants has been increasing from year to year and reached 132 million in 2006. A government survey estimated a total of 89.07 million rural migrant labourers in urban areas.[17] Taking into consideration the survey's 5 per cent margin of error, the real number was actually close to 100 million. The problem is that during the construction of the urban social security system the priority had been for urban residents. Hence these 100 million rural-to-urban migrant labourers are not getting any form of social welfare or assistance in the urban areas and at the same time, having left the rural areas, they are not benefiting from the rural poverty assistance programmes, hence turning them into a special community outside social welfare policy altogether. Furthermore, these rural-to-urban migrant labourers are mainly engaged in highly manual and high-risk jobs without any work security, with bad lodgings and hygiene conditions. They do not enjoy the same education and medical services as urban residents, and often suffer from discrimination. Without proper social assistance when living in poverty, and suffering from inequalities, this had led to these migrants being involved in crime and other serious social problems.

Poverty alleviation in the 11th and 12th Five-year Plan periods and the importance of social security support

During the 11th Five-year Plan period, China's poverty population decreased from 64.31 million to 26.88 million. (i.e. a five-year average annual reduction of 7.486 million). In the coming decade China placed the basic elimination of absolute poverty as the primary task of poverty alleviation and development. The ultimate target was to eliminate the phenomenon of absolute poverty by 2020. During the 11th Five-year Plan period, work on poverty alleviation was carried out in full force, leading to the country's poverty population being reduced to 26.88 million by 2010, with the incidence of poverty dropping to 2.8 per cent. Durin g this time, the poverty alleviation focus counties' rural per capita net income experienced an average annual growth of 10.28 per cent – i.e. 0.95 percentage points higher than the national average, reversing the situation during the 10th Five-year Plan period in which the rural per capita net income of these focus counties was lower than the national average. Such achievement was also reflected in the strengthening of infrastructure in poverty-stricken areas, more rapid economic development of the counties and further improvement of the ecological environment.

With the targets of the "China Rural Poverty Alleviation and Development (2001–2010)" framework considered as having been achieved, a new "China Rural Poverty Alleviation and Development (2011–2020)" framework was promulgated in the 12th Five-year Plan period, with increased standards for poverty alleviation. While much progress has been made during the whole reform period, China's poverty population size is still huge, and returning to poverty is presenting renewed challenges. Furthermore, the perennial serious threat of natural disasters and the difficulties of overcoming them in poverty-stricken areas has also contributed to China's still-widening income gap, increasingly apparent relative poverty, uneven regional development and the glaring contradictions in terms of the contiguous poverty-stricken areas. In view of this, the formidable task of the 12th Five-year Plan has been poverty alleviation which is seen to be entering a very critical stage, especially amidst the mounting social discontent manifest in widespread social unrest throughout the country in recent years.

According to the State Council Poverty Alleviation Office of Policy and Regulation Department, to ensure that no Chinese citizens are left behind in the progress into *xiaokang shehui* (formally translated as a "well-off society"), elimination of absolute poverty represents the prioritised mission during the

12th Five-year Plan period, with particular focus on the contiguous poverty-stricken areas. It is to be carried out through coordinated development which is centred on promoting employment, increasing income, improving people's livelihoods and accelerating development (Gu, 2011). In fact, other than the poverty assistance investment from the central government and local governments as well as state finance departments, social poverty assistance activities encouraged by the central government have in the past also collected a certain amount of funds from other channels. Such social poverty assistance funds have been estimated to amount to a quarter of the central government's poverty assistance funding, and since the mid-1990s, such social poverty assistance has invested 113.7 billion yuan in poor areas.[18]

A set of "Four Heightened Emphases" were put forward with regard to poverty alleviation during the 12th Five-year Plan period: a transformational development model to enhance sustainable development in poverty-stricken areas; human resource development to improve the overall quality of the poor population; enhancing equality of the provision of basic public services so as to improve production and living conditions for the poor; and overcoming the poverty problem of contiguous poverty-stricken areas in order to achieve better and faster development (Gu, 2011). Three characteristics have been emphasised for this new stage of poverty alleviation: the full implementation of poverty alleviation policy for the low-income population, mainly focusing on the absolute poor while also being concerned about the low-income population; setting up nationwide social assistance system of support for the rural old, disabled, orphans, and the poor and needy in a two-prong approach of developmental poverty alleviation plus livelihood assistance (in contrast to the mainly development-oriented poverty alleviation of the past); and earmarked/specific-item poverty alleviation, which is more specifically focused on increasing income and enhancing capacity compared with the relatively wide range of earmarked poverty alleviation in the past.[19] The reason that China has been adopting a mainly developmental approach to poverty reduction in rural areas is related to the level of development of the rural economy. Compared to urban areas, the level of development in the rural areas is in general relatively low. The urban-rural gap has been expanding. The direct result of the slow development is that the great majority of China's poor are living in rural areas. On the other hand, the relative concentration of the rural poor in geographically remote areas with resource and environmental degradation in the central and western regions tends to justify the focus on regional development in poverty reduction.

Such a regional development approach at poverty reduction is aimed at poor *regions* rather than poor families or individuals, which reduces the problem of identification. A developmental approach focuses on improving the conditions for production and living standards in the poor regions, and enhances agricultural and non-agricultural productivity via improving basic infrastructure and public services to increase income of the poor. The need for public financial resources is relatively low since the government just needs to focus its financial capability on building basic infrastructure and public services. At the same time, the government needs mainly to mobilise and encourage financial institutions to provide direct financial support to productive activities in rural areas. Finally, a regional approach could fully utilise the existing administrative system, thus enabling a reduction in administrative costs.

However, such developmental approach to poverty reduction has its limitations. In the long term, it may need to be combined with a rural social security system in order to more effectively overcome the rural poverty problem. Ignoring the construction of a rural social security system could result in a part of the rural population falling into extreme poverty – especially those who lose the ability to work and other unsupported populations, such as the disabled, the aged, orphans, the sick, etc. A government survey found that 25.42 million people belong to this special "problem community" in rural areas.[20] In addition, a lack of social security support may constrain the effectiveness of the developmental approach to poverty reduction. Those who have just moved out of poverty are still relatively economically weak, and can easily return to poverty due to calamities or illnesses. Without suitable social security support to cushion the impact of such vicissitudes, these families can easily end up being trapped in long-term poverty. Due to the realisation of the need for a synergy of developmental approach to poverty reduction and appropriate social security, China's government is aiming at a basic system of social assistance that will cover both urban and rural areas, with particular focus on the gradual construction of a social security system guaranteeing a minimum standard of living for rural residents.[21] However, in terms of institutional arrangements, the grave inadequacy in the efforts towards a rural social security system has always been apparent. Even the ongoing experimentation with social insurance for senior citizens is mainly dependent upon individual contributions, and hence represents a type of personal savings insurance and hence cannot really be considered social insurance as such (Tang, 2008: 316). Other than in the case of rural residents under the aforementioned *wubaohu*, people affected by calamities and some other special groups are not guaranteed a minimum standard of decent living, and with the exception of the *wubaohu*, standardisation of social assistance programmes has apparently not been achieved – even in the case of the new village cooperative health care security system, which has seen preliminary standardised institutional arrangements, rural residents in the majority of counties are yet to be covered, partly because its voluntary participation model poses problems for those in extreme poverty, especially some ethnic minorities in the country's western region (Gao, 2007: 160–1; Tang, 2008).

State Council's 101st Standing Committee meeting framework for the 12th Five-year Plan period

Deep-seated contradictions still exist at present to constrain development in poor areas. Huge numbers of the poor are under increasing danger of returning to poverty, the income gap is still widening, there is a prominence of the phenomenon of relative poverty, a severe imbalance in development and a serious threat of natural disasters with little ability to recover from them. Regarding developmental imbalance, the poverty problem has been particularly severe in specific areas including minority areas and frontier areas, old revolutionary base areas and mountain areas. These special types of poor area and poor population have always posed the most formidable challenges for poverty alleviation efforts.[22] As a matter of fact, with the further shift of focus on poverty reduction to the central and western regions earlier during the "eight-seven" (*baqi*) programme for poverty reduction.[23] distribution of poverty assistance funds has already further slanted towards the central and western regions. Between 1998 and 2001, the poverty counties in the western, central and eastern regions received an average (rural per capita) of 92 yuan, 63 yuan and 7 yuan of central poverty assistance funding respectively. Adding the local matching fund and other sources of poverty assistance funds to this gives a total poverty assistance fund per capita of 130 yuan, 101 yuan and 43 yuan for the poverty counties in the western, central and eastern regions respectively. On average, the central government poverty assistance funds received by the frontier regions are 37 per cent higher than the other poverty counties. In this regard, government analysis shows that the inter-poverty county distribution of poverty assistance funds depends mainly on a poverty county's condition of poverty, population size and type of county (e.g. whether it is in the frontier region).[24] For every increase of 1 percentage point in the incidence of poverty, a poverty county would receive a per capita increment of 0.9 yuan of poverty assistance from the central government. This shows the important consideration of the degree of poverty in the distribution of poverty assistance funds by the central government and provincial governments. For every increase of 10,000 people in the rural population of a poverty country, there would be a decrease of 2.44 yuan in per capita poverty assistance funds, which shows the inferior status of the more populous counties in the distribution of poverty assistance funding. As poverty assistance funds often use the county as unit of distribution, population size has not been given deserving consideration. For instance, the ethnic minority counties are getting 14 yuan per capita of poverty assistance funds – more than other counties with equivalent conditions, and frontier counties are getting 67 yuan more than other counties with other conditions equivalent.[25] In terms of targeting, China's rural poverty reduction programme has the peculiar characteristic of regional targeting, instead of directly targeting poor families.

Facing the new challenges, the State Council's 101st Standing Committee meeting decided to prepare a "poverty alleviation and development" framework for the following decade to further improve the national poverty reduction strategies and policies. Based on the basic direction of social security sustaining survival and poverty alleviation and development as key to getting out of the poverty trap, the new framework has aimed at developing a new, more adequate national standard for poverty alleviation and adjustment mechanisms for the following decade and the 12th Five-year Plan period, while allowing the provinces, *zhixiashi* and "autonomous regions" to fix local poverty alleviation standards higher than the national standard.[26] It is also planned to select during the 12th Five-year

Plan period some of the typical contiguous areas of severe poverty for the development of earmarked, specific plans to strengthen resource integration in carrying out poverty relief, and continuing the major support for poor villages of the frontier areas and ethnic minority areas. Given the large absolute number of non-Han minorities occupying vast expanses of often strategic land areas, poverty alleviation in ethnic minority areas has always been a major focus of the overall poverty reduction framework. Since the implementation of the "China Rural Poverty Alleviation and Development (2001–2010)" framework, the old revolutionary base areas, ethnic minority areas and frontier areas have been the key focus of poverty alleviation. In fact, from 2002 to 2009, the five "autonomous regions" of Inner Mongolia, Guangxi, Tibet, Ningxia and Xinjiang, as well as the provinces of Guizhou, Yunnan and Qinghai, which have large ethnic minority populations, have received central government poverty alleviation funds totalling 41.74 billion yuan, accounting for 39.87 per cent of the total investment of the country, while earmarked/special-item minority development funds amounted to 5.2 billion yuan.[27]

According to the rule of the management of poverty assistance funding, the central government requires local governments to provide matching funds for the central government-provided poverty assistance funding other than funding for poverty assistance loans. The requirement during the early stages is at the matching ratio of 1:1. However, this requirement is usually unfulfilled, a fact that can be attributed to the prevalent financial difficulties of the governments of the poor regions.[28] Hence, after the implementation of the rural poverty assistance framework in the 2000s, the central government has stopped setting such exact matching requirements, but has just asked local governments to increase poverty assistance investment.

It has been pointed out that the problem of poverty in ethnic minority areas features special causes, problems and manifestations, hence requiring constantly increasing inputs and efforts, and, in particular, enhancement of the relevance and focus of the measures. This is to be done by improving the basic quality of the labour force by way of poverty alleviation through education, developmental poverty alleviation through focusing on supporting the development of industries with special ethnic characteristics, channelling enterprises in the eastern region to found new ventures in the western region's ethnic areas, and the combination of poverty alleviation and ecological construction as well as other similar measures.[29] Regarding poverty alleviation through education, in the past, besides the standard poverty assistance funds, other government departments have also implemented some poverty assistance programmes and investments directly aimed at the poverty areas including the compulsory education projects for the government-designated poverty areas implemented by China's Ministry of Education. This compulsory education programme mainly focuses on the government-designated and province-designated poverty counties. The first phase of the programme began at the end of 1995, and the total amount of investment from the central government was 3.9 billion yuan by 2000.[30] The second phase was implemented during the 10th Five-year

Plan period of 2001–2005, with investment from central government amounting to 5 billion yuan.

Reform, decentralisation and poverty alleviation

Returning to the issue of fiscal decentralisation, Chinese revenue collection had been falling rapidly as the traditional tax base of the command economy eroded with the onslaught of market reform, and this fiscal decline continued well into the early 1990s. It was in this climate that the 1994 fiscal reform was introduced as an effort by the central government to regain control and recoup lost revenues via a new system of dual taxation (tax sharing) that redefined central government's and regional governments' revenues. The comprehensive reform in effect redefined the whole intergovernmental fiscal relations (fiscal IGR) by changing the structure of the main taxes, responsibilities in tax administration and revenue-sharing arrangements. This weakened the ability of the regional governments to employ surreptitious approaches for revenue mobilisation. China's proportion of local public spending in total national public spending is actually much higher than that of the major federal countries in the world. China's local public spending has since the mid and late 1980s been steady at about 70 per cent of total national public spending, whereas in federal countries such as the USA, Germany and Russia, the proportion of local public spending in relation to total national public spending is only 46, 40 and 38 per cent respectively (Yeoh, 2009: 246). Furthermore, the scope of China's economic decentralisation goes far beyond decentralisation in public finance, but even measured solely by the latter China has been said to be one of the world's most economically decentralised countries.

While Cai and Treisman (2006) challenged the claim that decentralisation had much to do with the success of China's reforms and subsequent economic miracle, von Braun and Grote (2000: 15)[31] warned that China's approach to administrative decentralisation, which relies on negotiations rather than rules to define relations between the central government and the four sub-national tiers (provinces, prefectures/cities, counties and villages/townships), might over time threaten the success of the reform process. Pursuing the second link outlined in their conceptual framework – whether public services for the poor are fostered by decentralisation, and by fiscal decentralisation in particular – von Braun and Grote (2000) commented that the 1994 tax reform seemed to have failed to arrest the trend towards worsening interregional inequality, as the loyalty of the local governments shifted away from the national government to the sub-national level,[32] since taxes belonged to the central government unless specifically assigned to the localities. As the local rural governments began to impose a host of fees and levies because the higher-level governments were not able to subsidise existing services due to fiscal strain, the poorer regions were likely to be victimised as they are less able to do the same (von Braun and Grote 2000: 20). In fact, in order to end the wanton charging of fees by schools and to further regulate and strengthen the fee management system of schools to reduce the economic burden of families with school-age children, especially the rural poor, the government began implementing the one-fee system (*yi fei zhi*) in poor areas. One-fee reform was remarkably effective in stopping education costs from rising too fast and in reducing peasant families' liabilities, as well as to a certain extent increasing the rate of enrolment. However, it had been warned that the fee reduction also has the tendency to compromise the quality of education, due to schools' financial difficulties and debts.[33] On the other hand, as one of the seven prongs of the western regional 2004–2007 plan to achieve comprehensive nine-year education and basically eliminate youth and adult illiteracy in the western region by 2007,[34] the "two exempts and one subsidy" (*liang mian yi bu*) scheme aims at solving the problem of children of poor families in backward areas attending school.

Under this scheme, the central government provided free textbooks, while the various tiers of the local governments took up the responsibility of exempting poor students from sundry fees and subsidising boarding expenses. *Liang mian yi bu* specifically targets compulsory education stage students living in rural areas (with the main source of family income being agriculture), studying in rural (including village, township and county town) primary and secondary schools, who are unable to pay for textbooks, sundry fees and boarding expenses due to economic difficulties of their families (also including county-level students with disabilities). The report indicates that central government expenditure for this purpose in 2004 amounted to 1.17 billion yuan, with 32 per cent of students from poor families in the central and western regions provided with free textbooks. The number of primary and secondary students from poor families in the rural compulsory education stage benefiting from free textbooks in the central and western regions reached about 30 million people. Nationwide, government expenditure for rural compulsory education amounted to 184 billion yuan in 2006, exempting all 52 million students at rural compulsory education stage in the western region and parts of the central region from school and sundry fees, providing free textbooks for 37.3 million students from poor families, and subsidising living expenses for 7.8 million boarding students. To further strengthen the development of rural foundational education, the report notes that the central government has also decided to extend the *liang mian yi bu* scheme to all rural areas nationwide to provide educational opportunity for more children from poor families.

Besides such schemes targeting education, whole-village development (*zheng cun tuijin*) – one of the three foci[35] of China's current rural developmental poverty assistance aims – on the other hand aims at using relatively large-scale capital and other resources to greatly enhance in a relatively short time the assisted village in terms of foundational and social services and amenities, living and production conditions as well as industrial development, leading to better coordination of various items to achieve greater integrated benefits, hence enabling the poor population to get out from poverty, and at the same time enhancing the integrated productive capability of the poverty community and population and their ability to withstand risks. Government statistics on 70,000 poverty villages in 16 provinces/*zizhiqu* (including Hebei, Jilin, Heilongjiang, Jiangxi,

Anhui, Henan, Hubei, Hunan, Guangxi, Hainan, Sichuan, Yunnan, Shaanxi, Qinghai, Ningxia and Xinjiang) set the average poverty assistance fund for each poverty village at 2.28 million yuan.[36] Of the 16 provinces/autonomous regions (*zizhiqu*), 12 have an average fund planned at between 1 and 3 million yuan, only Guangxi and Heilongjiang have more than 3 million yuan planned, with Guangxi having more than 13 million. On the other hand, two provinces (Hunan and Yunnan) have lower than 1 million yuan. According to the statistics, until mid-2005, the average poverty assistance investment for each poverty village was 0.34 million yuan, which met only 15 per cent of the demand. The report emphasised that even with the assumption that all these investments were used on poverty villages that have already implemented the whole-village development programme (only 32 per cent of the poverty villages have implemented the whole-village development programme), the average fund for each such village was merely 960,000 yuan. Hence, the actual poverty assistance investment and planned investment were seriously inadequate to meet the actual demand. Only Jilin, Jiangxi, Henan, Guangxi, Ningxia and Xinjiang have average poverty assistance investment exceeding 50,000 yuan, while Hubei, Hunan, Hainan and Qinghai have average investment of each poverty village of less than 20,000 yuan. These findings also show that except for a minority of poverty villages where the provincial/*zizhiqu*/*zhixiashi* units[37] and leadership were directly responsible for supporting the programme, most poverty villages were either not getting any poverty assistance investment at all or only very limited funds. Besides, the report's findings also show great discrepancy in income growth among different rural families in the *same* village under the programme, and the main beneficiaries from poverty assistance investment are the relatively richer rural families in the poverty villages, due mainly to the need for the rural families themselves to provide a part of the capital (matching fund) which is beyond the capability of those in absolute poverty.

Given the still grave situation of overall Chinese poverty even after the remarkable poverty reduction achievements over the last few decades, it is indeed pertinent to include the implications on poverty reduction and interregional disparity in further research on fiscal reform and dimensions of decentralisation. As poverty and inequality constitute one of the most, if not *the* most, critical challenges China faces in her next phase of politico-socio-economic development, and poverty in China has the properties of being concentrated in the western region and in the ethnic minority areas, ethno regionalisation of poverty inevitably ensues (Yeoh, 2009: 269–272), presenting China not only with economic challenges but also long-term socio-political security risks. The solving of the remaining problems of poverty and inequality, still daunting despite the impressive achievements of the last few decades, in this vast nation has duly been the focus of researchers and policy-makers, whether the policy suggestions, to give a few examples, be in the form of Woo's four points of implementing programmes that strengthen the three mechanisms of income convergence (i.e. free movement of goods, people and capital), that provide infrastructure, that focus on rural poverty and that mobilise the universities for growth (Woo, 2004), or Fan *et al.*'s seven points of increasing overall public investment in rural areas, increasing public investment in agricultural research and development, in rural education, in rural infrastructure, in improving the efficiency of existing public irrigation systems, as well as improving the targeting of funds to the poor and increasing fiscal transfers from the richer coastal region to the poorer western regions, in view of the country's decentralised fiscal system and the western region's small tax base (Fan *et al.*, 2002: 50–51), or *Zhongguo Fazhan Baogao 2007*'s nine points of establishing the "developmental poverty line" standard to readjust the long-term poverty alleviation policy, establishing a poverty alleviation credit system and ways for private finance institutions to participate in poverty alleviation, establishing a sound social security system both urban and rural, advancing the progress of urbanisation and the provision of social security and public services to rural-to-urban migrants, providing more equitable educational opportunity, expanding human resource development (including skill training and re-training) for rural labour, improving rural medical services, establishing a rational public finance system and strengthening public governance for poverty alleviation, and enhancing the role of non-governmental organisations in poverty alleviation (pp. 174–182).

The highly remarkable extent of fiscal decentralisation that exists in China should be further enhanced to aid the effort at poverty alleviation, especially in the context of the ethno-regional dimension of the poverty problem. In recent years, local and international organisations around the world have been increasingly advocating decentralisation to bring about more effective poverty reduction, with both the direct effects on the regional targeting of transfers and the indirect effects of overcoming the inefficiency in local public services and hampered economic growth related to sub-optimal decentralisation (von Braun and Grote, 2000: 2). Although theoretically there may not be a clear-cut functioning relationship between decentralisation and poverty reduction, most research findings in recent years definitely point to the positive. Von Braun and Grote (2000) pointed out that political, administrative and fiscal decentralisation need to be considered simultaneously, and the sequencing and pace of these three aspects of decentralisation seem to play an important role in impacting poverty reduction. While fiscal decentralisation shows ambivalent effects for poverty reduction and administrative decentralisation alone does not add power and voice to the poor, "political decentralisation often benefits the poor, because involving civil society in planning, monitoring and evaluating public programs and policies is crucial to ensure steady progress and that is facilitated in a decentralised system" (Von Braun and Grote, 2000: 25–26). Or, as Boex *et al.* (2006: 2) pointed out in their research report *Fighting Poverty through Fiscal Decentralisation*, "if the increasingly accepted wisdom that 'all poverty is local' is correct, then decentralisation policy and poverty reduction strategies could be closely intertwined and have synergetic positive effects on each other".[38] Kyei (2000), in his study of the case of Ghana, concluded that the rural poor in Ghana could only benefit with a much stronger commitment from the central government to decentralisation, especially in terms of power sharing and financial provision.

Vijayanand's paper on the Kerala state of India noted various advantages of decentralisation in terms of poverty reduction including the greater reach of resources with earmarking of funds for the disadvantaged groups, less sectionalism in decentralised programmes with greater convergence contributing to the reduction in the ratchet effect of poverty, greater emphasis on locally appropriate and affordable solutions, greater realism in tackling problems of poverty, improved accountability, etc. while decentralization "affords opportunities to the poor to grow in strength by continuous participation (learning by doing), constant observation of the exercise of power (learning by seeing) and accessing more information (learning by knowing)" (Vijayanand, 2001: 23). Hence, given the crucial ethno-regional dimension of China's poverty problem, it is pertinent that the poverty alleviation effort of the country should benefit from any possible progress in decentralisation – fiscal, administrative and, most importantly, political – since decentralised governments, due to their closeness both institutionally (e.g. ethnically) and spatially to citizens in the regional/rural areas, could be more responsive to the needs of the poor than the central government and hence more likely to successfully formulate and implement pro-poor policies and programmes in these regions and areas.

Problems in health care provision: the implication for decentralisation

Since the 1980s, China's fiscal system has gone through an evolution from the traditional highly centralised "unified revenue, unified spending" (*tongshou tongzhi*) system to a decentralised system of division of levels and taxes. The latter is a re-division of government expenditure responsibilities, in which the central government assigned more spending responsibilities to the local governments. Such large-scale decentralisation can also be seen in the health care sector. During the past decade, from the perspective of the expenditure structure, the central government's health budget only accounted for 5 per cent of the total health expenditure budget. The health expenditure of the central level is about 2 per cent, and the rest is from local government level, and counties and townships' total expenditure accounted for 55 per cent to 60 per cent of the budget. This shows that, in sharp contrast to most of the world's market economies where the central government and provincial government are bearing the main burden of expenditure on education and health care, in China the local government, in particular the grassroots level of government, represents the main body of public health spending.[39]

In the fiscal decentralisation reform, higher levels of government transferred responsibility for health financing to the lower levels of government. Facing financial constraints and a lack of effective measures to eliminate personnel redundancies, the lower levels of government in turn pushed the main task of financing to the health sector which in effect passed the problem to an originally failed market. The local governments' urge to unload this burden is an important motivating factor in market-oriented health care reform.

In this tiered structure of fiscal responsibility, China's health expenditure comes mainly from local budgets, while only a very small proportion comes from central transfers. With the expansion of the interlocal economic development gap and the interlocal fiscal capacity gap, the local government health expenditure gap is also continuing to grow. The declining ratio of government health spending has a clear regressive trend: the poorer a province economically, the greater the decline of its government's spending on health care, a trend leading to even more serious urban-rural disparity. The tax system reform implemented in 1994 represented a major adjustment mechanism, with policy documents further clarifying that health care competences follow the level of territory principle. However, the institutional reform in 1994, while increasing the proportion of central government revenues, also decreased the fiscal capacity of local governments. This is especially so in the case of counties and townships which represent the main body of health expenditure (55–60 per cent of government health spending actually comes from the county and township level), which is experiencing increasing fiscal difficulties in the face of tax system reform due to the concentration on financial resources at the higher level of government, with some only managing to maintain very basic operations, and this is causing a high degree of vertical imbalance in terms of health care responsibilities and fiscal capacity. In this situation, for some public health institutions, county and township governments have either decreased funding and subsidies or even resorted to selling them off directly in a forced step into marketisation, thus jeopardising public welfare.[40] After the fiscal reform, the proportion of public health expenditure in total public expenditure has been falling continuously, and its proportion in the total expenditure for science, education, culture and health has been experiencing the same falling trend. In other words, at a time of continuous economic growth, government spending on health is actually declining continuously. The proportion of government spending in total health payments decreased from 37 per cent in 1981 to the lowest level of 16 per cent in 2000, while during the same period personal health spending increased from 20 per cent in 1981 to 59 per cent in 2000.

Moreover, due to fiscal decentralisation, public spending on health has become the responsibility of local governments while fiscal capacity is exhibiting huge differentials between local governments – public health spending per capita of the province with the highest fiscal capacity is in fact more than 10 times that of the province with the lowest fiscal capacity. The impact of fiscal decentralisation on health expenditure has thus been shown to be significantly negative, indicating that the higher is decentralisation, the lower is the government's health spending. The relationship between GDP and health expenditure has also been shown to be negative, indicating that economic development does not lead to increased government health investment. This shows that the higher the decentralisation, the more the government will invest in the economic sector instead. As the local governments' major performance evaluation indicator is GDP, the use of public finance to develop the economy is thus much preferred to its use to more directly improve people's livelihood through health, as well as education, expenditure.

Nevertheless, also evident is that it could be too simplistic to blame decentralisation while the main culprit is actually what has been dubbed "GDPism". In other words, fiscal decentralisation itself might not have negatively affected government health spending, and the culprit is instead the incentive system which uses the simple pursuit of GDP growth as the target for assessment. In the present context, this has led to insufficient health care provision, while rapid economic growth is being applauded. Under the present fiscal decentralisation mechanism, in order to improve the conditions of public health care provision, introducing new standards of evaluation into the present assessment mechanism that focuses solely on GDP growth is of utmost importance in order to encourage local governments to pay more attention to public welfare spending. In addition, more attention should be paid to the negative impact on public welfare spending from the reform of the tax system as the government needs to introduce complementary measures to share the cost brought about by the tax system reform (Xiong and An, 2011). Similar phenomena can be observed in the case of the provision of education.

Decentralisation and compulsory (obligatory) education

From the point of view of the education funding and management system, from 1949 to the mid-1980s, the Chinese central government was the sole provider of public education, and local governments were but agents of the central government to implement the supply of public education; hence education expenditure was not much different between regions. By the mid-1980s, with the beginning of fiscal decentralisation, the supply of compulsory education gradually underwent a transformation whereby the local governments took over from the central government as the main providers, and also began to transfer the task of compulsory education to the next level of authority. The "Compulsory Education Law of the People's Republic of China", implemented in 1986, further officially confirmed the "local responsibility, different levels of management" for compulsory education. Besides the central government schools, the provision of most of compulsory education became the responsibility of local government with the province as the largest unit, but the specific responsibility continued to be shifted down to the next level which had to bear the ultimate responsibility of providing compulsory education – from the municipality all the way down to the county government. Due to the vague division of responsibilities between the village and county government, the provision of compulsory education expenditure was further shifted down to next level of authority, and many local village/township governments ended up being the actual fundraisers for and providers of local compulsory education, culminating in the situation that compulsory education was no longer obligatory and the benefit principle was brought into play when the cost of education ultimately fell on the shoulders of the rural families as beneficiaries of compulsory education. Though rural provision of education began to be partly shifted back to the county level after the 2001 rural tax reforms, the overall burden was still at too low a level (Sun *et al.*, 2010).

Under such a decentralised system, the basic education expenditure responsibilities originally shouldered by the central government have been transferred to the local governments. The central government, besides bearing the payment of salaries and other basic items, is no longer directly involved in local education decision-making. Among the local governments who are bearing the responsibilities for basic education, county- and township-level governments have become the most important source of funding for local public education expenditure. In stark contrast to most advanced countries where the central government bears the major portion of the cost of compulsory education, China's current pattern of fiscal burden distribution for compulsory education expenditure is as follows: 78 per cent being borne by the village/township-level government; 9 per cent by the county-level government; 11 per cent by the province-level government; and 2 per cent by the central government. It is clear that under such a system the existence of severe horizontal imbalance between localities would inevitably result in inequality in educational opportunity due to interregional and urban-rural disparities in the provision of education. In short, since the mid-1980s, in the 7th to the 11th Five-year Plan period, the Chinese government implemented the world's largest ever fiscal decentralisation of education, and the decentralised system thus established has negatively impacted upon the local governments' investment in basic education, leading to a rapid increase in the private burden of education cost and even to the "education-induced poverty" phenomenon in the poor areas, with many rural families struggling under the heavy burden of tuition fees (Yuan and Chen, 2010).

Concluding remarks: poverty reduction and social security challenges in the 12th Five-year Plan period

With the launch of the 12th Five-year Plan, one of the key elements of fiscal reform during the period is to overcome vertical imbalance – i.e. to enhance the matching of fiscal capacity and task responsibility. In this regard, the ultimate target is to increase equalisation in the enjoyment of basic public services and the main amenities, and improve intergovernmental fiscal relations so as to achieve the balance of task responsibilities and fiscal competences at all levels of government to enhance all levels public investment in basic public services. The particular focus is on rural areas and the central and western regions in an effort to enable urban and rural residents to enjoy equal basic public services. In other words, while the 12th Five-year Plan period is inevitably seen as a critical period for finally establishing a sound market economy, and tax reform will play a very important role in this process, solving vertical imbalance and achieving compatibility between task responsibilities and fiscal capacity/competences at all levels of government is a key element in this new round of fiscal and tax reform. This will inevitably involve the refinement by central and local governments of spending responsibilities and a clear delineation of the assignment of spending responsibilities to the different levels of government. Together with this, an important concomitant issue is to accelerate the development of a sound standard of vertical fiscal transfer payment system as well as ecological compensation and a horizontal transfer payment system to solve the present problem of intergovernmental distrust and the proliferation of earmarked grants, which are impossible to monitor to ensure their determined usage.[41]

In short, fiscal reform during the 12th Five-year Plan period in both timing and content will be basically set to follow two main lines – to serve the five years' overall framework of transformational economic progress and to focus on the three closely interrelated prongs of fiscal institution, budgeting system and tax system in an ultimate pursuit of the gradual perfection of the country's public finance system. Such fiscal reform will mainly involve the rationalisation of intergovernmental fiscal relations (fiscal IGR) as well as a sounder tax sharing system. Such rationalisation of fiscal IGR will inevitably involve dealing with the transfer payment system – the increase of the size and ratio of the regular general grants and the adjustment and reduction of earmarked grants (sub-provincial fiscal institutional reform), as well as moving towards direct provincial administration of counties so as to ensure and strengthen the county's fiscal capacity for the provision of public services, and exploring the institution of local government bonds. As declared in the 12th Five-year Plan framework, "to fully promote the reform in various sectors with heightened determination and courage", the fiscal institution and tax system are set to experience a series of critical reforms. Since the 1994 fiscal reform, after so many years of the implementation of the "tax sharing" system, many problems and weaknesses have emerged in the current fiscal IGR framework of the central-province-municipality-county-village/township five-tier public finance structure and the acute financial problems facing the counties and villages/townships have so far proven to be insurmountable. It is time, as the contents of the 12th Five-year Plan framework – in particular a potential framework of central-province-county three-tier public finance system linking to the proposals of "nationwide direct provincial administration of counties other than ethnic regions, 2012" and "county administration of village/township finance" as well as the exploration of a feasible local government bond system to overcome vertical imbalance[42] – shows, to tackle these problems head-on in order to fully realise the potential fruits of economic and fiscal decentralisation since reform began more than three decades ago.

Against the backdrop of this fiscal readjustment, and following the discussion in the preceding sections of this chapter on poverty reduction and social security challenges, especially in terms of education and health care, it is noteworthy that issues concerning income distribution, social security and rural development have led the main content of the 12th Five-year Plan. While neither the 12th Five-year Plan proposal declared in the communiqué of the fifth plenary meeting of the 17th session of the Central Committee and the subsequent lengthy and the detailed explanation by the former Premier Wen Jiabao gave clear quantifiable policy targets like those given by the 11th Five-year Plan, Wen's explanation has illustrated clearly the prominence of improving income distribution and enhancing social welfare in the policy implementation of the 12th Five-year Plan period that circles closely around the five major directions of economic development, structural adjustment, personal income, social construction and "open-door and reform", with the attainment of a comprehensive *xiaokang* (moderately prosperous) society by the year 2020 as the ultimate target. Of the five major missions of the 12th Five-year Plan for economic development delineated in Wen's explanation, two top the list – i.e. persistence in expanding domestic demand with due emphasis on advancing urbanisation, improving income distribution, expanding coverage of social security and perfecting basic public services, and promoting agricultural modernisation with due emphasis on enlarging farming land per capita, strengthening basic rural amenities and public services, raising rural residents' occupational skills and income-earning capability as well as increasing and diversifying rural residents' income sources.

In conclusion, in the case of strengthening the social security system, the emphas would be on housing protection and other social security reforms including those related to healthc are, education and the welfare of senior citizens. These, which would contribute to the overall attack on income disparity and social inequality that have risen to represent the most worrying issues in China's socio-economic development, in short, constitute a most important, and in fact overarching, component of the country's 12th Five-year Plan for economic development.

Acknowledgements

Part of this chapter is reprinted from "Fiscal Reform, Decentralisation and Poverty Alleviation in the Context of China's 12th Five-Year Plan", by Emile Kok-Kheng Yeoh, Susie Yieng-Ping Ling and Pik Shy Fan, 2012. Reprinted by permission of the *Journal of Asian Public Policy*.

Notes

1 Statistics from *Cong "liang shui fa" dao "fen shui zhi": zhongyang-difang boyi xia de caizheng shuishou zhidu* (From "two-tax regulation" to "tax sharing": tax system under central-local manoeuvre"), *Zhongguo jingjixue jiaoyu keyan wang CENET luntan*, 2009.
2 The term "*xiagang*" refers to redundant workers mainly at state enterprises, without directly describing them as "unemployed". Still officially attached to their work units or enterprises, the *xiagang* workers continue to receive basic minimum subsidies for their living and medical expenses, and are encouraged to change job, probably through state-run job and re-employment centres, or go into small businesses. In line with state enterprise reforms, the number of *xiagang* workers has been on the rise: 4 million in 1995, 8 million in 1996, 12 million in 1997, 16 million in 1998, 20 million in 1999, though dropping to 11 million in 2001 (Zhou, 2006: 289).
3 Information on poverty reduction here is mainly drawn from that provided by *Zhongguo Fazhan Yanjiu Jijinhui's Zhongguo fazhan baogao 2007 – zai fazhan zhong xiaochu pinkun* (*China development report 2007 – eliminating poverty through development in China*) (see especially pp. 92–93, Table 4.1). Such information and data in *Zhongguo fazhan baogao 2007* were in turn drawn from 151 Chinese and English source references and 24 background reports.
4 Data from *Zhongguo fazhan baogao 2007*.
5 See Note 3.

6 Data from *Zhongguo caizheng (Public finance of China)*, 2008, issue no. 4.
7 Statistics from *Zhongguo fazhan baogao 2007*.
8 "San Xi" (three "Xi") refers to China's poorest region represented by Dingxi in Gansu province, the Hexi corridor and Xihaigu in Ningxia province, designated since the early 1980s as the priority target for rural poverty reduction.
9 Statistics from *Zhongguo fazhan baogao 2007*.
10 These data from *Zhongguo fazhan baogao 2007* were for the year 2003.
11 Data from *Zhongguo fazhan baogao 2007*.
12 Statistics from *Zhongguo fazhan baogao 2007*, p. 99.
13 "Yuan" is the largest denomination of China's currency "renminbi" ("people's currency", RMB), roughly equivalent to US$0.146.
14 Data from *Zhongguo fazhan baogao 2007*.
15 Billion = thousand million.
16 Statistics from *Zhongguo fazhan baogao 2007*, p. 100.
17 Statistics from *Zhongguo fazhan baogao 2007*. The survey was conducted in May 2005.
18 Statistics from *Zhongguo fazhan baogao 2007*.
19 Data from *Guowuyuan Fupinban dangzu chengyuan Jiang Xiaohua: "shi'er wu" fupin kaifa nandu jiada* (Jiang Xiaohua from the Poverty Assistance Committee of the State Council: degree of difficulty of poverty assistance under the 12th Five-year Plan increases), *Xinjiang Shengchan Jianshe Bingtuan "shi'er wu" guihua zhuanlan*, 2010.
20 Data here are from *Zhongguo fazhan baogao 2007*. The survey mentioned was conducted in 2003.
21 See Note 20.
22 Data from *Guowuyuan Fupinban dangzu chengyuan Jiang Xiaohua: "shi'er wu" fupin kaifa nandu jiada, Xinjiang Shengchan Jianshe Bingtuan "shi'er wu" guihua zhuanlan*, 2010.
23 An anti-poverty programme launched in 1993, called 'eight-seven programme' meaning that China would eliminate the poverty of about 80 million people in seven years by the end of the twentieth century.
24 Data from *Zhongguo fazhan baogao 2007*.
25 See Note 24.
26 Data from *Guowuyuan Fupinban dangzu chengyuan Jiang Xiaohua: "shi'er wu" fupin kaifa nandu jiada, Xinjiang Shengchan Jianshe Bingtuan "shi'er wu" guihua zhuanlan*, 2010.
27 Data from *Zhongguo zhengfu wang: minzu diqu rengshi "shi'er wu" qijian fupin kaifa youxian didai* (China Government Net: ethnic regions are still the priority areas of poverty assistance development during the 12th Five-year Plan period), *Zhongguo zhengfu wang*, 2009.
28 Data from *Zhongguo fazhan baogao 2007*.
29 Data from *Zhongguo zhengfu wang: minzu diqu rengshi "shi'er wu" qijian fupin kaifa youxian didai, Zhongguo zhengfu wang*, 2009.
30 Data from *Zhongguo fazhan baogao 2007*.
31 von Braun and Grote (2000: 15) noted that in China "the allocation of responsibilities across tiers of government remains unclear, except for health and education which are controlled by the provinces ... While administrative discretion has helped preserve the momentum for growth and reform, it has also created opportunities for corruption."
32 As von Braun and Grote (2000: 20) noted, provincial tax officers, aiming to establish some tax autonomy, "entered into direct negotiations with enterprises for payments and transferred tax funds that would otherwise have been shared with the central government into local extra budgetary accounts".
33 Data from *Zhongguo fazhan baogao 2007*.

34 The seven prongs are (1) implementation of the rural boarding school system; (2) implementation of the "two exempts and one subsidy" system to assist schoolchildren of rural families with economic difficulties in the western region; (3) long-term modernisation of the rural primary and secondary schools; (4) greatly strengthening the teaching team in the rural areas of the western region; (5) deepening the reform in teaching and learning, and enhancing quality of education; (6) expanding and strengthening direct assistance in education; (7) clear demarcation of the responsibilities of various levels of government in implementing this plan.

35 This also includes labour retraining and loans. Poverty reduction through loans, including microcredits, has in general not met with much success.

36 See Note 33.

37 Referring to the 31 *sheng* (i.e. provinces of Anhui, Fujian, Gansu, Guangdong, Guizhou, Hainan, Hebei, Heilongjiang, Henan, Hubei, Hunan, Jiangsu, Jiangxi, Jilin, Liaoning, Qinghai, Shaanxi, Shandong, Shanxi, Sichuan, Yunnan and Zhejiang), *zizhiqu* (i.e. "autonomous regions" – each a first-level administrative subdivision having its own local government, and a minority entity that has a higher population of a particular minority ethnic group – of Guangxi of the Zhuang, Nei Monggol/Inner Mongolia of the Mongols, Ningxia of the Hui, Xizang/Tibet of the Tibetans and Xinjiang of the Uyghurs) and *zhixiashi* (municipalities under the central government – Beijing, Chongqing, Shanghai and Tianjin).

38 "Poverty is local and it can only be fought at the local level" (UNCHR Fifty-sixth Session – Item 10 of the Provisional Agenda, New York: United Nations Commission on Human Rights (UNCHR), 1999).

39 Statistics from *Guodu shichanghua yu gaodu fenquanhua shi Zhongguo yiliao weisheng gaige de shuangchong wuqu* (Over-marketisation and a high degree of decentralisation constitute the double danger zone of China's medical and healthcare reform), *Zhoukou xinwen wang – lunwen pindao*, 2009/*Dajia luntan*, 2010.

40 See Note 39.

41 Data from *"Shi'er wu" caizheng gaige zhuolidian'* (Focus of efforts in fiscal reform under the 12th Five-year Plan), *Liaowang xinwen zhoukan/Lianhe zaobao wang*, 2010.

42 Data from *Jiedu shi'er wu guihua gangyao zhiyi: caishui gaige de luoji* (Interpreting one of the essentials of the 12th Five-year Plan: the logic of tax reform), *Jingji cankao bao/Wenzhou wang*, 2011.

References

Boex, J., Heredia-Ortiz, E., Martinez-Vazquez, J., Timofeev, A. and Yao, G. (2006). *Fighting Poverty through Fiscal Decentralization*. Report for Fiscal Reform in Support of Trade Liberalization Project funded by the US Agency for International Development. Available at: http://pdf.usaid.gov/pdf_docs/PNADH105.pdf.

Cai, H. and Treisman, D. (2006). *Did Government Decentralization Cause China's Economic Miracle?* Available at: http://www.polisci.ucla.edu/cpworkshop/papers/Treisman.pdf.

Chen, J. S. (2006). *Tuigenghuanlin Yu Xibu Kechixu Fazhan (Defarming-Reforestation and Sustainable Development in the Western Region)*. Chengdu: Xinan Caijing Daxue Chubanshe.

Fan, S., Zhang, L. and Zhang, X. (2002). "Growth, Inequality, and Poverty in Rural China: The Role of Public Investments", *IFPRI Research Report 125*. Washington, DC: International Food Policy Research Institute.

Gao, J. (2007). *Woguo Xibu Nongcun Diqu Shehui Yiliao Baoxian de Zhengfu Gongji Yanjiu (A Study on Government Provision of Social Medical Insurance in the Western rural Region of China)*. Beijing: Xinhua Shudian.

Gong, B. (2009). *Lun Woguo Kaifashi Fupin de Tuozhan Yu Wanshan (A Discourse on the Expansion and Perfection of the Developmental Poverty Assistance in China)*. Available at: http://www.studa.net/china/090608/15000213.html.

Gu, Z. Y. (2011). *Guowuyuan Fupinban: Weilai Shinian Jiben Xiaochu Juedui Pinkun (Poverty Assistance Committee of the State Council: Essentially Alleviate Absolute Poverty in the Next Decade)*. Available at: http://news.eastday.com/c/20110307/u1a5765594.html#.

Kyei, P. O. (2000). *Decentralisation and Poverty Alleviation in Rural Ghana: Perspectives from District Elites and Voices of the Rural Poor*. Available at: http://unpan1.un.org/intradoc/groups/public/documents/idep/unpan003042.pdf.

Sun, B. Z., Chen X. J. and Yu, X. H. (2010). *Lun Caizheng Fenquan Beijing Xia Yiwu Jiaoyu Diqu Chayi Yu Caizheng Zeren de Zai Peizhi (A Discourse on the Regional Disparity in Compulsory Education and Re-allocation of Fiscal Responsibilities Against the Backdrop of Fiscal Decentralization)*. *Suiyue Lianmeng Luntan*. Available at: http://www.syue.com/Paper/Financial/Study/28398.html.

Tang, X. M. (2008). *Minzu Diqu Nongcun Shehui Baozhang Yanjiu (A Study on Rural Social Security in Ethnic Regions)*. Beijing: Renmin Chubanshe.

UNCHR (1999). *Fifty-sixth Session – Item 10 of the Provisional Agenda*. New York: United Nations Commission on Human Rights (UNCHR).

Vijayanand, S. M. (2001). *Poverty Reduction through Decentralization: Lessons from the Experience of Kerala State in India*. Paper presented at the Asia and Pacific Forum on Poverty – Reforming Policies and Institutions for Poverty Reduction, 5–9 February. Manila: Asian Development Bank. Available at: http://www.adb.org/Poverty/Forum/frame_vijayanand.htm.

von Braun, J. and Grote, U. (2000). *Does Decentralization Serve the Poor?* Paper presented at IMF Conference on Fiscal Decentralization, 20–21 November, Washington, DC Available at: http://www.imf.org/external/pubs/ft/seminar/2000/fiscal/vonbraun.pdf.

Wang, T., Di, Y. P. and Zhang, K. Z. (2010). *Caizheng Fenquan Xia de Jianpin Zhengce Yanjiu (A Study on Poverty Reduction Policy under Fiscal Decentralization)*. *Xianqu Luntan*, 32. Available at: http://www.ectime.com.cn/Emag.aspx?ADUQCount=4&titleid=14179&page=1.

Wang, Y. Q., Zhang, Y., Zhang, Y., Chen, Z. and Lu, M. (2006). *Shizilukou de Zhongguo (China at a crossroads)*. Available at: http://www.comment-cn.net/economy/analysis/2006/0807/article_16142.html.

Woo, W. T. (2004). *Some New Priorities in Reducing Poverty in China*. East Asia Program, Center for Globalization and Sustainable Development, Columbia University.

Xiong, X. and An, G. (2011). *Caizheng Fenquan Tizhi Xia de Gonggong Yiliao Gongji Shizheng Fenxi (An Empirical Analysis of Public Medical Provision under the Institution of Fiscal Decentralization)*. *Lunwen Daquan Wang*. Available at: http://www.11665.com/manage/caiwu/caiwuqita/201103/73877.html.

Yan, Y. (2010). *Shouru Fenpei Jiegou* (Structure of Income Distribution) in Lu Xueyi (ed.) *Dangdai Zhongguo Shehui Jiegou (Social Structure of Contemporary China)*. Beijing: Shehuikexue Wenxian Chubanshe (Social Sciences Academic Press (China)), pp. 173–214.

Yeoh, E. K. K. (2009). "Leviathan at a Crossroads: China's Reforms and the Pitfalls and Prospects of Decentralization", in E. K. K. Yeoh (ed.) *Regional Political Economy of China Ascendant: Pivotal Issues and Critical Perspectives*. Kuala Lumpur: Institute of China Studies, University of Malaya, pp. 241–303.

Yin, N. C. (2008). *"Shanghai Shehui Baozhang Fazhihua de Tedian Ji Wenti Fenxi"* [Properties and Problems of the Legal Institutionalization of Social Security in Shanghai], in H. Wang (ed.) *Shehui Baozhang Zhidu Gaige Yu Fazhan – Lilun, Fangfa, Shiwu.* Shanghai: Shanghai Jiaotong Daxue Chubanshe, pp. 268–274.

Yuan, C. G. and Chen, J. Q. (2010). *"Chen Jingqi: Ruhe Zouchu Fenquan Tizhi Xia Jichu Jiaoyu Touru Kunjing"* (Chen Jingqi: How to Get Out of the Dilemma of Basic Education Investment Under the Institution of Decentralization). *Quanjing Wang.* Available at: http://www.p5w.net/news/xwpl/201011/t3295048.htm.

Zhongguo Fazhan Baogao 2007 (2007) *China Development Report 2007 – Eliminating Poverty Through Development in China.* Beijing: Zhongguo Fazhan Chubanshe.

Zhou, L. (2006). *China Business: Environment, Momentum, Strategies, Prospects.* Singapore: Prentice Hall/Pearson.

12 Conclusion

Analysing the productivist dimensions of welfare: looking beyond the Greater China Region

John Hudson and Stefan Kühner

Introduction

Following the publication of Esping-Andersen's (1990) classic *The Three Worlds of Welfare Capitalism*, the comparative social policy literature has been dominated by the welfare state modelling debate. One of the thorniest questions here has been how best to classify East Asian states (an early criticism of Esping-Andersen's work was that it had misunderstood and so misclassified Japan, the only East Asian nation included in his typology – see Esping-Andersen, 1997) but as the welfare regimes debate has expanded to encompass a much wider geographic area the debate has become more complex still, with a wide range of rival typologies having developed (Abrahamson, 1999, 2011) and debates continued over the most appropriate indicators (Clasen and Sigel, 2007; Kühner, 2007) and methods (Hudson and Kühner, 2010) for welfare regime analysis. While Esping-Andersen (1999) acknowledges that all classifications rely on simplified ideal types that cannot fully capture the complex reality of actual welfare regimes, some have questioned their utility even as a broad heuristic device (Baldwin, 1996). The present chapter critically examines the productivist dimensions of welfare beyond the experience in the Greater China region by looking into other European countries' welfare development.

Welfare typologies revisited

There is, of course, always a danger that broad typologies of welfare risk over-simplifying real-world complexities, overlooking important differences between cases in the rush to create broad classifications that have proved to be incredibly useful in cross-national analyses of social policy. Typologies require us to identify the salient features of different cases, highlighting the features that divide nations into reasonably coherent but distinct clusters, a task that by definition means highlighting some key features which some nations share but which others do not. In other words, the process involves identifying, to borrow a phrase from Castles and Mitchell (1993), "families of nations". It is important to recognise here that such classifications do not need to encompass every dimension possible: while some typologies have aimed to be all encompassing, capturing the welfare regime in the round (as was the case in Esping-Andersen's study), some focus only on a discreet aspect of welfare, examining similarities and differences in specific policy areas (e.g. Bambra, 2005) or with respect to specific policy trends (e.g. Hudson and Kühner, 2009).

In this book there are two key issues that have been examined that are relevant to this debate. Firstly, there is the often implicit view that geography itself is one of the salient features we should look to in classifying welfare systems into different types. Factors such as shared culture linked to shared geography or a shared language have often been cited as partial explanations for links between regions and welfare. Secondly, and not unconnected in this instance, we have had a focus on the notion of "productive welfare" (see, e.g. Chang and Ku, Chapter 5). There has been a long-running debate over the notion of productive welfare, following an early contribution to the welfare regimes debate from several theorists – most notably Holliday (Holliday, 2000, 2005; Holliday and Wilding, 2003; Kwon and Holliday, 2007) – who argued that social policy regimes in East Asia can be seen as distinct from the three welfare regime types articulated by Esping-Andersen because of their *productive* – rather than protective – intent (other important contributions to this debate include: Aspalter 2006; Goodman *et al.*, 1998; Gough, 2004; Jones, 1993; Kwon, 2005; Lin, 1999; Wilding, 2008).

Both of these claims are open to challenge. Indeed, there are those who doubt whether geographic location is key factor in shaping welfare types (e.g. Walker and Wong 2005 contest the notion of an "East Asian model") and, independently of this, there are also good reasons to doubt whether "productivism" is either a distinctive feature of welfare in East Asia or, indeed, a feature at all (Hudson and Kühner, 2011). Indeed, "productivism" itself is not always conceptualised coherently with some treating as "productive" those policies which enhance formal labour market participation (Rudra, 2007), while others tend to focus on either supply-side workfare measures or active labour market policies in their entirety to depict changes towards or away from "productive" welfare (see e.g. Chan and Ngok, 2011). Emphasising the human capital functions of "productive" policies – i.e. education and labour market training investment, we offered in an earlier work (Hudson and Kühner, 2011) a theoretical and methodological framework for exploring such claims, also undertaking a limited empirical analysis that used the best data we could assemble that allowed for a comparison of long-standing OECD states with East Asian cases, including China, Hong Kong and Taiwan. In this concluding chapter we update the findings from this earlier analysis using the detailed case studies covered in this book, allowing us to offer a more nuanced analysis than was possible in our earlier contribution. Doing so allows us to also draw together the key arguments from each chapter in an explicitly comparative fashion. Before undertaking this task, however, we will first outline the framework we developed for assessing productivism in welfare states.

Classifying productive and protective welfare revisited

Theoretical and methodological backdrop

As noted above, an early critique of Esping-Andersen's (1990) typology of welfare regimes centered on the claim he had overlooked the key features of a fourth world of welfare located within East Asia (Goodman *et al.*, 1998; Jones, 1993) in which, broadly stated, governments emphasised economic development over social policy. Holliday's (2000, 2005; see also Kwon and Holliday, 2007) challenge was the most explicit, for he concluded that it is "impossible to place [East Asian cases] in Esping-Andersen's framework" (Holliday, 2000: 711) because a "productivist" world of welfare existed in the region. However, the concern with productive welfarism has not been limited to East Asia. Indeed, writing from a rather different perspective, some have argued that – in response to globalisation – all high income states have shifted the emphasis of their social policies towards that of a supporting and subjugated role *vis-à-vis* economic policy: indeed, Evans and Cerny (2003; see also Cerny and Evans, 1999; Horsfall, 2010) suggest the welfare state has been *replaced* by a "competition state", with traditional income protections gradually dismantled in favour of policies that can boost economic competitiveness. Jessop (1999, 2000) similarly argues that we have seen the death of the old style "Keynesian Welfare National State" and the rise of the "Schumpeterian Workfare Post-National Regime" in which the state constrains social rights in the face of an increasingly competitive global economy. Holliday (2000: 721) himself conceded such a trend may be visible, suggesting that globalisation "could help make productivist welfare capitalism something of an international standard in the twenty-first century". In short, as Kim (2008: 120) argues, "It is questionable whether the new mix of welfare is a unique feature only in East Asia, since it is increasingly found that every modern welfare state contains both protective and productivist elements".

Yet, one of the weaknesses in the productive welfare debate has been that few studies offer a systematic comparison of a broad range of nations, many offering case studies of a small number of countries within a single region. To rectify this we developed a framework for assessing the balance between productive and protective welfare that could be used to compare a broad range of countries (Hudson and Kühner, 2009). We began by examining OECD member states but then expanded our study to include five additional cases (Hudson and Kühner, 2011) and then a further 32 cases (Hudson and Kühner, 2012).

In each instance a central pillar of our work was the use of fuzzy set ideal type analysis. This has its origins in fuzzy logic and, more directly, in fuzzy set social science as articulated most extensively by Ragin (2000, 2008). Its starting point is that cases (in this instance, welfare states) are best understood as differing configurations of multiple, conceptually rooted dimensions. Researchers begin by specifying the key dimensions that are the focus of analysis and then proceed by viewing each of these dimensions as a "set" in which the cases can have varying degrees of membership. So, for instance, if a study is concerned with the generosity of welfare states and their redistributive intent, then these two concepts form the basis of two distinct sets and empirical analysis proceeds by establishing whether individual countries are members of both, one or none of these sets. Sets are "fuzzy" in this approach because in the real world there are rarely "crisp" boundaries: rather than falling into a simple dichotomy of "generous" and "not generous" types, welfare states are likely to have varying levels of generosity that fall between these two poles, and fuzzy set analysis reflects this by analysing cases on the basis of their graded, partial memberships of sets. These scores range between 0 (full non-membership) and 1 (full membership) for each set being examined. For fuzzy set ideal type analysis, the scores for each fuzzy set are essential but how multiple dimensions are combined is also key. Two key principles of logic are utilised to analyse combinations of sets: logical NOT (the negation principle) and logical AND (the intersection or minimum principle) (see Ragin, 2000, 2008 for fuller discussion).

In our initial study of 23 OECD nations (Hudson and Kühner, 2009), our classification was based on four key components of social policy activity: two reflecting the key protective dimensions found in employment and income protection programmes; and two reflecting productive dimensions found in education and active labour market programmes (ALMPs). Table 12.1 summarises the variables we used for these dimensions and the protocols used to transform them into fuzzy sets (fuller detail of the rationale can be found in Hudson and Kühner, 2009).

These four conceptually rooted dimensions were translated into four fuzzy sets that logically combine to a total of 16 types. Four of these are "pure" ideal types. Countries which score high on each of the four fuzzy sets – education investment, training investment, income protection and employment protection – combine both productive and protective elements successfully and constitute the

Table 12.1 Productive-protective indicators

Dimension	Indicator and source	Fully in	Fully out
Education investment	Public education spending as a share of total public social and education spending (*OECD Education at a Glance; OECD Social Expenditure Database*)	25%	15%
Training investment	Training component of ALMP budgets as a share of the total ALMP budget (*OECD Social Expenditure Database*)	80%	20%
Income protection	Net replacement rate of benefits (including social assistance payments) for a single, long-term unemployed worker without any children at average production worker wage (*OECD Tax and Benefit Models*)	80%	20%
Employment protection	OECD Employment Protection Legislation Index (version 1) (*OECD Employment Outlook*)	3.0	0.5

productive-protective ideal type. Countries that score high on both productive sets (education and training investment), but do not make it into the protective sets are purely productive ideal types. Equally, purely protective ideal types score high on income and employment protection but perform less well in education and training investment. Weak ideal types score low on both protective and productive fuzzy sets. The remaining types are hybrids; these are also relevant. Weak productive-protective types each score high only on one of the respective productive and protective fuzzy set variables – i.e. these cases show high education investment paired with either high income or high employment protection, or high training investment with either high income or employment protection. Those countries that score high on both productive sets and also on one of the two protective fuzzy sets are labelled productive-plus types. If a country only scores high on one of the productive and none of the protective countries, it is labelled weak productive. Equally, those countries with high scores on both protective and one additional productive fuzzy set are labelled protective-plus types. Weak protective types score high on only one of the two protective fuzzy set variables. Table 12.2 outlines the fuzzy set ideal type memberships of the productive-protective property space for the year 2003 (the most recently available data when we completed the 2009 study) for the maximum number of countries with available data (23 in total) as presented in Hudson and Kühner (2009).

Initial findings

Our original study presented a direct challenge to Holliday's (2000) productive welfare thesis in two key respects. Firstly, contrary to his suggestion that a focus on productive welfare forms the basis of an East Asian model, neither of the two included East-Asian countries actually qualified as a purely productive ideal type. Rather, the data suggested that Korea is merely a member of the weak-productive-protective hybrid type alongside countries like Greece, Ireland, Switzerland and Italy. Japan was characterised as a weak-protective hybrid alongside countries like Spain, France, the Czech Republic and Portugal. Secondly, the analysis placed two nations from outside of the East Asia region in our productive ideal type: the USA and New Zealand. Interestingly, Castells and Himanen (2002) suggested the USA represented an unbalanced informational welfare state focused primarily on investment in human capital and our analysis strongly supported this, the USA's fuzzy set membership score for this set being among the highest across all the countries and all the pure types in the sample, stressing the strong balance of its welfare state toward productive features. Finland was at the crossover point for the productive-protective ideal type, which is interesting since it matches another dimension of Castells and Himanens' (2002) thesis – they regarded the Finnish model as an "informational welfare state" that managed to combine both productive and protective elements simultaneously – and challenges Holliday's view that welfare regimes must choose between a focus on productive *or* protective elements. Our data suggested that both Korea and Japan shifted *away* from productive strategies over this time period.

Table 12.2 Fuzzy set ideal type country memberships (2003)

		Productive-protective: *Finland*		
	Productive plus: Denmark, Norway		**Protective plus:** Sweden, Netherlands, Austria, *Finland*	
Productive: USA, New Zealand		**Weak productive-protective:** Greece, Ireland, Switzerland, Italy, Korea		**Protective:** Belgium, Germany
	Weak productive: Canada		**Weak protective:** Spain, France, Czech Republic, Japan, Portugal, *United Kingdom*	
		Weak: Australia, *United Kingdom*		

Note: Italicised countries are at the crossover point of two ideal types

The follow-up study

While such findings created a strong case for detaching debates about productive welfare from debates about welfare in East Asia, we believed it evident that a full debate about both productive welfarism and the nature of welfare regimes in East Asia required a focus beyond the 23 OECD countries included in our original analysis. Our ambitions were, though, constrained by the parameters of the major data sets and, in particular, by the restricted number of East Asian nations and territories included in the OECD databases. To address this, in a follow-up study (Hudson and Kühner, 2011) we presented a tentative analysis of the balance between productive and protective welfare in seven East Asian nations/territories –

China, Hong Kong, Japan, (South) Korea, Malaysia, Singapore and Taiwan – on the basis of ADB/ILO data and indices compiled by other researchers.

Data limitations restricted our analysis in some significant ways in this follow-up study (see Hudson and Kühner, 2011), not least the lack of strictly corresponding measures for our four dimensions of welfare policy, but using a broad brush approach we were able to plot membership of these seven East Asian cases into our original productive-protective ideal types. Table 12.3 highlights the ideal type memberships for each of the seven East Asian cases on the basis of our

Table 12.3 Four dimension fuzzy set ideal type country memberships

		Productive-protective: *Finland*		
	Productive plus: Denmark, Norway		**Protective plus:** **(China), Taiwan,** Sweden, Netherland, Austria, *Finland*	
Productive: USA, New Zealand		**Weak productive-protective:** **Hong Kong, Korea,** Greece, Ireland, Switzerland, Italy		**Protective:** Belgium, Germany
	Weak productive: **Malaysia, Singapore,** Canada		**Weak protective:** **Japan,** Spain, France, Czech Republic, Portugal, *United Kingdom*	
		Weak: Australia, *United Kingdom*		

four-dimension model. Japan and Korea maintained their membership of the weak-protective and weak-productive-protective ideal types respectively. Interestingly, two of the new cases – mainland China and Taiwan – were clearly placed on the protective side of our model (both are members of the protective plus type), while Hong Kong joined Korea in the weak-productive-protective ideal type. In short, five of the seven cases had protective elements strong enough to allow them to join one or more of our protective sets. Clearly this runs contrary to the suggestion that East Asian welfare regimes favour productive, over protective, social policies. Malaysia and Singapore appeared nearer to the purely productive ideal type: this, in some ways, matches with Holliday's (2005: 152) claims, for he viewed Singapore as "perhaps the best fit with the productivist type". In our analysis, both nations were placed in our weak productive type on the basis of their membership of the education investment set alone. Indeed, the extremely high scores for education investment across East Asia as a whole should be emphasised here. With the exception of Japan, all cases in the region were full members of our education investment fuzzy set. The raw values for the education data showed some exceptional numbers when compared to the OECD nations, stressing the balance towards education spending in the region. Expansion of social security and health care provision has resulted in a rebalancing of social budgets in some East Asian countries during the last decade (see Figure 12.1). For example, using the latest OECD data reduces the education share for Japan to just over 14 per cent in 2009 compared to 16 per cent in 2003; the scores for Korea were 33 (2009) and 41 (2003) per cent respectively (OECD 2012a, 2012b). Nevertheless, the share of education investment remained such that all East Asian countries bar Japan would remain fully in the education investment fuzzy set at the end of the 2000s if we were to recalculate memberships with the latest data.

Taken alone, it would be easy to see why the figures make a strong case for viewing the productive intent of the region's welfare regimes as exceptional. However, in fuzzy set ideal type analysis, variation above full membership does not matter conceptually and high scores on one variable cannot be used to compensate for low scores on another (see Hudson and Kühner, 2010). It is precisely because of this that our approach suggests the USA and New Zealand are better examples of productive welfarism than Singapore or Malaysia: the low score in these East Asian nations for training investment – what ought to be a key pillar of productive welfare strategies – matters in our analysis.

However, we faced significant barriers in assembling our classification in the follow-up study and noted at the time that detailed case studies were required to test the classification. One of the major problems we faced was that some nations in our extended sample had high levels of informal employment, meaning that many workers were not covered by key social insurance schemes. We suggested that this was particularly problematic for the classification of mainland China and Malaysia; according to ADB (2008) the distributional effect of social protection (i.e. the percentage of poor receiving some social protection) at the time point for our analysis was relatively limited in these nations, with only 69 per cent of the poor in China receiving some form of social protection and just 44 per cent in

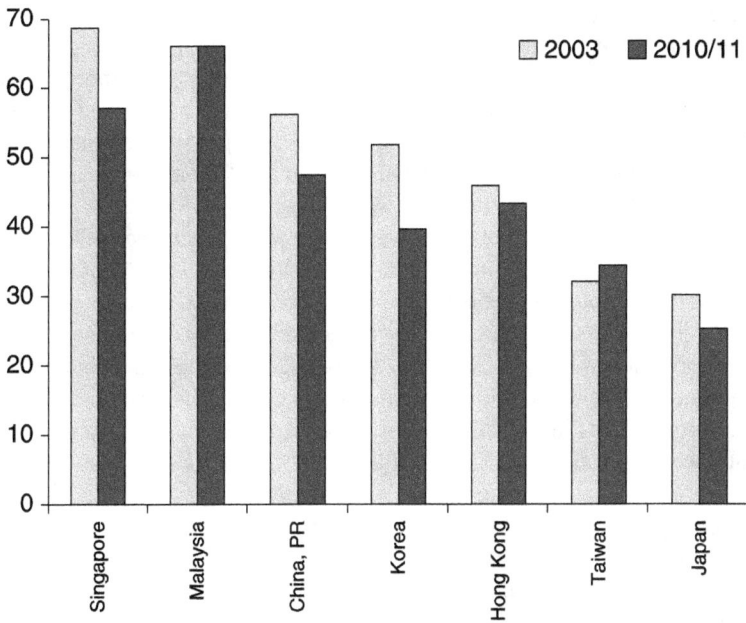

Figure 12.1 Education investment in selected East Asian economies, % of total public social protection, health and education spending, 2003 and 2010/11.

Source: Asian Development Bank Statistical Database System, accessed 23 December 2012; own calculations.

Notes: Data for China refers to 2006 and 2010; central government spending only – except Japan: consolidated general government spending.

Malaysia. Similar observations could be made about limitations of the employment protection index we used to capture the strength of employment protection, for it was based on laws that may not be fully or evenly implemented in each case. Naturally, Ngok (Chapter 6) shows that existing social insurance programmes in China have increased their coverage considerably, while a series of new measures have been introduced to cover farmers and migrant workers in particular in recent years. Ambitious goals by the Chinese government to extend old age pension coverage to all senior citizens by 2015 and complete reforms to provide basic health care as a public service to all of its citizens by 2020 promise to alter the distributional impact of social policies in China further in the future. Added to these limitations, data was available for a very restricted set of time points; in each case we used the latest data available at the time; while this was 2006 or 2003 in most cases, for some indicators the data related to 1997 and so did not reflect the most recent policy changes. We also noted that both Esping-Andersen's and Holliday's classifications were concerned with *welfare capitalism*. This, of course, raises questions about the inclusion of mainland China in our sample, which, despite economic reforms of recent decades, has an employment policy that still relies a great deal on state-owned enterprises (SOEs). Given these issues, we suggested that the analysis of mainland China be "bracketed": we included the case because of the broader significance of mainland China, but accepted that its omission would produce a more coherent sample and, perhaps, a more robust set of findings. Again, Ngok (Chapter 6) argues that China has moved beyond an "occupation-based social insurance model", which might indicate that our treatment of China and our worries about the inclusion of China in broader comparative work have been mitigated to a degree by recent policy changes.

Most problematic of all, though, was that there was a severe lack of high quality data concerning active labour market policies – allied with some doubts about the validity of this dimension for the nations being considered – which meant we also presented a revised set of classifications that excluded this component. Despite recent important additions to case study knowledge (see Chan and Ngok 2011), it is symptomatic that ADB (2008) excluded skills development and labour market training programmes in its definition of social protection and hence the calculation of social protection index scores for East and South East Asian economies. Table 12.4 outlines the revised model and Table 12.5 summarises the ideal types for each of our cases. This table heavily echoes the patterns in the four-dimensional model, though by disaggregating the weak-productive-protective type it suggests that Hong Kong and Korea balance their education investment with different types of protection: the former favouring income protection, the latter employment protection. Indeed, this difference is rather pronounced, for Hong Kong is fully out of our employment protection set. This disaggregation serves to underline the diversity of welfare strategies deployed across East Asia, from Japan's

Table 12.4 Three dimensions model

Ideal type label	Characteristics and model
Productive (P)	Membership of the education investment (EI) set only: EI•~EP•~IP
Productive protective (PP)	Membership of the education investment (EI), employment protection (EP) sets and income protection (IP) sets: EI•EP•IP
Productive plus employment protection (PEP)	Membership of the education investment and employment protection sets, non-membership of the income protection set: EI•EP•~IP
Productive plus income protection (PIP)	Membership of the education investment and income protection sets, non-membership of the employment protection set: EI•~EP•IP
Not productive (N)	Non-membership of the education investment set: ~EI

Note: In Boolean logic•denotes AND while ~ denotes OR (see Ragin, 2000).

Table 12.5 Three dimension fuzzy set ideal type country memberships

	Productive: Malaysia, Singapore	
	Productive-protective: (China), Taiwan	
Productive + **employment** **protection:** Korea		**Productive +** **income** **protection:** Hong Kong
	Not productive: Japan	

non-productive approach, through varying mixes of high education investment with employment and/or income protection and to the more productively oriented strategy of Malaysia and Singapore.

Building in case study evidence

Given the various (data) limitations in our analysis of welfare productivism across East Asian economies, the chapters in this volume provide us with the opportunity in this concluding chapter to challenge our initial findings in three regards: first, the more detailed case evidence allows us to complement our (mainly quantitative) evidence base with up-to-date and detailed information on policies and policy change; second, while enabling us to revisit country classifications in general terms, this also enables us to consider whether the membership of individual East Asian economies may have changed over time; third, the focus in the previous chapters on Greater China allows us to extend our previous analysis by adding Macao into our analysis. In the remainder of this chapter, we will briefly summarise the main findings of each of the territories covered in light of the above discussions.

Hong Kong

In our previous study, Hong Kong was classified as a member of the productive-protective ideal type, scoring high on the education investment and income protection, but not the training investment and employment protection fuzzy set. Mok and Ramesh (Chapter 2) argue that the policy responses of the Hong Kong government to economic and political pressures as well as socio-economic and labour market transformations has not resulted in any real shift of the predominant welfare paradigm – "big market, small government" – and hence, any concerted attempt to alter longstanding institutional welfare arrangements towards a "long[er]-term . . . social protection commitment". Lee and Law (Chapter 4) also ascertain that the social policy responses to the 2007 financial crisis were decidedly short-term, targeted and time-limited and therefore unlikely to alter the overall institutional welfare arrangements in Hong Kong.

Still, there have been a series of policy innovations that suggest the Hong Kong government has not entirely shied away from implementing controversial legislation to extend the social protection of Hong Kong citizens. Lau (Chapter 3) raises the question whether the "small government" approach in Hong Kong is fit to meet the challenges posited by growing income disparities, the consequences of growing instances of casual employment among those lacking general/academic skills, rapid ageing and other socio-economic transformations. Although not aimed at pooling social risks in the same way as social insurance in Western Europe, the Mandatory Provident Fund (MPF) was introduced in 2000 after decades of controversial discussions – yet, the MPF does not provide benefits to the increasing number of elderly who are already retired, or will retire soon, and suffer from low income and social exclusion due to the absence of adequate family support. After cautiously setting up a time-limited minimum wage scheme after the SARS outbreak in 2003, a minimum wage policy was finally implemented in 2011 – yet, this has led to mixed results for labour market insiders and outsiders. While the so-called Task Force on Economic Challenges promoted an industrial strategy to rebalance the Hong Kong economy, Lee and Law (Chapter 4) add that the Hong Kong government – "despite damaging its non-interventionist image" – also implemented Keynesian-type public works and infrastructure projects in the wake of the 2007 financial crisis.

The reoccurring emphasis on supply-side workfare measures that is drawn out in the chapters on Hong Kong is particularly interesting. Mok and Ramesh (Chapter 2) show that the introduction of welfare-to-work programmes after 1997 was mainly intended to curb raising social assistance spending by extending the conditions attached to benefit receipt and emphasising the "self reliance" of Hong Kong citizens (see also Lau, Chapter 3). To date, receipt of social assistance payments in Hong Kong remains subject to participation in the "Support for Self-reliance Scheme", which offers recipients a mix of personalised employment assistance, an obligation to participate in unpaid community work and the provision of disregarded earnings (HK Social Welfare Department 2008; SSA 2012).

Demand-side activation measures predating the 2008 financial crisis, such as the Transport Support Scheme, the Job Search Allowance or the On-the-Job Transport Allowance remained small in scale. The initial responses to the 2007 financial crisis, such as the Hong Kong government's pledge to create 62,000 jobs and internship opportunities – including the controversial Internship Programme for

University Graduates – were further reaching and aimed at affecting unemployment more directly. However, Lee and Law (Chapter 4) stress that the majority of these training and internship places were offered merely on a temporary basis, aimed at easing the immediate fallout of the crisis.

More generally, Lee and Law (Chapter 4) question the effectiveness of the existing job-search and (re-)training measures in Hong Kong as survey evidence suggests many participants are simply pushed into low-skill, low-paid jobs; existing activation measures very seldom trigger upward labour market trajectories in Hong Kong. Similarly, despite the introduction of several programmes specifically geared towards assisting low-income families with the costs of education, such as the School Textbook Assistance Scheme or Student Travel Subsidy Scheme, we learn from Lau (Chapter 3) that public provision has continued to fall short of improving educational outcomes of children with such family backgrounds and hence effectively facilitating social mobility. The creation of the Child Development Fund in 2008 stands out as one of the few policy measures with a longer time horizon, attempting explicitly to raise the human capital and asset accumulation of children from disadvantaged family backgrounds via mentored "Personal Development Plans" and "Targeted Savings" programmes. While Mok and Ramesh (Chapter 2) emphasise the "self-reliance" character of the targeted savings programme in particular, the persistent reluctance of the Hong Kong government to subscribe to large-scale *public* policy initiatives and was reaffirmed – amongst others – by its decision to opt for a one-off cash allowance of $6000 to all citizens to address the intensified problem of working poverty in 2012. Although Hong Kong has witnessed considerable policy innovation and experimentation in recent years, it is – on balance – difficult to justify a re-classification of its productive-protective intent. The welfare system may continue to be strained to the point where – by means of more systematic evidence – membership of the social protection fuzzy set in particular will need to be re-evaluated, but due to the increased focus on supply-side workfare there is little to suggest that Hong Kong should join either the employment or labour market training set at this juncture.

Macau

Mok and Ramesh (Chapter 2) point out that there are similarities between Hong Kong and Macau in regards to the policy responses to the various regional and global crises since the late 1990s. Similar to Hong Kong, welfare policies in Macau have been characterised as "reluctant" and ultimately "developmentalist"; while emphasising supply-side workfare measures to tackle the burgeoning social and economic challenges, the public demand for expansions of social and employment protection legislation has been met tentatively by a mix of flexible and short-term measures unfit to challenge the persisting welfare paradigm. The reduction of salary taxes together with the payment of cash allowances to every resident in 2008 and 2009 are – as in the case of Hong Kong – symbolic of the aversion – from a comparative perspective – to the implementation of a longer-term, more progressive programme to extend existing welfare arrangements. What is more, Lai (Chapter 8) points out that while the replacement levels of old age pension and unemployment benefit payments remain comparatively low – merely 18.2 and 19.1 per cent of Macao's median wage in 2011 – the Macau SAR has thus far merely introduced non-mandatory individual savings accounts under the Central Provident Fund scheme and postponed a decision on contribution and fund management regulations. Finally, the introduction of temporary income supplements in 2008, which have subsidised the incomes of a considerable number of (low-wage) workers, can be seen as a less rigid alternative to the introduction of a minimum wage that, although advocated by trade unions and popular among Macau SAR residents, is strongly opposed by employers for the fear of its possible impact on labour costs.

These developments stand in contrast to the decision by the Macau government to extend compulsory free education and to increase financial support of students in tertiary education in 2005. Indeed, Mok and Ramesh (Chapter 2) stress that government spending on education more than doubled in Macau between 2003 and 2008 – a trend that seems to go against the trajectory of social spending in other East Asian economies. This is indicative of Mok and Ramesh's (Chapter 2) and Lai's (Chapter 8) implicit suggestion that labour market and low income policies in Macau – because of the special features of the Macau economy and the demand for a more skilled labour force after 1997 – were more holistic in the sense that they combined attempts to increase work incentives with an emphasis on vocational training and lifelong learning – at least initially.

For instance, the 1998 expansion of the Social Security Fund included investments in training and special youth allowances alongside more protective employment subsidies and unemployment relief. The introduction of a social literacy course in 2001 and the Four Hundred Million Fund for Vocational Training in 2002 suggest a concern of the Macau SAR government to equip the unemployed with the skills needed in a changing social and economic context. Yet, Lai (Chapter 8) also points out that support for these programmes started to wane once the economy recovered in the 2000s. The purpose of the Allowance for Supportive Training for Employment, which was introduced in 2004 to replace social literacy courses, despite its name was – as Lai (Chapter 8) argues – increasingly intended to encourage work discipline among recipients and to put pressure on trainees to re-enter the labour market.

Whether the seemingly more productive intent of the policy approach of the Macau SAR after 1997 constitutes a longer-term, institutional feature or a necessary, short-term response to an exclusive social and economic legacy is hard to tell at this juncture and without further empirical evidence. Certainly, compared to the other economies in Greater China, the subordinate role of protective social policies indicated by the lack of mandatory CPF, a minimum wage and the repeated ad-hoc payment of cash payments appears to be in accordance with Lai's (Chapter 8) assessment stressing the regulatory approach to social policy-making by the Macau SAR government. As for our framework of productive-protective welfare, there is little to suggest that Macau SAR is close to becoming a member of either our income or employment protection fuzzy sets in the short and medium term. Macau's tentative active labour market policies implemented after the 1997 crisis have arguably lost some of its training and human capital-centred components after introduction of the Allowance for Supportive Training for Employment. Instead, supply-side workfare measures have played a bigger role in recent years, which suggests it would also be difficult to classify Macau as a member of our labour market training set. Given further investments in the education sector in recent years, this would then suggest that Macau is more similar to countries like Malaysia and Singapore, which were classified as weak-productive in our original four dimension fuzzy set classification.

China

The clearest suggestion of a fundamental regime change – "the coming of the era of social policy" – is entailed in Ngok's discussion of social policy developments in Mainland China (Chapter 6). Indeed, the list of newly introduced or amended welfare programmes to increase the coverage of social programmes, particularly among the rural population and migrant workers, is significant in scale. The New Agricultural Cooperative Medical System was introduced in 2003 and by 2006 the Chinese government actively pursued the development of a rural health service system. A health care insurance scheme for those not covered by occupational insurance was introduced in 2007 and the Chinese government – for the first time in its recent history – acknowledged basic health care as a public good and its provision as a government responsibility in 2009. As a consequence of these developments, Ngok shows that around 95 per cent of China's population was covered by one of its key health insurance systems by 2011.

Mok and Huang (Chapter 7) provide a case study on Guangzhou, a relatively economically developed city in South China, examining how the local government responds to changing social welfare needs and expectations in the city. With particular reference to what major strategies the Guangzhou government has adopted in managing/addressing people's welfare needs, the chapter focuses on how far the new measures would have met the changing welfare expectations of citizens in China mainland. The case of Guangzhou has clearly indicated how the Chinese government has begun to take people's needs and interests into consideration when they design social policy and find measures appropriate for addressing the growing social welfare needs against the context of a widening gap between the rich and poor and a deepening intensity of poverty, inequality and other unintended social consequences when China has tried to quest for GDPism without striking for balanced economic and social development. The authors in Chapter 7 highlight that even though the government in Guangzhou has taken people's needs and interests into serious consideration, we must note that welfare regionalism and social policy variations do exist in China mainland since the implementation of social policy/social protection measures highly depends upon the political will and capacity of local governments under the policy context of fiscal decentralisation in social policy and social welfare.

Ngok (Chapter 6; but also see Yeoh and Ling, Chapter 11) also describes how more migrant workers have been included in the existing urban social insurance schemes in recent years, while other public services have increasingly opened up for migrant workers and their children. In 2007, the Minimum Living Standard Scheme was extended to include the rural population with dramatic consequences: the number of recipients increased from 2.65 million in 1999 to 47.6 million in 2009 (Ngok, Chapter 6). In 2005, the decision was taken to improve basic old age insurance for urban workers and employees – including a shift away from PAYG towards partial accumulation system, but the crucial change in Chinese old age pension policy was implemented in 2006 when the State Council decided to introduce a new funding mechanism for rural pensions under the "five guarantees" system. In 2008, new measures were implemented to enhance incentives for rural and informal workers to join social insurance schemes and the new rural pension insurance scheme has operated in China since 2009 (Ngok, Chapter 6). All of these measures, Yeoh and Ling (Chapter 11) tell us, were introduced alongside large-scale coordinated fiscal investments into the local economies of poorer regions in an attempt to eliminate absolute poverty in China by 2020.

In our initial analysis of East Asian economies, China – although bracketed for reasons discussed above – was classified as a member of a productive-protective ideal type, scoring high in regards to social protection (for urban workers) and education investment, and low in regards to its employment protection and training investment. While Ngok (Chapter 6) argues that China has overcome its occupation-based social insurance model, he shows that – while the central government has begun to take more fiscal responsibility in terms of funding protective social policies, government spending on education has continued to increase during the 2000s. Indeed, Ngok shows that educational inequality has been firmly on the agenda in China and has resulted in increased investments, particularly in rural areas and poorer regions. Thus, the initial decision in 2004 to abolish tuition and other school fees in some poorer regions was extended to the whole western region of China in 2005. Similarly, the initial decision in 2007 to implement free compulsory education in rural areas was extended in 2008 to the whole country.

While there is not a great deal of evidence to suggest that the previous assessment of mainland China as being in our social protection and education investment fuzzy sets was false and no longer valid, there are other developments which may indicate a shift in terms of its employment protection and training investment. The new Labour Contract Law, from July 2007, added to the changes in the Labour Law two years prior by entailing a series of new standards in regards to the strictness of labour contracts, including temporary and short-term fixed work, severance payments and – importantly – facilitated the role of trade unions and workers' organisations in labour relations. The new Employment Promotion Law, which was enacted only one month later in 2007, prohibited any discrimination against job-seekers, required local governments to invest in vocational training programmes and employers to offer on-the-job as well as pre- and re-employment training in an attempt to raise the skills of workers. Public employment offices were legislated to provide their service free of charge to any job-seeker from that time on. While probably not far-reaching enough to suggest a change of membership, the trajectory of these measures goes against our initial classification of the productive-protective intent of mainland China. While Ngok (Chapter 6) rightly stresses a "reposition[ing of the state's] role in public welfare and social justice", we would reserve judgement – at this point in time and from our specific analytical perspective – as to whether a complete reorientation has already occurred. Similar observations are also found in Chapter 7 by Mok and Huang but we should not over-generalise the findings in these two chapters to make any claims that Chinese people in the mainland nowadays enjoy significantly improved social protection since regional variations are common in social welfare provision and social protection in China.

It is also worthwhile mentioning at this point some of the challenges that China faces moving forward. Chen and Yang (Chapter 9) stress that the fragmented retirement benefit system has led to severe underfunding of pension schemes in some municipalities, which is particularly worrying given the projected increases in the elderly population in China in the very near future. While the aim of the Wen Jiabao administration was to reach full pension coverage by 2012, the level of benefit payments and questions about their effectiveness in protecting the elderly has increasingly been on the agenda. Not least, Chen and Yang show that adequate old age care and social insurance arrangements have become more of a concern for Chinese citizens in recent years – and interestingly in tandem with an equal degree of concern about the future economic development of China. It will be interesting to follow how the incoming Chinese administration will deal with these popular calls to expand its reach in providing key social policies beyond the immediate aftermath of the global economic crisis.

Taiwan

Chang and Ku (Chapter 5) highlight comparative regime research that clusters South Korea and Taiwan together sharply. They also suggest – as with South Korea – that broad economic and political changes have underpinned a gradual expansion of welfare provision in recent decades. In particular, they highlight the move towards a more post-industrial economy and democratisation as key factors in understanding the development of social policy which, as they rightly note, does not develop in a vacuum.

With respect to the economy, they point to labour market changes that have brought rising levels of pre-state redistribution inequality, partly due to an increase in the level of unemployment and partly due to rising rewards at the top. This has created greater pressure for social intervention and although state transfers have expanded, they note that rising underlying inequalities mean the overall effect has been one where post-transfer income inequality has risen. Meanwhile, with respect to politics, increased party competition has helped some social policy issues rise up the political agenda, but also created a challenge that they suggest politicians have failed to adequately address: how to meet the demand for increased welfare expenditure without also advocating electorally unpopular tax rises. While expenditure has risen, so too has the level of public debt as a consequence of a failure to increase tax in line with expenditure.

What this suggests, perhaps, is that there has not been a paradigm shift in Taiwan's social model in recent years, with incremental changes expanding key elements of the model and expenditures rising in part because of rising client numbers. Indeed, Chang and Ku list the many promises made by the parties at election times but note agendas have often remained largely unimplemented by the winning party by the time of the subsequent election. Yet, if radical change has not been in evidence, whether Taiwan was correctly classified as "productive protective" in our earlier work is a moot point.

Chang and Ku's evidence certainly supports Taiwan's membership of the education investment set, the crucial role of education in supporting the economy being noted. Indeed, they suggest that in the 1970s and 1980s it was the key policy above all others, describing it as the "preferred" policy. If this remained so, then it would suggest classification in the productive type is more appropriate. Yet, their chapter also highlights the gradual yet considerable development in social policy since the 1980s that has moved Taiwan away from a developmental state model. At a minimum, consideration of classification beyond the mere productive type seems justified.

However, they perhaps note as many weaknesses in the protective dimensions as they do strengths. So, for instance, with regard to employment protection, they highlight the increased social pressures that have arisen from rising unemployment which, in turn, they in part attribute to increased global competition and the movement of investment from Taiwan to cheaper locations elsewhere (particularly mainland China). The failure of successive governments to protect jobs resulted in an increase of unemployment in the 2000s to around double the rate of the early 1990s. At the same time, though, the protective aspects of the labour market are also highlighted elsewhere in this chapter. In particular, the significant voice of labour movements is flagged in their data on the number of disputes and the complaints of enterprise owners. Moreover, that businesses are moving jobs on the basis of labour costs implies that Taiwan's social model incorporates protections absent in those of neighbouring economic rivals. Of course, trade disputes could be seen as a sign of labour weakness (a failure to achieve goals by negotiation) and the existence of an economic rival with lower labour costs does not mean protections are strong in Taiwan, so we need to be cautious here. With regard to income protection, the authors note that there have been gradual improvements in schemes in order to bring them in line with international expectations. They highlight increased investment and the stronger role the state now plays in redistributing incomes.

Yeh and Shi (Chapter 10) document the evolution of pensions in Taiwan, noting that its economic model has facilitated the growth of a set of public pensions – and relatively modest private pensions – over recent decades. Significantly, they contrast this position with Japan, where the inverse is true, suggesting strong public pension protection is a significant feature of Taiwan's social policy framework. However, both Yeh and Shi, and Chang and Ku also flag problems with respect to income protection schemes, including gaps in coverage, rising income inequality occurring due to widening pre-intervention inequality and an increased fear of poverty and unemployment, with a large proportion of society recently reporting that they feel impoverished. Interestingly, Chang and Ku also note how increased unemployment rates and, more particularly, increased job search periods, have highlighted gaps in active labour market policy and led to increased activity in this productive dimension of welfare, with new schemes such as the Employment Promotion Programme (launched in 2009) being introduced to support the unemployed.

In short, the evidence presented in this volume provides some degree of support for Taiwan's classification as productive-protective, though weaknesses in some aspects of provision muddy the overall picture. That said, our initial model was never intended to be a commentary on the efficacy of policy, merely on where the balance of activity lies.

Conclusion

Our earlier classification of East Asian welfare systems concluded there was evidence of considerable diversity with regards to productive versus protective elements but noted that detailed case study evidence would be needed to unpick the nuances of each case because our analysis had relied on mainly simplified quantitative indictors. Each of the chapters in this volume provides additional clues that add to the broad bird's-eye view of welfare systems captured in our quantitatively rooted analysis. However, because each chapter reflects the different concerns of each case and, to a significant degree, the concerns of each author, the picture that emerges lacks the clarity provided by a quantitatively informed bird's-eye analysis. Indeed, the detailed discussion of ongoing local policy reforms and local policy debates highlights the localised differences: this certainly helps us to understand the nuances of each case, but presents new challenges for us in trying to ascertain how knowledge of these local differences might then feed back into our bird's-eye analysis. For example, many authors rightly focus their analysis on identifying the weaknesses in existing frameworks or planned reforms, but this does not always help us to pinpoint the overall nature or level of provision in the round. Indeed, a recent reform widely attacked for its deficiencies by political actors in one country might well still offer a more extensive framework of support than that found in another country. This, of course, is a limitation of all single country case studies. While multiple country comparative analysis risks presenting a naïve perspective because it lacks depth of case knowledge (in Chapter 5 Chang and Ku suggest some studies are based on a simple "browsing" of East Asian cases), single country cases offer us the more nuanced view by exploring detailed local debates, but in so doing risk, as Eardley *et al.* (1996: 19) put it, presenting a "native" analysis that does not provide the contextualised data required for a systematic general analysis of trends. Certainly there is an element of this evident in the chapters within this volume.

Yet, perhaps this is helpful in confirming one aspect of our original findings nonetheless: that diversity with regards to systems, reform plans and policy challenges is evident. In Greater China – as in East Asia or Europe or North America – geography is an important factor in shaping policy, but its influence is far from direct. Chang and Ku, for instance, note the role of regional trade in shaping the context for social policy in Taiwan. But deeper impacts are evident and many of these vary by place: the role of (differing) past policies in shaping current debates is a clear theme within the book as is the role of (differing) institutional arrangements, (differing) economic challenges and, in some regards, (differing) social challenges. It may be that we have erred in our classifications of some cases within our productive-protective framework or, indeed, that the framework is too simple and misses key areas of activity. Irrespective of this, however, we feel the chapters within the book underline the diversity of policy frameworks in Greater China. They also, we might add, highlight what appears to be the gradual but significant expansion of income protection in all cases. Both these factors together lead us to believe that the simple labelling of the region as being home to a common "productive welfare" model remains too simple to be convincing.

References

Abrahamson, P. (1999). "The welfare modelling business", *Social Policy and Administration*, 33: 394–415.

Abrahamson, P. (2011). "The Welfare Modelling Business Revisited", in G. Hwang (ed.) *New Welfare States in East Asia: Global Challenges and Restructuring*. London: Edward Elgar, pp. 15–34.

ADB (2008). *Social Protection Index for Committed Poverty Reduction, Vol. 2: Asia*. Manila: ADB.

Aspalter, C. (2006). "The East Asian Welfare Model", *International Journal of Social Welfare*, 15(4): 290–301.

Baldwin, P. (1996). "Can we define a European welfare state model?", in: B. Greve, C. Bent and C. Bambra (eds) (2005) "Worlds of welfare and the health care discrepancy", *Social Policy and Society*, 4: 31–41.

Bambra, C. (2005). "Worlds of Welfare and the Health Discrepancy", *Social Policy and Society*, 4(1): 31–41.

Castells, M. and Himanen, P. (2002). *The Information Society and the Welfare State: the Finnish Model*. Oxford: Oxford University Press.

Castles, F. and Mitchell, D. (1993). "Worlds of Welfare and Families of Nations", in F. Castles (ed.) *Families of Nations: Patterns of Public Policy in Western Democracies*. Aldershot: Dartmouth.

Cerny, P. and Evans, M. (1999). *New Labour, Globalization, and the Competition State*. Working Paper No. 70. Cambridge, MA: Center for European Studies, Harvard University.

Chan, C. K. and Ngok, K. (2011). *Welfare Reform in East Asia: Towards Workfare?* London: Routledge.

Clasen, J. and Sigel, N. (eds) (2007). *Investigating Welfare State Change: the 'Dependent Variable Problem' in Comparative Analysis*. London: Edward Elgar.

Eardley, T., Bradshaw, J., Ditch, J., Gough, I. and Whiteford, P. (1996). *Social Assistance in OECD Countries: Synthesis Report*. London: HMSO.

Esping-Andersen, G. (1990). *The Three Worlds of Welfare Capitalism*. Oxford: Polity Press.

Esping-Andersen, G. (1997). "Hybrid or Unique? The Japanese Welfare State between Europe and America", *Journal of European Social Policy*, 7(3): 179–189.

Esping-Andersen, G. (1999). *Social Foundations of Post-Industrial Economies*. Oxford: Oxford University Press.

Evans M. and Cerny P. (2003). "Globalisation and Social Policy", in N. Ellison and C. Pierson (eds) *Developments in British Social Policy 2*. Basingstoke: Palgrave.

Goodman, R., White, G. and Kwon, H. (eds) (1998). *The East Asian Welfare Model*. London: Routledge.

Gough, I. (2004). "East Asia: the Limits of Productivist Regimes", in I. Gough and G. Wood (eds) *Insecurity and Welfare Regimes in Asia, Africa and Latin America*. Cambridge: Cambridge University Press.

HK Social Welfare Department (2008). *Comprehensive Social Security Assistance Scheme – Support for Self-Reliance Scheme*. Hong Kong: HK Social Welfare Department.

Holliday, I. (2000). "Productivist Welfare Capitalism: Social Policy in East Asia", *Political Studies*, 48(4): 706–723.

Holliday, I. (2005). "East Asian Social Policy in the Wake of the Financial Crisis: Farewell to Productivism?", *Policy and Politics*, 33(1): 145–162.

Holliday, I. and Wilding, P. (eds) (2003). *Welfare Capitalism in East Asia*. London: Palgrave.

Horsfall, D. (2010). "From Competition State to Competition States?", *Policy Studies*, 31: 57–76.

Hudson, J. and Kühner, S. (2009). "Towards Productive Welfare? A Comparative Analysis of 23 Countries", *Journal of European Social Policy*, 19(1): 34–46.

Hudson, J. and S. Kühner, S. (2010). "Beyond the Dependent Variable Problem: the Methodological Challenges of Capturing Productive and Protective Dimensions of Social Policy", *Social Policy and Society*, 9(2): 167–179.

Hudson, J. and Kühner, S. (2011). "Analysing the Productive Dimensions of Welfare: Looking Beyond East Asia" in: Hwang, G-J. (ed.) *New Welfare States in East Asia: Global Challenges and Restructuring*. "Globalisation and Welfare" series. London: Edward Elgar.

Hudson, J. and Kühner, S. (2012). "Analyzing the Productive and Protective Dimensions of Welfare: Looking Beyond the OECD', *Social Policy & Administration*, 46: 35–60.

Jessop, B. (1999). "The Changing Governance of Welfare: Recent Trends in its Primary Functions, Scale, and Modes of Coordination", *Social Policy & Administration*, 33(4): 348–359.

Jessop, B. (2000). "From the KWNS to the SWPR", in G. Lewis, S. Gewirtz and J. Clarke (eds) *Rethinking Social Policy*. London: Sage.

Jones, C. (1993). "The Pacific Challenge: Confucian Welfare States", in C. Jones (ed.) *New Perspectives on the Welfare State in Europe*. London: Routledge.

Kim, Y.-M. (2008). "Beyond East Asian Welfare Productivism in South Korea", *Policy & Politics*, 36(1): 109–125.

Kühner, S. (2007). "Country-level Comparisons of Welfare State Change Measures: Another Facet of the Dependent Variable Problem within the Comparative Analysis of the Welfare State?", *Journal of European Social Policy*, 17(1): 5–18.

Kwon, H. J. (2005). "An Overview of the Study: The Developmental Welfare State and Policy Reforms in East Asia' in H. J. Kwon (ed.) *Transforming the Developmental State in East Asia*. London: Palgrave.

Kwon, S. and Holliday, I. (2007). "The Korean Welfare State: A Paradox of Expansion in an Era of Globalisation and Economic Crisis", *International Journal of Social Welfare*, 16(3): 242–248.

Lin, K. (1999). *Confucian Welfare Cluster: A Cultural Interpretation of Social Welfare*. Tampere: University of Tampere.

OECD (2012a). *Social Expenditure Database*. Available at: www.oecd.org/els/social/expenditure.

OECD (2012b). *Education at a Glance*. Paris: OECD Publishing.

Ragin, C. C. (2000). *Fuzzy-Set Social Science*. Chicago: University of Chicago Press.

Ragin, C. C. (2008). *Redesigning Social Inquiry: Fuzzy Sets and Beyond*. Chicago: University of Chicago Press.

Rudra, N. (2007). "Welfare States in Developing Countries: Unique or Universal?" *The Journal of Politics*, 69(2): 378–396.

SSA (2012). *Social Security Programs Throughout the World: Asia and the Pacific*, SSA Publication No. 13–11802. Washington: US Social Security Administration.

Walker, A. and Wong, C. K. (eds) (2005). *East Asian Welfare Regimes in Transition: From Confucianism to Globalisation*. Bristol: The Policy Press.

Wilding, P. (2008). "Is the East Asian Welfare Model Still Productive?", *Journal of Asian Public Policy*, 1(1): 18–31.

Index

For Product Safety Concerns and Information please contact our EU
representative GPSR@taylorandfrancis.com
Taylor & Francis Verlag GmbH, Kaufingerstraße 24, 80331 München, Germany

9 781138 579187